# THE COUNTER-REFORMATION

A.D. WRIGHT

# THE COUNTER-REFORMATION
## CATHOLIC EUROPE AND
## THE NON-CHRISTIAN WORLD

St. Martin's Press
New York

Printed in the United States of America

First published in the United States of America in 1982

ISBN 0-312-17021-1
ISBN 0-312-17022-X (pbk.)

---

**Library of Congress Cataloging in Publication Data**

---

Wright, A. D. (Anthony David)
  The Counter Reformation.

  1. Counter Reformation.
2. Catholic Church—Missions—history.   I. Title.
BR430.W7   1982      270.6      82-3210
ISBN 0-312-17021-1      AACR2
ISBN 0-312-17022-X (pbk.)

---

# CONTENTS

# PREFACE

THIS BOOK is not designed to challenge existing brief introductions to the Counter-Reformation. It is however intended for interested readers new to the subject as a guide to the issues involved in any serious study of those developments in Western Christendom and beyond, which have been known by that name. The inclusion of some consideration at least of events beyond the confines of Europe is of crucial importance, for it is arguably that dimension which has most been lacking in many earlier studies, with a corresponding absence of adequate attention to the reciprocal effects of European and missionary experience in the evolution of Catholicism. Further information about the persons, places and events mentioned here can be found in other works: a guide to existing literature is provided in the Select Bibliography.

I should like to record my gratitude to Professor J.M. Roberts, Vice-Chancellor of the University of Southampton, for stimulating me to write on a subject and in a way which I had been considering for some time, but without the necessary spur to commit my views to paper. Other debts of gratitude are too numerous to record individually, but collective mention must be made of those fellow historians and pupils with whom I have discussed the subject of this book, to my undoubted advantage and not, I hope, to their disadvantage.

A.D. WRIGHT
9 June 1980

CHAPTER I

# INTRODUCTION:
# THE COUNTER-REFORMATION AND
# AUGUSTINIAN EUROPE

THE COUNTER-REFORMATION was originally the creation of modern historians. The negative view, adopted by nineteenth-century German, and essentially Protestant, scholars, of those developments in Western Christendom which were opposed to the sixteenth-century Reformation, was characterized by the term 'anti-Reformation'. Since such opposition to the spread and consolidation of the Protestant Reformation was seen, not without reason, as a largely political and military story, the concept of a movement designed to counter the true Reformation of religion seemed natural. Historical study, not least of the great figures of the Reformation such as Luther himself, could not overlook the literary and polemical campaigns of Western Europe in the age of religious division, and the mixture of theological learning and personal abuse. But the Reformation and Counter-Reformation were regarded as clearly antithetic, utterly distinct, and having no common ground. For even the arguable antecedents of the Protestant reformers, among the Christian humanists of the beginning of the sixteenth century, had been condemned, ever since the days of Luther, Bucer and Erasmus, or Pole and Vergerio themselves, in those cases where commitment to the reformed faith did not in the end follow.

More recently, in the twentieth century, appreciation of a more positive aspect of the Counter-Reformation became evident, even among Protestant writers in England, for example. The enthusiasm of Catholic reformers of the later sixteenth century for purifying their own Church, as well as their zeal for persecuting Protestants, was acknowledged. But this intermediate understanding of the Counter-Reformation still shared with the pristine picture the portrayal of Catholic action, remedial as well as repressive, as a reaction to the challenge of Protestantism. Only gradually, in English historical writing at least, was the singularity of the Protestant Reformation reduced, together with the reactionary quality of Catholic reform,

and a more accurate perspective provided. By the time of the posthumous publication of Evennett's penetrating discussion of the spirit
of the Counter-Reformation, it could clearly be seen that both Reformation and Counter-Reformation had common origins. The continued attempts at reform of the medieval Western Church, despite
the disappointed hopes aroused by Conciliarism, produced, at the
end of the fifteenth century and beginning of the sixteenth century,
a religious revival that was both institutional and personal. While
some leaders of this revival, such as Savonarola at Florence, preached
the need for individual conversion of life, only subsequently becoming involved in wider questions of Church and state—with tragic
results in his case – other friars, and monks and laymen, cardinals
and bishops, inquisitors and rulers, promoted institutional reform in
different parts of Europe. The restoration of discipline was in each
case confined, to a religious order or to a diocese, or to the spontaneous activity of those seeking a new form of religious life entirely,
rather than the strict observance of an ancient rule, as in the case of
the Brethren of the Common Life in the Netherlands, or the first
oratories in Italy. The nationalism of fifteenth-century Western
European states and language-areas, evident in the General Councils
of the century, and encouraged by the papal schism which those
Councils had originally been designed to resolve, divided such efforts
for Christian renewal. But such dissipation of effort was to some
extent at least countered by the new common language and learning
of the humanists, whose revival of classical ideals soon extended to the
recovery of Christian antiquity, and the resurrection of the Church.

Different Protestant reformers, like Luther or Bucer, thus owed
much to the twin developments of the late medieval and Renaissance
Western Christian revival: the institutional and the intellectual.
These two men, for example, had both been friars, and had experience of the internal struggle to reimpose a properly regular life on
the Augustinians, the Dominicans and the Franciscans, carried on
in different ways in the German lands, in Spain, in Italy and elsewhere. Both men were also at one time participants in the common
correspondence of Christian humanists, before precisely doctrinal
questions separated them from Erasmus. The denunciation of their
former companion did not however mean their dissociation from the
biblical and patristic learning of the Christian humanists. That was
neither desired nor possible, any more than Luther's desire to shed
all remnants of medieval scholasticism proved possible. The Nom-
inalism which he so despised not unnaturally continued to influence
his thinking. Luther's original call for the reform of the Church, not

the creation of a new one, was, for a brief time, the same as the search of Erasmus or Colet to rediscover the truly Christian life, by studying the evidence of the Bible and the Fathers of the Church. The elevation, by Luther first, and then by other magisterial Protestant reformers, and even by the literalist as opposed to the spiritualist wing of the radicals, of the Bible to a unique position as source of faith and revelation of the divine, did not in fact end Protestant attention to the writings of the Fathers of the Church. The age of the division of Western Christendom and the accompanying religious polemic was that of a continued patristic revival. Both Catholic and Protestant writers made selective use of the Fathers of the Church, in an effort to prove, in the one case the continuity of the traditional Church from the apostolic age to the contemporary era, in the other the discontinuity caused by papal power and other medieval developments, necessitating a recreation of the one true Church.

The patristic revival of the fifteenth and early sixteenth century was thus a common inspiration for both the Protestant Reformation and the Counter-Reformation, since both in fact emerged from the single movement for Christian revival, personal and communal, of the late medieval and Renaissance period. The Protestant Reformation, in its search for a purified Christian life, and the authority of the Fathers for that, was thus in one sense, and for all its early and continued internal divisions, a continuation of important aspects of immediately pre-Lutheran religious reform. The Counter-Reformation too was a direct development from the pre-Lutheran attempts at renewed devotion, restored religious observance, and reformed diocesan government, whatever the additional elements of reaction to Protestantism which soon became evident. Among the Fathers of the Church whose writings were thus consulted by those in pre-Lutheran and by those in religiously divided Europe, in their search for a reform of Western Christendom, the figure of Saint Augustine was clearly predominant. This was not, perhaps, simply the result of his prolific composition, or even of his stature as arguably the greatest of the Western Fathers, whose experiences were more immediately applicable to the conditions of later Western Christendom than those of the Eastern Fathers. The fifteenth-century disillusionment with institutional reform, as Conciliar, papal and political power struggles divided the endeavours of those seeking practical reform in common, suggested an interior approach to the problem of salvation. Here Augustine's confessional discussion of personal conversion, his obsession with the doctrines of Justification and predestination, proved of compelling attraction. After Luther's own private doctrinal development, on a scriptural basis, had started, Augustine seemed to provide support for Luther's personal convictions, from the age of the Fathers; while to Catholic writers the importance of Augustine as a resident bishop, countering heretics by force as well as by argument, had an equally obvious authority.

The authority of Augustine had, in one sense, never been lacking in the Western medieval Church. But the incorporation of his views in medieval thought, by the process of textual inclusion, the reproduction of sentences from an authority, but often at second-hand, via another author, remained ultimately fragmentary. What was new, in parts of Europe at least, in the fifteenth century, was the apparent revival of attention to Augustine's views *in extenso*, above all to his doctrinal discussions, as opposed to quotation of his views in a political or philosophical context. The medieval evolution of a largely Aristotelian philosophy, not least in the work of Aquinas, represented the accumulation of Augustinian references. The search for some notional separation of Church and state, increasingly in later medieval Western Europe, produced a particular concern with the *City of God*. But in the fifteenth century, even before the advent of printing had had its effect, a new attention to the essentially theological views of Augustine seems to be evident. The argument from the numbers of manuscript copies of a work made at any time is inevitably uncertain, because of the migration of manuscripts and the accidents of survival. But it is still striking that for most works of Saint Augustine it would seem to be the fifteenth century which, in Italy at least, produced the largest numbers of complete manuscript texts. With the exception of the *City of God*, there seems to have been something of a caesura, in the tenth and eleventh centuries in Italy, in the production of complete manuscripts of his works. The interest in his views which could motivate such copying revived only gradually, it appears, in the twelfth and thirteenth centuries: more in the fourteenth, but a clear revival, on a different scale, in the fifteenth. Moreover two works which are well represented in these fifteenth-century Italian manuscripts are the *De gratia et libero arbitrio* and the *De libero arbitrio*, both on questions of grace and free will, such as were to divide Erasmus, Luther and Calvin: the one work dating from 426 AD, the other from 388 AD. These two works, in other words, are compositions from either side of the division in Augustine's life, identified by historians of the Augustinian era as occurring from 417 AD, which produced a changed outlook, and a more distinctively and unreservedly 'Augustinian' view of man's fate, in the later works.

Such evidence of a new concern with Augustine's opinions on salvation and predestination is admittedly less clear for other parts of Western Europe. In the British Isles, again allowing necessarily for the chances of manuscript migration and survival, the fifteenth century produced the greatest number of copies of some works of Augustine, but for other works more appeared in the fourteenth or earlier centuries. In the Iberian peninsula the greatest number of manuscript copies of Augustine's works often dates from the fifteenth, but sometimes from earlier centuries. But the Italian example is the most striking, given the importance of Italy, together with the Netherlands and other parts of Northern Europe, in the patristic revival which characterized Christian humanism, alongside Catholic 'evangelicism', of a more purely scriptural inspiration. This was evident in Italy as early as Gregory of Rimini (d. 1348) and Petrarch (1304-74), despite their different religious and intellectual concerns. In the Netherlands the importance of manuscript copying in the new regular activity of the Brethren of the Common Life led, again, to the reproduction of Augustinian as well as scriptural texts; while the associated canons of Windesheim represented, in their observance, the attempt to revive the purity of the primitive rule attributed to Saint Augustine, in a way common to parts of other religious orders elsewhere, at the end of the fifteenth century and beginning of the sixteenth century, which followed versions of that rule.

The advent of printing encouraged scholarly comparison of texts of the Fathers, in the preparation of editions, just as it encouraged critical exegesis of scriptural texts. The Christian humanism of the Netherlands was again influential here, not least by virtue of the heroic work of Erasmus as a patristic editor, as well as biblical commentator. Erasmus published an edition of Saint Jerome in 1516, of Saint Cyprian in 1520, and of the commentaries on the psalms of Arnobius the Younger in 1522. Like the other patristic editions of Erasmus, his Hilary was first published by the Froben press at Basel. This edition, of 1523, improved on that edited by Robert Fortuné and published by Bade in Paris in 1511. The improvement was based precisely on Erasmus's comparison of the Paris edition with other manuscript copies. His work on an edition of Augustine naturally proved long, but a complete edition was finally published in 1529 in ten folio volumes. Such a monument to the religious preoccupations of divided Christian Europe was not left without competition, however. At the end of the sixteenth century an edition of Augustine emerged, again in the Netherlands from the Catholic university of Louvain: an edition which was to be regarded as a 'Jansenist' one, in the light of Louvain's importance from the time of the commentary on the *City of God* begun there by Juan Luis Vives in 1520, which was condemned by local and papal authorities. Louvain was the place where Baius taught, and a centre of Catholic Augustinianism. So in seventeenth-century France another edition of Augustine was published, in answer to the 'Jansenist' one: this 'orthodox' edition (1669–1700; 11 volumes) being the work of the Maurists, the French Benedictine congregation dedicated to renewed standards of study and scholarship. The works of Augustine had thus become, in the space of two centuries, a contested field, occupied not only by Catholics and Protestants, with their differing interpretations, but also by rival groups of Catholics, claiming the validity of their own reading of the Saint, on the basis of their own editions. The climax of this polemical appropriation of Augustine's authority, within the Catholic Church, may be seen in the portrait of Saint Cyran, who can be regarded as in some ways the founder of French Jansenism. His portrait by Philippe de Champaigne, a painter associated with the Jansenist communities of Port-Royal, shows him supported by the authorities of the Bible and of Augustine. In this restrained triumph of the Word over more external Works, from within the Catholic, not the Lutheran tradition, the authority of Augustine is finally assimilated, in splendid isolation, to the status of the scriptures.

The preoccupation of Western Christendom with the views of Augustine, then, was not a product of the Protestant Reformation, nor a concern confined to the confrontation between Catholics and Protestants. The 'Augustinian moment' lasted rather from the mid-fifteenth to the mid-eighteenth century, symbolizing an obsession with the most central problems of the Christian faith, salvation and grace, Justification and predestination, which finally alienated many minds, not so much because of the terrible cost of supposedly religious wars and civil strife in Western Europe, in the sixteenth and seventeenth centuries, as because of the increasingly sterile and embittered struggles of factions within Catholic society itself, each claiming unique access to the true statement of doctrine. The political overtones of these struggles, and the involvement above all of the Society of Jesus, led eventually to the transformation of a doctrinal into a jurisdictional dispute. So that what had once been a debate about belief became increasingly a conflict over the rights of Church and state within Catholic Europe. The questions once faced by Augustine in the *City of God* were again more topical, not least in France; just as they had already been for the Venetian friar, Sarpi, at the beginning of the seventeenth century, with his interest in

Gallican thought from Gerson onwards, in his own conflicts with the papacy.

The genesis of the Augustinian age, in the mid-fifteenth century, is arguably more obscure. The possibility of the mutual recriminations of Luther and of Catholic theologians, as at the Council of Trent, denouncing their opponents as Pelagians, perhaps gives a clue in this context. The theological revolution effected in Western European belief by Saint Anselm (c. 1033–1109) had at first meant a greater degree of personal involvement in the salvation of the individual, a refinement of the dependence on the victory of Christ over sin and death, in the cosmic struggle against the demonic forces. But by the fifteenth century, in popular religion at least, the concentration on the human sufferings of Christ, in the redemptive process, seemed once again to have been dissociated from the terrible demands of God as judge: destroying the subtle union of debt and redemption demonstrated by Anselm in *Cur Deus Homo*. This dislocation of Christ's sacrificial person is possibly shown pervasively in fifteenth-century religious art, with the separate dominance of scenes of judgement, dances of death, and the apocalyptic vision of Dürer and Cranach, at the beginning of the sixteenth century finally disseminating a millenary expectation by means of the new techniques of mechanical reproduction; while the elaboration of physical torture in the sequences of Christ's passion is equally distinct.

This dissociation of religious sensibility has sometimes been seen as the result of temporal suffering, in Western Europe terrified by the effects of war, plague and famine. But such a materialist explanation, vague in its chronology, is perhaps less satisfactory than a more strictly theological account. Among the marks of popular belief and practice in fifteenth-century Western Christendom, from Italy to England, the growth of the devotional as opposed to the sacramental is striking. The golden age of the indulgence and of the indulgenced relic, of sermon and pilgrimage, of continued confraternity activity, including both the charitable and the flagellant, is the age of the devout layman, rather than of the priestly administration of the sacraments of the Church. Quite apart from the emergence of the Brethren of the Common Life, or subsequently of the lay and clerical membership of the Italian oratories of Divine Love, or the mixed lay and regular circles in early sixteenth-century Venetian piety, the predominance of the priest is already qualified. For while it is true that pervasive anti-clericalism in Western Europe was distinct from the Lollard and other survivals of specifically heterodox attacks on the sacramental powers and status of the priesthood, the increasing independence of lay devotion is undoubted. While lay literacy, to some extent, was the basis for orthodox, even if suspected mysticism and piety in fifteenth-century England or the Netherlands, and not in fact a monopoly of Lollardy, the illiterate faithful were gaining a relative freedom from clerical mediation in practice, though not in doctrinal theory. The popularity of sermon and of pilgrimage demonstrates the efficacy of lay action in common, especially where the preachers were chosen or licensed by civic authorities: a process reaching a climax of international importance during the years of Savonarola's influence within the Florentine Republic. The growth of the system of paying for an indulgence gave a greater assurance to the purchaser of the value of his acquisition, no longer entirely dependent on the assertion of hierarchical authority over souls in life and in eternity by verbal promise alone. The confraternities chose their own preachers and confessors, so that even the sacramental ministrations of their chaplains were at the ultimate disposal of those who employed them. In the chantries of fifteenth-century Europe, finally, the orthodox doctrines of priestly sacramental powers, efficacy of prayers for the dead, and validity of requiem masses were all asserted in conclusive triumph. But the individual or family or guild who erected and maintained the chantry once again exercised an economic selection in the choice of clergy to serve as mass-priests and singers. They were no more necessarily dependent on the parish priest than was the peasant who sought absolution rather from the itinerant friar.

The lack of confidence in the secular clergy which is thus demonstrated in immediately pre-Lutheran lay devotions is not surprising, in the light of the known deficiencies of a clerical caste characterized by legal privilege rather than by vocational formation. The pre-Lutheran reformers in Spain, France, England and elsewhere who endeavoured to provide some specific training for the clerical profession, especially for the non-graduate clerical proletariat, drew attention to this problem themselves. But the moral deficiencies of the parochial clergy, which in the German lands, for example, led so readily to civic approval of a return to an older German tradition of a married clergy, were perhaps more influential than the educational disabilities. The growth of self-administered devotions among the laity – as in the case of devotion to the human sufferings of Christ, as well as in Marian piety and veneration of the saints – and the elaboration of extra-parochial provision of mass and the sacraments, reduced lay dependence on the parish clergy, and allowed for individual or group employment of priests thought sufficient for the needs of the faithful. Precisely where the sacraments were still required, for mass – even if not for lay communion – whether for the living or for the dead, and for confession, the choice of priest mattered most. The official teaching of the Church, that the efficacy of the sacraments depended on the validity of the priest's ordination, but not on his individual moral quality, had never won perfect acceptance in the popular mind. The rejection of the services of the priest living in sin, or at least lingering suspicion of the worth of his services, could not be entirely eradicated. In this way the confrontation between the Donatists and Saint Augustine, centuries before on the North African littoral, was still repeated in Western Europe on the eve of the Protestant Reformation. The admission, in the age of papal schism and Conciliar response, of the need for reform of the Western Church, underlined an unease which was both learned and popular. The failure, in effect, of the Conciliar programme for reform, was made more acute by the equal disillusionment which followed the theoretic reunion of Eastern and Western Christendom, in the face of imminent Islamic victory, at the Council of Florence, in the mid-fifteenth century.

The final adoption – largely for conspicuous reasons of political necessity – of the reform programme by the papacy, at the beginning of the sixteenth century, produced in the decrees of the Fifth Lateran Council public recognition of standards acknowledged to be largely absent in the Church, which were obviously as far from general implementation as ever on the eve of Luther's challenge. While popular reaction retreated still to the external works which lay piety could provide for itself, without priestly ministration, the learned response was rather to consult the earliest traditions of the Church, in the search for the true identity of the Christian life: a search conducted not, until Luther, in the scriptures alone; but in the Fathers of the early Church too, as guides to the apostolic as well as to their own age. The genesis of Erasmus's guide to the devout layman, the *Enchiridion*, which was to prove in some ways his most widely influential work – even, for a while, in Spain – is a symbol of the twin reaction of learned and intuitive religion to the state of the official Church in Western Europe at the beginning of the sixteenth century. The works of popular piety attacked by the Christian humanist élite, by Erasmus and, originally, by Luther, were viewed with concern precisely because of their popularity. In place of a religion where man's salvation once again turned on his own efforts, in the debasement of Anselmian theology, a truly Christian life, relying on the merits of Christ, was proposed, not only by Luther but also by Erasmus. The latter stressed the co-operation of man's free will; Luther condemned such qualification as Pelagian still, to be in turn condemned as Pelagian himself by Catholic critics of his interior Justification, and its dependence on an intuitive realization of saving grace. But this double concern for the real nature of salvation, and the consequent questions of Justification and of pre-destination, stemmed from a natural return to the doctrine of the Fathers, and above all to the theological works of Augustine, where such questions were so exhaustively examined. It is perhaps in this light that the beginnings of the Augustinian obsession, from the mid-fifteenth century, in Western Europe, are best explained. Anselm's theology, which in its pristine state had heightened lay as well as clerical spirituality in Western Christendom, was replaced, because of the practical effects of its debased form, by a revived Augustini-anism, among the theologically literate at least.

The respect paid by the Christian humanists to the authority of the Fathers did not cease with the first generation of Protestant Reformers. The attention given, from the evolution of Luther's own beliefs onwards, to the Pauline doctrines of Atonement and predes-tination, necessarily perpetuated interest in the interpretation of such subjects in Augustine. In Calvin's *Institutes* the selective quotation of patristic authority, especially Augustine, is pervasive. The contin-ued evolution of Protestantism, after Calvin, produced further pre-occupation with the problem of predestination. International atten-tion was attracted by the debates of the Synod of Dort, at the beginning of the seventeenth century. The doctrinal differences of the Dutch Calvinists over this issue were feared, by Protestants elsewhere in Europe, to symbolize a weakening of their successful struggle against the power of Catholic Spain. The Arminians, who favoured the logically difficult concept of a mitigated predestinari-anism, were denounced as fifth columnists, not only by the Dutch intransigents, but by more politically minded sympathizers with Dutch resistance to the European hegemony of Spain elsewhere, such as the Venetian Sarpi. The Pauline-Augustinian topic of pre-destination was thus to become a weapon for the attack on supposed fifth-columnists within each major division of Western Christendom, since precisely the same type of accusation was to be made against the Jansenists, charged with representing a crypto-Calvinism within the Catholic Church in the Netherlands and France – both areas of divided religious allegiance – at least until Louis xiv attempted to eradicate both Protestant and Jansenist dissidence within his king-dom. The sensitivity of Calvinists at the beginning of the seventeenth century to charges of compromise in doctrine was explicable, given the dangers of voluntary or involuntary collaboration with non-Calvinist authorities. In the first two decades of the century the hitherto triumphant forces of Calvinism seemed to be under attack, by violent oppression or by insidious toleration, in France, Savoy, the Valtelline, Bohemia and the Palatinate. In Scotland concern was equally strong over the outcome of the debates at Dort, since a king educated as a Calvinist in doctrine was nevertheless supporting an attempt to impose episcopal discipline on the Scots Presbyterians. The succession of James VI to the English throne, in 1603, heightened English interest in the fortunes of continental Calvinism, whether in the question of Dutch doctrinal disputes, or in that of the defence of the Palatinate, lost by the king's daughter and son-in-law. But English domestic controversy on the question of predestination preceded the reign of James I. In the last decades of Elizabeth's reign the possibility of a mitigated predestinarianism had been discussed at Oxford, anticipating the Dutch quarrels, and subsequently attacked at Cambridge. The gradual triumph of Puritanism in Elizabethan England, eclipsed by the unresolved questions of Church discipline, involving both Presbyterian sympathizers and more constant loyalists, saw the almost universal adoption by English Protestants, including the official hierarchy, of some form of predestinarian belief, by the beginning of the Stuart regime. The centrality of such belief in the lives of members of the Anglican state Church was shown precisely by the fury with which supposed abandonment of the doctrine, among the Laudian episcopate, was greeted, until the attempted suppression of public controversy over the question by Charles I.

After the Council of Trent, Catholic writers showed a disposition to select favoured patristic authors for quotation, above all Saint John Chrysostom or Saint Gregory, or Gregory Nazianzene, to strengthen argument in support of a hierarchic Church. But Augustine was again of central importance, as himself a resident bishop, even if his relations with the see of Rome were of ambiguous interpretation. The determination of Elizabeth, in mid-sixteenth-century England, to retain an episcopal Church, in the face of both papal and Presbyterian opposition, necessitated, for Anglican apologists, an equally selective use of the Fathers in the search for historical support. The definition of disciplinary structure before comprehensive doctrinal position, which characterized the Elizabethan settlement, whether or not representing a return to the priorities of the Henrician period, was akin to the desire of the emperor to see the Council of

Trent reform the disciplinary abuses of the Church, rather than proceeding to define doctrine in the face of Protestant disagreement. But the Anglican Church could thus not in fact rely on the sole authority of the scriptures, as Calvin in theory at least might do. The final evolution of an Anglican declaration on predestination, in the Articles of Religion, seemed unambiguous enough until the doctrine was deemed to be endangered in the early seventeenth century, when a doubtful uncertainty was detected. The eclectic composition of Anglican definitions, doctrinal and disciplinary, was further hampered by the implicit clash between predestinarianism, favouring an elect, and the Tudor insistence on a comprehensive national Church. Since the latter concern was the original object of Henry VIII and Cromwell, and remained the accepted policy pursued by Elizabeth and her ministers, any attempt to make visible the presence of a possible elect was at variance with the royal will: this incompatibility was as true of the Exercises or Prophesyings of Elizabeth's reign, even where conducted by loyalists, as of the premature separatists during her life.

The further evolution of English Puritan·thought, during the first half of the seventeenth century, even if drawing on earlier sources, saw the transformation of the Covenant theory of salvation. Whether or not under the stimulus of Scots Presbyterian rebels against the continued attempt by the Stuarts to reimpose episcopacy and an effectively English liturgy in the Northern Kingdom, the English Puritans of the Interregnum managed, for all their varieties of independence in matters of belief and practice, to transform the theory of a predestined elect from individual to national application. Either version allowed for, and might be said to require, the existence of the reprobate; but the earlier contradiction, experienced at Geneva itself, between the élitism of pristine predestinarian doctrine and the demands of a comprehensive state Church, to which all should be made to conform, was thus resolved. This resolution of theory proved possible only when the search for a single national Protestant Church, with an enforced monopoly of religious activity, had finally proved a failure in fact. But the abolition of the episcopal hierarchy of the English Church, after long and growing opposition, drew attention equally to the previous potential discrepancies in the composition of that Church. The search for patristic support for the necessary presence of bishops in the Church had finally led, in early Stuart England, to formulation of the *jure divino* theory of episcopacy; even if such an assertion differed from the proposition of those Catholic bishops at the Council of Trent who favoured such a pronouncement, since in the one case the contest was over the exaction of tithes in England, in the other over the much graver issue of the relationship between the papacy and the episcopal hierarchy of the Church. With the disestablishment of Protestant non-conformity in Restoration England gradually but decidedly made certain, the theoretical problems of election and salvation returned, to be finally resolved, in the late eighteenth century, only by Wesley's adoption of a General, as opposed to Particular, doctrine of salvation: an instance of the effect of foreign missionary effort, in his case in America, on the development of European religious belief and practice.

The Western European obsession with the Pauline–Augustinian problems of salvation and predestination can thus be seen to have begun before the Protestant Reformation, and to have continued in the Protestant world, into the eighteenth century. Moreover the use of such concepts and their various interpretations to accuse opponents of crypto-sympathy with an external, Catholic opposition is also clear. In the peculiar circumstances of England, the attempt to maintain an episcopate, not in obedience to the see of Rome, allowed particular opportunities for such attack: here the reliance on patristic authority proved an ambiguous support. The later history of sympathetic contacts, in the seventeenth and eighteenth centuries, between French Catholics, whether Gallican or Jansenist, and Englishmen, whether Anglicans or Catholics at odds with the dominant authority within the confusion of a proscribed community, is a further reminder of the ambiguous authority provided by the Fathers for episcopal hierarchy. Sarpi's criticism of the Council of Trent, in his history of the Council, first published in London in 1619, was based, from the first page, on the view that the Catholic bishops at Trent had voted away their own lawful independence, enslaving themselves to the power of Rome. Such criticism proved welcome in the eccentric world of Jacobean England, even if for reasons more strictly political than theological. The deployment, from the end of Elizabeth's reign, of a Cecilian policy of dividing English Catholics by the formal demands of a public profession of loyalty to the Crown, had been complicated by the postures of James as an international theologian and statesman. The royal debate with Bellarmine, a Jesuit cardinal supposed to represent the heights of papal pretensions to secular power and the depths of jesuitical policy in support of those claims, was published and publicized, oblivious of the irony of Bellarmine's own temporary disgrace, and the brief inclusion of his work in the papal Index of prohibited books, for its too tempered assertion of papal rights.[1]

The political association of James with Gallican France and with republican Venice, a principality devoutly Catholic but facing a papal Interdict in 1606-7, was largely designed to balance Spanish power in Europe, but royal policy made much of the dangers to European rulers, Catholic and Protestant, allegedly caused by Jesuit promotion of regicide. The additional remarks of a polemical nature, provided for the first edition of Sarpi's history of the Council of Trent, by Marc'Antonio de Dominis, reflected the practical disillusionment of many bishops in the remote sees of the Venetian empire. The practical difficulties caused by the conflicting demands of the Venetian state, in Istria and Dalmatia, Crete or the other islands, and the papacy and its representative, the Nuncio in Venice, during the decades after the conclusion of the Council of Trent, at the end of 1563, hampered episcopal attempts to implement the reforms decreed by the Council. But while few of these sees were well remunerated, only de Dominis, after the earlier episode of Vergerio's flight from Capodistria, imagined that the peculiar isolation of Anglican England would prove agreeable. The more telling involvement, in the publication of Sarpi's polemic history, of its translator into English, Nathaniel Brent, underlined the real uncertainty of English episcopalian independence. Brent was a lawyer, like many of Sarpi's international correspondents. His continued services as vicar general to Archbishop Laud, on his succession to the discredited Calvinist Archbishop Abbot, did not prevent him from providing evidence against Laud, when the attempts to extend and realize metropolitical power in the English Church finally collapsed. Sarpi's view of the defeat of episcopal rights at the Council of Trent, by Roman aggrandisement, echoed official statements of the Venetian republic after, though not during the Council; but represented in fact rather the practical concern of the state, after the Council, with its own power and independence, believed to be threatened by papal policies which furthered the designs of the Habsburgs.

The reassertion of episcopal authority in Catholic Europe after the Council of Trent was in the event more hampered by secular rulers, jealous of their traditional control over the Church in their territories, than impeded by papal prerogatives or even by undoubted Curial centralization. The apparent compromise of episcopal rights, by virtue of those many disciplinary decrees of the Council ordering bishops to reform aspects of diocesan life not by virtue of their ordinary powers, but as apostolic delegates, enabled bishops to attempt at least the restoration of their authority over those once exempt because of peculiar privileges obtained from the holy see.

Cathedral canons and, in some respects at least, male and female religious, were now subject to diocesan government, while the plenitude of papal power to grant exemptions was not openly diminished. Such intentional compromise naturally meant decades of difficulty for resident bishops, after the Council, even if not on the scale of the obstacles caused to reform by the Council's realistic abandonment of plans for an outright attack on the privileges claimed by secular rulers in ecclesiastical affairs. The equally contrived ambiguity of wording, with which the major dispute at Trent, over the relationship between papal power and episcopal office, was finally resolved, ended the danger of the Council's disruption by open dispute, even after the refusal of the presiding legates, repeatedly throughout the long and interrupted course of the Council, to allow explicit debate of the question had reduced the discussion to one, in form at least, confined to the nature of a bishop's duty to reside in his see. By comparison with such contested issues, the purely doctrinal decrees of the Council of Trent are often regarded as a consolidated success, ending previous doubt as to the identity of true Catholic teaching. The relative ease with which the doctrinal definitions of the Council were accepted in Catholic Europe, as opposed to the disciplinary reforms, or the areas of mixed doctrinal and practical implication, such as the decree on marriage, and the possibility of reducing the careful formulae of the doctrinal decrees, soon after the end of the Council, to a systematic catechism, certainly support such a view. The catechetic campaigns of the Catholic Church, from immediately after the end of the Council, spreading from Europe to the overseas missions, and lasting until the French Revolution, arguably transformed, however gradually, popular Catholicism, from a ritual to a creed, even if at the most elementary level of comprehension. Yet, by a great paradox, the doctrinal definitions of Trent, with all their care to balance existing traditions within Catholic thought, failed in fact to end internal debate over Catholic belief and its formulation, within the same period, among educated believers, not least professional theologians. It is in this context that the continued preoccupation, in Western Europe, with the Pauline–Augustinian topics of salvation and predestination, beginning before the Protestant Reformation, is revealed as maintaining itself, into the eighteenth century, in Catholic just as in Protestant religion.

Before the end of the sixteenth century a doctrinal dispute arose in Catholic Spain, which was to disturb the peace of the post-Tridentine Church both there and in Italy. The controversy *De Auxiliis*, about the means of grace, was essentially about salvation. But the

Spanish origins of the conflict reflected less theological issues. While the opinions attributed to the Jesuit theologian Molina by Dominican and other opponents were attacked for Pelagian laxity, the Dominican theologians of Salamanca, led by Bañez, defended an Augustinian rigorism. The opposition of the friars to the Society of Jesus in Spain was based in part on an objection to the Society's entry into the world of university education. The friars in Spain attempted to maintain a monopoly of the chairs held by mendicants, causing continual problems for bishops, as at Salamanca, and the papal Nuncio at the Spanish 'court, by their quarrels against the Jesuits. Orders from Rome to suspend public controversy were disregarded in effect; and topics for argument were freshly sought, as, for example, the question of whether or not *castrati* singers might legitimately marry. The entry of the Jesuits into educational activity proved problematic elsewhere, as at ancient Italian universities such as Padua and Bologna, where traditional privileges were defended against the attractions of enterprising initiative. The Paduan difficulties were ultimately resolved by the expulsion of the Society from Venetian territory, following the Interdict of 1606–7, during which the Jesuits had taken a conspicuously pro-papal position. The attractions of Jesuit colleges, maintaining a constant tutorial supervision of pupils, in a way which the old universities in continental Europe did not provide, continued to persuade parents in Venetian territory to risk the penalties prescribed for sending children out of the state, to such colleges, for education. The state monopoly of higher education which the Venetian republic thus attempted to conserve for Padua was effectively breached; while in Venetian Dalmatia funds were clandestinely collected to send children across the Adriatic, to be educated by Jesuits at Loreto, in the papal states.[2]

The irony of the pervasive triumph of Jesuit education, creating problems with episcopal and university authorities elsewhere, as in Prague, after the Counter-Reformation triumph of the battle of the White Mountain, was the reluctance of the Society's superiors to recognize this activity as proper to the Jesuit purpose. The rapid spread of Jesuit colleges, from Sicily to Northern and Eastern Europe, and overseas both Eastwards and Westwards, took place in the face of official disapproval within the Society, until, at the end of the sixteenth century, the force of public demand for Catholic education of the male children of the upper levels of society was acknowledged. The colleges for lay education, complemented in some areas, as in Hungary, by universities directly under Jesuit control, were thus in the end more successful than those for clerical education.

The specialist seminaries, created for areas where diocesan seminaries were obviously impossible, as with the English College at Rome, underwent internal difficulties as a result of contested Jesuit direction, when the papacy entrusted such institutions to the Jesuits. The diocesan seminaries for the vocational training of the secular clergy, which gradually began to be erected, following the decree of the Council of Trent ordering such institutions to be set up, were at first placed under Jesuit direction, by bishops still lacking an adequate supply of able clergy of their own. But accusations that the Jesuits undermined the whole purpose of raising the quality of the ordinary clergy, by enticing the most promising students into their own Society, frequently led to a revision of such initial arrangements. In Spain the opposition of vested interests, not least the friars', prevented, unusually, the successful competition of the Jesuits at university level, and their educational enterprises, in the Spanish kingdom, took the uncharacteristic form of colleges catering also for middle to lower levels of society, training boys in the literary skills necessary for further legal education; even if that again demonstrated the versatility of the Jesuits' curricula, which varied from country to country, and continued to change in the seventeenth and eighteenth centuries, until the suppression of the Society in 1773.

The apparent paradox of Ignatius Loyola founding his Society outside Spain, even if subsequent Generals included Spaniards, and indeed highly born Spaniards, suggests another reason for the bitterness of the doctrinal disputes which marked the immediately post-Tridentine decades in both Spain and Italy. The difficulties encountered by the young Loyola in central Spain, at a time when all religious independence and enthusiasm were suspect, should be remembered together with the influences of the Iberian periphery in his life: his birth and early life in the Basque provinces and Navarre, and his chosen retreat at Montserrat, in the Catalan heartland. The accusations made, not least by Dominicans at both the Roman and Spanish courts, that the Society should not receive papal approval – which was indeed withheld for some time, because the Jesuits lacked the characteristics of a religious order – represented in one sense an accurate assessment of the Loyolan search for the essence of an ordered yet active religious life, independent of the regular traditions of any existing orders, even the mendicant orders. The suspicion of Erasmian contempt for the regular orders thus lingered, together with the insinuation that a peculiar form of meditation, in the Spiritual Exercises, was reminiscent of the mystical idiosyncrasies of the 'enlightened' in early sixteenth-century Spain, sub-

sequently suppressed on the grounds of alleged crypto-Protestantism
or of Judaizing. Such suspicion even the strictly enclosed reformed
Carmelites led by Saint Teresa of Avila had to face too, in their
search for a renewal of the properly contemplative life. The Society
of Jesus, however, was marked out for special distrust, because of its
singular appropriation of the divine name, and, finally, with the
eventual approval of its constitution by the papacy, because of its
close links with the papal office. The friars had, in the later medieval
Church, partly replaced the monks, as those whose intimate connections with Roman privilege chiefly obstructed the normal functioning
of the episcopal hierarchy and parochial system. But the Jesuits'
extra vow of absolute obedience to the pope of the day inserted the
new Society between the orders of friars and the holy see; this was
just at the time when the privileged exemptions of monks and mendicants were under attack by the assembled bishops at Trent. At the
Council the theologians provided by the Jesuits, alongside those
provided, in accordance with tradition, by the older religious orders,
defended the powers of the papacy against episcopal claims, following their vow of absolute obedience. But the prominence of the new
Society's representatives, and their influence, even if on separate
debates and decrees, and not in all cases as a united force or in a
constant direction, remained a source of disquiet. Such issues combined, in the decades immediately following the Council, in a clear
challenge to Jesuit autonomy in Spain.

The crown Inquisition in the Spanish kingdoms was the creation,
in effect, of the fifteenth century, when the reform of the Spanish
Church was combined with the beginnings of the final stage in the
reconquest of the Iberian peninsula for Christianity. The expulsion
of the Jews, at the end of the fifteenth century, the conquest of the
last Moorish kingdom on the Northern shore of the Western Mediterranean, Granada, by the Catholic monarchs, and, ultimately, the
expulsion of the Moriscos at the beginning of the seventeenth century, were stages in the reimposition of Christian purity, conceived
in racial as much as in religious terms. The effective extension of
Castilian dominance over the other kingdoms of the peninsula, which
this process also represented, despite the very real assertions of local
rights which continued in Aragon, also reached a climax. This was
achieved by the succession to the Portuguese kingdom and its overseas possessions of the Spanish crown, between 1580 and 1640,
before the collapse of complete Castilian hegemony caused by the
attempts of Olivares to make the union of the Iberian crowns a
political and economic reality. The reform of the Spanish Church

and the Christian reconquest of the peninsula were thus equally extensions of the crown's effective control over Iberian life, and the financial resources of the Military Orders, originally destined for the fight against Islam – which did still continue in the central and Eastern Mediterranean, and, more briefly, on the North African coast – contributed directly to the crown's needs, by a similar extension. Other ecclesiastical sources of revenue were granted by the papacy to the crown in Spain, while the papal grant of patronage rights over the newly founded Church in Granada was amplified by the greater grant of patronage rights to the Spanish and Portuguese crowns over the new worlds to be discovered and the new Churches to ʾe founded and funded by royal authority overseas. To this extent, the fifteenth-century alliance of popes and national rulers, which survived the schismatic years of rival popes, and was strengthened by the restored Roman papacy's search for support against the Conciliarist claims of bishops and cardinals, reached its logical extension in the new territories of the Iberian crowns. While the alliance had its equally effective elements in France, or in England, overcoming obstacles in either case, to last, in the latter, into the earlier part of Henry VIII's reign, the empire, alone of major European powers, remained isolated; both because of the effective dissipation of authority within the empire, among principalities and cities, and because of the long-standing distrust of imperial authority at Rome, and the reciprocal view of the papacy in Germany.

The special control over religious, and indeed secular life, exercised by the Spanish crown, depended, however, on the papal grant of competence in Inquisition against heresy. The original use of the crown Inquisition against Jews rather than against Christian heretics was not at issue, given the extensive use of the institution precisely against alleged Judaizers. The control once granted proved impossible to recover, as the papacy discovered at the time of the Council of Trent. The supposed exemption of bishops from the attentions of the crown Inquisition, and the theoretical reservation of cases involving them to Rome's own tribunals, were openly challenged at the highest level. The arrest of the primate of Spain, Carranza, archbishop of Toledo, enabled the crown to benefit for a long period from the revenues of one of the richest sees in Christendom. But the successful attack on the newly appointed archbishop, fresh from struggle against Protestant heretics in Marian England, in the service of his master, Philip himself, by a combination of rivals, episcopal and mendicant, was a sign that the crown Inquisition in Spain recognized neither primatial nor papal superiority. The triumph of the

Dominicans was above all established, since the mendicant rivals of Carranza included those from his own Dominican order, and the Dominicans were powerful in the crown Inquisition, as in the old medieval Inquisition. Elsewhere, in areas where the revived Roman Inquisition, reactivated by Caraffa in the mid-sixteenth century, operated, Dominicans and sometimes Franciscans were commonly the Inquisitors; while the royal council of the Inquisition in Spain, which included lay councillors, was headed by the Inquisitor General, usually a Spanish cardinal or at least an archbishop, whose powers on the Supreme Council were nevertheless limited. The Dominicans were thus peculiarly associated with the exercise of Inquisitorial authority in Spain, even if other connections with royal power were shared with other orders of friars.[3] The Augustinians were also prominent, alongside the Dominicans, in Spanish intellectual life and in the overseas missions; while the Augustinian offshoot, the Hieronymites, were powerful at the royal court, and were to occupy the purpose-built Escorial of Philip II, both court and convent. For, with the defeat of the *comuneros* revolt under Charles, and the arrest of Carranza, the end of Toledo as imperial capital was marked, and, despite signs of the old peripatetic character of the monarchy being revived, after Philip II's death in 1598, with the use of Valladolid once again and of Madrid, the Spanish crown settled in the centre of Castile. The offence of the Jesuits, in this period, was thus to challenge openly the absolute powers of the crown Inquisition, newly demonstrated in the case of the primate, by claiming that their special relationship with Rome exempted them from the authority of that tribunal. A careful persecution was launched, to establish their subjection to the crown Inquisition, which was mitigated in its effects only by the intervention of the papal Nuncio in Spain. There were to be no exemptions from the authority of the crown Inquisition in the Iberian peninsula. The controversy over the means of grace thus takes its place in the origins of Jesuit-Dominican rivalry, part of a wider rivalry between Jesuits and friars, the latter sometimes acting alongside other opponents of the Society, whether Jansenists in Catholic Europe, or diocesan bishops, there or in the overseas missions. For, with the early extension of Jesuit activity to the missions, and even to the Far East, a new dimension of rivalry appeared.

The post-Tridentine papacy failed in effect to resolve or suppress the doctrinal disputes between Jesuits and Dominicans. The decrees of the Council of Trent itself were in a way no more effective. The Conciliar debate on Justification, and the final definition on that subject, are often described as having marked the final separation of Catholic and Protestant faith in Europe, the exclusion of chances of compromise represented by Contarini's proposal of a Double Justification theory, and the defeat of Catholic Augustinianism represented by Seripando. In fact none of these suppositions proves accurate. A more fundamental disagreement between Catholic and Lutheran, from an early stage of the Council, was established as that concerning the source of faith, for the determination of all other contested doctrines: scripture alone, or scripture and the traditions of the Church, the one supporting the Lutheran theory, if not entirely practice, of the priesthood of all believers, the other implying the traditional concept of an hierarchical Church. This ultimate division also reflected Luther's own evolution, from his original appeal from pope to General Council, in the way taken by other dissidents such as the Dominican friar Savonarola, to his final view, as a married ex-Augustinian friar, at the time of the Council's belated meeting, that such a Council was irrelevant. It was indeed precisely on the nature of the Church that the debates conducted at Regensburg by Contarini were shown to have failed, since the impossibility of compromise, over the doctrine of the Eucharist, even with the moderate Lutherans primarily represented at the Colloquy, drew attention to the inextricable link between an hierarchic Church and one rejecting any concept of a priesthood with sacrificial and mediatory powers. The connection between eucharistic doctrine and the doctrine of the priesthood had been demonstrated at least since the time of Wyclif, even if Luther had not always been immediately aware of the necessary association, from his first surprise at finding himself following the arguments of the despised Czech heresiarch, Hus, to his obstinate defence of the theory of Consubstantiation. Neither Contarini nor the Lutherans viewed the Regensburg discussions as a successful prelude to compromise in fact.

The Conciliar debates at Trent on Justification, in their extended development, excluded one personal position on the subject; but since that position was suspected, but not known, the exclusion could hardly represent a failure to allow open debate. The refusal of Cardinal Pole to reveal his own private belief on the subject heightened suspicion of him among opponents who were never to be permanently reconciled with him, within the Church, Caraffa above all; while it added to his dangers by allowing critics from the Protestant world, led by Vergerio, to accuse him of hypocritical silence, thus confirming the doubts of Catholic conservatives about the English cardinal. The revelation, in recent years, that Pole's views on Justi-

fication were virtually identical with those of Luther sheds light on
those contemporary manœuvres; but it does not alter the fact of
Pole's preference to retreat from the Council and submit implicitly
to the new formulation of the teaching of the Church, rather than
expose and defend his personal opinion at Trent. The Conciliar
debates, whether on Justification or on the source of faith, as also on
eucharistic doctrine, were in any case a careful search for expressions
which would do justice, as far as possible, to all legitimate forms of
existing Catholic thought, as has also been demonstrated in detail in
recent study. The idea of the Council's search always for the most
extreme statement of traditional views, in an attempt to delineate,
with the greatest possible clarity, the distinction between faith and
heresy, is thus inaccurate. The incompatibility of Catholic teaching
and Protestant errors was certainly demonstrated, by the intentional
conclusion of the doctrinal decrees with formulae of anathema, ad-
dressed to specific heretical statements; but such antithetical structure was traditional, from the earliest Councils of the Church. Nor
were the doctrinal decrees of the Council a defeat for Catholic Augustinianism, and the triumph of a revived scholasticism. On the
crucial issue of salvation an Anselmian, rather than purely Thomist
view of the Redemption was reasserted.

The Conciliar doctrine of original sin, and identification of the
fallen state of man, were in fact an outlook shared by Calvin, as well
as obviously, if in a different way, by Luther. The consequent necessity of infant baptism, asserted in words parallel to those of Calvin in his *Institutes*, even if providing nevertheless some grounds
for Calvinist criticism, marked the more important European division between the Catholics and magisterial reformers, Calvinists
included in this case, on the one hand, and the radical sectarians on
the other. The notion of Justification entertained by the Augustinian
General, Seripando, who remained a cardinal of the Church and
legate presiding at Trent after the conclusion of the Conciliar debate
on this topic, was never intended as an eirenic gesture to Protestantism, however. Unlike those from the Augustinian orders who fled
to the Protestant world, like Peter Martyr, seeking a quasi-Lutheran
independence and the possibility of clerical marriage in Edwardian
England, Seripando explicitly condemned the views of Lutheran
theology on the subject. The defeat of his own proposals and the
victory of a more Thomist approach was not simply a Dominican
triumph against the rival Augustinian theologians, though. Those
Italian bishops present who had some pastoral experience, or at least
sensibility, preferred a modified Augustinianism, stressing the way

of salvation open potentially to all men, and so joined the Dominican critics of Seripando. The outcome was thus certainly not a reassertion of scholasticism, under Jesuit inspiration, despite the importance of the contribution to the debate of the Jesuit theologian Salmerón. For, in any case, the Dominican school of Salamanca was about to launch its attack on the innovation of Jesuit theology as well as of the Society's rule. Seripando's own views, too, were influenced by Thomism, as well as by anti-Aristotelianism acquired both from the neo-Platonism he found in Augustine and independently from his own studies in Platonism. The Council's implicit condemnation of a Catholic theologian at the university of Louvain, Baius, spared him the indignity of public association with heresy, quite apart from the sensitivity of a Catholic institution in the Netherlands which Spanish rule was trying to retain for the Church. The interpretation of the doctrine of grace and salvation which Baius defended could be described as Augustinian, in an unqualified manner.

The further, papal condemnation of Baius, in 1567, coincided with the final elevation to the status of Doctor of the Church of Thomas Aquinas, associating the Dominican authority in this way with the learning of the Fathers. This symbol of Dominican victory against rival theological schools should, however, be considered in the light of subsequent events. While this victory strengthened Dominican morale in the struggle against Jesuit influence, the outcome of the dispute *De Auxiliis*, as has been seen, proved ambiguous. Moreover the Dominicans, both in Spain and subsequently in France, represented a rigorism, opposed to Jesuit alleged laxity in pastoral theology, which was shared by the Catholic Augustinians of Louvain and later of France. So that it is impossible to see the condemnation of Baius as further evidence of a scholastic revival, let alone one led by the Jesuits, at the expense of a Catholic Augustinianism supposedly defeated at Trent. While theological tradition certainly rested to some extent on the rivalry of religious orders, Thomism and Augustinianism were to a degree complementary, certainly not mutually exclusive. The use made by Aquinas of certain Augustinian ideas, however much selective, or Arabized, led to partial Dominican defence of Augustinian theology, while the Dominicans' own rule was a further example of one claiming Augustinian inspiration. The medieval predestinarian tradition of the Augustinian friars, represented by Gregory of Rimini, was naturally appreciated by Luther, but the parallel Augustinian tradition of the Franciscans was traced through Bonaventura and Duns Scotus. It was not surprising that Erasmus, in editing the Fathers, should urge respect for both Aquinas and Scotus.

Although friars, both in the Germanic and Hispanic worlds, were among the most voluble enemies of the Christian humanists, not all opponents of the humanists were friars, as the examples of the young Luther and Bucer should recall. The defeat of Erasmian humanism in Spain, at the hands of the crown Inquisition, could never be attributed however to the Jesuits, for obvious chronological and institutional reasons. The virtual independence of the Spanish Inquisition, as in its condemnation of the Catechism which Carranza had intended for the true conversion to Catholicism of England, during the Marian restoration of the old religion, was a reminder that the Tridentine assertion of doctrinal determination by the central hierarchy of the Church alone was never accepted in fact throughout Catholic Europe. The enforced rapidity of the Council's conclusion, despite Spanish episcopal protest, with the supposed danger of revived Conciliarist claims in the event of the pope's death during the sessions of the assembly, left to the papacy wide powers of confirming and completing the decrees passed at Trent. This explicit decision of the bishops, reflecting the experience of the unenforced reforms adopted at Constance, at Conciliarist Basel, and at the papal Fifth Lateran Council, showed a mature consideration of practical reality. The speedy confirmation of the Conciliar decrees, after examination by a commission of cardinals at Rome, left the papacy as the theoretic sole source of subsequent doctrinal interpretation, as well as the single authority for the decision of disputed cases arising from the implementation of the disciplinary decrees. The practical results were inevitably very different. The Council's realistic rejection of a plan to remove all existing privileges in Church administration and finance from those rulers still owing allegiance to Catholicism left popes as well as diocesan bishops restricted in the enforcement of disciplinary reform. But even in the realm of doctrine, where explicit refusal to accept the Council's decrees did not so apply in Catholic Europe, the papacy proved unable to enforce its monopoly of declaratory decision. The medieval tradition persisted of alternative sources of doctrinal arbitration, not least the universities, or their theological faculties. Henry VIII's marital difficulty had been the subject of public consultation in the European universities; while the intervention of university theological authorities in the disputes involving the Christian humanists and their traditionalist opponents led to the involvement of the same authorities, as well as of the Council of Trent itself, in the genesis of the Index of Prohibited Books, ultimately (outside Spain) a papal preserve, again in theory.

In fact book censorship in France, where the jurisdiction equally of the Roman Holy Office was never accepted, remained rather a matter for national authorities, not least secular. The independence of Louvain university was proudly preserved in the Netherlands, and Baius died a Catholic. But the influence of the Louvain school of Catholic theology persisted, and was enshrined in the exhaustive *Augustinus* of Jansen, bishop of Ypres, which was to become the fount of French Jansenist inspiration. In the Netherlands, the assertion of episcopal rights, associated with an interpretation of independence from Rome based on patristic study, lasted until its final transformation into the schism of the Church of Utrecht in the early eighteenth century. On the borders with France, the territory captured by Louis XIV, or at least incorporated into the possessions of the French crown, provided the opportunity for Fénelon, as archbishop of Cambrai, to persecute the Jansenists of the diocese, after his own fall from favour at the royal court. In France, the involvement of the Paris theological faculty, the Sorbonne, complicated the resolution of the Jansenist controversy. The transformation, though hardly the solution of the problem, eventually followed shifts of position among other participants, the king, the Gallican clergy, and the lawyers of the Paris *parlement*, in the early years of the eighteenth century. For French conditions in fact allowed the intervention of such forces, as well as that of the Sorbonne, in an originally theological dispute. Anti-Jesuit feeling over their educational influence was once again involved here, in the genesis, for example, of opposition to the Society in the Arnauld family. By the end of the seventeenth century the French Oratory, founded by Cardinal Bérulle as a pro-papal force in the Gallican Church, had come to include Jansenist sympathizers and opponents of the Jesuits, not least because of the rivalry between the Society and the Oratory in French Catholic education. The French province of the Jesuits was also by then no longer a unitedly pro-papal group, but included its own Gallicanists, supporters of royal power against both Jansenists and the *dévot* representatives of the pristine Catholic reform existing before the division of revived Catholic devotion between the Jansenists on the one hand, and the non-Jansenist varieties of Catholic rigorists on the other.

The rivalry of the Society and of the French Oratory thus represented a contest for influence, not least over the direction of seminaries for the diocesan clergy. This was a problem already experienced elsewhere, before the innovations of Saint-Sulpice, another foundation of the early seventeenth century in France, designed to begin the belated reform of the Catholic Church there and strengthen its links with Rome against the revived Gallicanism which accompanied the new Bourbon dynasty. The brief expulsion of the Jesuits from parts of France during the reign of Henri IV, on suspicion of complicity in one of the assassination plots which ultimately brought him to the same end as his last Valois predecessor, had not sufficed to satisfy feeling against the Society. Once again issues less than purely theological were involved, as with the comparable genesis of anti-Jesuit feeling from the earlier years of the Society in Catholic Spain, in the mixed religious society of seventeenth-century France. The papal policy of support, until the decision of Clement VIII to make diplomatic advantage from necessity, for the ultra-Catholic League in France, as opposed to the Bourbon candidate of Navarre, led to a revival of Gallicanism among the moderate supporters of Henri, the *politiques*, powerfully present among lawyers and *parlementaires*. Such considerations, with their implication for public attitudes towards an order closely connected with the papacy, are very far from questions of grace and predestination. It was not a triumph of neo-scholasticism which was originally feared from the Jesuit presence in France. The Christian humanist tradition, which barely survived in Spain, in biblical, patristic and even Erasmian references, was not at risk in early seventeenth-century France, recovering gradually from the civil wars of the past half-century. Nor was Catholic Augustinianism at first at issue in France, except inasmuch as the influence of Augustine combined with that of Aquinas originally in the thought of both Bérulle and Antoine Arnauld.

Bérulle's eclectic theology demonstrated receptivity to the traditions of Bonaventura and modern Jesuit writers too, as well as an emphasis on selective biblical study: at the origins of the Oratorian development of scriptural criticism in seventeenth-century France. Religious orders after the Council of Trent were not in fact confined to the defence of a single theological tradition. Jesuit admiration for the works of Augustine was found even in Spain, as well as in the writings of Bellarmine; while Benedictines were loyal to Thomist thought, both in Spain, and at the university of Salzburg, founded in the early seventeenth century by a reforming prince-archbishop. The original French supporters of Antoine Arnauld against the Jesuits included those who were not favourable to the supposed theology of the Jansenists, but who nevertheless objected to the method of condemnation of the five propositions, alleged to be drawn from the *Augustinus*. The original leader of the French Jansenists, Saint Cyran, had admirers who were not of his theological opinion, among the *dévots* involved in Catholic reform and charitable activity, such as Vincent de Paul. Such admiration had to face political suspicion, since the circles of *dévots*, and the Jansenists who subsequently emerged from those circles as a distinct group, never lost their association with criticism of the main tradition of French foreign and domestic policy in the seventeenth century.

This was not simply because of the pro-papal attitudes of the first founders of the French Oratory or of Saint-Sulpice, who regarded some check to revived Gallicanism as necessary in the practical reform of the abuses of the French Church, after the disruption of civil war, and in a country where a Calvinist presence had finally been granted royal recognition. The opportunities for Catholic reform, appreciated even by Richelieu, as a young bishop, resident in his diocese, before his emancipation from the political patronage of the Queen Mother, first arose in the regency which followed the assassination of Henri IV, the king whose throne rested, in part at least, on the recognition of the Huguenot religion. The return in the regency to a pan-Catholic, pro-papal and pro-Habsburg foreign policy, directed by Marie de'Medici and her Italian and other servants, represented the ideals of the French Catholic reformers, including those who were later to emerge as Jansenists. But the reaction, promoted by Richelieu in the name of Louis XIII, to the royal tradition of an anti-Habsburg policy, marked a permanent division between the Gallican crown and the circles of both *dévots* and Jansenists. The association of *dévots* and Jansenists with the *frondeurs* in the regency of Anne of Austria represented another attempt to redirect French internal and external policy. The attitudes towards the Jansenist controversy struck at this time by the rival prelates, Mazarin and Gondi, in their search for political support at Rome and in Paris, were a further reminder of the political complications of an apparently theological issue. At the end of Louis XIV's reign, the attempt to suppress the Jansenists, following the supposed solution of the problem of the French Protestants, coexisted with the adoption of an equally rigorist, but non-Jansenist, moralism at the royal court, under the influence of Mme de Maintenon.

Yet this royal rigorism, at a court where the king's confessor was a Jesuit, was again distinct from the partly anti-Jesuit rigorism of the deutero–*dévots*, such as Saint-Simon and Fénelon, associated with the successionary interest. The critics of the internal and external devastation caused by the policies of Louis's later years drew their inspiration, in the cases of such men, from the traditions of Christian humanism and Catholic reform; but they, like Vauban, were dis-

graced for their political opposition rather than for their religious
attitudes exactly. Nevertheless, it was the order of Louis to Fénelon,
to retire to his diocese, which allowed the archbishop of Cambrai to
begin his anti-Jansenist campaigns there, and to make that singular
gesture, in the history of the French Church of the seventeenth and
eighteenth centuries, his own public submission to papal censure of
his Quietist views. The Jansenists themselves, until the end of the
seventeenth century, strove to represent their position as one of
loyalty to the papacy, as befitted their common origins in the world
of Catholic reform in the early decades of the century. Their use of
casuistry, supposedly a weapon of their Jesuit opponents, to maintain
a distinction between 'fact' and 'right', in the condemnation of allegedly Jansenist error in Augustinian interpretation, was thus not
originally the legalism of jurisdictional controversialists. The desire
to be recognized as obedient to the Church was natural, in the light
of their attempt to claim as Catholic their version of Augustinian
theology. Yet such doctrinal questions, by the beginning of the
eighteenth century, in France and the Netherlands, were complicated
by divisions more serious than those between the mendicant orders,
which, for example, fuelled the dispute at and after the Council of
Trent, in Spain above all, over the Immaculate Conception: a singular case of the problematic definitions of the effect of grace. The
royal Gallicanism of Louis XIV, which attempted the extension of the
*régale*, against the interest of French diocesan bishops and their
selection of suitable parochial clergy, saw the resistance naturally
look for Roman support, even when the bishops concerned were, in
some cases, sympathetic to Jansenism. But the later wars of Louis's
reign, and his increasing diplomatic isolation in Europe, necessitated
his own search for papal support, in turn. The Jansenist alliance
with the Gallicanism of the French clergy and lawyers was then
effected, as the only alternative for survival, in the face of papal
condemnation and royal persecution. The final transformation of an
originally theological cause, even if never lacking political implications, into a jurisdictional campaign was thus brought about. In the
Netherlands, the disputes over the exercise of hierarchical authority,
which had characterized the proscribed Catholic communities in
both England and the Northern Netherlands throughout the
seventeenth century, finally created the schism of Utrecht in the
early eighteenth century. But in France, and eventually in Spain, in
Italy, influenced both by France and directly by the Netherlands,
and in the Austrian lands influenced in turn by Italy as well as
by the Febronianism of the princely German bishops, eighteenth-

century Jansenism was marked by anti-Curialism and even anti-Romanism. Such attitudes were largely jurisdictional, despite the still present Augustinianism of bishops and theologians, including those from certain orders, especially Augustinian and Oratorian.

The anti-Jesuitry of eighteenth-century statesmen and rulers in Catholic Europe thus drew on complex sources. The reservations about papal power which the effect of the Tridentine reforms had rather excited among secular lawyers and politicians were still live; and the association of the Society of Jesus with papal claims was maintained by the existence of the Society's special vow, even if taken only by the élite of an order which, in any case, had grown to such a size as to present many competing signs of allegiance, as within the French province by the beginning of the century. The rivalry of religious orders for educational influence in Catholic society, apparently won on a universal scale by the Jesuits, in Europe and overseas, was overtaken by secular concern at the effects of ecclesiastical formation of lay society, and the accompanying accumulation of wealth, represented by all aspects of the Church, including the contemplative as well as the active orders. The rivalry of the religious orders in Europe, especially that of the friars with the Jesuits, was fatally increased by a new factor, contributing to the successful campaigns against the Society, which ultimately led to the expulsion of the Jesuits from one Catholic state after another and the virtually enforced suppression of the Society, ironically by the papacy itself. The European conflicts of Church and state, in the post-Tridentine Catholic revival, reached a climax in this way, and in the similar defeat of the long, post-Conciliar attempts by the papacy to enforce application of the revised bull, *In Coena Domini*, which threatened automatic excommunication against all who obstructed ecclesiastical rights or jurisdiction in any way. But the tensions caused in the overseas missions by the entry of the post-Tridentine papacy, from the early seventeenth century, into activity previously granted as a monopoly to the patronage of the Iberian crowns, were a reminder that the pastoral and jurisdictional problems within areas of Christian division in Europe, whether France, the Netherlands or England, were mild compared with the difficulties of missionary enterprise among non-Christian peoples.

The Council of Trent, despite its originally proclaimed purpose of reuniting Christendom against Islam, did not give attention to specifically missionary problems, as opposed to the doctrinal challenge of European Protestantism. The fluctuations of Habsburg and of papal policy, as demonstrated in the question of the French succession, prevented the successful creation of a Catholic alliance of pope and rulers against Protestants, whatever the political and military threats experienced by the latter. Papal financial contributions to Habsburg enterprise, against Elizabethan England or in early seventeenth-century Germany against native and Swedish Protestants, did not prevent constant conflicts over policy, whether in Germany in the sixteenth and seventeenth centuries, in the Netherlands, or towards England or France. The military, or rather naval confrontation with Islam was not markedly successful, despite the brief triumph of rare Catholic co-operation at Lepanto, and Spanish attention was increasingly diverted from the Western Mediterranean to the Atlantic and the Netherlands. The defence of Malta, though heroic, did not compensate for the loss of Cyprus, least of all, naturally, in Venetian eyes. The second strand of papal policy in the post-Tridentine decades, that of reunion, was only partially more successful than this first pursuit of confrontation, whether with Islam or Protestantism. The most extreme attempts to unite non-Protestant Christians in Roman obedience, involving contacts with the Russian and Ethiopian Churches, failed. Relative success was obtained in the patronage of the Maronites. The formation of a Uniate Church among the Eastern-rite believers of Poland was the outstanding victory, a part of the general and largely Jesuit triumph in recovering Poland for the Roman allegiance. But the cultivation of Greek Christians, in Sicily and Southern Italy, and the training of Greek-rite clergy loyal to the papacy, in a special seminary at Rome, had as little effect as the optimistic publication of the *Acta* of the Council of Florence on the view of Roman claims entertained among the Greeks of the Venetian Mediterranean empire. The Republic, always anxious to maintain the allegiance of its Greek subjects, protected their effective independence from Roman interference. It feared their contacts with the Orthodox patriarch of Constantinople, resident at the capital of the Turkish enemy, might otherwise become too close, as a reaction against Roman intervention.

The third aim of papal universal policy, from the beginning of the seventeenth century, was however to intervene in the conversion of non-Christian peoples in the overseas missions. The lack of resources for this task eventually led to the political complication of French support for the papal missions, organized under the Congregation *De Propaganda Fide*, as the decline of the Portuguese empire in the East, particularly, led to the danger of Anglo-Dutch Protestant influence in the area triumphing against Catholicism. The confrontation of the papal missions of the *Propaganda* and the crown missions of the Spanish *patronato* and Portuguese *padroado* were thus, in a way, part of the rivalry of European powers in areas of overseas expansion, creating in effect, a French quasi-patronage in place of the Portuguese. While such political considerations sometimes played a crucial part in the fortunes of the Catholic missions, as with the Dutch encouragement of Japanese suspicions about the Jesuit presence in their islands, the Catholic Church exported to the overseas missions its own internal divisions experienced in Europe after the Council of Trent. The rivalry of bishops and regulars, competing for limited financial resources above all, and the conflicts of friars and Jesuits, were not effectively controlled by the Iberian royal councils, nor could they be in fact by the papacy, whose powers in the overseas missions were almost non-existent until a late date.

The problem of converting non-Christians had arisen at an early stage, even in the missions of the friars in America. Las Casas, the Dominican defender of the rights of the native Indian population of America, stressed the rationality of potential converts to Christianity. He was influenced in this by the views of Augustine, especially on free will, finding, in the *City of God*, consideration of the fate of infidels. A similar concern about the eternal destiny of virtuous pagans naturally arose among the Christian humanists of fifteenth-century Italy, where, as has been seen, attention to Augustine was revived, alongside attention to the classical authors and to scriptural texts. But a practical preoccupation with the problem of converting non-Christian peoples had already been caused, in the expanding dominions of the Spanish crown, by the reconquest of Granada, where a population was to be changed from Islamic to Christian loyalty as swiftly as possible. The missionary experience of friars, directed by Talavera, the first archbishop of Granada appointed by the Catholic monarchs, was a short-lived preparation for the problems of the overseas missions. For the impatience of the primate, Cisneros, and the introduction of a more abrupt procedure, changed the issue of the Moriscos from a missionary to an Inquisitorial one. The Inquisition was indeed exported to the overseas territories of the crown, though its competence was originally, and in theory, there confined to the European settlers, including those of Jewish stock. The transformation of approach to the Moriscos of Spain indeed owed much to the rise of the crown Inquisition itself in the fifteenth century, originally as a weapon against *conversos*. The extension of crown power and financial gains which its use allowed followed from the divisions of nobility and financiers, many of *converso* blood, under the rule of the Catholic monarchs. Christians of *converso* origin were sometimes themselves the loudest in calling for a more rigorous approach to alleged Judaizing among their own number. The Augustinian preoccupation with the problem of the Church's duty to convert by reason, but to protect the flock by force, was reflected in the demands of the General of the Hieronymites, an Augustinian order. Oropesa's treatise on the impossibility of coexistence for the Christians and Jews in Castile led eventually to the expulsion of the Jews. In the American missions the original determination of the friars to eradicate all signs of pagan practice, destroying much of the visible culture of the Indian civilizations, gave way to the belated beginnings of serious study of the society and languages of the native population. This more positive transformation reflected the unsatisfactory experience of mass conversion, and the problem, even in a society lacking a true written language or sacred texts, of translating Christian concepts, without assimilating them to the pagan pantheon.

The only solution to this last problem was considered to be the imposition of European terminology, Latin or Spanish nomenclature, even in explanations of the Catholic faith delivered in the vernacular. The friars' concern to protect their native converts from colonial exploitation, as well as to maintain their own monopoly of native services, not least building work, as opposed to the demands of the parochial system and tithe exported from Europe with the settlers, led to resistance to episcopal rights over their missions, despite the extension of episcopal authority over pastoral work by mendicants at the Council of Trent. Even specific papal rulings, ultimately if not consistently in favour of episcopal government in the American colonies, were unenforced, given the control of royal authorities overseas. The papal concern about the abuses of the *encomienda* system, and consequent lack of adequate pastoral care for both Indians and imported slaves, which led to these rulings, was fuelled by the few reports of missionary conditions which the royal authorities failed to prevent reaching Rome. The Jesuits were particularly anxious about royal and mendicant opposition to the creation of an indigenous priesthood in America, and this concern too was shared by the papacy, despite the acquiescence of the Jesuits' superiors in the policies of the crown. The Jesuit search for unconquered territories to colonize free of European secular influence was successful, in the area of Paraguay, until, by the eighteenth century, the convergence of the Spanish lands and the Portuguese settlements meant the end of these exemptions from crown control. The friars' desire to move their missions ever further from the frontier of colonial settlement, creating in effect similar enclaves free from the full effects of crown patronage, had similar limits, ultimately, of a geopolitical nature. In the Far East, the Portuguese empire, unlike the Brazilian settlements, was one of trading stations on the edge of native states and continental empires in India and China.[4] The effective control of the crown's patronage was limited to these enclaves, and to the movement of missionaries from Europe to the field.

The continued identity of the Council of Portugal, promised at the time of Philip's accession to the Portuguese throne in 1580, created, even between then and 1640, a rivalry with the Spanish Council of the Indies, which resulted in the presence of both Jesuits and Franciscans in Japan, with tragic consequences. The arrival of the friars from America, by the Pacific route controlled by the Council of the Indies, was uncoordinated with that of the Jesuits, under Portuguese patronage, by the Cape route. The conflict of Jesuits and friars, at a distance beyond the control of the papacy, despite its success in averting a similar clash in China, could not be resolved by Portuguese prelates confined to Goa or Macao. The solution of a Jesuit bishop in Japan naturally was seen as the worst of all possible worlds by the Franciscans, determined to avoid both Jesuit and episcopal direction in their missionary work. The Portuguese crown missions in the East made little progress at first. The choice of bishops made by the Council of Portugal for overseas dioceses was often poor, while some European missionaries, including Jesuits, at first despised non-European or half-caste peoples, and resisted any idea of a native priesthood. In Japan, however, the Jesuits, independent in all senses except, fatally, in economic terms, so that they proved vulnerable to accusations of involvement in trade, were more free to adapt missionary methods to a relatively sophisticated civilization. The insistence on the liturgical use of Latin, which the Council of Trent had reasserted, in the face of Protestant attack, and without thought for the problems of missionary areas, as opposed to those of union with Christians of the Eastern rite, hampered Japanese progress in the new faith. But adoption of Japanese for training as priests and members of the Society was proposed, and a deputation of noble boys, converted to Catholicism, was proudly paraded through the Italian centres of the Counter-Reformation, Rome and Milan, at the close of the sixteenth century by the Jesuits. The conversion of the Far East was praised from the pulpit, by the archbishop of Milan, with the same fervour which attached there to watch on the fortunes of the English Catholics.[5] Yet the Recusants survived persecution in England, in a culture common to them and to their oppressors, while

the Christian century, in the other island Church of Japan, came to
a sudden and tragic conclusion.

The relatively minor problems of cultural distinction, the use of
foods and fasts, were faced by the Jesuits in Japan with some success.
But the major problems of culture and caste, in China and India,
were more difficult to resolve. The Jesuits were accused by rival
missionaries, not least friars, of indiscriminate conversion of natives,
without proper preparation, of forced conversion, and of conversion
by the bribery of charity: the creation of 'rice Christians'. But such
accusations paled before the charges which were ultimately to end
all serious chances of Jesuit conversion of the great Eastern civilizations in China and India. The caste system of India prevented
Christianity from appealing simultaneously to those of high and low
caste; while in China the Mandarin class could hardly be persuaded
of the attractions of a popular religion, even during the period when
missionary work was allowed in the provinces, before the Jesuit
mission was confined to Peking. Assimilation was attempted, in one
sense, in India, when the native Christians in the Malabar, the
Christians of Saint Thomas, were Latinized, under the influence of
missionaries from the regular orders, especially after the death of
their last native metropolitan; even so a schism was not prevented.
But assimilation in a more drastic sense was practised by Jesuit
missionaries, Nobili and Ricci, in the Brahmin and Mandarin societies of India and China. Social scandal was perhaps the original effect
among European colonists in India; but the Confucian ceremonies
practised by the Mandarins raised theological issues. The veneration
of ancestors might be regarded as compatible with Catholic doctrine
of intercession for the souls in purgatory or else condemned as
incompatible paganism. The civic or religious status of the cult of
ancestors was thus contested. After many reports, prepared by the
papal visitors and vicars apostolic, who were trying to realize their
powers in the declining Portuguese empire, at the expense of the
prelates appointed by the crown to the sees of the trading enclaves,
lengthy lobbying at Rome finally resulted in the condemnation of the
Chinese rites. The conclusive prohibition of the Eastern rites, since
assimilation in India was also condemned, at the beginning of the
eighteenth century, marked the failure of Catholicism, as a European
religion re-Latinized at the Council of Trent, to penetrate the sophisticated civilizations of the Far East, with their written languages
and sacred texts. The future relations of East and West were affected,
and the universality of the Roman Church restricted. The growth of
Catholic overseas missions was in a way hindered, until the post-

Revolutionary expansion of the nineteenth century, with its new missionary orders of an activist nature and its resurrection of the Society of Jesus. The accusations of Jesuit laxity in pastoral theology, however, had a more immediate effect on the Society in eighteenth-century Europe, not least in France, which so contributed to the work and investigations of the papal *Propaganda* and its vicars apostolic in the Far East.

The French Catholic missions of the seventeenth century in North America, despite the eventual creation of an independent diocese for colonial society there, and the spread of the new orders of the Catholic revival of that century in France to the overseas territories of the crown, experienced their own particular problems. The nomadic nature of the North American Indian prevented the relatively successful catechism and conversion of the native population which the friars in Mexico and South America had achieved. But the difficulties heroically encountered in North America did not prepare the French Catholics of a rigorous disposition to view with favour the efforts of the Jesuits in the Far East, as opposed to those elsewhere of products of the *Missions Etrangères*. As the internal European controversies of a theological nature were transposed in France, at the beginning of the eighteenth century, into essentially more jurisdictional struggles, a renewal of the practical issues involved in anti-Jesuit sentiment among Catholic critics was encouraged by the reports from the East. The Jesuits were accused of favouring lax standards of spirituality at home, with indiscriminate access to the sacraments, ready absolution and too frequent communion; and of being ready to compromise true Catholic teaching abroad. The Catholic Augustinians could thus turn the tables on those who had accused the Jansenists of distorting Catholic doctrine. The combined charges were to further anti-Jesuit campaigns in Catholic Europe throughout the century.

The Counter-Reformation, both as a reaction to Protestantism, and as the continued movement to reform the Catholic Church, thus represented a period of doctrinal debate, as well as one of jurisdictional controversy over the disciplinary implications of practical reform. That doctrinal debate continued within the Catholic Church, as well as in confrontation with Protestant theology. The absence in fact, contrary to widespread views of the Tridentine doctrinal achievement, of monolithic Catholic formulae of faith which were beyond controversy caused accusations of fifth-columnist deviance from the true teaching of the Church to be the more bitter. While Jesuits were accused by Catholic rigorists of Pelagian laxity, Jansenists were accused of being crypto-Calvinists. In the same way the Arminians were charged, even by Bayle, at the end of the seventeenth century, with being anti-Augustinian, reflecting the allegations in the Netherlands and in England that they were politically and theologically counter-revolutionaries. To stress the common inheritance, from late medieval reform movements, and from the revival of patristic standards by the Christian humanists, of both Catholics and Protestants, at the level of articulate doctrine, is not to deny the reality of the religious divisions of sixteenth- and seventeenth-century Western Europe for which men died. The religious wars of the period, certainly involving motivation of a political and economic order, like the theological disputes within the Catholic and Protestant worlds themselves, achieved a rallying of the less articulate to the slogans of denominational division: the veneration or breaking of images; the sacrifice of the mass or the communion of the Lord's Supper; the use of Latin or the translations of the vernacular in worship. The accounts of more critical contemporaries, not least in the French civil and religious wars of the second half of the sixteenth century, acutely reflected in Montaigne's works above all, reveal the certainties preached, until the last days of the armed friars of the Catholic League, directing the 'poor whites' of the times, in Paris and other Catholic urban strongholds, against the privileged beneficiaries of Navarre's succession: the prosperous *politique* Catholics, and the Huguenot former co-religionists of the king. Religious riot also represented opportunities for the settlement of local rivalries, in France at least; even if that element was strangely absent, according to contemporary accounts of the amazing restraint in redressing economic grievance, in the iconoclastic incidents in the Netherlands.

Popular marks of identity, and enmity, as with the Marian cult, were fostered by more pacific preachers of the Counter-Reformation, both in Italy and Spain, and in more divided territory: in the Jesuit reconversions of Austria, Bavaria and Poland, for example. But institutional change, *de facto* irreversibly made by the Protestant Reformation, as in the striking instance of Marian England and the failure to re-establish monastic life except at royal foundations, also created divisions in Christian society which were not purely cultural. The anti-Hispanic, but not necessarily anti-Catholic feeling aroused in Marian England by the prominence of a few foreign friars, agents of an alien king, in the cloister at Westminster, in the purge of Oxford university, or in the organization of conspicuous celebration of Corpus Christi, by processions of a more mediterranean than insular colour, paled beside the vast consequences of monastic dissolution in the Protestant world, whether at first *de jure*, as in England, or rather *de facto* as at first in Scotland. The absence of organized communities of celibate regulars, especially male religious, represented not merely a readjustment of economic resources, reflected eventually in Catholic society too, from the anti-mortmain legislation of early seventeenth-century Venice to the sweeping confiscations of Josephine reform in Austria and Italy, anticipated also in France, even before the Revolution. The lack of such potential missionaries for overseas expansion notably delayed serious Protestant mission abroad until the organization of the missionary societies in the eighteenth century, with the evolution of the colonial empire of England, above all. The valuable insistence of historians, such as Jean Delumeau, and, in a more qualified manner, John Bossy, on the cohesion of Catholic and Protestant religious experience in sixteenth- and seventeenth-century Europe must thus be set against the signs of social separation and distinct development. Both traditions were heirs to the Christian humanist attempt to impose credal comprehension on the uneducated, and especially the rural, poor of Western Europe, in place of rituals reclassified as heretical or superstitious. But the episcopal leadership which characterized that attempt in the post-Tridentine Catholic Church, and in a very limited way in the Anglican, rather than in the Recusant, community in the insular conditions of England, was necessarily distinct from all Protestant campaigns, in Scotland and continental Europe, to eradicate the remains of Rome and purge the people of pagan practices. The Augustinian rigorism of Catholic reforming bishops, resident in their dioceses and investigating in person the religious conditions of remote rural areas after long periods of episcopal neglect, was thus part of a complete patristic revival: just as the reform, from Luther's youthful trip to Rome and earlier, into the later sixteenth century, of the orders based on the rule attributed to Saint Augustine, was equally a part.

The Protestant Reformation, lacking monastic orders and, normally, episcopal authority in any real sense, remained necessarily a less complete representation of that revival. On the other hand, the concern of Wyclif and Hus with the pristine nature of the Church, the operation of grace and the workings of predestination owed much to Bradwardine's virtual Augustinianism, but cannot be seen as pointing to a subsequent defence of Christian humanism, biblicism and patristic standards by Protestants alone. The view that in Catholic Europe, after the Council of Trent, only dissidents maintained such ideals, in the face of some supposed assertion of scholasticism, is clearly untenable, unless the whole history of Jansenism is distorted, by an inversion of historical perspective. The Jansenists emerged from Catholic debate, continued in post-Conciliar controversy, over central theological concepts, radical in their implications for the Christian view of man; only separation of their position from that of other Catholic rigorists and premature identification of their aims with those of eighteenth-century jurisdictional polemicists can permit the equation of the Counter-Reformation with the reimposition of scholasticism as a solely acceptable theology and philosophy, in the sixteenth and seventeenth centuries, even if editions of Aquinas continued to be produced in Venice, Paris and Antwerp. As will be seen, the Jansenists originally struggled to remain a part of the world of Catholic Augustinianism, which, beginning with pre-Lutheran theologians and religious reformers like Nicholas of Cusa, in the German-speaking world, continued to embrace Italian episcopal activists, typified by Saint Charles Borromeo, and French Catholic rigorists, like the non-Jansenist reformer of La Trappe, Rancé, in the sixteenth and seventeenth centuries. The Catholic reassertion, after Trent, of the necessity of popular participation in the sacraments complemented the new direction of confraternity devotion and control of local cults attempted by diocesan bishops and by the Roman Curia; while a liturgical uniformity previously unknown in Western Christendom was more successfully imposed, despite surviving rites peculiar to religious orders of ancient foundation and a few primitive sees, and the independence of pastoral liturgical experiment shown on occasion in eighteenth-century France, Germany and England. The social implications, and economic calculations, raised by the persistence of weekdays observed as holy days by abstention from work, were a reminder, in Catholic Europe, that governments were as determined to impose their own erastian controls on the population of their states, increasingly so in the eighteenth century, as were Protestant rulers.

Conformity to the religion of the ruler remained the law, from the first separation of Lutheran princes in the empire onwards, even before the formal enunciation of the doctrine *cujus regio ejus religio* in the mid-sixteenth century. Thomas More had recognized this permanent disruption of Western Christendom, refusing to acknowledge the right of the ruler to determine religious belief in this way, at the cost of his own life, while accepting the particular alteration of the English succession dictated by the requirements of Tudor government. The conflicts, after the Council of Trent, of Church and state in Catholic Europe were chiefly over areas of contested control of lay society, its composition by marriage and inheritance, and its economic resources, typified by disputes over episcopal supervision of confraternities and female convents, both institutions involving substantial secular investment; as well as over revived claims to clerical immunity in legal and fiscal terms. The adoption of diocesan bishops as formally agents of the holy see thus strengthened anti-Roman feeling in Catholic states, in the long-term evolution of post-Tridentine Catholic Europe. Such a result, though partly reversed by the reaction to Revolution at the end of the eighteenth century, was of more lasting importance, for the evolution of Catholic society in Europe, than either the rise of modern science and the end of the great witch-craze, or the largely independent evolution of the performing, literary and visual arts in the Mannerist and Baroque, Rococo and proto-Romantic or early neo-classical styles.

CHAPTER 2

# RELIGION AND MAGIC IN
# AUGUSTINIAN EUROPE

THE AUGUSTINIAN REVIVAL, common to Catholic and subsequently
to Protestant Europe, from the mid-fifteenth to the mid-eighteenth
century, was the concern of an educated élite. The objection to
popular misconceptions of Christian belief and practice which stimulated the revival, especially in the Erasmian circles of the early
sixteenth century, was a sign, even before the religious division of
Western Europe and the political insistence on national uniformity
in religion, of the desire of the educated to impose new ways on the
less educated. This élitist preoccupation coincided, chronologically,
with the external threat to Western Christendom posed with particular immediacy from the mid-fifteenth century by the power of
Turkish Islam. The convocation of the Council of Florence, in an
attempt to restore the unity of Eastern and Western Christendom
against that imminent threat, brought new opportunities for the
study of Greek, and especially Platonic texts to Italian and above all
Florentine scholars. But the failure of the reunion to win acceptance
in the East, despite the continued efforts of those, led by Bessarion,
who remained in the West, was a dramatic indication of the dangers
which, after the fall of Constantinople, came to face the Western
Church itself. The invasion of Hungary, and the consequent menace
to the empire from that quarter, were a major distraction, in the
sixteenth century, to Charles V in his efforts to reconcile Catholics
and Lutherans in his territories, not least with a view to presenting
a united front to the Ottoman enemy. The recession of the Turkish
threat was delayed, whatever the internal weaknesses of the evolving
Ottoman empire, until the later seventeenth century. While Venice,
once again, suffered on behalf of Christian Europe – losing Crete, in
succession to the loss of Cyprus a century earlier – the campaigns of
Prince Eugene, and the brief restoration of Venetian rule in parts of
Greece, represented the beginnings of Islamic retreat. The successful
relief of Vienna, in 1683, marked the failure of the Ottoman advance

at its most ambitious extent. The Polish support of Sobieski for the resistance of Vienna more than compensated for the failure of the French king, Louis XIV, to respond to European appeals for a modification, in this danger, of the Bourbon policy of alliance with the Turks against the Habsburgs.

By the middle of the eighteenth century the serious danger to Christian Europe from Islam was past, and the internal wars of Western Europe, and their colonial extensions, were equally free of any serious religious connotations. Precisely the same period, the mid-fifteenth to the mid-eighteenth century, saw the rise and decline of the great witch-craze in much of Western Europe; though the dualism at least implied by some manifestations of the craze almost never disturbed the religious tradition of the Orthodox Churches of the East, even under Turkish rule. The Manichaean background of Augustine left him, after his conversion to Christianity, with a concern to establish the identity of lesser forces in the universe, the demonic, whatever their ultimate subjection to divine omnipotence and prescience. The pagan deities of the late Roman world he identified as having such a subordinate existence. Their reality, even though in subjection to divine purpose, was asserted in the *City of God*. For this reason Augustine condemned the public plays and games of antiquity as being religious ceremonies, designed to honour these demonic forces, pagan ritual in a true sense, and not just the public demonstration of civil values. His association of the plays and games with temple worship also suggested another ground of condemnation: they were perversions, in a moral sense, carrying associations of sexual licence. Tertullian, in his work *On the Shows* (c. AD 196–7), condemned them for the same combination of reasons. The charges of blasphemous idolatry and of sexual immorality were precisely those which were to be made against the supposed coven of witches, in the great craze of Western Europe from the mid-fifteenth century. The predominant image of the coven as a female gathering was also a remarkable inversion of the male confraternity which post-Tridentine bishops sought, with varying and only partial success, to bring under the control of the hierarchical Church, and the supervision of the clerical profession. The essentially male confraternity in post-Tridentine Catholic Europe proved ultimately compatible with the authority of the Church; not so the supposedly diabolic inversion of the female coven.

Such considerations, of origins and external threats, are important, because the rise of the great witch-craze clearly predated the division of Western Christendom by the Protestant Reformation. The rivalry

of the Reformation and Counter-Reformation may indeed have
heightened the obsessions which perpetuated the craze, but that was
not the original cause. The identifications of alleged witchcraft with
heresy certainly followed: Catholic witch-hunters accused witches of
heretical diabolism, not merely of the *maleficium* supposedly caused
to persons and property by indulgence in the magic arts. Protestant
witch-hunters saw the persistence of alleged witchcraft as a sign of
the presence of the old religion, uneradicated remains of Roman
superstition. In the three centuries of the great craze, the friars, in
Catholic Europe, were particularly prominent in witch-hunting,
especially the Dominicans, as well as, in places, their Jesuit rivals.
The association of the Dominicans in particular with the Inquisition
went back to the medieval tribunal, before the revival of the Roman
Inquisition in the mid-sixteenth century to meet the new challenge
of Protestantism, and to the origins of the order. The original task
of confronting heretics in Languedoc, in a world where Cathar heresy
had political and also social connotations and complications, as has
been shown in the detailed examination of one locality, extended
eventually to the aim of confronting pre-Lutheran heretics elsewhere: not least in other areas of relative remoteness and potential
independence, such as the Alpine retreats of the Waldensians. It was
precisely in the Alpine world, at the head of the Italian peninsula,
and at the cross-roads of Western Europe, that the efforts of the
Dominicans and other friars to identify and eradicate both heresy
and witchcraft produced apparently conclusive and seminal evidence
of diabolic complicity, in the later fifteenth century. The final elaboration, in printed edition, of the manual for witch-hunters prepared by friars (*Malleus Maleficarum*, 1486) was produced in these
new circumstances.

The literature of witch investigation was thus established, before
the Lutheran challenge to Catholicism, in the age of printing, and
continued to find acceptance in both Catholic and Protestant lands
after the Reformation. The tests for witchcraft proposed in the manual were successful, because they were largely self-fulfilling, not least
when questions were of a leading nature, and supported by the threat
and use of judicial torture. The publicity given to witch-trials and
the sequence of denunciations which could cause the spread of trials
in a given locality to sex, ages, and social classes normally immune,
made familiar the supposed activities of the coven, even to the
illiterate. The admission of the practices of the coven could thus
occur, with detailed authenticity, in appearance, and remarkable
exactitude in repeating the descriptions of the manuals, as far away

as Scotland, at periods far removed in time from the first edition of the manual. Only the inclusion, among those denounced, of too many from the normally prosecuting classes, the educated of the clerical and legal orders above all, would act as a brake on the cycle, as has been demonstrated for parts of South-West Germany. Political considerations could also further or terminate a trial, as was shown in France, in the seventeenth century, by Richelieu's use of the Loudun trial against his enemies, and by the suppression of evidence, in a later trial, associating the court of Louis xiv with diabolism. The witch-craze was more normally, however, the persecution of the relatively uneducated or the illiterate, by the clerical and legal élite, and commonly, though not invariably, an accusation of females by males. The prominence of unattached and elderly females, widows or aged spinsters above all, among the victims is not necessarily a sign of the guilty resentment against those in need, creating social demands on the family structure of a community, at least as the sole motivation for their selection. Such social denunciation of neighbours, in settlement of doubtless many grievances, was necessary before witch-hunters could act in a given locality; but the local accusation of *maleficium*, reflecting a popular belief in the magic powers of certain individuals, often elderly surviving females, persisting long after the decline of the learned witch-craze, was not the same as the charge then preferred by the learned judges, of demonic conspiracy, the satanic pact, of heretical diabolism, in fact. The fear of vendetta, however, restrained many charges against males, or against females protected still by the existence of relations: only the single female could be supplied as victim to the visiting judges without fear of reprisals.

The period of the Augustinian revival in Christian Europe, both Catholic and Protestant, was thus also a period of learned obsession with the demonic. Only as the theological controversies internal to both major religious divisions of Western Europe, as well as between them, faded, to be replaced by more jurisdictional concerns, by economic considerations and more frankly political ambitions, did the demonic preoccupation also decline. The decreased danger from the external threat of Islam, and the reduction of heresy as a political source of unrest within Western Europe, saw a relaxation in the search for fifth-columnists among the uneducated, largely rural poor; just as it did in the acrimonious accusations of Arminians and Calvinists, Jansenists and Jesuits, that their opponents were a fifth-column within their own religion. The problem of identifying pagan practices, of assessing their reality, which could only mean their

invocation of the demonic, even if in Augustinian terms of subordinate deities, was increasingly a concern of the overseas missions; rather than the backward areas of Europe, such as those which early Jesuits on internal mission had christened 'the Roman Indies'. The revival of episcopal residence after the Council of Trent, in Catholic Europe, and the personal visitation of dioceses, even in their remote or mountainous areas, aroused alarm at the state of superstition which passed for Christianity. The diocesan synods, which enacted decrees aimed at eradicating popular ritual which was now conceived of as pagan, stressed the importance of the official sacraments of the Church, even for the humble laity, the need for control of confraternity devotions and their subordination to parochial liturgy, the necessity of clerical approval for popular cults and processions. The vernacular sermon to expound the faith, as a credal and comprehensive system, to the laity, became the hall mark of Catholic as well as Protestant devotion in the sixteenth century. The pulpit, as well as the confessional, the prominent high altar and subordinate side altars dedicated to individual saints, was a visible characteristic of the Counter-Reformation church; just as the broad naves, borrowed from the tradition of the late medieval friars' churches, built in the new churches of the post-Tridentine age allowed clear acoustics for the preacher, as well as an unimpeded view of the altar for the faithful.

The campaign to catechize children but also adults, not least in rural areas, was another Catholic activity of the post-Conciliar period, even before the development of the Sunday School in Protestant countries, by dissociation of the catechism there from secular elementary learning in Latin and literacy. The Tridentine decree that sermons must be preached at mass on Sundays and major feasts was complemented by a reminder of the bishop's obligation to provide preaching of the faith in his cathedral and the parishes of his diocese. Many post-Conciliar bishops, with their erudite training in classical literature and humane studies, found vernacular preaching to the less educated a problem; and financial and patronage complications delayed, in many cases, the provision of a canon at each cathedral specifically trained in theology, rather than in the more common canon law.[1] But new and reformed orders, especially the Jesuits and Capuchins, specialized in internal missionary work in Catholic Europe, as in areas to be reconverted from Protestantism; so that the eloquence of the Jesuits complemented the practical charity which accounted for the popularity of the Capuchins at every level of society, from rulers and their chief ministers, to the poor who first fell victim to the epidemics of the growing cities of Mediterranean Europe. Episcopal concern in Catholic areas – including those where the witch-craze never seriously took root, as in peninsular Italy, or only peripherally and briefly, as in Spain – for eradicating superstition was thus a tradition continued by the rigorists of the immediately post-Tridentine decades, and by the more liberal-minded, often aristocratic, prelates of the eighteenth century. The absence of heresy did not mean the absence of popular misbelief and malpractice, even if it did allow relative freedom from the identification of witchcraft as an intentional diabolic deviance from Catholicism. In Spain the independence of the crown Inquisition, and its desire to demonstrate the continued necessity of its existence, provided a late example of the hunting of superstition and magic, in the eighteenth century, when native objects of attention, Jews, *conversos* and Moriscos, were as lacking as Protestants; this was just when the witch-craze was in decline elsewhere in Catholic Europe. After the obsessive search for the solution to the supposed bewitching of Charles II of Spain, the concept of satanic covenant, expressed elsewhere in Europe at an earlier date, as in the myth of Faust, was hardly alive in the Spanish peninsula, though.

The attention to neo-platonic learning in Italy, after the Council of Florence, naturally involved interest in the demonic, even if the demonic was in this context the neutral term for subordinate intelligences, acting under divine permission. The Christian platonism, found in sixteenth- and seventeenth-century Europe, both Catholic and Protestant, also led the Jesuit syncretists of the Far-Eastern missions to claim an Augustinian basis for their attempts at assimilation: a basis opponents denied. Despite the attack on offshoots of neo-platonism among Catholic critics of cabbalistic studies, as opposed to veneration for Hebrew and Oriental Studies as aids to exegesis of the scriptures, among both Catholic and Protestant ecclesiastics, Christian platonism remained important in both parts of religiously divided Western Europe, alongside revitalized Aristotelianism.[2]

It has been argued that a scholastic reassertion of Aristotelianism, in the Counter-Reformation, accounted for the rise of the witch-craze in Catholic Europe. But the pre-Reformation origins of the crucial identification of witchcraft with diabolism, not simply with *maleficium*, and the continued Protestant reliance on procedures laid down by late medieval friars, do not seem to support such a view. The Augustinian and neo-platonic contribution to the classic form of witch belief seems more prominent. The Council of Trent, in any case, did not represent the triumph of scholasticism, as has been seen. The case of Federico Borromeo is an interesting test for the theory of the Catholic witch-craze as a product of an Aristotelian cosmology. The prolific compositions of the archbishop of Milan (1595–1631) include demonological writings, in which many of the classic opinions on witches are expounded. The possibility of attempted *maleficium* being ineffective is accepted, but the serious nature of diabolism stressed. The existence of the coven, and its usual location in remote places, are assumed, and the evidence extracted from the accused in witch trials is cited as proof, with the refinements of theories about demonic eradication of memory in participants in the coven. The relative freedom from witchcraft of Italy is thankfully noted, but vigilance is called for against any spread of the infection. In practice, too, Federico was careful to promote a watch by his priests for signs of witchcraft, especially in illness, and the increased activity in this context at times of social distress, with the arrival of troops from north of the Alps in the late 1620s, in the overspill of the Thirty Years War into Northern Italy, is certainly notable. The epidemic which also arrived at this time, striking Milan in 1630–1, after the food shortage of 1629, led to civic and popular belief in the existence of witches devoted to spreading the plague by means of infectious ointment. Federico, by contrast, doubted the existence of such agents of the devil, on this occasion, and gave his attention to urging social relief on the more prosperous classes, the provision of sacramental and devotional services in such a way as to reduce the risks of contagion, and the arguments against charms to ward off infection, as ineffective.[3] His humane concern for spiritual and charitable relief of the infected and the isolated thus matched his earlier involvement in a plan to open a house for reformed witches.

The example of his theoretical belief and practical concern about witchcraft is striking, however, because his cosmological views, expounded in other works, were Copernican not Aristotelian. This was natural in a friendly correspondent of Galileo, who followed the theories of the astronomer by means of his own observations through a telescope, and accepted his writings for the Ambrosiana library, which the archbishop had opened to the public in Milan. Before the beginning of Galileo's final trial, Federico had become entirely preoccupied with plague relief in Milan, and the end of the epidemic had been closely followed by his own death; but the cardinal had continued to support Galileo, despite the earlier difficulties encountered by the latter with the Inquisition in Florence. At a later date, in the Protestant world, the pervasive influence by the end of the eighteenth century of Newtonian cosmology did not prevent Wesley from urging the existence of witchcraft and the dangers of disbelief in its actuality. The episcopal reforms of Federico Borromeo, on the other hand, though following the model of the ideal bishop, identified by contemporaries in the life of Charles Borromeo (archbishop of Milan 1564–84), even before his early canonization, at the beginning of the seventeenth century, in witch-hunting as in all else, also suggested a possible cause for the eventual decline of the witch-craze. The description of Charles as ideal bishop in the works of Agostino Valier, friend of the Borromeo archbishops, and himself a resident and reforming bishop in Venetian territory, at Verona, was eventually to be followed no longer in the particular of detecting and eradicating witchcraft.[4]

The decrees of the Council of Trent placed on diocesan bishops responsibility for supervising female convents, and the papacy after the Council continued a policy of attempting to impose strict enclosure and a more truly religious life in female communities by means of encouraging episcopal control, in place of the oversight of male regulars, monks and friars.[5] The resistance of nuns to a more strictly observant life, to enclosure above all, was marked and sometimes dramatic, in Italy, Spain and elsewhere. The relations of such nuns also objected to the replacement of male regulars' supervision of female convents by episcopal control, on the grounds that such reform suggested improper behaviour in the past: an implication which was all too often true in fact. Family honour was thus at stake, and the economy of noble and middle-class society too, in fact, since the presence of nuns, in numbers, who had no true vocation to an ascetic life was openly acknowledged by both bishops and secular authorities, but defended with determination by lay interests. For the rising level of marriage dowries in polite society, and the need to limit family inheritance by the confinement of marriage to an heir or to one daughter alone, in the sixteenth and seventeenth centuries, produced a surplus of gentlemen and ladies without means of employment or support. Celibacy, often prolonged, as in the Venetian Republic, allowed male cadets to seek their fortunes indifferently in Church or state, in the clerical or military life. The survival, after the Council of Trent, of a celibate clergy in the Latin Church, and of religious orders, old and new, thus had a lasting social effect, despite the Tridentine attempt to regulate the admission to beneficed positions or to wealthy abbacies of those without a tested clerical vocation and a professional education. Such attempts, in any case, were hardly successful in Italy, in the Venetian state above all, let

alone in France, or in Spain, where a numerous clergy continued to
provide a large part of the crown's civil service in effect. The undowered females who were placed in convents by their families, since
concepts of honour demanded the visible maintenance of chastity by
the unmarried females of a family, which was thought difficult to
demonstrate in society at large, had less choice.

The lower levels of dowry paid by a family on the entry of a
daughter or dependant into religious, as opposed to married life,
gave an interest to the laity in the conduct of such convents, in the
question of a house's economy above all. The fixing of rates for entry
dowries, the decision as to the number of nuns which a convent's
endowment and income could support, remained matters of lay concern, because of the investment of resources and of family honour.
The attempt to make of female convents less a particular part of lay
society, and more a part of the hierarchical and professional Church,
with clerical male control of funds and persons, was not a success:
arguably the least successful campaign of the Counter-Reformation.
The conflict was more fierce than in the case of lay confraternities,
where lay investment of funds was also involved – whether for internal use to the benefit, spiritual and physical, of members and their
families alone, or for external use, to the benefit of secular society
and its particular needs, the sick, the aged, or the orphaned – because
the economic survival of gentle families depended on the traditional
use of convents as discreet depositories for undowered dependants.
Social status was at stake, not merely a humane, or even less consciously perhaps, self-interested desire to ameliorate the conditions
of the less fortunate in society and reduce the dangers of unrest. The
attempt of reforming bishops to test the vocation to the properly
religious life of girls presented for entry to convents was thus largely
a failure: the pressure of family decision proved too strong, in most
cases, to circumvent.[6] Female conventual life remained in Catholic
Europe, in the seventeenth and eighteenth centuries, a notably relaxed part of the post-Tridentine Church: this was in spite of the
heroic rigour of some communities, like those of Port-Royal, eventually suppressed by the French government of Louis XIV, because
of their importance at the heart of Jansenist circles, clerical and lay.
Since the numbers of nuns could not be reduced to the few with a
true vocation to the conventual life, even where this was imposed –
against the wishes of nuns and their families to maintain within the
convent a style of life sufficiently indicative of the nuns' social origins
– conscientious bishops had to devise ways of transforming the
religious outlook of such inmates, by more lengthy processes. The

spiritual direction of nuns was thus not necessarily confined to the choice of chaplain and confessor, which the bishops after Trent increasingly took out of the hands of the monks and friars; while the new orders of the Counter-Reformation left their female offshoots to episcopal supervision.

The correspondence which Federico Borromeo maintained with various nuns, mainly in his own diocese, was designed, on his part, to provide a further means of direction in the religious life, and a gradual education of involuntary regulars in the way of true spirituality and devotion. His observation of individual and collective female psychology in this way caused him to note a connection between enforced enclosure of females who had not strictly chosen their way of life or their companions and the possibility of group hysteria. He thus urged caution in accepting all cases of apparent demonic possession as real, suggesting the possibility of false possession whether consciously or unconsciously feigned.[7] Possession and exorcism were obsessions of the Catholic world in the Counter-Reformation, as the reality of the demonic was once again stressed, with the dangers of external and fifth-columnist attack on the true faith. But Protestant preoccupation with the literal identity of Anti-Christ, from Luther to the Fifth Monarchists of Interregnum England, also denoted a heightened reawakening to the actuality of the diabolic: Milton's epic centred on the satanic anti-hero grew out of this. In England, despite the absence of the witch-craze in its classic form of detecting demonic association behind mere *maleficium*, except for isolated instances, again mainly in the abnormal conditions of the Interregnum, Recusant priests and Puritan preachers competed to prove their spiritual powers by exorcising possessed persons. The official clergy of the Anglican Church, excluded from this charismatic exhibition in areas like Lancashire, where Recusants and Puritans effectively faced each other in a religious division more akin to continental European conditions, were not supported by any public teaching on witchcraft, despite the importation from Calvinist Scotland of the demonological theories of King James. In the areas, Catholic and Protestant, of Europe, outside England, where the witch-craze found expression, possession was taken as a signal test of demonic invocation: physical *maleficium* to a victim was merely a supporting sign of the diabolic invasion of body and soul caused by witchcraft. The convulsions which marked both possession and exorcism, the oral blasphemy which was a release for the victim in perhaps more senses than one, were dramas of the Counter-Reformation Church less innocent than the moralized classical plays of the

Jesuit collegiate theatres or the sacred music dramas of the original Roman Oratory staged by Philip Neri.

But these scenes were repeated in Protestant Europe and even, as is notorious, exported to the Puritan colonies of the New World; precisely in areas where the Covenant theory was longest maintained, the inversion of the diabolic pact was most feared. The distinction between real possession and possible false possession obviously undermined the certainty of such evidence against accused witches in a serious way. In France, where the decline of the witch-craze was first markedly apparent, by the end of the seventeenth century, cases of alleged witchcraft were commonly tried by the lawyers of the secular courts. It seems possible at least that the decisive role attributed to the legal profession in France, in the decline of willingness to prosecute in such cases, was encouraged by confusion over the validity of such crucial evidence as possession. The clerical and legal élite of Europe was arguably responsible for the decline of the witch-craze, as opposed to the persistence of popular belief in witchcraft on the simple level of *maleficium*, just as for the promotion of witch-hunting in the first place. The Roman law adopted, in varying degrees, in continental Europe and Scotland – but not in the same way in England with its common-law insularity – represented a procedure and principles identical in both Catholic and Protestant states. The use of judicial torture, until the eighteenth century, in Roman law areas favoured the apparent confirmation of evidence in witch trials by the admissions of the accused, and the further denunciation of accomplices; while in England, judicial torture, though not unknown, was not in regular use. The lay justices who heard cases of alleged witchcraft in first instance, in England, shared the beliefs of the less educated in the possibility of *maleficium*, even if aware of neighbourly grievance as a potential incentive in such accusations. But their own legal training, at the Inns of Court, was more likely to be kept alive, in the country, by exercise in the law of property, essentially a matter of the common law, than in meditating on the possibility of demonic conspiracy. Cases of alleged *maleficium* decided at sessions by the justices of the peace thus did not normally reach the higher jurisdictions in which professional judges presided. The duty of detecting un-Christian and unlawful behaviour was imposed, with varying degrees of success, by English authority on Church-wardens in the Tudor period, as on confraternities in Catholic Europe. But this did not, therefore, lead to a witch-craze, in the peculiar conditions of England.

The desire of reforming bishops in post-Tridentine Catholic

Europe to eradicate popular superstition was equally distinct, it is clear, from witch-hunting. The attempt to implement the mixed doctrinal and disciplinary decrees of the Council on the sacraments proved especially problematic. It has been noted that the assertion of parochial mass on Sundays and feast days at the expense of confraternity devotions, which were to be reduced to subordinate importance, reversed the late medieval development of confraternity independence. The support of secular authorities for the resistance of confraternities to episcopal control represented, again, concern about the security of lay investment in guild funds, distinct from the still increasing wealth of the Church; though the foundation of new confraternities in the Counter-Reformation gave some opportunity for episcopal control, as ordered at Trent, from the start. Thus even at Venice, where the economic and political links between the rich guilds, the *Scuole grandi*, and the state were vigorously defended by the Republic, the humble sodalities founded in the parishes to promote the Counter-Reformation cult of the reserved sacrament were allowed to remain under the direction of the patriarch. Some new confraternities of the period, elsewhere, were under the supervision of regulars, however, which led to tension with episcopal or equivalent authority, as in England, where the use of sodalities reinforced Jesuit influence in the household churches which re-emerged in the peculiar conditions of Recusant clandestine activity. In the Venetian republic, after the Interdict of the early seventeenth century in particular, the influence of regulars over the laity was intentionally reduced, not only by virtue of the expulsion of the Jesuits and, more briefly, of other new or reformed orders, the Theatines and Capuchins, but because even old orders were prevented from continuing to direct lay confraternities. The guild associated with lay support for the Roman Inquisition was doubly suspect, given the Republican aim of reducing still further the independence of the Inquisition in Venetian territory after the Interdict; even if the problem of declining law and order, in Venetian mainland possessions, as across the border in Spanish Lombardy, was not complicated by the privileges of the lay familiars of the Inquisition, in the latter state, in the carrying of arms. The attempt of the Spanish authorities in Milan to prevent guild members processing in public in the traditional habit which concealed the face, by a hood, was ostensibly based on a similar concern for the danger of violence and lawlessness.[8]

Both bishops and regulars, in the post-Tridentine Church, encouraged confraternities, especially new foundations, to extend their charitable work, on a more specialized basis, such as provision for pilgrims on route to Rome, for example, to society beyond the membership of the guild and immediate families, as well as insisting on the devotional duties and, in some cases, the flagellant purpose of the sodalities. The danger of lay confraternities becoming, without clerical control, inadvertent sources of superstition or even heresy was clear. In the singular conditions of the diocese of Turin, which extended to territory, in the mountains, where both old Waldensians and new Calvinists were to be found, confraternity celebration of Maundy Thursday, in a commemoration of the Last Supper and institution of charitable service which was clearly innocent of any intentional heresy, had nevertheless declined into bibulous banquets held in church. The use of new confraternities in the Counter-Reformation to repress blasphemy was a negative complement to the organization of lay sodalities to teach catechism and literacy in the Schools of Christian Doctrine, held on Sundays and feast days. The detection and prevention of violence and vendetta by lay guilds were also encouraged, in an effort to help stem the growing wave of violent crime in many parts of Italy – at the end of the sixteenth century and the beginning of the seventeenth – from the supposedly well-ordered territories of Venice, and the Lombard states of the Spanish king in the North, to the papal states and kingdoms of Naples and Sicily in the centre and South. Bishops were active themselves in trying to mediate in family feuds, not only in the perennial violence of Corsica, but in the apparently more polite society of the Venetian mainland cities, like Padua and Verona.[9] The Capuchins too, each of whom adopted a name in religion which seemed to mark him out as singularly free from family pressures, even compared with other regulars, were involved in attempts to settle such feuds. They were also involved in delicate political representation, to the Spanish crown above all, conveying the laments of Italian subjects oppressed by rising taxes.[10]

The attempt of the Counter-Reformation Church, in these ways, to insist that Catholicism meant a Christian way of life, involving Works which were practical and altruistic, as well as purely devotional or even sacramental, should be a sufficient reminder that Christian humanism of an Erasmian pattern was not something suppressed at Trent. The desire, as at the very heart of the Counter-Reformation, in the Milan of Charles Borromeo, to purify the lay practice of religion, as something more than debased ritual, led to the elaboration of new and rigorous codes for confessors. Far from representing casuistry, as that term was later and pejoratively used, the Borromean consideration of cases of conscience was strict in the extreme. The sin of dancing on Sundays or feast days was one for which absolution was reserved to the archbishop in person.[11] The Borromean view of usury, money-lending at interest, was at the most restrictive of the range of post-Tridentine Catholic theological opinion; though even in Vicenza, in Venetian territory, a city suspected of Lutheran leanings even after the Council of Trent, the laity of the city would not accept a slight rise in the rate of interest allowed on deposits at the *Monte di Pietà* without assurance of papal approval.[12] The promotion of such charitable institutions, intended for the relief of the poor, was taken up in post-Conciliar Italy by reforming bishops, intent on reducing reliance on Jewish money-lenders, and the necessity of contact between Christians and Jews; even if, at Rome itself, for financial reasons, the ghetto was maintained, alongside the new *Monte di Pietà*. But in Venetian territory, where the *Monti* had already become a more established feature, as opposed to the city of Venice, which repeated Rome's dependence on a ghetto as well as a new *Monte*, episcopal control of such accumulated lay investment was absolutely prevented. Yet the lay management of these institutions, as revealed by the Venetian representatives in the mainland cities themselves, was a constant story of peculation and maladministration: which made an interesting comment on the Tridentine assertion that all pious legacies, and by extension the funds of confraternities and *Monti*, remained a matter for ecclesiastical investigation and enforcement. In the kingdom of Naples, after a prolonged struggle over such ecclesiastical intervention, a compromise was reached, in the post-Tridentine decades, by which episcopal oversight of confraternities and pious institutions with a charitable purpose was to be accepted, but auditing of the revenues excluded from this.[13] The dispute was connected, elsewhere, with the contested control of female convents, for reasons which have been considered; while the Tridentine reservation of royal rights, in the case of foundations of a conventual or charitable nature at Naples, allowed increased possibilities of resistance to episcopal intervention.

Elsewhere the conflict over female tertiaries, whom the post-Tridentine papacy was intent on enclosing as regular nuns, linked the two types of dispute explicitly; and in Spanish Lombardy, at Varese and Novara, the Ursuline nuns, whose original aim had been to maintain freedom from strict enclosure, in the pursuit of their educational work among girls, resisted Borromean implementation of the papal policy, with the support of the Milanese senate, invoked by virtue of the nuns' claim to be a lay foundation, not a religious order.[14] The similar search for an active female life, in religious

education, was successful only in the abnormal conditions of Recusant England, for Mary Ward, where proscription paradoxically
meant freedom from effective episcopal authority. The rigorism of
Borromeo's *Instructions to Confessors*, following that of Saint Antonino, was maintained in the French Catholic revival of the seventeenth
century, but not in any way as a monopoly of the Jansenists. The
distribution of the *Instructions*, which were reprinted to the end of
the eighteenth century in Catholic Europe, was ordered in France
by the assembly of the French clergy in 1657, which condemned
casuistry. The Jansenist insistence on care in the giving of absolution
was certain. But it was precisely in the 1650s that they temporarily
accepted a compromise, based on a Thomist, that is a scholastic
argument, in the dispute in which they were involved; just as the
distinction of 'fact' and 'right' suggested a legal, if not theological
casuistry. This hardly supports the association of legalism and
Augustinianism suggested by Bouwsma, any more than does the
mechanical view of excommunication and absolution adopted by the
lawyers of the Venetian state, in Sarpi's circle, or the counsel of the
Spanish crown, at Naples and the royal court. The patristic pastoral
standard of Borromeo was acknowledged, by contrast, in seventeenth-century France by Le Camus, the heroic bishop of Grenoble,
even if Jansenists in France took a rigorist view of usury, as opposed
to the divided opinions of Jesuits, and of the later schismatic Jansenists of Utrecht, on this issue.

The imposition of social order, by means of the confessional, was
certainly not abandoned in the Counter-Reformation, in other
words. The new regulation of the sacrament, in the post-Tridentine
Church, involved the use of the confessional box, and the replacement, arguably, of a social ritual of reconciliation by an ecclesiastical
investigation of the individual soul and clerical formation of personal
spirituality. But the confessional box in open church was obligatory
particularly for the hearing of female penitents' confessions, while
the design of the box in fact allowed, in both Roman and Milanese
usage, continued conversation face to face between confessors and
male penitents. The assertion of the necessity of infant baptism, by
the Council of Trent just as by Calvin, certainly led to new practical
prescriptions in the post-Tridentine Catholic Church. The care, in
episcopal visitation, to note the presence of midwives reflected the
needs of emergency baptism, the danger of popular superstitions
connected with the afterbirth or with still-born babies, and the papal
campaign, after the Council, continued against abortion, as against
infanticide concealed as accidental suffocation, or the exposure of

unwanted children in an ancient Mediterranean tradition. The limitation in choice of godparents, more perhaps by character than by number, and the assertion of the primacy of the rite of baptism over family celebrations of the occasion, arguably represented a stress on the dominance of a hierarchical Church over the individual member, despite the undoubted stress on the catechetical duties of the family, and of mothers above all.

But a sacramental parallel was more visible in the contested question of marriage regulations in the post-Tridentine Church and Catholic society. The Conciliar insistence that only sacramental marriage in the presence of priest and witnesses constituted a legitimate contract resolved the ambiguities of marriage in medieval traditions. But the prohibition of clandestine marriage alienated more than the Catholic rulers who objected to such interference with the political necessities of diplomacy and internal rivalries. The registration of acts which remained civil as much as religious in their effects was not a Catholic innovation alone. While the tabulation of sacraments and services, the listing of personal details of the flock in the *status animarum* and the records of episcopal visitation, represented the new care of the Catholic Church to record its personal as well as its propertied resources, the desire to assess and control population strength and movement led to Tudor orders for parochial registers in Anglican England; there poor relief similarly moved out of the sphere of voluntary parochial collection into that of a rate compulsorily levied under the supervision of the secular justices. The peculiar conditions of the English Catholic community allowed clandestine marriages to continue, along with other pre-Tridentine forms of the old religion: so much of the Conciliar reform planned at Trent depended on episcopal implementation intentionally, and that remained far from easy in a proscribed community with the conflicts over authority engendered by the rivalry of missionary priests, Jesuit, regular or secular. The assertion by the Council of Trent of the essentially sacramental, not purely contractual nature of marriage led to conflict, in Naples and elsewhere, in the post-Tridentine Church, over matrimonial offences. The competence of episcopal or Inquisitorial tribunals to hear cases of bigamy was asserted, in Italy and Spain, since such an offence, which could rarely be accidental, was argued to denote a consciously heretical view of marriage, and a rejection of Conciliar doctrine. But secular tribunals, concerned that marriage was the key to family possessions, legitimacy and inheritance, continued to assert civil competence in matrimonial cases, unless further evidence of heresy were established. In Venice, the city tribunal dealing with simple cases of blasphemy similarly resolved matrimonial questions, among the lower orders at least, despite the claims of the patriarch to jurisdiction over marriage regulation.[15]

Blasphemy was indeed another area of contested competence, since the Inquisition, in Venetian territories and elsewhere, claimed, after the Council of Trent, that it necessarily implied heresy; while Venetian secular authority, encouraged by Sarpi, asserted that simple blasphemy represented social disorder alone, unless further proof of intentional heresy were forthcoming, and, as an offence to the Republic, should be punished by civil penalties solely.[16] The Venetian representatives in the mainland territories, and the Council of Ten at the centre of republican government, extended this theory, in practice, to try to reserve even more evidently serious cases to their own jurisdiction. Blasphemy, like usury, was a crime contested by ecclesiastical and secular tribunals at Naples;[17] while episcopal assertion of authority at Milan and Florence was extended to usury. In Sicily the Spanish crown Inquisition was established, but it was rejected by both episcopal and popular native resistance in Naples and Milan, where the Roman Inquisition continued to exist, tenuously in the Kingdom, but under effective archiepiscopal direction in the North. The Inquisition in Sicily was obliged to prove the necessity of its existence, in the period between the expulsion of the Jews at the end of the fifteenth century, and the arrival of Protestant ships' crews, with the English truce at the beginning of the seventeenth. Reconciliation of those who escaped from Turkish captivity, after conversion to Islam which was more or less voluntary, was hardly sufficient to warrant the large number of armed familiars who represented an organized source of crime and violence in the island, and refused to accept the jurisdiction of the royal courts, other than the Inquisition tribunal. To counter the complaints of successive viceroys to the crown the Inquisitors sent to the royal court in Spain lists of those they had sentenced to long galley service for blasphemy which was clearly, from the details provided, the common currency of ill-educated working men, without any intention of heresy. The lack of effective episcopal care, in the peculiar conditions maintained in the isolated Sicilian Church, even after the Council of Trent, and commented on by royal officials themselves, was hardly likely to provide catechism or confraternities devoted to eradicating blasphemy. The selection by the crown of Spanish prelates, who allegedly did not learn the native language, reinforced largely pre-Tridentine characteristics of the Church. So did the refusal to allow episcopal contacts with Rome, prevented by the exclusion of nuncios, visitors or vicars apostolic, and the limitation of appeals to the royal insular court of the *Monarchia* held by a lawyer in the name of the viceroy, representing the legatine status claimed by the Sicilian crown. The mountainous interior of the island was feared to harbour Judaizing deviance from true Catholicism, as well as the Basilian communities of monks following the Eastern rite. Roman attempts to intervene in Sicilian affairs produced the worse result of long vacancies in episcopal sees, while papal dependence on Sicilian grain for the provisioning of the city, especially in years of harvest failure in the papal states or of pilgrim crowds for a Jubilee, reduced the efficacy of complaints made about crown interference there or elsewhere in the Spanish possessions in the affairs of the Church.[18]

The Tridentine defence of auricular confession, in response to Protestant attack, suggested that the sacrament as an individual rite of penance, rather than as a communal act of reconciliation, was already established in the medieval Church, before Protestant objection to this personal discipline as obligatory. The retention of public penance was not in fact the lasting result of Borromean regulation, but the singular survival of the Anglican Church, in Tudor and early Stuart England, for matrimonial offences at least. For there the discipline of the external forum, the Church courts, was maintained on the basis of the presentation of offenders by Church-wardens, as with other aspects of the medieval Church which survived in the absence of either a thorough Reformation or a completed Catholic reform. In Presbyterian Scotland there was a possible parallel. But in post-Tridentine Catholic Europe the episcopal campaign to enforce the Conciliar doctrine of marriage as a sacrament of the Church met with popular resistance, given the tradition, especially in remote and mountainous areas, of periods of extended pre-marital cohabitation being regarded as a contractual union. The post-Conciliar claim of the Church to reassert its competence over both matrimonial questions, as with prohibited degrees of affinity or closed seasons for the solemnization of marriage, and all testamentary cases, once again involved conflict with secular concern to protect the transmission of lay property.

The examination of lay witnesses in Church courts, unless with the licence of secular authorities, was resisted at both Venice and Naples. The reciprocal ecclesiastical attempts to prevent the summoning of clerics to secular courts were not always successful.[19] The legal immunity claimed by the clergy in the medieval Church was a source of renewed conflict with Catholic states after the Council of

Trent, as bishops tried to realize the powers over their diocesan clergy finally restored by the Conciliar decrees. The restoration of prestige to the ecclesiastical courts was promoted at Trent, by the decrees ordering excommunication and spiritual penalties, as opposed to pecuniary fines or imprisonment, to be reserved for properly religious or moral offences, as opposed to cases involving temporal interests, and implying that they should be pronounced only by judges in holy orders. A similar attempt was made in the Anglican Church in the same period, with hardly more marked success. The right to determine clerical immunity, in first instance, was maintained by the secular courts at Naples, while at Venice the Republic extended its papal privilege – originally applicable to the city and lagoon alone – to the mainland possessions, of trying clerics accused of atrocious crimes in the secular courts. This question, like that of the extension or restriction of ecclesiastical property, lay behind the genesis of the Interdict. But at the rival maritime republic of Genoa, less independent than Venice, because of the closer involvement of Habsburg interests in the Western port, measures including a law to limit mortmain, within the rocky and partly sterile littoral of the republic, were rescinded under papal pressure. Within the confines of the inland republic of Lucca, despite a previous history of heresy, a similar retreat before papal protest took place; while in the Medici state of Florence, a law on the lines of Venetian legislation was specifically proposed and explicitly rejected. The Medici alliance, active ever since the restoration of the family at Florence following the fall of the Savonarolan republic, brought benefits to the papacy at the Council of Trent, in the form of Medici orders to the bishops of Tuscany to support papal powers against episcopal attack. Despite the refusal of two successive bishops of Fiesole to comply, because of their first-hand experience of the problems of resident government of episcopal sees, not only in their own diocese, but in that of Florence – which they administered for the great figures who drew the revenues of the archdiocese – the papacy rewarded the Medici, after the Council, with the desired title and precedence of grand-duke, to a chorus of protest from other Catholic states.

The problems of criminal clerics and of Church finance were inevitably linked, in the post-Conciliar just as in the medieval Church, despite the Council's qualification of clerical legal immunity. The episcopal attempts to abolish corruption in the Church courts, as urged at Trent, did not mean only the careful licensing of lawyers fit to plead in them. The payment of regular salaries to presiding judges, the clerics acting as vicar civil and vicar criminal in the two types of case coming before ecclesiastical courts, was necessary if bribes and unofficial exactions were to be successfully eliminated. The efficient working of diocesan administration similarly required not only able chancellors and archivists, but a salaried cleric of outstanding ability to act as vicar general. The emphasis on episcopal responsibility for reform, in the disciplinary decrees of the Council, made such considerations more important than ever. The powers of the vicar general were not uncontested by secular authorities, however. The Venetian secular authorities did not, by their own admission, always observe the letter of the papal privilege, which required the presence of the vicar general at the trial of a secular cleric, as of a religious superior at the trial of regulars, over whom the Nuncio otherwise claimed jurisdiction.[20] The proprieties of judicial procedure were not always maintained, in the breakdown of law and order which affected the Venetian mainland from the 1580s, just as much as other areas of Italy, from Spanish Lombardy to Sicily.[21] The preliminary degrading of the cleric, before execution of sentence, was not always performed. Bishops in Spanish Lombardy complained, at the end of the sixteenth century, that a new papal ruling on the right of secular courts to deal with clerics accused of more atrocious crimes did not preserve ecclesiastical privileges, but, on the contrary, gave new scope for secular interference.[22]

The immunities of sanctuary were also debated, in different parts of Italy, after the Council, with reference to cases of different severity, in terms of the charges to be brought. Neither at Venice nor in Sicily was the immunity of ecclesiastical prisons always respected. The decrees of the Council of Trent had realistic reference to the reliance of the Church courts on the secular arm; but they also contained a more optimistic assertion of the bishop's right to enforce his own jurisdiction by means of an independent court official or police. Instances of such a force in action, in post-Tridentine Catholic society, would not seem to be common. At Piacenza careful secular watch allowed an episcopal officer on this model. At Milan a prolonged struggle between the Borromeo archbishops and the Spanish authorities ended with virtual ecclesiastical victory, and the recognition of an armed archiepiscopal police force, despite conflict over its size or the nature of its arms.[23] But the Spanish crown was adamant that other bishops in Lombardy – already considered dangerous to native obedience, by virtue of their noble status – and areas of temporal jurisdiction attached to sees, as at Tortona, should not develop similar forces. Such conflict was distinct from that

between different parts of Spanish government itself, as with the
rivalry of viceroys and crown Inquisitors or crown Visitors, in
Sardinia and Sicily, for example.[24] The fear that Italian bishops, in
Spanish Lombardy and most sees in the kingdom of Naples, might
prove to be leaders of native disaffection was peculiar to Spanish rule
in Italy.[25] But the more general point about Church and society in
Catholic Europe after the Council of Trent was equally clear: that
the Church did not in fact possess the power to enforce its authority
unequivocally on all clergy, let alone the laity.

A similar limitation was evident in the financial resources of the
Church. The cost of salaries for diocesan officials, or of rebuilding
episcopal residences after long periods of absenteeism, was problematic, but two further difficulties compounded the troubles of
bishops. The major innovation of the Council of Trent, in decreeing
the erection of diocesan seminaries for the training of secular clergy,
authorized a bishop to tax his clergy for the purpose, as well as
contributing a part of his revenues. The delay in the creation of such
institutions, in Italy itself – let alone in other parts of Europe, like
France, where seminaries only evolved in the seventeenth century,
and under the influence rather of New Orders, that of Saint-Sulpice
above all – was not least caused by financial problems. The reluctance
of existing clergy to contribute to the training of their successors was
understandable: disputes with bishops arose over this, as Bollani,
bishop of Brescia after the Council of Trent, found. Bishops themselves were not always in a position to afford easily their part of the
costs. Even in well-endowed sees, or rather especially in well-re-
munerated dioceses, the face value of the bishop's revenue was much
above his real income often. The Conciliar assertion of episcopal
residence, after long struggle over the expression of the relations
between pope and bishops, left the power of the papacy to summon
prelates to Curial service at Rome intact, while urging respect for
the care of dioceses. The papacy after Trent in fact maintained the
spirit of the Conciliar decrees surprisingly well, by distinguishing
between diocesan bishops, even if cardinals, and officials of the Curia.
The end of the medieval and Renaissance system, of supporting the
work of the Curia and its members from the revenues of sees and
benefices throughout Catholic Europe, was thus, in one sense, to a
large degree effected. The result however was a search for new means
of financial support for the Curia, especially as its centralized powers
grew rather than diminished, with the decision that Rome alone
should be the place of arbitration in all questions arising from the
interpretation of the Council's decrees. The papal states generally

were made to yield such taxation as they could, at some cost to agricultural productivity, even if sensitive areas, like Bologna, were rather protected in their existing privileges. The new papal funds, the *monti*, based on low rates of interest, were created in Rome to attract investors. But the papacy also continued to extract financial provision for Curial officials from the revenues of dioceses by the use of 'pensions'. These were paid to the Curialist by the resident bishop, according to the terms of provision drawn up at Rome for a newly appointed diocesan.

The Spanish crown, which was used to funding the work of its own central administration from the revenues of the Church, by the simple expedient of using dignitaries of the Church as civil servants who supported themselves from the income of their see or canonry, made a similar adaptation. Pensions were reserved, just as at Rome, on the revenues of sees to which the crown had the right of nomination, in Spain itself or in some of the other Spanish territories, at the time of a cleric's preferment. The pensions in this case sometimes supported lay servants of the crown, rather than ecclesiastics; just as, in Elizabethan England, bishops were ordered to support courtiers by grants of land or unfavourable exchange of properties. The Spanish crown also paid pensions to ecclesiastics who supported its policies and promoted its interests at Rome or elsewhere, or who might be expected to do so. Some cardinals at the Curia, whether Spaniards or Italians, were thus in receipt of Spanish pensions, whether or not the services they rendered to the crown, in papal conclaves above all, were in the end regarded as satisfactory. The freedom of papal policy, let alone of papal elections, was nevertheless compromised in this way, quite apart from the question of the composition of the electoral college of cardinals, and the influence of the recommendations of Catholic rulers. The ironic result, at Bologna, after the Council of Trent, where Gabriele Paleotti was active as a reforming diocesan, was that so independent a cleric was in receipt of a Spanish pension. For his resident activity, on a model of Tridentine reform compared by contemporaries with that of Charles Borromeo at Milan, in the same period, was hampered by his shortage of funds, after the reduction of his revenue by a papal pension; and the reorganization of diocesan income more generally proved impossible, because the Curia, in its role as government of the papal states, feared the effects of any alteration in Bolognese traditions, and obstructed Paleotti in this, as in many of his proposed reforms.

The French crown similarly continued to reward clerical and even lay servants with the revenues of rich abbeys, by the device of commendatory abbacies, quite apart from the implicit support of the nobility which continued access to the economic resources of diocesan bishoprics represented from the wars of religion in the later sixteenth century to the pre-Revolutionary decades of the eighteenth. The Council of Trent had opposed the granting of commendatory abbacies to laymen and discouraged their use by clerics who were not regulars. But in France the tradition continued unchanged, and in Sicily the Spanish crown continued to grant such abbacies to ecclesiastics, including cardinals at the Curia, and even papal nephews.[26] The desire of Scipio Borghese to accumulate such resources, in support of his cultural patronage and despite the disapproval of the pope, created conflict, at the end of the Interdict, with Venice, over the abbey of Vangadizza. The Venetian Republic effectively continued the use of commendatory abbacies for the benefit of noble ecclesiastics, but confined this benefit to natives, patricians of Venice itself, not least where the extensive property of monasteries in sensitive, border areas was concerned. The Republic, even before the Interdict, was concerned about the weakness of its land frontiers, not only with the Spanish and Austrian Habsburgs in Lombardy and Istria, but, from 1598, with the papacy itself, after the papal annexation of Ferrara. Conflict over control of the mouths of the Po, and over rival shipping interests in the Adriatic and relations with the papal port of Ancona, continued to disturb the Venetian government. The French support of the Gallican Bourbon, Henri IV, after his reconciliation to the Church, did not alter the fact that he had acquiesced in this papal annexation, in return; while Venetian claims to have produced the papal recognition of Henri, belatedly, as legitimate Catholic ruler of France, to the exclusion of Spanish claims, had to be balanced in fact against the diplomatic intervention of the Medici, in the same cause. Added to this was the decisive influence on Clement VIII of independent clerics, such as Paleotti and the Venetian Valier, but above all the Oratorians, the Florentine-born Neri and the subject of Spain from the kingdom of Naples, Baronius.

The search, by this diplomatic volte-face, to secure greater independence for the post-Tridentine papacy from Spain, was never acknowledged at Venice. But the acquisition of a potential alternative, in France once again officially Catholic, to the power of Spain as sole supporter of the papacy, did relieve some of the pressure felt by the popes of the immediately post-Conciliar decades, despite their assertions of independence. The formal right, claimed by Spain as by other Catholic sovereigns, to exclude candidates from the papal throne who were not acceptable to the crown, was never recognized at Rome; although successful intervention in papal conclaves by cardinals representing the views of the Spanish king or the emperor continued to be made. Reform of the procedure at papal conclaves, in an attempt to reduce the possibilities for such dictation, was made in the early seventeenth century by Cardinal Ludovisi, papal nephew, and Cardinal Federico Borromeo, archbishop of Milan; he was a victim, like Baronius, of the opposition of Spain to the election of those who opposed the claims of the crown over the Church in Italy.[27] The financial benefit which the crown gained from allowing sees in its nomination, in Spain and Sicily, to remain vacant, for extended periods, paralleled that derived from the same device by the crown in Elizabethan England. But papal representation of such similarities produced outrage at the court of the most Catholic monarch. The desire of the Spanish crown to maximize its income from such sources was nevertheless one of the most persistent causes of conflict in Lombardy, between Church and secular government, in the post-Tridentine period and into the later seventeenth century.

The Council of Trent had legislated clearly for control of diocesan revenues, during vacancies, by cathedral chapters. But in the duchy of Milan, inherited by Spain from Charles v, an alternative tradition existed, of the sequestration of vacant sees and benefices by an administrator appointed jointly by Rome and the temporal authority.[28] The attempt of the Spanish government to continue the operation of this system in the case of bishoprics failed, in the face of Roman respect for the Conciliar decree, and local opposition from cathedral chapters and from the bishops of the area, led by the Borromeo archbishops of Milan. The extension, by these episcopal opponents of the old sequestration system, of the struggle to the vacancy of benefices produced less clear success. The issue involved in this case was not so much financial as pastoral and political, since the secular involvement in admission to the temporal possession of a benefice allowed a policy of favouring natives of Lombardy or subjects of the crown at the expense of the Tridentine programme of admitting to livings only the best qualified after open competition and episcopal examination. Other areas of Catholic Europe, such as the city of Bologna, wished to reserve parochial and other benefices for natives; this was quite apart from the self-selection of noble cathedral chapters, which opposed episcopal attempts at imposing reform, both before and after Trent, in Italy, Spain and the German lands. The Venetian state similarly wished to limit the access of those who were not subjects of the Republic to incumbencies by control of the grant of temporal possession: and this policy was reinforced after the Interdict, just as was the exclusion of those not native to the state from headship of religious houses in its territories or of provincial office-holders in the religious orders who were not subjects. The loyalty to Venice of many, though not all, of the bishops of the mainland dioceses, drawn from the Venetian patriciate in the richer sees, and from the citizens of Venice or the local nobility of its territories in other cases, was demonstrated in the Interdict; and more consistently the obedience of vicars general, especially in the absence of diocesan bishops, who were subjects of the state. The attempt of Spain to exclude diocesan officials at Milan who were not subjects of the crown was, by contrast, a failure, in the face of determined opposition from the Borromeo archbishops;[29] though Spain recognized the effect of Venetian bishops being native nobles.[30]

The recovery of Church property and revenues was as much a campaign characteristic of post-Tridentine Catholic Europe, as of Anglican England in the Laudian era. The proportion of land held by the Church in Catholic Europe varied from area to area, as did the relationship between the extent of surface area and the real value of such lands. In parts of Northern Italy, it has been suggested, the loss of Church lands to lay ownership was marked in the pre-Tridentine period, but this argument has not won entire acceptance. Even if it were agreed that the proportion of land in ecclesiastical hands in the Milanese area had been reduced to at most 15 per cent by the middle of the sixteenth century, the proportion in Southern Italy is estimated to have remained as high as 70 per cent. In 1587, the Venetian representative at Milan regarded the ecclesiastical lands of the area as forming one seventh of the total surface area, but as worth a third of the total value of landed property in the state. An early eighteenth-century survey of land in Lombardy nevertheless suggests the extension of Church property, between the middle of the sixteenth and the middle of the seventeenth century, by about 12 per cent. Archiepiscopal action would thus seem to have contributed to the result, at the time of the survey itself, of ecclesiastics holding about 22 per cent of land in the state, except in the most mountainous areas. At the end of the sixteenth century, the Spanish authorities regarded ecclesiastics as possessing a third of the land in the state, including all the best properties, however; and such vague assertions were repeated in the food shortage of 1629.[31] Monetary inflation clearly increased competition for land in which to invest; while economic competition in general between ecclesiastics and laity was the more pronounced in a period of price rises, absolute and relative, of which contemporaries were well aware.

The violent clashes which resulted, between families and their clerical members, were evident in the Venetian areas of Bergamo, Brescia and Padua, at the end of the sixteenth century and in the early decades of the seventeenth.[32] In 1605 secular authority represented the property of the Church, of hospitals and other religious institutions as forming two-thirds of the surface area of the Bergamasco, a poor and sterile region, and as being still on the increase.[33] Detailed archiepiscopal investigation of Church property in the diocese of Milan, as in the mountainous area of Lecco in 1608, revealed many small properties bequeathed to support devotional and charitable activities; but not all were in the real possession of the Church in fact.[34] In Lombardy the productivity of Church lands was in any case contested, since some soil would support only rice cultivation, which the Spanish authorities were intent on limiting, in part because they feared a health hazard from the water-fields. Dispute over such cultivation broke out between secular and ecclesiastical authorities, as also over the free movement of grain produced on Church land, where concern for profit was at odds on occasion with the securing of an adequate supply for the populous city of Milan. The contested quartering of troops on ecclesiastical property similarly affected the potential income from tenancies, and in Lombardy the taxation of lay tenants on Church land was resisted by the Borromeo archbishops.[35] The free disposal of grain for sale was at issue elsewhere in Catholic Europe, in Sicily for example,[36] while the Roman Curia claimed from the kingdom of Naples supplies of wine, grain and silk. This symbol of the suzerainty of the papacy over the kingdom was a reminder of the claims which anti-Curial and even anti-papal legal opinion at Naples resented and resisted, both before and after the Council of Trent. The taxation of clerics by the papacy was unsuccessfully resisted at Naples,[37] whereas clerical contribution to military subventions, as with the cost of improved fortifications, in the early seventeenth century, was disputed in Spanish Lombardy and across the border in Venetian territory.[38] The relatively high proportion of land owned by ecclesiastics in the Bergamasco, where poverty was a serious problem, was thought by the Venetian authorities to account for a lack of enthusiasm, among the laity as opposed to the clergy, for the papal interest in the Interdict.[39]

But while some parish clergy were susceptible to the pressure and propaganda brought to bear in the area by Federico Borromeo, archbishop of Milan, and the writings of Bellarmine and Baronius, the canonries of Bergamo itself were always an attraction for the sons of local nobility, deprived of much other means of support. The richer canonries of Padua, on the Venetian mainland, were shared by the native nobility of the city with Venetian patricians, with consequent disputes over the distribution of revenues, and the post-Tridentine attempt to enforce canonical residence by daily distribution of stipend. The involvement of clerics in the rising tide of violence on the Venetian mainland in the decades from 1580 similarly marked an increasing competition for resources in an area, around Padua particularly, where Venetian patricians were taking over land, as they diversified from maritime investment. The clergy in the Venetian state were in any case subject to normal indirect taxes, while the papacy allowed the collection of *decime* by the Republic, at agreed intervals and rates, which were designed to support, from the clergy's wealth, the stand of Venice against Islam. The grant of such subsidies was naturally an occasion for intense negotiation over ecclesiastical rights and state interests, and the failure of the Republic to maintain an anti-Turkish policy at all times put the grant at risk occasionally. The exemption of the revenues of cardinals and of some religious orders, not least the Jesuits, from their property within the state, was also a contested aspect of the collection of the *decime*. In Spain a similar subsidy was granted, from the wealth of the Spanish clergy, to the crown by the papacy, with similar negotiations at intervals, in which Sicilian grain for Rome might be effectively bargained against Spanish ecclesiastical income for the monarchy. A complication in this case was the levy of a part of this subsidy by the papacy itself, for the fund dedicated to completion of the fabric of Saint Peter's Rome.[40]

Luther's original objection to sale of an indulgence in Germany theoretically designed, in part at least, for this purpose was in one sense met by the decree of the Council of Trent forbidding the sale of indulgences, and limiting their grant to the powers of pope and bishops. The post-Tridentine episcopate did not always find it easy to end the attraction to the laity of the indulgences still claimed to be disposed freely by religious orders and confraternities, especially the arch-confraternities of Rome itself.[41] But in Spain an indulgence was, in effect, still sold, as was recognized at Rome, in discussion of the 'Crusade' indulgence, which raised revenue from the laity for the crown in Spain, Sicily and America.[42] The purchase of this benefit, supporting, supposedly, the crusade of the crown against Islam and heresy, was considered to free the owner from all ecclesiastical penalties, including those imposed by bishops or their courts. The institution was thus regarded by active Spanish bishops, after the Council of Trent, as disruptive of their authority; while in Sicily the commissioners of the 'Crusade', who were on occasion the crown Inquisitors themselves, represented a further obstacle to the exercise of both episcopal and viceregal authority.[43] In Sicily the Church contributed to the crown's needs, and took the lead, as the first estate, in voting subsidies in the island parliament, although in a rare association with Roman authority, the clerical estate's grant was supposed to be confirmed by the pope.[44] The wealth of the Sicilian abbacies was in some cases considerable, as was that of the virtually titular see of Monreale, at the monastery above Palermo, which was held by ecclesiastics whom the crown wished to favour, and who were usually absentees.[45] In France the first estate supported the needs of the state by its grant of subsidies, even if at a rate below that increasingly imposed in the seventeenth century, from the rise to power of Cardinal Richelieu as minister of the crown, on the third estate. The territorial interests still involved in many bishoprics and abbacies in the empire remaining in Catholic hands at the end of the sixteenth century, quite apart from the states of the electoral prince-archbishops, presented an inextricable link between ecclesiastical administration and temporal government. The attempt, in the Thirty Years War, of the emperor to ensure the restitution of Church lands taken by Protestants since the Reformation caused resistance among the princes of the empire, who feared to lose their acquisitions of economic and political authority, to the profit of reasserted imperial power. The genesis of the revolt in the Netherlands against Spanish rule similarly involved, in part, the fears of the native nobility that reorganization of the sees of the area, to reduce the size and wealth of dioceses, and to increase their number and the effectiveness of episcopal action against heresy, would mean the exclusion of their own families from such sources of traditional authority in the Low Countries, and the intrusion of foreigners chosen by the Spanish crown. There was thus a parallel with the opposition of the cities and states of the Netherlands to the economic consequences of uniform taxation on the Spanish model and the overriding of local judicial and fiscal privileges by the Inquisition.[46]

The size of German dioceses impeded the implementation of Tridentine reform in many cases, despite the zealous work of Jesuit and other internal missionaries from the religious orders, old, new and reformed. In Bavaria ducal patronage of the Counter-Reformation was marked in both its positive and negative aspects: the work of Canisius and the influence of the Jesuits, on education and the revival of popular Catholic piety as well as on politics, was accompanied by direct action by the ruler against heretical subjects. While a similar combination characterized the lands of the Austrian Habsburgs at the beginning of the seventeenth century, and Bohemia, recovered by the Habsburgs for imperial and Catholic rule after the Battle of the White Mountain (1620), early in the Thirty Years War, the prince-archbishopric of Salzburg provided another example. The inevitable preoccupations of state during the Thirty Years War did not prevent the activity of archbishops intent on reforming their clergy and monasteries, while rebuilding the churches and cathedral of the city in an Italianate style, and patronising the earliest opera north of the Alps, at a court which was certainly princely, as well as possibly archiepiscopal in its luxury. Later in the seventeenth century, during the attempts continued by Louis XIV after the Thirty Years War, to maintain French diplomatic power in German affairs, in the face of Habsburg authority and papal interests, the electoral archbishopric of Cologne demonstrated the lack of freedom for purely ecclesiastical action in the empire. The interference of Louis in the selection of an archbishop was natural, from the point of view of the political balance on the Rhine, but it openly ignored the interest of the Church, even if neither the cathedral chapter nor the papacy were free to overlook the political character of the appointment.

For dynastic reasons as much as religious, German bishoprics continued to be held in plurality after the Council of Trent on some scale. But the advancing absolutism of prince-bishops in German-speaking Europe in the later sixteenth century and in the seventeenth century, despite the attempt of noble cathedral chapters to maintain their privileges, allowed practical reform to be pursued by diocesan officials as well as Jesuits. This was generally true from the period immediately after the Council, despite the delays – often considerable and caused, as elsewhere in Catholic Europe, chiefly by financial problems – in creating diocesan seminaries for the training of parochial clergy. Changes pursued in Italy, for example, by reforming bishops were also enforced in German lands, despite the disruption of war. Archdeacons were subordinated to episcopal control, as were rural deans, in their exercise of supervision over the clergy.[47] Popular devotions, including pilgrimage, were encouraged but carefully controlled, and not allowed to compete with the obligations of the laity in receiving the sacraments at their parish church. Similar supervision of confraternities and charitable institutions was attempted by bishops, who also promoted catechetical instruction by means of

Sunday schools and the rebuilding of churches. The practical reform of Catholic life in this way was achieved through diocesan synods and visitations, despite the complication of the continued existence in German-speaking Europe of great independent abbeys and their extensive areas of temporal and ecclesiastical jurisdiction.

At a level below that of international politics, and in Catholic Europe from the end of the Council of Trent, the reassertion of the independence of the institutional Church, within Catholic society, by the recovery of its economic resources, was clear from the records of episcopal visitations, held according to the Tridentine decrees. The registration of the property and rents of each parish, as well as of legacies for the support of mass-priests, and for charitable concerns, usually to the benefit of the laity, was detailed, in an efficiently administered diocese. By contrast the occasional request of Venice to buy grain from the papal Romagna was not always sure of success, because of the concern of the temporal government of the papal states to ensure the supply of the native population.[48] Similar contrasts existed elsewhere in Catholic Europe. Redistribution of capitular revenues to ensure daily canonical residence and duties proved problematic in post-Tridentine Portugal.[49] In Savoy, ecclesiastical property notably increased between 1584 and 1738, even if not in proportion to noble accumulation. So too in Piedmont, between 1619 and 1717, clerical possessions were enlarged by a figure representing 3 per cent of the cultivated land area; and clerical income from rents equally increased in early eighteenth-century Piedmont, if again not in the same proportion as noble investment. Episcopal visitation records in Northern Italy, in the early seventeenth century, carefully noted the laity of each parish capable of providing charity to others.

The inheritance of the estate left by deceased bishops in Catholic Europe represented a further cause of dispute, in some states, over ecclesiastical and secular rights. Whereas in Anglican England a married episcopate, for all the disapproval of Elizabeth I, posed a further threat to the conservation of episcopal property, the post-Tridentine papacy, in Catholic Europe, maintained the view that the accumulation of property personal to a bishop, as opposed to the possessions of his see, was unsuitable in an office bound to the duty of charity. The *spogli* or 'spoils' of a deceased bishop's personal estate were thus claimed by the papacy in parts of Catholic Europe. In the Venetian territories little trouble arose over this; and the patrician bishops of the Republic were indeed noted for their charity, especially at times of particular poverty and shortage, after the Council of Trent. But in the kingdom of Naples and in Spain such papal claims were contested by secular authorities, in defence of the rights of inheritance asserted by a bishop's relations and servants. The physical contest which could ensue, in the house of a dead or dying bishop, did little for the repute of the papacy, which it was the Nuncio's duty to defend. The difficult task of collecting the *spogli* was, for a while, given to the separate papal office of Collector, in order to maintain the diplomatic prestige of the Nunciature in both Naples and Spain; in the latter, indeed, the Nuncio's tribunal had extensive judicial as well as financial powers, which were recognized except at moments of great tension as serving the interests of Spaniards who, in many cases, were thus saved the cost and difficulty of promoting their business at the papal court. But the disputes between Nuncios and Collectors proved a more damaging complication for papal diplomacy, and the Collector in Spain, lacking the diplomatic status of the Nuncio himself, was effectively expelled by the Spanish authorities in one dispute.[50]

At Naples prolonged dispute over the exercise of the Nuncio's faculties arose with the viceregal authorities; the presence, at times, of cardinals in Spanish service as viceroys at Naples did little to alleviate this problem. The *spogli* at Naples also represented the revenues of a see, *sede vacante*, and the estate of other ecclesiastics. The Gallican Church claimed exemption from the collection of *spogli*, while the dioceses of Piedmont mostly made agreements with the Curia for compounding, by the mid-seventeenth century. So that in this, as in other ways, as over the reception of the Tridentine decrees or the bull *In Coena Domini*, the contrast between Savoy and Piedmont represented the different evolution of the Catholic Church in French and Italian tradition. Despite the occasional concession by the papacy of clerical *decime*, the dukes of Savoy remained intent on reorganizing the provinces of religious orders, as these affected their own states, in a way comparable to Venetian and Spanish preoccupations.[51] But, as again in the Iberian peninsula, diocesan bishops in the duchy found their control of parochial benefices much reduced by monastic appropriations and peculiars.[52] The Medici of Florence lost their claim to the *spogli* of bishops in the Tuscan state. But the good relations nevertheless maintained between Rome and Florence were in contrast with the serious conflicts, in the Neapolitan kingdom, over the summoning of laity before ecclesiastical courts, in the post-Tridentine campaigns to recover Church tithes which had not been paid. The concern of the Medici over any form of Catholic reform, involving regulars, which seemed to echo the republican strains of Savonarolan enthusiasm, was more akin, in its effects, to the determination at Naples of the secular authorities not to allow episcopal intervention to reform those convents and charitable institutions which claimed to be royal foundations and, as such, to benefit from the concessive clause in the Tridentine decrees about royal patronage rights. Elsewhere in Catholic Europe the extraction of tithes from the laity proved problematic, vital as the tithes were for the maintenance of the parish clergy; except as in France, where they were sometimes alienated, or impropriated by monastic or other ecclesiastical institutions.

The cost of maintaining the physical state and equipment of the church, which could fall largely on the parish priest in a rural area, where the population lived at subsistence level, increased after the Council of Trent, as bishops on visitation of their dioceses ordered a higher standard of liturgical observance, requiring the correct plate and vestments, as well as the new, standardized liturgical texts, and the other books prescribed for clerical use. The resistance of laity in the area of Padua was supported by the Venetian government in a dispute over tithes with the cathedral chapter.[53] In Venetian territory there were also disputes over redistribution of parochial benefices, which the Council of Trent had empowered bishops to undertake, to meet the needs of changes in population and settlement. Local feeling was genuinely opposed, on occasion, to the abandonment of a building maintained by the residents' ancestors; but Venetian patrician interests and patronage rights were also sometimes rather at stake, where a beneficed cure had been reserved for a noble cleric. Since such redistribution was usually authorized or confirmed by Roman authority, a challenge to papal power was thus implicit, as also in the prohibition of free circulation or publication in Venetian territory of papal bulls, and of Inquisitorial edicts, without the prior permission of the Republic. The care taken to prevent the public reading in the vernacular of the bull *In Coena Domini*, within the Venetian state, suggested the concern of the Venetian government over its right to tax the clergy. A similar opposition to publication of this bull was marked in Spain, where a preacher who expounded it at Santiago was penalized by the secular authority.[54] In all these ways, it is clear, the hold of the Church over society in Catholic Europe after the Council of Trent, even in those states, in Italy and Spain, where society remained solidly and undoubtedly Catholic, as was indeed true of Venice itself, was far from complete: whether measured by reference to moral questions arising from the mixed decrees of the Council, as on marriage, or in respect of the assertion of financial privilege and legal immunity by the institutional Church.

Any assessment of the Counter-Reformation in practice must take account of this serious qualification of the more traditional picture of the reassertion of clerical dominance over lay society. The hierarchical structure of the Church itself was hampered in its workings, even where relations within the clerical order were concerned, by the intervention of secular authority. In parts of the kingdom of Naples, any claim of bishops to dispose of the *spogli* of their parochial clergy was at odds with papal interests; while in Lombardy the royal *placet* was necessary for the succession of newly appointed bishops to their temporalities and entry into their sees. More far-reaching was the royal assertion in the Neapolitan kingdom of the need for the *exequatur*, before a Nuncio's orders even to the clergy were to be permitted to take effect; this was a licence given after examination of the brief or other document in question by the royal chaplain general, who was a Spanish subject. In Sicily, similarly, all documents arriving from Rome were examined by viceregal authorities, and required the *executoria* for their validity in the island, according to secular claims.[55] In Spain, the possibility, for clergy against their bishops, and regulars against their superiors, even for bishops against the Nuncio, of appeal to royal tribunals existed;[56] while in France secular courts investigated claims of ecclesiastical subordinates against the orders of their superiors, by the appeals *comme d'abus*. The royal council in Castile also examined bulls and briefs arriving from Rome in fact, whatever the limitation of this practice in theory; and in Spain an Index of prohibited books, or of books requiring expurgation, was maintained independently of the Roman Index.

The Venetian Republic increasingly took control of book censorship in the seventeenth century, despite the concern of bishops and Inquisitors. The carefully confined enclave of Protestant merchants at Venice, at the German Warehouse, represented a minor threat of the spread of heresy in the city; and the English embassy, at the time of the Interdict, was an outlet for heretical books. But the Republic resisted a plan to revive its maritime fortunes, decaying under the pressures of piracy and rival shipping in the Adriatic, as well as the Turkish threat in the Mediterranean, by making the city a free port, as the Tuscan government was to do at Leghorn; and this resistance arose from a concern to preserve the religion of the state. More serious, in the eyes of the Church, was the presence of numbers of Protestant students at the University of Padua, the Venetian state university. The Venetian magistrates defended the right of these students to refrain from Catholic observances, not only in worship, but in such matters as abstinence from meat on prescribed days, and during Lent, provided that no offence to the Catholicism of the town population was caused, and that, in theory, episcopal permission was obtained for any breach of the abstinence regulations. Problems arose over the burial of any students who died as non-Catholics in Padua, and over the attendance on such students, when ill, by medical practitioners, since the Tridentine Church required doctors to refuse to attend more than once at the beds of those who did not profess the Catholic faith and receive the ministrations of a priest. The Inquisitor and bishop found themselves obstructed, in any intervention against Protestant students, by the Venetian magistrates, intent on maintaining the international reputation of Padua, at a time when the numbers of students attending from within the state were falling.[57] The chief concern of the Nuncio was that Protestant students from Germany and elsewhere north of the Alps were taking their doctorates without subscribing to the formula of Tridentine faith imposed by Conciliar authority on those taking degrees at Catholic universities. The doctrinal prescriptions at other universities in Europe, such as those in England, remained an effective obstacle to the graduation of Catholic students, even if that in turn helped to maintain the attraction of the Catholic colleges in exile, on the continent of Europe.

The educational provisions of Catholic Europe, below university level, were to be supervised by the bishops of the Church, according to the Council of Trent. But the absence of resources in fact left such education of the laity most commonly in the hands of the New Orders, both the Jesuits, and others, like the original Roman Oratory and the French Oratory, which sometimes catered for a wider social group of male pupils. The educational purpose of Neri's pristine oratorios was matched by the attraction of the collegiate theatres at many Jesuit colleges in the seventeenth century. But the social exclusiveness of the Jesuit colleges for lay students was rather reinforced, in response to secular demand, in the seventeenth and eighteenth centuries, with the broadening of the curriculum, in some cases, to include the gentlemanly skills of fencing, riding and music, alongside an academic education. There were colleges of non-Jesuit origin and direction which educated boys of good birth not necessarily designed for the clerical life. An early foundation of this nature was the Collegio Borromeo at Pavia, founded by Saint Charles, and directed subsequently by clerical members of the family, for which there were more applicants than places available. At other universities, as at Bologna, Jesuit and ecclesiastical influence was maintained among students not resident in such a college by means of sodalities of a devotional nature. The popularity of the Spiritual Exercises of Saint Ignatius, as a directed form of meditation and spiritual formation, among those who were not Jesuits nor even clerics, was a notable source of influence for the Society in Catholic Europe. Increasing lay literacy, below the levels of noble and upper-middle class society, by the eighteenth century, meant more use of books of devotion; these had equally sustained the faith of English Recusants, in the isolation of their households, at the end of the sixteenth century. While in England some of these works represented an unbroken tradition of late medieval vernacular piety, the new forms of devotion promulgated in continental Europe in the Counter-Reformation stressed again the cult of the reserved sacrament, of the Madonna, and of particular saints. Marian devotion and veneration of saints and their relics were reasserted by means of the rosary and the revival of pilgrimage. Popular imagery maintained the familiar depictions of the Madonna and Child, and of the Passion, as well as the portraits of new Saints of the age itself, newly canonized by the Church: Saint Teresa, Saint Ignatius, Saint Philip Neri, Saint Charles Borromeo, all raised to the altar soon after their death.

The episcopal campaign against superstition required, however, not merely the rejection of images which suggested a misrepresentation of true belief or classicizing paganism, or immoral distractions, but also the removal of images from unsuitable locations, where proper reverence could only be lacking. But such removal could disturb the popular mentality. At Naples, the removal of a sacred image from a customs shed at the port, by officials of the archbishop, was taken by the populace as a signal for an anti-tax riot, in which the shed was demolished. The danger, in Spanish eyes, was compounded by the cries of the crowd against taxation and in favour of the archbishop, an Italian from an important native family. The attacks, from time to time, of the royal authorities on the archbishops of Naples after the Council of Trent were unsuccessful, though on this occasion severe reprisals were taken against the archiepiscopal officials involved. The reform of the Dominican convent at Naples was similarly complicated, because of its use as a centre for the resistance of native nobles to the policies of the Spanish viceroy Ossuna, three decades before the revolt of Masaniello, of 1647-8, which eventually involved both popular and noble elements.[58] In France, in the Catholic reform of the seventeenth century, bishops removing popular images which they considered liable to cause superstition rather than correct devotion, faced charges of Jansenism and crypto-Protestantism. But such rigorism, as with objection to dancing on Sundays and holy days, was in fact adopted from the unqualified orthodoxy of the model reform carried out by Charles Borromeo at Milan.

The objection of Borromeo, and of other Italian reforming bishops, such as Paleotti at Bologna, after the Council of Trent, to the popular abuses of Carnival, at the start of Lent, and of comedies was less successful. The object of the attack, in the case of comedies, was the unscripted tradition of open-air representation by itinerant actors, inherited from the *Commedia dell'Arte*, which prevented pre-censorship by the Church. Bishops were constrained to note with care, in the records of episcopal institutions, the presence of such sensitive professions as doctors or midwives, musicians and school-masters, booksellers and lawyers; but the peripatetic nature of the acting profession resisted such classification. Carnival, as a pre-Lenten celebration of riot, expense and disorder, survived and flourished in Catholic society, into the eighteenth century, not least in Italy itself, and even in Rome, as well as in Venice. It proved impossible, in fact, to impose restraint and austerity on all of society throughout every season of the year, whether in the cause of Jansenist teaching, or in the activation of a rigorist Catholic reform. Popular superstitions survived, in rural France or Southern Italy, for example, until the Revolution, despite episcopal attempts at re-education; while heterodox enthusiasm broke out at the end of the seventeenth century and the beginning of the eighteenth, among the Camisards, revolting in their last mountainous retreat against the suppression of French Protestantism by Louis XIV, and among the Convulsionaries, in the urban retreat of a Paris cemetery, in response to the government attempt to repress Jansenism, otherwise noted for its intellectual austerity. The imposition, among the more normal activities of Catholic society, of observance of holy days by abstention from work, and the closure of shops, proved problematic for the Church, in Italy and Portugal for example, in the immediately post-Tridentine decades, in the face of opposition from secular authorities to the intervention of ecclesiastical courts in such matters; while in the eighteenth cen-tury Catholic governments attempted to reduce the number of holy days marked by abstention from work, with or without papal co-operation.[59]

Episcopal campaigns to regulate lay behaviour in churches proved, at times, as difficult in Catholic Europe as in Laudian England. There was lay resistance to the prohibition of proprietary pews, or to the exclusion of the laity from seats near the altar by means of altar-rails. The regulation of funerary display proved problematic, as

Catholic obsequies remained an occasion for the display of family honour and the achievements of the deceased. Attempts to limit the conspicuous expenditure characteristic both of funerals, and the solemn entry of noble nuns into their convents, were still made in the eighteenth century, but bishops never finally achieved their aim of reducing such ceremonies from social to purely religious occasions. Royal and noble funerals and marriages remained occasions for conspicuous display, as well as for the oratorical and literary panegyric expected from the Church, in the case of obsequies. The removal of funerary monuments from churches caused obvious opposition, while attempts to prevent the monumental celebration of martial prowess or profane triumphs were skilfully circumvented in Venetian territory by the disguising of traditional wall-tombs as side-altars to the saints.

The institutional Church itself was not a united force in such questions. The great families of Rome, celebrated for their cardinals and popes, continued to commission the elaborate decoration of side-chapels in the churches of Rome, which depicted the glories of the family as much as those of the titular saint. Even the originally austere décor of the great churches built in Rome by the New Orders was thus transformed, as the orders achieved popularity among polite society. The decrees of the Council of Trent did little in fact, for all their clarity, to end the medieval abuses of competition at death beds and in the conduct of funerals between regular and secular clergy. The proximity of dioceses characterized by active episcopal reform, and those lacking such improvement, was epitomized in the case of Borromean Milan itself. The neighbouring diocese of Como lay outside the ecclesiastical province of the archbishop, and the state of episcopal administration left much to be desired.[60] The flight of clergy who objected to the rigour of Saint Charles was made worse when apostate religious fled from the discipline of reformed convents to the Valtelline, where political sensitivities made ecclesiastical authority virtually non-existent and defeated, in the end, even the heroic labours of Jesuit missionaries. The design of Charles Borromeo to bring Como within the ecclesiastical province of Milan never succeeded, and his influence in the Valtelline was reduced, even by comparison with other Alpine valleys outside his own diocese, which he visited as apostolic visitor, to the training of priests to serve in the Swiss cantons and Alpine valleys generally, for which the special Swiss seminary was founded at Milan. Similarly the gentle admirer of Borromeo, Saint Francis de Sales, who represented a more humane face of Catholic reform and the encouragement of lay piety, was forced to exercise an admittedly extensive influence, by his spiritual writing, from Haute Savoie and French territory outside his nominal seat as bishop of Geneva.

The spread of Counter-Reformation devotion, typified by the new cult at the beginning of the seventeenth century of Saint Charles Borromeo himself, was nevertheless evident in Venice (for all its erastian tradition) and in its Dalmatian littoral empire, as well as in Alpine territories, where the family of Hohenems, connected with that of the Borromeo archbishops, founded a chapel dedicated to the saint at their family seat. Relics of the saint were sent to Spanish courtiers and all over Europe, even if Charles's canonization was too late to arouse the peculiar interest of Philip II, who gathered relics for his personal collection with the mania of an absolute monarch, and whose love of the prize exhibit could be imperious in its demands; so that the city of Messina, in Sicily, thought wisely in proffering voluntarily a mere copy of its treasured relic, an autograph letter of the Madonna to the early city fathers.[61] The collection of rare manuscripts, at the Escorial, the Vatican, or the Ambrosiana Library in Milan, as well as for Laudian Oxford, was a more scholarly pursuit by comparison; but the cult of Saint Charles Borromeo found favour as far away as Poland, as well as in France, in the spread of the Counter-Reformation. By contrast, the ducal attempt to recapture the city of Geneva for Catholicism and Savoyard rule, at the beginning of the seventeenth century, represented an inevitable failure of the purely military and political campaign against Protestantism in Europe. The fortunes of Catholicism in the Valtelline, and the power of the Protestant Grisons, were similarly not permanently protected and reduced by the papal garrison sent by Urban VIII, in an attempt rather to prevent Italy from being engulfed in the European conflict of Habsburgs and Bourbons, in the first half of the seventeenth century. For the importance to the Spanish Habsburgs of the land routes from Italy to the Rhine, by which troops were moved from Naples as well as Lombardy to the Palatinate and the Netherlands, was not diminished, after the Elizabethan maritime war had been ended by peace with England. So that French concern to intercept the route through the Valtelline led to the expulsion of papal troops by French forces, at the orders of Cardinal Richelieu in his policy, criticized by more pro-papal Catholic reformers in France, of putting the struggle against Habsburg power in Europe before considerations of Catholic solidarity.

The popular iconoclasm of sixteenth-century Netherlandish crowds was identified by the Spanish authorities as indicative of heresy; but the identification of heresy with rebellion came to be self-fulfilling as draconian legislation against heresy encouraged the native noble leadership of the Netherlands to abandon the local tradition of moderate Catholicism for the forms of Protestantism which might hope to attract international, above all, Calvinist support.[62] The aid of Elizabethan England in the end proved as limited as that of the French forces, for the encouragement of rebellion was not entirely to the taste of the English Queen; while the attempt by the vestigial authority of the royal government in France, under the influence of Catherine de'Medici, to redirect the conflicts of Catholics and Protestants inside France to the external arena of the Netherlands was hardly successful. The papacy, which feared the lack of action against the heretics of the Netherlands, on the part of Philip II immediately after the Council of Trent, and called for more severe measures, soon came, in the following decades, to deplore the alienation of loyalties caused by draconian policies; and complained ineffectually that the Inquisition in the Netherlands was not under Roman control. The revolts of unpaid troops in the fearful Spanish mutinies of the Netherlands were in any case a major cause of further loss of the religious and political allegiance of the cities and states, leading to the eventual independence of the Northern Netherlands.

The loss of the Northern states of the Low Countries to the Catholic Church and the Spanish crown represented the most dramatic defeat of the Counter-Reformation, confirmed by the terms of the Peace of Westphalia in 1648 at the end of the Thirty Years War. The papal protest, unheeded by the European states, at the terms of the Peace was directed not so much to the extension of rights in the empire to Calvinist as well as Lutheran princes, as to the final recognition of the system of *cujus regio ejus religio*. The end of the Thirty Years War effectively marked the failure of political and military pursuit of Catholic restoration and the defeat of Protestantism, only in part at stake during the war; and the continuing conflict of Habsburg Spain and Bourbon France – until Mazarin's conclusion of the Peace of the Pyrenees in 1659 – was between two Catholic powers. The last demonstrations of military power by the papacy, in the pontificate of Urban VIII, were equally ambiguous: the annexation of Urbino incorporated a desirable enclave within the papal states; but the attempt on the territory of Castro was a failure, concluding papal ambitions. In the reign of Louis XIV, the French crown, before its need of papal support in European diplomatic alignment, inflicted humiliation on the papacy in the city of Rome itself; even if the monument to French pride and papal impotence merely redressed the account for the papal statue at the Lateran basilica, cathedral church of the city, recording the succession of the Bourbons to the French throne by virtue of reconciliation to, and recognition by, Rome. The threats of Louis to the survival of the papal enclave at Avignon followed the king's extension of his royal rights over the French Church, which further damaged episcopal government, by reducing bishops' control over clerical appointments, quite apart from the absence of episcopal administration caused in some sees by the dispute with Rome over the royal rights.

The virtual retreat of the king's pretensions, in the more drastic attempt to make the 'Gallican Articles', adopted by a clerical assembly in 1682, compulsory teaching in French seminaries, reduced the danger of formal exposition of doctrines of Conciliar supremacy over papal power in the French Church. But the threat to the crucial training of priests in the Catholic Church was already evident; to be revived, with more real effect, by the reorganization of seminary education, under state direction, by the Emperor Joseph II, at the end of the eighteenth century, in the Austrian lands. The quality of seminary training varied, not least with the passage of time. The comprehensive institutions for youths of a wide age-range first erected in the post-Conciliar decades, in late sixteenth-century Italy, had a narrow curriculum; even if this was sometimes broadened, as in seventeenth-century Milan, under Federico Borromeo, by the sending of seminary students to the classes of a Jesuit college, for instruction in subjects beyond the strictly professional training and the formation of individual spirituality.[63] The pre-Tridentine, and more haphazard education of clerics, by which they acquired the practical skills of the priesthood by parochial service, continued in places for a long time. The creation of a diocesan seminary in Paris was accomplished relatively late in the seventeenth century; although the New Orders in France specializing in the direction of seminaries contributed to the sophistication of Catholic clerical training, by the division of minor and major seminaries, for different age-groups to acquire elementary and more academic learning, already practised by Bascapè in Novara, at the beginning of the century. The parish clergy of the city of Venice continued into the eighteenth century to learn their profession by service as parochial clerks, though a diocesan seminary was eventually established under patriarchal control. The seminary attached to the ducal chapel of Saint Mark, on the other hand, represented a source of clerical formation independent of patriarchal control; and, despite the initial involvement of the Somaschi, it represented a possible source, at the time of the

Interdict, of Sarpian influence on clergy educated there. Lecturers were associated with the dissident friar and republican counsellor, and candidates were admitted to holy orders by the *primicerio* of the chapel, a state appointment, or by the patriarchal vicar, a friend of Sarpi's, who administered the diocese during the Interdict.

Conflict, as at Venice, between Church and state in Catholic Europe could only damage the quality of religious life in fact. This was recognized, in a specific sense, of the religious life of female convents in the city and lagoon, which caused concern to the Republic itself, by the increased laxity which developed during the Interdict in their way of life.[64] Strict enclosure was not entirely restored after that interlude, despite the existence of a state magistracy charged with precisely this task. The difficulties which arose in the training of missionary priests for English service, in continental colleges, were not entirely the result of Jesuit direction. The financial patronage of the Spanish crown – most obviously in the case of those colleges in the Iberian peninsula itself, whether at Valladolid, Lisbon, or elsewhere, which trained priests to return to England and Wales, Scotland or Ireland – led to conflict, among English Catholics at least, over the nature and aims of the mission. The alternative paths for the Counter-Reformation were epitomized by the difficulty of distinguishing religious ends, in the maintenance of the old religion and reconversion of individuals, from political means, of insurrection or invasion. A similar difficulty arose with the attempt, at the end of Elizabeth's reign and the beginning of the Stuart regime, of some members of the English Catholic community, to assert the possibility of such a distinction, even in the face of papal disapproval. The resulting strains, not least between Jesuits and secular priests on mission, were compounded by peculiar complications, such as the demand of the exiled English Benedictines to be recognized as forming a congregation in its own right, and to be admitted to a share in the work of the mission, replacing Benedictine contemplative ideals by an activism which thereafter became the mark of the province.

In Catholic Europe the admission of clerics, once trained, to parochial livings never entirely matched the prescriptions of the Council of Trent for competition and episcopal examination of candidates for preferment.[65] Just as the papacy found it difficult, in the face of Venetian and Spanish opposition, to examine candidates for provision even for Italian dioceses at Rome, before accepting crown nominations to Sicilian or some Neapolitan sees, or Republican nomination of the patriarch of the city of Venice, so bishops found it difficult to control the choice of parish priests entirely. Quite apart from the extension of royal intervention in some French sees, the holding of open competition and the conduct of examination proved difficult in Spain even.[66] In the Spanish and Portuguese kingdoms large numbers of livings were in the gift of the military orders of the peninsula, or of the Knights of Malta. Patronage rights, in fact, whether enjoyed by rulers, individual nobles or ecclesiastics, or by clerical or regular institutions, remained extensive; and it required the determination of rare diocesans, like that of Federico Borromeo at Milan, to examine the suitability of candidates presented by lay or other patrons.[67] The choice of bishops, too, reflected considerations which were often social and political as much as religious. Yet the aristocratic bishops of many seventeenth- and eighteenth-century French dioceses proved conscientious administrators and resident reformers of clerical and conventual life; while noble bishops appointed to sees in Venetian territory, by consultation between Rome and Venice, included examples of devoted pastors, who preached and visited in their dioceses, at the end as well as at the beginning of the seventeenth century. More problematic was the implementation of the Tridentine decree ordering provincial councils and diocesan synods to meet at regular intervals, to interpret the Conciliar legislation in the light of local needs, before eighteenth-century papal concern that such assemblies might encourage national and aristocratic anti-Roman episcopalism. Successful examples appeared across the Catholic globe very soon after Trent, not only at Milan, but at Lima, Mexico and Goa; but enforcement of their decisions, in Venetian territory for example, was more contested, where lay interests were affected. In Spain itself the crown showed little favour to such promotion of episcopal authority, and in the kingdom of Naples attempted to impose viceregal representatives on any such assemblies of bishops or clergy.[68]

The summoning of bishops to Rome at regular intervals, to report on the state of their dioceses, was intended to ensure the implementation of Catholic reform throughout the Church, after the Council of Trent. But such *ad limina* visits were opposed, at times by the Venetian state, and more consistently by the crown in Spain;[69] while visits to Rome by bishops from the overseas Spanish empire were effectively prevented, by the control of the Council of the Indies. The uniformity increasingly imposed, nevertheless, on the Counter-Reformation Church, after the Council, was sufficient to cause resentful comment by the dissident Servite friar, Sarpi, at Venice. This centralization of administration and standardization of

practice were the achievements of the new congregations of the
Curia, reorganized by the papacy from the end of the Council. The
relations of bishops and regulars required a separate congregation,
apart from the general competence of the Congregation of the Council, for the interpretation of all Tridentine decrees. The authority of
the Holy Office and of the Congregation of the Index was in practice
limited, both in geographical and in other terms. But the influence
of the Sacred Congregation of Rites, not only over liturgy, but over
the lay piety which devoted attention to saints and their cult, was
enormous. Only those saints officially recognized by the Roman
Church were accepted, increasingly, for public veneration. The
popularity of specific images of favoured saints and scenes was a
popular mirror of the scholarly labours of the Jesuit Bollandists in
undertaking a monumental, standard hagiography. The Oratorian
Baronius was, already, involved in the revision of the Martyrology,
as well as in the compilation of the equally monumental Church
history, the *Annales*, designed, by papal command, to counter the
Protestant polemic of the ecclesiastical historians of Magdeburg.

The religious life of Catholic Europe, even as practised by the
laity, was never free from polemical overtones, whether of confrontation with Protestantism, or subsequently, of conflict between
Church and state in Catholic society. The noble and *dévot* Compagnie du Saint-Sacrement, in the French Catholic revival of the earlier
seventeenth century, saw its considerable charity among the poor as,
in part, a counter-demonstration against the self-help of the Huguenot
communities. But the political disfavour encountered by the Compagnie, and its offshoots designed to investigate and resolve tensions
and feuds in lay society, led to its official dissolution, at the very time
of the foundation of a seminary at Paris to train priests for the foreign
missions. This represented the transformation of Catholicism, in and
beyond Europe, in a way not reflected by the outmoded attempts of
James II in England, against papal advice, to pursue policies which
suggested to his subjects a plan to restore Catholicism by prerogative
action; while the support given, if not consistently, to James's attempts to recover the throne by Louis XIV was not matched by any
help from the papacy. The relative decline, in eighteenth-century
France, of both conventual and confraternity life, marked areas of
religious practice where the hierarchy of the post-Tridentine Catholic Church had had least success in imposing reform according to
its own ideals. The survival of Catholic lay independence, which this
effectively represented, is a further reminder that the post-Conciliar
Church, for all its undoubted attempts, never in fact established

anything approaching complete dominance over society. The renewed attempts, towards the end of the eighteenth century, to recover a real religion, in terms of Christian living, in Catholic practice, involved the co-operation of some bishops, particularly anti-Curial aristocrats of Jansenist sympathy, in their concern for the purity of belief and morals, with secular authorities. The pastoral preoccupation of such relative rigorists sought afresh high standards of Christian education, of lay piety free from superstition, and freedom for episcopal action from the interference of regulars as well as from Roman intervention. The evolving aims of Muratori, of the Josephinist ecclesiastics in Austria, or the Febronian episcopate in the empire, of the Synod of Pistoia in Tuscany, represented in this sense a revival of the immediately post-Tridentine rigour and impatience for reform characterized by Charles Borromeo. They did not represent merely the episcopalian assertion which continued in the post-Conciliar Church against Roman authority in practice. That ultimately issued in schism, not in an assuredly Catholic area of Europe, but in the divided Netherlands, in conditions which combined the problems of the missionfield with those of the European Church.

CHAPTER 3

# SCHOLASTICISM AND SCIENCE

SCHOLASTICISM and experimental science were never two mutually exclusive and opposed intellectual forces in Counter-Reformation Europe, any more than were Augustinianism and scholasticism. It has been at times suggested that the Protestant world, particularly the maritime states of England and the independent Netherlands, were more open to the development and application of experimental science in the seventeenth century than were the Catholic parts of Europe. The complexities of such questions are demonstrated by the relative technical advance of France in the eighteenth century, despite the loss of its skilled Huguenot workers, and the comparative decline of the Dutch economy. In England, the interest of polite and learned society in scientific experiment has been traced to Oxford circles of the early and mid-seventeenth century, free of commitment to political or religious innovation, as well as to metropolitan and émigré life in London. The range of intelligence in the Catholic dissident at Venice, Paolo Sarpi, undoubtedly included an interest in natural science, demonstrated by his connection with Galileo. Yet the report of the English ambassador in Venice, Henry Wotton, to James I, on the subject of Galileo's invention of the telescope, stressed the use of the new apparatus in the more accurate casting of astrological calculations. The intellectual inheritance of both Catholics and Protestants in the seventeenth, as in the sixteenth century was common to all educated men, and only rarely, as in the thought of Francis Bacon, was innovatory questioning carried to any systematic ends. Even the 'new' philosophy of Descartes – as much as the assumptions of Erasmus in the previous century – owed much to medieval methods of argument; while the *Summa* of Aquinas, arguably the chief monument to systematic medieval discussion, was influenced by neo-platonic as well as by the more commonly recognized Aristotelian philosophy.

It has already been noted that appreciation of Copernican or

Galilean cosmology did not preclude participation in the great witch-craze of seventeenth-century Western Europe. In the demon-ological writings which inspired the witch-hunt, Bodin's composition drew on both scriptural and Aristotelian authority, but also on the sources associated more commonly with Christian humanism, Saint Paul and Saint Augustine. The attitude of the Counter-Reformation Church, in any case, towards the emergence of experimental science needs to be distinguished from its treatment of scientific theory or of mathematical or philosophical calculation and speculation. The origins of experimental science lay as much in the world of practical alchemy and astrology, as in more rational pursuit of induction. The fears of Descartes, that his conclusions might endanger his personal freedom, were connected, it has been argued, with his alchemical associations with the world of the Rosicrucians. But the traditional opposition of the institutional Church to alchemical experiment, and formal disapproval of astrology, were reinforced in the sixteenth century by the new Protestant attack on magical charms and rit-ual. The eirenic overtones of the Rosicrucian circles, or of the court of Rudolf II at Prague, with its promotion of astrology as well as incidental support of astronomy, could only arouse suspicion among both Catholic and Protestant ecclesiastical authorities, intent on maintaining the distinctive denominational creeds of Western Europe. Political considerations were also involved. While the burning of Bruno at Rome for heresy demonstrated Catholic repres-sion of speculative theory, of a largely mystical nature in this case, but not of experiment, the papal concern over Campanella's views was increased by the delicacy of Roman relations with the Spanish-ruled kingdom of Naples. The involvement of Campanella and of other ecclesiastics in the Calabrian revolt of 1599 led to unusual papal acquiescence in the investigation and trial of these figures by the secular authorities in the kingdom. The possibility of heresy being involved suggested, certainly, the involvement of the Holy Office as necessary too; but Roman reliance on Neapolitan co-oper-ation in the attempt to suppress the growing problem of banditry on the southern borders of the papal states, at the end of the sixteenth century, promoted the grant of unusual freedom for the viceregal officials, to prevent any repetition of such risk to the stability of the Italian peninsula.[1]

The appreciation of Galileo's work extended, in the Catholic Church, to the great patron of the arts and of learning, Cardinal Maffeo Barberini, even after his election as pope in 1623, continuing the policies of his Ludovisi predecessor. The Dominican opposition to Galileo's theories at Florence was a prelude to his eventual condemnation at Rome. But the charge against him at his last trial arose not from an account of experimental work performed in fact, but from his refusal to abide by the order not to publish arguments in favour of Copernican cosmology. The condemnation was for a work of theory, not for a report of scientific experiment. Medical investigation, on the other hand, was approved by the Church, whatever the doubts of individual prelates, like Paleotti at Bologna, about unrestricted practical anatomy. The Venetian state university of Padua, at the beginning of the seventeenth century, attempted to maintain its declining attraction for Italian and foreign students, by reviving the practical anatomy classes of Acquapendente, a venerable professor associated with Sarpi.[2] In the absence of anatomical demonstrations, students had been leaving Padua for Bologna. The troubles over the anatomy course had not been raised by the Church, however, but were internal to the university. The lack of corpses for regular demonstration had led students to raid the Jewish cemetery in search of material for their own, unlicensed dissections. The fame of the anatomy theatre at Padua was such that the rebuilding of the papal university at Rome, *La Sapienza*, with the church of Sant'Ivo, of mathematical complexity as well as ecclesiastical symbolism, by Borromini, at its centre, included a similar theatre, copied from that at Padua. Medical training at Padua in fact continued to attract students from outside Italy, from as far away as Ireland, into the eighteenth century. In the same way the university of Leiden in the Dutch Netherlands was exceptional, in the seventeenth century, in attracting a reputation which surmounted denominational distinction, not least for its scientific work. At such universities, as well as at Rome or in Oxford, botany was pursued with systematic care, by the creation of a botanic garden, regulated, in the case of Padua, by the Venetian authorities, who also controlled the college of medical practitioners in the city of Venice itself. The parish schools of the city were staffed by schoolmasters, often clerics, but appointed and salaried by the Republic, who taught classes of unusual social composition, by non-Venetian standards, since children of nobles could be found alongside citizens' sons, learning Aristotle free of charge.[3] The later creation of a noble academy on the Giudecca reinforced noble distinction, for an older age-group. But the attempt to inculcate gentlemanly skills, such as horsemanship, taught in noble academies elsewhere in Europe, failed to produce lasting existence for a noble academy at Padua, despite the increasing movement of the Venetian patriciate to the life of landowners on the mainland.

The careful control of the materials, not least for the history of the Republic, collected at the public library in Venice, matched the state's censorship of books, from the seventeenth century, on political grounds, and the appointment of official historians to record Republican achievement. But the differences of opinion with Rome, as over control of the city's book-trade, declining for reasons of commercial competition as much as of censorship, did not prevent comparison with the official libraries at Florence and the Vatican, as a guide to the running of the Venetian library. Special collections in Catholic Europe continued to include material generally prohibited, but reserved for licensed readers, such as polemical writers commissioned to answer Protestant attack. This was true of the Ambrosiana library founded at Milan, as the first European library open to the general public, by Cardinal Federico Borromeo. His attempt to add the Pinelli collection from Venice, in this context, to the holdings of the Ambrosiana, was frustrated to the extent of seeing the Jesuit house at Naples carry off a large part of the collection, only to be lost at sea.[4] The polemical basis to the acquisition policy of libraries was not a Catholic preserve. Early lists of purchases to be made at the Bodleian, also a library founded in the early seventeenth century, at the university of Oxford, were based on the Index of Prohibited Books. Private patronage or public benefaction thus remained vital for the intellectual life of Europe. The reputation of universities, with the possible exception of Catholic Padua and Protestant Leiden, did not, arguably, stand as high in the seventeenth century as in the high middle ages; and, even after Laud's reforms at Oxford, the eirenic minds of Falkland's circle preferred the clearer air of Great Tew. At Merton College, Warden Savile, editor of *Chrysostom*, collected the first volumes of Baronius's *Annales* as they were published at Rome, as well as maintaining contact with Greek Orthodox scholarship.

Manuscript copying, as well as collection, continued to furnish the libraries of Europe, such as that at the Escorial. But the decline of the Spanish universities – after Philip II's prohibition early in his reign of Spaniards studying abroad, even in the Catholic world, without permission – soon became evident. The anti-Erasmian drives of the crown Inquisition had already ended the international circles of scholars at the university of Alcalá, founded by Cisneros, for the promotion of clerical learning, not least biblical scholarship. In the wake of the arrest of Carranza, some vestige of earlier learning, reflecting interests not confined to the Iberian peninsula, persisted in the circles of clerical study and diocesan reform at Toledo, in

which El Greco moved and found commissions for his church paintings. The relative failure of his search for patronage at the royal court
was the more marked, because of the employment on the decoration
of the Escorial of other foreign artists, such as Pellegrino Tibaldi,
associated with the ponderous Italian mannerism favoured by
Charles Borromeo. The demand of the papacy for Spanish scholars
to join the team of international *scrittori* in the Vatican library, after
the Council of Trent, embarrassed the crown and its ministers.[5]
They doubted if scholars who could hold their own against foreigners
at Rome, in humane letters, were to be found in the peninsula, even
if Coimbra as well as Alcalá and the other Spanish universities were
considered.

In Italy, too, learning to some extent removed from the universities
to learned societies, such as those of seventeenth- and eighteenth-
century Tuscany. That these were not entirely confined to the literary fantasies of Baroque imagination is suggested by Milton's
appreciation of his introduction to academic society in Florence;
even if the far-reaching speculations of patrician circles at Venice, in
the sixteenth century, were discouraged, by the Republic itself, from
the beginning of the seventeenth century. In the Interdict the Venetian state pursued a policy of demonstrating by more than usually
conspicuous celebrations the undoubted Catholicism of the Republic, and not solely from doubt as to the policy of Spain, hesitating
between qualified and tacit support for Venice, and armed hostility
on behalf of the papacy. The Spanish authorities in Italy did indeed
fear that Venice might allow the entry of 'liberty' into the peninsula,
but this reflected the common assumption of European states, Catholic and Protestant, in the early seventeenth century still, that religious pluralism could only lead to political unrest. The connection
of heresy and rebellion seemed proven in Calabria as well as the
Netherlands, in the empire as well as in France, everywhere, in fact,
from Scotland to Poland; just as Elizabethan and Jacobean assumption that religious disobedience was synonymous with political disaffection seemed to be confirmed by the risings and plots promoted
by elements in the Catholic Recusant community. Venice, too,
shared this view, and demonstrated increasing guard against Protestant contacts and infiltration, even before the end of Sarpi's life,
while ceasing to use even the threat of schism, and of continuing its
episcopal succession from the Greek patriarch of Constantinople, in
its relations with Rome.[6] In Rome itself academic life was famed
chiefly for the international reputation, among painters, of the Academy of Saint Luke, founded by cardinals who patronized the visual

and theatrical arts. But the scholarship of the Barberini cardinals, as of Baronius earlier, and of Federico Borromeo, extended also to the preservation of earlier Christian art – representing the pristine state of the Roman churches – and the first systematic exploration of the catacombs, as further evidence of early Christian life in the city. The continuity of the Catholic Church was certainly the argument which inspired such concerns; but the theatrical commissions for the Barberini theatre involved technological skill as well as the painter's art and the virtuosity of musicians and dancers. Hydraulics as well as mechanics helped the management of stage effects, in the musical dramas which paralleled the court masques of the Caroline court in England. The continued political alliance between the French court and the Barberini, after the death of Pope Urban VIII, furthered the taste for Italian style in the performing arts promoted by Mazarin; even if the subsequent treatment of Bernini, in the France of Louis XIV and Colbert, suggested the opposition, in the visual as well as in the dramatic arts, of French native artists and patrons to any reminiscence of the cardinal's power in the regency of Anne of Austria.

The prominence of learned societies, rather than of traditional universities, in the promotion of knowledge, was not confined to Italy in the seventeenth century. The patronage of the state, both in Catholic France and in Protestant England, encouraged the spread of scientific study. The utilitarian interest of governments was demonstrated by Richelieu's concern with hydrography, in the service of maritime expansion. In such study, Jesuit scholars and their pupils proved the worth of the relatively broad education provided in the Society's colleges, which could in places include mathematical and technical subjects. The astronomers and skilled technicians of the Society itself took their observations and creations from Europe to China, where clock repair remained the key to tolerance of the mission at the imperial court. Optics and the study of perspective were connected not only in scientific and artistic circles in the Dutch Netherlands, where the high quality of lens grinding necessary for the new telescopes and microscopes could support the highest philosophical activity, but also in Catholic Europe. The *trompe-l'œil* ceiling of the Jesuit church of Sant'Ignazio in Rome was created by the Society's own 'Padre' Pozzo. The illusionistic decorations of the type found in the convent cloister in San Trinità de'Monti, at Rome, were the device of the French Minim friars who inhabited it. Their Paris house became a centre of international scientific correspondence, in the lifetime of Mersenne; while the Rome cloister also incorporated

an ingenious meridian. The order of Minims in France produced
scientific work in zoology as well as botany which reflected the
increasing interest of Europe in the missionfields overseas: the movement of the crocodile's jaws was first demonstrated in this context.
The sometime members and the friends of the French Minims pursued scriptural exegesis too, and the bibliophilic activity represented
by Naudé. The advertisement by the Society of Jesus of its own
missionary achievements was supported, in seventeenth-century
Rome, by the more solid beginnings of ethnography made by Kircher
at the Collegio Romano; even if the magical attributes of scientific
knowledge were once again still present in his mystical approach to
supposed Egyptology. Humane letters were still an object of cultivation at Rome, not only in the attempt of Urban VIII to deploy his
poetic talents on a more classical style for breviary hymns, but in the
acquisition for the Vatican library of the Urbino collection, in succession to that of the Palatine. The dramatic conversion to the Roman
Church of Queen Christina of Sweden left its mark on the city of
Rome, by the monuments to her triumphal reception, even if her
emancipated patronage of heterodox minds and collection of ambiguous paintings subsequently embarrassed the papal court.

The decline of the European pre-eminence of an early university,
in the case of Bologna, had caused grave concern to Paleotti, as
bishop of the city, though his authority did not extend in effect to
the affairs of the university. He similarly was concerned to encourage
high standards of critical scholarship, in works of hagiography for
example, not always with success. The difficulties of maintaining
excellence in printing and publishing at Rome were known to him,
as were the reasons for that, both economic and arising from the
rigours of ecclesiastical censorship. His own studies on ecclesiastical
and philosophical questions were published without difficulty, except for his ill-fated attempt to write on the history of the Council of
Trent. But the growth of printing and publishing centres outside
Italy could not be resisted, despite the attempt of the Republic of
Venice to prevent the export of fount from the city or the emigration
of skilled workers.[7] The post-Tridentine enforcement of liturgical
uniformity in Catholic Europe reinforced the monopoly claimed by
Roman printers for the publishing of liturgical texts, thus harming
the Venetian book-trade, at a time when censorship was limiting the
range of vernacular and non-devotional literature. The reworking of
Italian classics, in the vernacular, to exclude anti-clerical references,
and sometimes to improve the moral content of the works, became
an exercise involving some serious writers, such as Salviati, in Tus-

cany. But the independence of Spain in Inquisitorial and Index matters allowed clerics to remain figures not above criticism in the prose and drama of the late sixteenth and seventeenth centuries in the Iberian peninsula, despite the protests of the Nuncio.[8] The decline of traditional university standards in both Italy and Spain was typified by the state of the Spanish College at Bologna, which came to concern the crown itself.

It has been argued that the Jansenists associated with Port-Royal, not least the mathematical genius and original spiritual insight of Pascal, demonstrate an openness to Cartesian thought; and that the government of Louis XIV, by contrast, promoted a scholasticism of Jesuit inspiration, used to support the hierarchical structure of society under a supposedly absolute monarchy. It has already been noted that the Thomist Dominicans, who most nearly represent scholasticism in the post-Tridentine Catholic world, were as opposed as the Jansenists to the innovatory philosophy and pastoral theology of the Jesuits. At the beginning of the seventeenth century, Catholic and Protestant rulers saw the Jesuits as proponents of limited sovereignty. The arguments of Cardinal Bellarmine, which were taken to typify Jesuit views, were nevertheless condemned, for a while, by the papacy; so that Jesuit scholasticism, as far as it existed in political controversy, was hardly attractive to the supreme authorities of either Church or state. By the end of the seventeenth century, certainly, a part of the French province of the Jesuits represented a royal Gallican policy in practice; and there was a possible extension of this in the circles advising James Stuart, subsequently James II of England. But the criticism of absolute rule, as far as such rule ever existed in seventeenth-century France, or more precisely of Louis's policies, was not a Jansenist preserve. The scriptural selectivity of the courtier prelate, Bossuet, in his political maxims, distinguished tyranny from royal supremacy, even if refraining from explicit criticism of Louis XIV. But his rival Fénelon, an anti-Jansenist, in theory and practice, was not so restrained. The sources of inspiration of Catholic leaders did not determine the outcome of their own thinking. The Jesuit Bellarmine admired Augustine, while the eclectic spirituality of Bérulle drew on Bonaventura and Jesuit writing, as well as on scriptural selections. The increasing objections of Gallican bishops to alleged laxism in Jesuit confessional practice were not necessarily the result of clear Jansenist sympathies, but represented the struggle, from the Council of Trent onwards, to reassert episcopal control over the hearing of confessions by regular clergy.

The early dissolution by the French government of the educational

work of Port-Royal suggested a desire to limit the social influence of
the Jansenists. But this suppression of 1660, preceding the destruction of the Port-Royal convents themselves in 1709 and 1710, should
be seen in the context of royal reaction to the political disruption of
the Frondes; which also led to the attack on the *dévot* Compagnie du
Saint-Sacrement, formerly the rival of Jansenist piety in the performance of public charity. The lay *solitaires* of Port-Royal were
thought to represent, by their alienation of property, rejection of
state service and acceptance of manual labour, in derogation of their
superior social status, an element of political disruption, certainly.
But, where members of the privileged classes made the final retreat
to a properly religious life, no such political complications arose.
The members of Rancé's community, refounded on lines of extreme
asceticism at La Trappe, eventually excited royal admiration; but lay
associates, as opposed to fully professed regulars, were carefully
limited. Rigorism in religious devotion and private morals was not
a Jansenist preserve, as the royal court under the influence of Mme
de Maintenon demonstrated. The moralism of La Rochefoucauld
was also, in this sense, Augustinian, but developed independently of
his friendship with Port-Royal. The élitist concern with a Hidden
God, not accessible to the lax superstition of the many, is attributed
by Goldmann to the alienation of a relatively privileged class, nevertheless excluded from the final benefits of the social hierarchy as
reimposed by Louis XIV. The lay relations and supporters of the
nuns of Port-Royal were not however from a single social group.
Despite the importance of lawyers and intellectuals from the *noblesse
de robe*, the attachment, at times at least, of members of the ancient
nobility of birth, the *noblesse d'épée*, particularly those suffering from
political or economic misfortune, was also evident. The precocious
brilliance of Pascal had been formed in the *dévot* world of his father;
and he, as much as Saint Cyran, was attracted to the assertion of
episcopal authority against Jesuits, in France and in the English
Catholic community, as well as being influenced by the involvement
of Jansenism, for all its intellectual rigour, in the miraculous and
thaumaturgic. His individual originality cannot easily be contrasted
with royal disapproval, however clear, of public promotion of Carte-
sianism in French universities; especially as he came to reject the
religious reasoning of Descartes.

    The non-Jansenist rigorism of Rancé, on the other hand, can only
be described as ultimately anti-intellectual. For his own reformed
Cistercians, at least, he opposed the revival of scholarship represented by the reformed Benedictine congregation of Saint Maur. His

debate with the Maurists did not deter them from continuing their studies in Church history, to new levels of critical examination of evidence, in this matching the more critical approach to ecclesiastical history and to hagiography of Baronius, at the Roman Oratory, and of the Jesuit Bollandists in the Netherlands. Rancé nevertheless admired the French Oratory, outside the Benedictine community, for its scholarly and educational work. Jesuit education, in France as elsewhere in the eighteenth century, however, continued to exert a dominant influence, even if its products, as with some of the anti-clerical or sceptical thinkers of the French Enlightenment, reacted chiefly against the teaching received. The influence of Jesuit classical education and regard for vernacular literature extended to the public theatres of court and metropolitan life, overriding, in a way, the quarrel of Ancients and Moderns. The use of the best manuals of style was demonstrated by the employment, in one Jesuit college for English boys, in the Low Countries, of Ascham's guide to Latin elegance; only the eulogies of Elizabeth I were corrected, to castigate the queen as a heretic instead. An early and most striking change in literate society, arguably attributable to the influence of Jesuit schools, was evident in Italy and Spain, from about 1590 onwards: the replacement, except among the most elderly, of a highly con-tracted Italic hand by a simple and clearer form of copperplate, free from the elaborations of eighteenth-century script.

The influence of Paracelsus on medical practice, arguably accepted in more eirenic circles at the beginning of the seventeenth century, free from the constraints of religious polemic, was equally to be found outside European universities. For his theories of medical prescription, based on alchemical analysis and the idea of sympathies in nature, were at odds with learned opinion; just as academic med-icine excluded surgery, as opposed to anatomical demonstration. The original aim of Cardinal Allen, in founding the English college at Douai in 1568, on the other hand, was to repeat the collegiate existence which religious tests at Oxford and Cambridge denied to Catholic Recusants. Although his creation became involved in the subsequent development of clerical seminaries to train priests for the English mission, the pristine ideal of Catholic scholarship was pur-sued in the translation of the Bible, producing the New Testament in 1582, and the whole Rheims–Douai Bible in 1609–10. The English and Welsh exiles, like Gregory Martin and Owen Lewis, who were involved in the translation, or in Catholic reform and the problems of English clerical education in Italy, thus maintained, for the singular conditions of confrontation and controversy with literate

Protestants in England, a means of access to the vernacular scriptures, despite Tridentine opposition to unrestricted lay access. Such access in Protestant universities did not, however, necessarily create a liberality of mind, in the seventeenth century. While Cambridge produced the sober optimism of the Platonist school, it also supported, in Newton's case, a mind capable of original scientific argument, and of apocalyptic obsession: of a pessimism as marked as that of some of the Jansenists in France.

Catholic stoicism, free of Jansenist overtones, was represented by Lipsius in the Netherlands, in the early seventeenth century. His correspondence with Federico Borromeo of Milan kept him in touch with the Italian centre of the Counter-Reformation, despite his own difficulties in the Netherlands, where religion divided the scholarship of Louvain from that of Leiden. Religious division in Europe was rather a stimulus to the creation of international law, however. Grotius continued the work begun in this subject by Gentili, an Italian who professed law at Oxford. England typified the Protestant rejection of canon law as a major subject of university study, though the largely unreformed nature of the Anglican Church necessitated a continued application in practice of much existing canon law in the ecclesiastical courts. Secular antiquarianism did not always have the nationalist and patriotic aim represented in England by Camden; the attachment of Stow, in his survey of London, to ancient institutions seemed to suggest a more dangerous love of the 'old religion'. In Catholic Rome and Florence, the study of classical literature and archaeology continued without interruption into the eighteenth century and the age of the Grand Tour. The ease of access, by then, for Protestant tourists prepared for the further attractions of the South, with the progressive discovery of Herculaneum. By then, too, Geneva had become associated with the debates of the Enlightenment, rather than with the religious intolerance which had led to the burning of Servetus, the Spanish exile who proved too heterodox for Calvin.

Such developments did little to upset the world of the less educated. Vernacular literature, or imagery, at popular level was to a degree undisturbed by religious division, despite the polemical woodcuts of the Reformation decades, and the connection of elementary education with catechetical instruction in both Catholic and Protestant Europe. The store of folk and fairy tales, containing a popular 'moralism' often at odds with Christian orthodoxy, was in a way common to the Western half at least of Europe, with whatever local variation. Popular astrology featured in the almanacks, while in

France the *bibliothèque bleue* of Troyes illustrated homely wisdom and a sometimes disconcerting fantasy of alternative forms of society. In Friuli, to the end of the sixteenth century, Protestant clandestine literature continued to reach the lowest levels of literate society, couched in the vernacular.[9] Among the educated of sixteenth- and early seventeenth-century Europe, the heuristic methodology of La Ramée might seem free of divisive religious connotations; but the association with heterodoxy prevented the adoption of his scheme generally in Catholic society and particularly in the Society of Jesus. The court academy promoted by Henri III of France had equally been suspect, despite the conspicuous and extravagant piety of the king, which did not prevent his assassination, the result of ultra-Catholic alarm. Mathematics on the other hand represented a form of ratiocination truly free of denominational overtones. The advances made by both Catholic and Protestant mathematicians in the later sixteenth century and first half of the seventeenth, in the simplification of calculation and ease of expression, not least symbolic, alone allowed the precision in complex quantification necessary for the proof of scientific theories advanced by the major discoverers who followed.

In one striking instance, however, religious prejudice prevented the ready acceptance of new learning, where the cycle of religious observance was also involved. The papal reform of the calendar, after the Council of Trent, rectified the anomaly between the lunar and the liturgical year. But reception of the Gregorian calendar was resisted for more than a century in parts of Protestant Europe; and the divergence of the Greek and Latin Easter caused problems in the Venetian Mediterranean empire from the start.[10] The secular priest and scientist, Gassendi, defended Copernican theory against attack at the Sorbonne in 1631, though he was later to be critical of Cartesian ideas; but the intellectual divisions within Catholic Europe were less hard to overcome than those between Catholic and non-Catholic states. Galileo, after his condemnation in 1633, was still able to publish work on sound, studied also by Mersenne, a reversion, in Galileo's case, to the musical theories of his father. Harvey's contributions to the theory of circulation of the blood were, however, prepared by his medical education at Padua under Acquapendente, including his use of mechanical analogy. Ideas were exported from Catholic Europe, just as much as the alum of the papal states, used in the processing of Protestant wool. The fantastic water jets of Italian and Austrian gardens used the same knowledge of hydraulics as did the fountains of formal gardens in Northern Europe; while botanic classification was extended by the discoveries of the mission-fields overseas.

But, in both Catholic and Protestant Europe, fear of an allegedly growing atheism was not strictly connected with scientific ideas, certainly not with scientific experiment, as the case of Mersenne proved. From Bodin's private speculations onwards, the sources of detachment from Christian orthodoxy were rather philosophic, and a reaction against religious intolerance, between the main Churches or within them. Such fears did not prevent the circulation of learned journals on an international basis, as with the early *Journal des Savants*, in the second half of the seventeenth century. By the eighteenth century Italy was once more exporting influential views to the rest of Catholic Europe and beyond. The historical rationalism, expressed in different ways, of Vico and Muratori, provided an alternative outlook to that of the French *philosophes*. Muratori's writings were influential in the development of Josephinism in Catholic Austria, which was also the product of views on Church and state traditional at Naples and revived both immediately after the Council of Trent, and again from the late seventeenth century into the period of Austrian rule in the Kingdom, preceding the Bourbon regime. In scientific knowledge, the work of Newton and Boyle eventually won acceptance on a European scale, at the expense of Cartesian theories. But the method of Descartes was as important as the programme of Bacon in inspiring later scientists, Catholic or Protestant. By the end of the seventeenth century leading thinkers, as with Leibniz, could openly pursue eirenic schemes, particularly in the recovery of the German lands from the effects of military destruction in the name of religious division. In the eighteenth century the classical scholarship of Germany was put to the service of Roman patronage, in the tragic career of Winckelmann.

The argument that Catholic Europe, in and after the Counter-Reformation, suffered economic stagnation and relative decline is based, however, on more than an antithesis between scientific discovery and the neo-scholasticism of Suarez and certain other Jesuits. The failure to apply technological advances to manufacture, and the perpetuation of a large, and celibate, clerical estate in Catholic society, are taken to be two aspects of the deleterious effects of Catholic reassertion. Indiscriminate charity has been supposed to have encouraged pauperism and endemic poverty. But in a number of ways, as has already been seen, such circumstances did not in fact exist in Catholic Europe as a whole, in the sixteenth and seventeenth centuries. The limitation of marriages among the upper class, particularly in Italy, in response to social and economic forces, was not promoted by the Church, which opposed its practical results, in the case of female conventual life. A large number of both rich and poor were certainly directed by need as much as by vocation to the ecclesiastical profession or religious life; and such factors were openly recognized, by the papacy, in discussion of the monasteries of the Sicilian interior, for example.[11] This very fact, though, whether in Sicily or Spain, Venice or France, meant that the institutional Church, and its extensive acquisitions of property in mortmain, by lay bequest, supported a substantial part of the otherwise surplus male, and to an extent female, population. The contest for possession of monastic and ecclesiastical property in the French wars of religion, or the concern of the Netherlandish nobility for their traditional sources of ecclesiastical support, at the same period, at the end of the sixteenth century, are reminders of that. Whereas in Scotland and, ultimately, in England, the aristocracy rather than the crown benefited from the process of full monastic dissolution, in Spain the crown gained control of the wealth produced by the estates of the military orders. In such ways, as too with the international properties of the Knights of Malta in Catholic Europe, the maintenance of a large, celibate clerical class helped to maintain the economic existence of the leisured and educated, as well as the less fortunate in society, not least by limiting the transmission of property beyond certain bounds.

The existence of a class or classes not supported by manual labour of their own was not, however, a characteristic of Catholic society alone in Europe of the Old Regime, before the French Revolution; nor did it imply economic decline or stagnation in all areas. While the Church, as much as lay aristocracies, provided employment for tenants as well as servants, whether of large monasteries or individual clerics, the desire of Colbert, in the reign of Louis xiv, to turn idle nuns into productive manufacturers faced opposition which was social rather than ecclesiastical. The nuns of Naples or Toledo might specialize in the lady-like confection of sweets, but to use conventual discipline in systematized factories proved difficult, given the social background of families who had placed their daughters in the institution. The resistance, in this case, was much like that which faced other attempts to involve the French nobility in at least large-scale commercial enterprise. While speculation, as in the notorious case of John Law's scheme, in the regency following the death of Louis xiv, had the aristocratic virtue of gambling, commercial venture remained to a large extent still unacceptable socially. Areas of Catholic France did in fact respond to the opportunities of overseas trade and investment, not least the Atlantic and, more briefly, the Mediterranean ports. The development of communications, canals and roads and bridges built, at whatever social cost, to a high standard of civil engineering, characterized eighteenth-century France. The Catholicism of France no more impeded such progress than the Protestantism of the Dutch Netherlands prevented relative economic decline in the same period, leaving Atlantic and Indian competition to Anglo-French rivalry. The previous obstacles to French economic improvement were, arguably, the high cost of European wars indulged in, during the reigns of Louis XIII and Louis XIV, in terms of the fiscal burdens on a peasant productivity already barely sufficient to support the subsistence of the rural working class itself, and the damage to agriculture caused by troop movements; together with the ultimately sterile recycling of investment, through the closed circuit of tax farming, venality of office, and the *rentes*, which were in effect, if not in name, government bonds. The fiscal system which combined the disadvantages of a regressive scale in general, but a progressive scale for the tax-paying third estate, thus produced a clear disincentive to continued investment in any activity which might not, eventually, bring noble status and tax exemption.

Such a contrast between France on the one hand, and the different fortunes of the English and the Dutch on the other, suggests that relative tolerance in religion was, again, not the sole or sufficient key to economic prosperity. The Dutch Netherlands, and eventually the English, for all their own internal division over religious issues and related political questions, provided a relative haven for religious dissidents, not least the Huguenot refugees from the France of Louis XIV. The loss of skilled manpower in parts of Spain, however, after the expulsion of the Moriscos early in the seventeenth century, was thought even by contemporaries to have harmed the economy of some areas, Valencia in particular. The Spanish court debated a proposal to import Christian labourers from Dalmatia to replace the Moriscos; even though no action followed, any more than in the case of the proposal to revive the failing economy of Sicily, by readmitting Jewish merchants to the island.[12] Venice maintained the presence of Jewish communities in the ghetto of the city, but this did not prove a sufficient preventive against maritime depression. The luxury arts of Italy in any case suffered from the mercantilist competition promoted by Colbert, in Catholic France, quite apart from the cost of Spanish wars, in terms of the tax burden in Lombardy, Naples and Sicily. The export of surplus manpower from the first two of these states to the Spanish forces might represent an economic advantage;

but the rising level of taxation was a cause of complaint not only in Naples and Sicily, but in the formerly more prosperous Lombardy, in the first third of the seventeenth century. The expulsion of almost all the Jewish families of Lombardy, in the decades at the end of the sixteenth and beginning of the seventeenth century, was recognized by the Spanish crown to pose a further risk to the ability of Spanish government in Northern Italy to maintain credit; but the decision for the expulsion was finally taken at the Spanish court.[13] Despite the argument advanced that papal Rome still harboured a ghetto, the ecclesiastical authorities in Milan had no objection to the expulsion; but it was not the Church which decided on this policy.

In Spain itself the long series of wars of the sixteenth and seventeenth century, in Europe and overseas, in which the crown was involved, produced a similar burden of taxation, in Castile at least, until the attempts of Olivares to extend the burden on the kingdoms of Portugal and Aragon produced the revolts which led to the regaining of Portuguese independence but the failure of the attempt to achieve Catalan autonomy under French protection. Ecclesiastics took a part in the promotion of Catalan separatism, although the Church in Castile, and elsewhere in the peninsula, had long contributed to the crown's needs, balancing the help given by the Balearic privateers not to the Catalan rebels, but to the Castilian crown, because of fears of French competition in the Mediterranean. The use of ecclesiastical wealth did not, in any case, prevent the royal bankruptcies of the sixteenth century in Spain. But by the end of the seventeenth century a real, if relative, economic revival was apparent after a long period of recovery from the ruin of native enterprise and exhaustion of Genoese credit. The accumulated profits of Genoese enterprise, among the city's ruling class, were expended on conspicuous display, from the later seventeenth century onwards, in the building and decoration of palaces and churches; and the same was true in the city of Venice, even while the city patriciate continued the development of mainland properties and villas, later paralleled by the Protestants of Amsterdam. Such undertakings were not directly productive perhaps, except in terms of the building and decorative trades and the employment they maintained; and much the same was true of papal Rome, from the Sistine to the later Baroque rebuildings of churches, palaces and public monuments, which prepared for the pilgrimage as well as the later tourist industry, from the end of the sixteenth century onwards. In Spain the growth of a rural as well as of an urban nobility was marked by the spread of the sculptured *blasón*, over the doors of modest stone houses; and the *juros* provided a form of investment which shared the economic disadvantages of the French *rentes*. The strengthening of fiscal and judicial powers over the provincial population, granted by the Spanish crown to the nobility of the Neapolitan kingdom, damaged economic prosperity; though the stone buildings of the Puglian ports suggest a comparative vitality maintained until the early seventeenth century. The Portuguese overseas empire suffered neglect, not least in the failure of defence against Dutch and eventually English competition in the Far East, during the period of union with the Castilian crown. The over-extension of the Renaissance state, for all its attempts, in both Catholic and Protestant Europe, to control every aspect of the subject's life, including religious belief and economic activity, was nowhere more evident than in the results of Spain's commitment to land and sea warfare in Europe and across the globe.

The promotion of charity in Catholic Europe, in the Counter-Reformation, was, furthermore, not merely indiscriminate. The rejection of Protestant arguments about the reason for charity, in the Lutheran attack on salvation by works, was accompanied by innovations in philanthropy, as original as the Tudor distinction between the idle and the truly poor. Catholic calls for charity by means of casual alms were successful beyond doubt, but some advocates of this nevertheless urged the value of limiting such casual giving, on any one occasion. The episcopal and regular promotion of charitable enterprise, usually by confraternities, to benefit society at large, in place of the internal benefit to members and their families, has been noted. Specialization was also a characteristic of the new charities of the Counter-Reformation, as with the foundation of institutions for the *incurabili*, usually syphilitic. The foundation of New Orders specifically devoted to medical work was another factor aiding such specialized care, even if the association of pastoral and medical service could lead to the differences of opinion experienced with diocesan authorities by the Ministers of the Sick, founded by Saint Camillo de Lellis.[14] Bishops in late sixteenth-century and early seventeenth-century Italy were involved not only in charitable provision from their diocesan and personal income, but in the work of moral recovery in institutions, known as the *convertite*, for prostitutes who had been persuaded or forced to abandon their profession. A seminal distinction between remedial and preventive care was added, when discrete homes for girls in danger of being forced by economic pressures into that livelihood were set up, building on the existence in Italy of lay bequests to provide dowries for girls from families unable to pay for their marriage. The involvement of regulars and laity in such enterprises, alongside bishops, was continued, so that Italy at least still represented, as at the beginning of the sixteenth century, one of the areas of Western Europe where social welfare was most adequately provided; this was quite apart from civic employment of medical practitioners as public officers of health, with varying degrees of responsibility, as demonstrated during the epidemics of the seventeenth century.

The Catholic revival of that century in France saw the lead of Saint Vincent de Paul in charitable work, and his success in employing females, who were in effect if not in name religious, in that work, despite papal disapproval of female unenclosed activism. The development of Catholic charity in the Counter-Reformation had some effect in Spain too, where *Monti*, hospitals and hospices for poor girls, existed; so that the diversion of ecclesiastical rents and property to educational and charitable use in the Reformation, in the German cities and to a much lesser extent in England, was not the only change in philanthropic provision in sixteenth-century Western Europe. The shift of lay resources from devotional or ultimately self-interested spiritual endowment, as in the chantry supremely, to educational or charitable bequests for social benefit at large, was already evident before the advent of Protestantism, in England at least, in the view of Jordan. The absolute as opposed to the face value of such bequests, in an inflationary age, whatever the role of Spanish bullion in the causation of sixteenth-century inflation, has been questioned; but a more persistent question perhaps arises from the destination of many chantries, in London as surveyed by Stow at least, to support private wealth rather than public need. No clear distinction seems possible, at any rate, between Protestant selectivity in the continued performance of charitable works, and an alleged lack of discrimination in Catholic philanthropy as a result of the Counter-Reformation. Only gradually, outside Italy, did secular authority, in Catholic Europe, come to rival or replace the Church as the sole source of charitable relief.

Such extrovert Catholic action was very different, not only from the reassertion of contemplative and mystical values in the religious life of the Counter-Reformation, but also from the revival of interiorized spirituality by the Quietists of the seventeenth century. Whereas the work of Saint Teresa and Saint John of the Cross among the discalced Carmelites in Spain, male and female, had in the end won official approval, against internal and external opposition to their reforms, the secular world of Mme Guyon and of Fénelon, outside the cloister, remained suspect to the hierarchy of the Church.

In part the association of uncontrolled female enthusiasm with moral licence was feared, at least in the case of Christina of Sweden, in her Roman exile, and her patronage of Molinos, however respectable the relationship of the French prelate and lady. The court rivalry which finally separated Mme Guyon from Mme de Maintenon, and which haunted the relations of Fénelon and Bossuet, also represented differences of political and personal faction. But the departure of Quietism from the practical reassertion of sacramental practice at the Council of Trent divided its protagonists from both Jesuit spiritual direction and Jansenist regard for the sanctity of the sacraments. The emphasis on individual illumination and divine inspiration seemed to recall not only the 'enlightened' mystics of early sixteenth-century Spain, but the dangerous evolution of Protestant independence from the Erasmian search for a lay piety true to Christian principles. The mysticism of the Quietists, condemned by the Church, was nevertheless the antithesis of the scientific spirit of active experiment and practical discovery. It might accord with Pascal's individual and interior religion but was otherwise more akin to late medieval piety in the Anglo-Dutch world, before the impact of Protestantism or the influence of much of the Renaissance learning of Southern Europe. In the formation of Counter-Reformation spirituality, as in the direction of charitable care, the Church in Catholic Europe generally promoted an active approach to religion, not a passive. The approved enclaves of purely contemplative existence, in the older and reformed orders, cannot be seen as symbols of resistance to a practical and investigative age, however subordinate the role of the laity in the institutional life of the post-Tridentine Church. The literature which clergy were ordered to possess and consult, in the immediately post-Conciliar reforms, certainly represented liturgical and devotional, rather than scriptural or philosophical study. The manuals for confessors and guides to canon law complemented the editions of Tridentine and diocesan or provincial synodal decrees. But by the eighteenth century, in Piedmont, the books possessed by parochial clergy included some patristic collections, as well as a continued predominance of devotional and casuistic works; and also represented were practical works on agricultural and other topics, reflecting the technical interest in social improvement of the eighteenth century. Piedmont indeed represented a Catholic state where, from the seventeenth century, secular rather than ecclesiastical authority took the major role in directing society and controlling moral and educational life.

The decrees of the Council of Trent had been concerned not only with the mixed area of the sacraments and morals but also with purely theological doctrine; but, as has been seen, pure scholasticism was not imposed or reasserted in the doctrinal decrees. In the debate on the eucharist, defence of the doctrine of the real presence of Christ in the sacrament of the altar and of the explanation of this involving the term transubstantiation, against Lutheran theories of consubstantiation, and other Protestant views, nevertheless aimed to avoid too literal a reproduction of Thomist terminology. In the debate on the sources of faith, the decree reaffirming the authority of both scripture and the traditions of the Church was the outcome of a similar desire not to insist on a definition too narrow, which would exclude legitimate schools of Catholic thought. Such examples raise the question of the freedom of debate at the Council. There were instances where speakers were interrupted, and forced to abandon their line of argument. But these interruptions came from the floor of the Council, rather than from the presiding legates. More serious, however, was the control, from the very start of the Council, of the business and debates of the assembly by the legates, appointed by Rome. The determination of the legates to retain control of the Council restricted the freedom of the bishops to settle their own procedure and agenda; this was crucial because the legates refused to abandon their rule that motions could only be put from the chair, 'the presidents proposing', as this was called. By this means the legates managed, despite serious and continued opposition, to prevent at any stage an open debate on the relations between the authority of bishops and that of the papacy; although in the end such a debate was largely conducted by means of that on the necessary residence of bishops in their sees. The papal concern about this issue, which threatened a revival of Conciliarist declaration of the supremacy of episcopal assemblies over the papacy, had been an important factor in the reluctance of Rome to call a Council at all. Orders to the legates to prevent such an open debate were, on one or two occasions, supported by the removal of particularly obstinate proponents of episcopalist views from the Council. The selection of new legates, to fill vacancies caused by death, also gave the papacy an opportunity to try to maintain, by this indirect means, control of the course of the Council; while in the later stages of the Council, in 1562–3, daily letters from the papal nephew, Charles Borromeo, directed the action of the legates, and they reported frequently to Rome in return. The arrival, belatedly, of French bishops at the Council, led by the Cardinal of Lorraine, threatened to overthrow the whole work of the assembly, since the French regarded the achievements of earlier sessions as having been made without their approval and as therefore of no force. Only the association of Lorraine with the presiding legates, by papal intervention, modified this proud position.

The composition of the Council, before the arrival of the French, indeed raised the question of the representative character of the bishops assembled at Trent. The predominance of Italians and Spaniards allowed for serious debate of practical reforms and the assertion of episcopal rights, since at Trent, as previously at the Fifth Lateran Council, held in Rome at the beginning of the sixteenth century, the Spanish delegation included vigorous spokesmen for the activity of resident, reforming bishops. The dangers to Spanish independence of mind came rather from the pressures by the crown and its representatives. The ambassador at Trent attempted to interfere with the voting of bishops from Spanish territory, when the interests of the king were thought to be involved; though when rebuked for such action he denied it. The choice of bishops attending the Council from the kingdom of Naples was made by the viceroy. The hurried conclusion of the Council – when the death of the pope was feared, and the spectre of a Conciliarist claim to elect a successor, in place of the conclave of cardinals, threatened – was supported by the Spanish crown, in the face of Spanish episcopal protest that the reforming work of the Council should be completed. For a division of the Church, along national lines, was the likely outcome of any attempt at a Conciliar papal election, instead of the conclave which could more easily be made aware of Spanish wishes. It was, too, the Spanish representative at Trent who protested at the interference of the Council with the privileges of the crown, typified by the use of the crown Inquisition against the Spanish primate, Carranza; whereas both pope and bishops protested at the continued imprisonment of the archbishop, and intervened, at the time unsuccessfully, to secure his transfer to Italy. The number of Italian bishops attending the Council was natural, not only because of the choice of Trent for the assembly, at the northern extremity of the peninsula, but within imperial territory, to satisfy papal concern to be able to exert some control over proceedings, and imperial demands for a 'free' Council.

The ancient division of Italy into many small dioceses, some indeed rich, but many poor in their revenue, also created a preponderance of Italian prelates, which was not new at the time of the Tridentine Council. The poverty of some of these prelates, as also of a few exiled from their sees, who had lost their revenues to Protestant hands, was a problem increased by the inflation of prices for food and lodging at Trent, which the influx of many bishops and their retinues as well as diplomats and their servants into the small town caused. Papal subsidy of poor prelates, and more general provision of funds for the transport of foodstuffs and other necessities at Trent, raised a further question over the independence of the assembly. But, as was clear in the case of the bishops of Fiesole, the prelates from small and relatively poor sees were not necessarily inhibited in their criticisms of papal privileges or Curial practices, even when further pressure, in this instance the instructions of the Medici to Tuscan bishops, was also applied, in an attempt to ensure support for papal policies as opposed to episcopal demands. The Venetian bishops who attended the Council were also on occasion subject to pressure from the Republican authorities and their representatives at Trent. While the doctrinal questions and even that of the general relation of papal to episcopal power in the Church were matters left to the conscience of the bishops, any supposed interference with the existing rights of Catholic states, or reflection on the orthodoxy of Venetian prelates, individually, produced grave concern among the Venetian patricians, and attempts to investigate the position of bishops from the Republic attending the Council. The French bishops' belated arrival raised even more strongly the danger, feared from the start by the papacy, of the Council's division into the national blocks of political or linguistic nature, which had in the end characterized and ruined the reforming activity attempted by the great Councils of the fifteenth century. The doctrinal negotiations conducted independently of Rome, within both France and the empire, under royal and imperial supervision, suggested a permanent division of the Western Church into national churches, which were likely to prove heretical in belief, as well as schismatic. The success of the Council of Trent was not least the eventual reunion of the remaining Catholics of Western Europe against Protestantism, defeating the creation of independent French or German national Churches. The continued attempts of rulers, the emperor and the duke of Bavaria in particular, to impose religious compromise by their own authority, within their territories, were resisted by the Council and the papacy, by the rejection of the grant of communion in both kinds to the laity, offered by local secular authority, and for a while contemplated with tolerance by ecclesiastical authority.

The belief of the emperor, that such a gesture of practical compromise as the granting of the chalice to the laity could heal the religious divisions between Catholics and Lutherans, or prevent the further loss of adherence to the old faith, lay behind his insistence, from the beginning of the Council in 1545, that disciplinary reforms should be pursued, rather than the divisive definition of orthodoxy. The lack of realism which such a view represented was made clear by the development of debate at Trent during the brief period, in 1551-2, when Protestant representatives from Germany were present. The primary decisions of the Council, concerning the sources of faith above all, represented an obstacle to any agreement on individual doctrines disputed by Catholics and Protestants. The Council was well aware of Protestant opinion, as the range of clauses in the doctrinal decrees, condemning varieties of non-Catholic belief, demonstrates; and these were based on reading of Protestant texts by the expert theologians at the Council. By the middle years of the sixteenth century, insufficient common ground, in doctrine, existed between Catholics and Lutherans, let alone other Protestants, for agreement to be reached by any amount of debate. The attendance of Protestant representatives, even if briefly and belatedly, was a surprising triumph for diplomatic pressure, inasmuch as Luther's own view, at the end of his life, was that any Council meeting, even in the imperial town of Trent, at the summons of the papacy was not a free Council such as had originally been demanded for and by the German Church and people. While the representation of Western Christendom, after the departure of the Lutheran representatives from Trent, still included those from Poland or England, the papacy did not abandon attempts to secure recognition of the Council as an assembly of general authority for all Christians still. For the reconvening of the Council in 1562, unsuccessful invitations had been sent to the English Church, recently resubjected to royal government. The unity maintained within the Council itself was also a surprising achievement, however. The schism which threatened at the time of the removal of many of the bishops, as of the presidents, from Trent to the papal city of Bologna, following fears of an epidemic in the North, was not solely the result of imperial objection to this departure from the empire. The German bishops who remained at Trent were in the end implicitly successful in forcing the return of their colleagues from Bologna; even if the assembly at Bologna had spent much of its time registering the fact of its own authentic existence as the continued Council, as opposed to those remaining at Trent.[15]

The limited presence of bishops from the empire, not least the result of military preoccupations and the need to defend principalities from Protestant attack, had raised a problem from the very start of the Council, when a vote as well as a voice had been demanded for the proctors of those unable to attend. The refusal of this demand,

and the insistence that the Council was to remain a strictly episcopal assembly, in which theologians, other than bishops and the heads of certain religious communities, would advise but not be given a vote, was the decision of the assembled bishops themselves. In contrast to the Fifth Lateran Council, which had virtually been forced on the papacy, before the appearance of Luther as a problem in the Western Church, by the political manoeuvres of the French king and a few disaffected prelates, the chief obstacle to the continuation of the Tridentine Council proved to be not the temporary disruption of the Bologna interlude, but the European warfare and permanent hostilities between the emperor and France. The Fifth Lateran Council had pursued plans for ecclesiastical reform, under the direction of the papacy, as an answer to the Conciliarist call for reform of the French assembly, aided by a few Italians, at Pisa and subsequently at Milan. The *conciliabulum* of Pisa was intended to lead to the deposition of Pope Julius II for simony; but the papal counter-move, at the Lateran, led to perfectly serious discussion of disciplinary reform, not least under Spanish inspiration. The grave failing of the Fifth Lateran Council, however, was the lack of reconsideration of doctrinal questions which, even if as yet only implicitly, lay behind practical abuses in clerical and religious life. The only doctrinal error to be condemned was that of the revived fashion for doubting the immortality of the soul: a crucial enough article of faith, but a matter at issue only in limited circles of largely academic debate within Italy itself. By contrast, the eventual papal determination to hold a general Council, which led to the opening of the Council at Trent, was from the first successful in insisting that the assembly was to clarify orthodoxy, as well as discussing practical reforms, despite imperial opposition. The Council itself, once the bishops had assembled, even if at first in small numbers, determined that doctrine and discipline were to be debated concurrently, and that policy was followed in alternate decrees throughout the sessions of the Council. At no time did any condemnation of cosmological views, such as the Copernican, arise. The work of the expert theologians was as strictly doctrinal as the previous conflict of Gropper and Melanchthon over the interpretation of Augustine.

The prevention of further schism, despite the expression of fundamental disagreements at the Council, and the persistent refusal, until the last years, of the French to entrust themselves to imperial authority at Trent, was in a way the greatest achievement of the papacy in the direction of the Council. The concluding vote, confirming the decrees of the assembly and explicitly requesting and requiring papal approval for their validity, was impressive for its unanimity, in this light. The unconcluded nature of the practical reforms, which left some important issues for papal determination, proved the point of previous Spanish episcopal protest. But the confirmation of the decrees passed in all earlier sessions represented a triumph against the divisive disputes, at the time of the reconvening of the Council, in the early 1560s, over whether or not the Council to be resummoned was a new assembly, and whether the doctrinal decrees previously agreed, against Protestant heresy, still had validity. Spanish and imperial disagreement divided Habsburg opinion on this point, since the emperor was once again intent on the pursuit of doctrinal compromise with the Lutherans. By this date the imperial attitude to the use of Trent had also changed, in contrast to the earlier refusal to accept Bologna as a substitute for the imperial town. Again the papacy persisted in its determination to continue the earlier sessions of the suspended Council; and there was no revival of the earliest plans, which had reached no more than an abortive preliminary ceremony, before the assembly at Trent ever began, for the use of Vicenza in Venetian territory, situated on navigable waterways, and nearer the supply of necessities at Venice itself. The unanimous expression of agreement at the end of the Tridentine Council can also be contrasted with the result of the First Vatican Council, in 1870, when a group of bishops left the Council prematurely, rather than be present at the declaration of papal infallibility. While the disruptive effects of international diplomacy and hostilities were felt at the Vatican Council, the Council of Trent had also faced the disruption caused by Franco-imperial hostilities, and the long suspension between 1552 and 1562 was in large measure a result of this. The suspension also indicated papal reserve about the achievement of the first sessions, it is true. During the years of suspension the pursuit of papal independence in divided Europe was undertaken by political means which closely resembled, at times, the family aggrandisement attempted by earlier popes. The example of Caraffa's dispute with the Habsburgs, not least in the kingdom of Naples, was instructive, however, because belated repudiation of self-interested behaviour by the pope's nephews eventually followed. Caraffa's concern to promote ecclesiastical reform by papal, as opposed to Conciliar, authority was also demonstrated by his ending of some abuses at the papal court and Roman Curia, as well as by the reactivation of the Roman Inquisition in Italy. The emergence, from the later sessions of the Council, resumed in 1562, of papal authority not only preserved but strengthened, by the explicit decision of the bishops themselves, was unexpected, and certainly seemed unlikely when the resumed assembly was almost disrupted by the violent clash of opinion about the residence of bishops, reflecting the deeper issues of papal and episcopal rights. For all these reasons the account of Sarpi, in his history of the Council of Trent, is misleading, in that papal policy was for long concerned with the preservation of Roman independence, rather than with any hopes of enhancing Curial control of the Church at the expense of bishops.

The doctrinal decrees of the Council were hardly innovatory. Only the condemnation of certain Protestant views produced the specification of orthodox belief and practice under pain of anathema which created doctrinal definition, in place of common tradition. Continuity of Western Christian belief was expressed in decrees on ecclesiastical authority, including penitential and matrimonial, and, to a large degree, in the assertion of the eucharistic real presence. Practical questions were involved on occasion, as with defence of the sanctity of the canon of the mass, and the recitation of this most central part in a voice not intended to carry to the laity. The defence of clerical celibacy was again a strictly disciplinary question which nevertheless took on a quasi-doctrinal aura, in the reaction against Protestant attack. The reassertion of the liturgical use of Latin in the Western rite similarly marked a positive pronouncement stemming not from a desire to innovate, but from a reaction to Protestant criticism. The defence of the seven traditional sacraments of the Church involved clarification of previously unclear questions, as to the conditions for valid marriage, or as to the precise purpose and nature of Unction; but no innovation was involved in the restatement of the necessity of auricular confession. The criticisms of Sarpi, alleging novelty in the Church as a result of the Council's decisions, turn not on strictly theological questions, but on the ecclesiological, and by extension political issue of the relationship of the Roman see to the Church elsewhere in Catholic Europe.

The Protestant teaching against which the Tridentine decrees were reacting was in one way hardly innovatory. Luther condemned the Copernican theory, because it conflicted with biblical literalism. The complaint of Catholic opponents of Lutheranism, from the 1520s and 1530s onwards, was, however, that the reformers' teaching was innovatory, because of the new interpretation applied to selected biblical passages. Both Luther and Calvin, even if followed by Catholic apologists too, were in fact selective in their treatment of scriptural texts, maintaining a literal translation at times, to the exclusion of the allegorical and figurative interpretations made in parallel by medieval commentators; but at other times avoiding an inconvenient literalism, and interpreting scripture figuratively. In neither the Catholic nor the Lutheran case, though, was an unbending literalism maintained which, in the immediate period of Reformation controversy, caused any conflict with all new teaching, in social or political terms, for example, or in economic thought. Thomas More, as a conservative proponent of reform within the existing institutional Church of Western Europe, summarized the Catholic objection to Protestant reliance on the salvation of the believer by scripture alone. The determination of what the canonical scriptures were was itself the result of the traditions of the Church: the authority of recognized scripture depended on that of the Church. The Council of Trent asserted the contested canonical authenticity of the apocryphal books of the Old Testament, which Protestant critics rejected; but this was a symptom of the problem to which More astutely drew attention, not the crux of the matter. In More's own lifetime, before either his execution or the convening of the Council of Trent, it was clear that Luther's doctrine of Justification by faith alone, without good works, could only be supported, from Pauline texts, if the status of the Epistle of Saint James was to some degree undermined, which Luther attempted to do.

More's conservative prescience enabled him to see the varieties of opinion which reliance on individual interpretation of the scriptures, for which Luther claimed to stand, was producing and would continue of necessity to produce; this would happen even without the complication of the Spiritualists, as opposed to the literalists, among the radical Reformers, who rejected the bibliolatry, as they saw it, of magisterial Protestants, in favour of reliance on the work of the Holy Spirit still inspiring men's minds and hearts. The concept of unrelieved and unique inspiration in the canonical books of the Old and New Testament, as More saw, created the problem of explaining the accident of a single revelation, at some date after the earthly life of Christ, which was never repeated, never reproduced in the Councils of the early Church for example. The conservatives of the Christian humanist movement, faced with the challenge of Luther to the concept of free will which they themselves had at first defended against deadening misinterpretations of Christian duty and religious observance, saw the link between the evangelists and the Fathers as inextricable; More himself relied more on Augustine than all other Fathers, and on Chrysostom most of all the Greeks. To the patristic age was first owed the definition of what the canon of scripture included and excluded, whatever the faults of Jerome's translation, the Vulgate, which the Protestant critics attacked. The reaction to technical innovation, in the production of the printed book, differed, in a subtle way, between Erasmus and More on the one hand, and Luther and Tyndale, for example, on the other. To the conservative Christian humanists, the scriptures would have been books like any other, no more and no less authoritative, but for the traditional teaching of the Church, from the Fathers onwards, as to what distinguished the inspiration of the authentic Holy Scriptures from other early Christian writing; in the same way the printed text of a work made no improvement to its sense, unless a printed edition corrected misreadings and other errors. Editorial authority was ultimately decisive, for the text and meaning of works produced in past ages. But for the would-be literalists, among the Protestant Reformers of humanist background, the canon of Holy Scripture was self-evidently authoritative, just as a passage was clearly correct from its context in one book, and clearly at fault in another. The proper reading of the inspired Word had been originally recorded, and was, by an equally singular moment of Special Inspiration, unerringly recovered at the invention of printing: only the conservative editors resisted the 'true' reading of controversial passages of scripture. The editorial authority of the Reformers themselves was thus asserted to be equal to or superior to that of the Fathers. The Fathers on occasion lapsed into error, but the Reformers themselves were happily able to detect that, and restore the true reading and meaning of scripture. In this sense, it was true, the figures of Saint Augustine and the other early Fathers could never have the same decisive authority which they had for conservative commentators and controversialists.

Luther's practical opposition to the individual variety of belief which followed the freeing of scripture for personal interpretation was resolved by his gradual evolution of the balancing theory of the authority of the Christian ruler to determine religious behaviour in his state. In place of the authority of the Church's teaching, that of the prince's legislation was introduced, to counter the literalism of the radical Reformers and of the peasants of Germany who rose in revolt against economic oppression, as they termed it, on the basis of an equally selective use of scripture. The attempt at antiquarian exactitude, in Protestant reliance on scripture alone, without the distortions of the intervening centuries of Christian life, produced in the end a new support for the absolute power of the secular ruler, beyond the theories of medieval writers, with the possible exceptions of Marsiglio of Padua; and of Wyclif, who had first attempted a similar reliance on the text of scripture, clarified in the vernacular by

his followers. Protestant, and indeed lay Catholic objection to supposed Jesuit political theory, by the beginning of the seventeenth
century, was, indeed, to turn precisely on the Society's opposition
to such absolute and divinely accorded power, and the maintenance
of a more balanced, Thomist view of the relations of Church and
state. The rejection, in Luther's fully evolved theory, of intermediary
powers of the priesthood, between God and man, led to the similarly
Wycliffite conclusion that all men, including churchmen, must be
subject to the lay ruler in every respect. The original claim of Henry
VIII in England, against the clergy, had indeed involved a demand
for recognition of royal power not only in jurisdiction but in the
pastoral care of the faithful: at the source of priestly status in fact.
The Council of Trent, on the other hand, in the stress on priestly
ministration as a necessity, for example, in the valid marriage of two
lay persons, was reasserting a claim already made in the medieval
period, by the claim of Church courts to have competence over all
matrimonial cases, as well as testamentary. The heretical implications of offences against the marriage regulations of the Church, as
being in breach of a sacrament, were already asserted by the Western
Church in the middle ages. Catholic argument against Protestant
practical changes in religion, before and at the Council of Trent, was
thus historical, in the sense of being traditional; while Protestant
innovation was defended by appeal to antiquarian recovery of a lost
original. Neither Catholics nor Protestants wished to accept the
charge of novelty. At the Council of Trent, the suggestion that the
Protestants were correct to state that scripture contained all things
necessary to salvation – even if incorrect in denying the worth of any
practice or belief they asserted not to be found in scripture – was
rejected; this was logical enough, given the argument that the final
source of inspiration lay in the determinative traditions of the
Church, as well as in the very words of the recognized scriptures. The
Tridentine reassertion of the authority of the Vulgate also followed.

The Catholic view of Protestant religious belief and practice was
thus that it lacked authentic authority, being based on private interpretation alone, and, as such, represented change. The practical
changes which many Catholics resisted after the Council of Trent in
the organization of the Church's life were not the same, in the official
view, given the joint source of Christian authority in both scripture
and the teaching of the Church. That magisterial authority had
hitherto been exercised above all, though not exclusively in fact, by
popes and Councils; the Council of Trent justified its own actions,
and simultaneously submitted its decisions to papal authority for

confirmation and implementation. But to a Catholic dissident, like Sarpi, the magisterial Church was not simply the hierarchy of pope and bishops, let alone the sole post-Conciliar authority of Rome. Sarpi's view of Christian authority included the jurisdiction of the Christian ruler, supreme in all things temporal, but not in things spiritual. This medieval form of distinction between ecclesiastical and secular jurisdiction, in which Sarpi, like Protestant controversialists of the sixteenth century, made use of the arguments of the medieval Gallican, Jean Gerson, was not, however, innovatory in the sense that Lutheran and Anglican erastianism was: it was, by comparison, antiquarian.

Protestant religious practice, which Catholics rejected as human innovation, against divine institution, seemed to involve the abandonment of works which were not merely incidentals of life, but sacramental necessities, at occasions in life or at entry into a new form of life. The final form of Lutheran teaching rejected as necessary sacraments all but baptism and the eucharist, and other varieties of Protestantism followed suit. But beyond the sacraments themselves, ways of Christian behaviour were also attacked, as not merely unnecessary but even corrupt, which raised central doctrinal issues nevertheless. The transformation of Protestant objection to the regular life and conventual vows, following Erasmian criticism of their abuses, led to the attack on the whole concept of the religious life apart. The marriage of former nuns and monks, or of friars like Luther himself or Bucer, thus demonstrated the view that the vows of regulars were improper, invalid, and of no force. But the question of other religious vows was thus raised, as in marriage, for example; and divorce, as distinct from medieval annulment, appeared *de facto*, if not yet *de jure*, in Protestant practice. Luther himself was worried about this. The clerical celibacy of the traditional Church was also ended, but this in turn raised questions about more than property and the support of a clerical ministry. The attack on the necessary celibacy of the clergy could not be separated from Protestant rejection of the distinct mediatory powers of the priesthood. For in the same way, and again in fact following a Wycliffite tradition, original objection to the abuses of indulgences, not least their sale, led to rejection of the doctrine of the apostolic power of the keys, over souls in life and in death, and so of the doctrines of purgatory and of the priestly power to forgive sins. The practical regulations of the Church, as on fasting or matrimony, could not be dissociated from this doctrine either, since breaches of these regulations had been seen, formerly, as involving sin. In this light, the Council of Trent was unable to accept as a definition of the eucharistic real presence the Lutheran doctrine of consubstantiation, as an alternative to the theory of transubstantiation, since the maintenance of the reality of the appearances of bread and wine could surely lead, as had been the case with Wyclif, to attack on the whole concept of priestly sacramental power.

It was ultimately such considerations which divided Catholic sympathy with the need for reform of abuses, whether before Trent, as with Erasmus and More, or at the Council, from Protestantism. More, for example, could accept the idea of vernacular scriptures for the literate, but only if such translation were authorized by the hierarchical Church. The private commentaries of individual Reformers, whether implicit in their translations or explicitly provided in notes and glosses, could not be accepted. Thus works of Erasmus, innocent of any conscious Protestantism, necessarily came to appear on the Index of Prohibited Books, for Erasmus, as a pre-Lutheran scriptural scholar, had made private comments public. Printing alone produced that effect. The radical Protestants, on the other hand, accepted that they were trying to recreate immediately a new Christian society of true believers. They rejected explicitly the authority of the ruler to coerce the individual, whether the believer were inspired by the Word or directly by the Spirit. The radical Reformers were attacked by both magisterial Protestants and Catholics, because they represented dangerous innovation, based on human reason, unrestricted by recognizable authority expressed by clerical or princely voice. This was clear from the rejection of infant baptism, and assertion of the need for adult, personal decision. The interiorization of spiritual experience begun by Luther, in his stress on subjective awareness of the objective operation of purely divine Justification, was taken further. But the novelty awaited with expectation by the literalists within the radical world, and by some of the Spiritualists, was exterior: a millenarian existence. Only in some later transformations, of the seventeenth century, was this modified to schemes for the utilitarian improvement of existing society. Optimism was more generally enthusiastic not rational in the radical world, just as it had been in the later medieval forms of Western heterodoxy, in which persecution had fostered zealous expectation. The later medieval heresies had, however, often been traditionalist, in another, distinguishing sense: for the asceticism and utter poverty pursued by offshoots of the literalist party in the Franciscan world, followers of the letter of the founder's rule, as they understood his intentions and example, were not at first or always pursuing the more

fundamental rejection of the natural order found in the Manichaean
outlook of the Cathars, for example.

The doctrinal division of Western Christendom was not, though,
an immediate and final outcome of religious revival at the beginning
of the sixteenth century. It was not only Pole whose views on salvation were comparable with those of Luther. The return of Christian humanists and evangelicals to study of the scripture, relatively
free from the preoccupations of medieval commentators, naturally
produced a range of theological interpretation, unrestricted, before
Trent, by any certain limitation of the bounds of orthodoxy. In Italy
itself, not all saw the doctrinal distinction between orthodoxy and
heresy as clearly as the lay lawyer, More, did in England. The
North Italian religious revival, based on a biblical piety, a concern
for the true following of the regular life, and a realization of episcopal
authority and responsibility, was prominent above all in Venetian
territory, from the late fifteenth century; and especially in the reformed Benedictine movement, later the Cassinese Congregation,
the chief house of which was Santa Giustina at Padua. In the last
two decades of the century, the biblical and particularly Pauline
studies of the members of the congregation and monastery were
complemented by an attention to Greek patristic writing, not least
the works of Saint John Chrysostom. The copying of Greek texts
led, in the sixteenth century, to views for which members of the
congregation were denounced for favouring Lutheran doctrines on
sin and salvation, and for placing a Pelagian reliance on man's part
in salvation; for the Council of Trent was later to accuse Luther of
Pelagian exaltation of man's centrality in the divine work of redemption. Another Benedictine writer in sixteenth-century Italy, Benedetto da Mantova, was instrumental in the composition of a text on
the redemptive work of Christ, the *Beneficio di Cristo*. This work,
the authorship of which has been the subject of uncertainty and
debate, reflected also some views found in the Neapolitan circle, of
the early sixteenth century, formed around Valdés. In his teaching,
stress was placed on the redemptive love of God, almost to the
exclusion of the worth of man's co-operative work, although the
systematic denigration of human existence and implicit leaning towards predestination found in Luther were lacking.

Later in the sixteenth century, the attacks of doctrinal conservatives on such teaching, suspected of heresy, produced the dispersal
of the followers of Valdés, who fled, in some cases, from Italy to the
supposed havens of Alpine Protestantism; while the circle attached
to Pole's household at Viterbo was similarly suspected of harbouring

views which were beyond the bounds of possible orthodoxy. Such
bounds remained unclear, however, until the formulation of the
Tridentine doctrinal decrees, although individuals who were convinced of their own orthodoxy, such as Caraffa, never regarded Pole
without suspicion, despite apparent reconciliation of personal rivalry. The suspicions entertained by some Spaniards, against Pole
and other activists within practical reform movements, such as Carranza, were also of long standing. Yet the persecution of Protestant
heretics, under Pole, in England of the Marian restoration, and the
co-operation of Carranza in that, could do nothing to revise such
opinions. In Spain itself, the search for deviation from Catholic
orthodoxy produced a similar flight, of those who escaped the attentions of the crown Inquisition, to Protestant centres. The fate of
Italian exiles like Peter Martyr or Spaniards like Servetus was not in
all cases the same. Peter Martyr helped, at Oxford, to form the mind
of English Protestantism, in the Edwardian Reformation; but other
Italians found the bounds of orthodoxy at Geneva, or elsewhere, too
narrow, and went further East in Europe, in the search for room to
follow their anti-Trinitarian beliefs or their assertion of the right to
polygamy. Servetus was executed in Calvin's Geneva, for failure to
conform to Calvinist orthodoxy. Pole, while suspected of heterodoxy,
was further harmed by Protestant accusations that his remaining in
the Catholic Church was hypocrisy. Calvin denounced those in Italy,
believed to be numerous, who adopted a Nicodemist policy: maintaining outward conformity to the Church's rites, though thinking
the doctrinal teaching of Protestantism to be true. Such a denunciation confirmed the belief of the zealous, such as Caraffa, that crypto-
Protestantism was indeed a danger in Italy. Yet the origins of views
suspected of being identical with those of Protestant leaders were
often independent of the writings of those leaders, reflecting instead
a common study of certain earlier texts.

The theology of the *Beneficio*, however, did owe something to a
reading of Calvin, while its view of man outdid even Calvinists in
pessimism. The emphasis on Justification by faith, among Italian
evangelicals, was thought to be a crucial test of orthodoxy or heresy,
because mere conformity to the rites of the Church could, on a
Nicodemist view, be regarded as a matter of indifference. The question, therefore, was as to the necessity of the sacraments of the official
Church. The suspicions entertained against those active in practical
reform within the institutional Church, such as Morone, friend of
Pole and bishop of Modena, were thus logical if not necessarily
accurate. Caraffa's imprisonment of Morone revealed the familiarity

of the accused with the person and the beliefs of some who had fled or been condemned for heresy. Morone's patronage of preachers at Modena who stressed the essentials of faith and Justification brought the danger of heresy close to the papal states themselves. In the same part of Northern Italy, Ferrara had produced, in Renata d'Este, a princely patron of heterodoxy, which she subsequently fostered in France. Pole's circle included Vittoria Colonna, the noble lady whose friends extended not only to reforming bishops, and to Michelangelo, but also to preachers accused of clear heresy. The concern with the spread of opinions which were beyond the possible bounds of orthodoxy was not new in Caraffa's pontificate, however. For all its failure to open debate on theological questions, the Fifth Lateran Council emphasized the need to control the free transmission of private opinion by the new printing press. Behind the question of belief lay that of authority. The distinction between those who remained Catholics, and those who became Protestants, in Italy and, as Pole's case suggested, more generally, thus came to turn on attitudes to the Church: its nature and its authority to determine doctrine. Yet the common sources of inspiration, of both Catholic reformers and Protestants, were traditional: the scriptures and the Fathers, not the stimulus of new ideas of a non-theological nature. The division of Catholics and Protestants reopened old questions of Western Christendom, and of the Church, both Eastern and Western; it hardly reflected the new challenges of non-European missionary areas. On the contrary, as More recognized in his attack on Tyndale, what was at issue was the nature of the true Church, as it had previously existed; or as a new creation claimed by certain Reformers in Western Christendom.

The question of freedom of thought is thus different, in the case of sixteenth-century approaches, Catholic and Protestant, to theological teaching on the one hand, and to questions not strictly doctrinal on the other. The Venetian Republic, as well as the pro-papal Medici of Florence, were willing in the end to hand over to the Roman Inquisition major figures whose heresy was beyond doubt. Bruno should thus be seen in company with Carnesecchi, not with Galileo. The belief that heresy would lead to revolt against secular authority was absolute and seemed to contemporaries both logical and proven. Not only had Savonarola suffered as a heretic, but, from the development of Czech Hussite offshoots and of the later English Lollards, in the fifteenth century, heterodoxy seemed associated with rebellion. In the case of Savonarola, the remaining doubt in fact concerned his heresy, actual or alleged only as the result of political opposition; hence his unofficial cult, continued in orthodox Catholic circles of Italian reformers, religious and others, to the end of the sixteenth century and beyond. But the careful confinement of inquisitorial power in Venetian territory, especially from the end of the century and after the Interdict, did not alter the Republic's determination to eradicate heresy in its territories; only a belief that the process had largely been successful allowed this divergence from Roman policy. So too in seventeenth-century France, Catholics were united in considering the Huguenots to be in error; the difference of opinion was as to the best methods to apply to the problem of their persisting presence in the kingdom, in order to produce a true and comprehensive conversion to Catholic orthodoxy. In the German lands and Habsburg territories of Eastern and central Europe, the terms of the Peace of Westphalia, against which the papacy vainly protested, nevertheless allowed Catholic rulers to continue the vigorous re-establishment of Catholicism as the sole religion tolerated in their states. Only in Poland was the identification of national unity with Roman allegiance delayed – by the weakness of an elective monarchy and the power of individual landlords – until Swedish invasion, in the seventeenth century, completed the work of re-conversion begun by the Jesuits: the Protestant Vasas of Sweden represented a threat at once to throne and altar. The relative and enforced toleration of Polish pluralism, before that, had not produced any scientific sequel to Copernicus, however.

The case of Sarpi is also enlightening. For all his genuine scientific interest, and the independence of speculative thought on religious questions, in his private papers, his public position remained that of a Servite friar. The Republic could not countenance any suggestion that he died other than as a Catholic, since he had been theological and legal adviser to a state proclaiming itself unquestionably ortho-dox. His correspondence with non-Italians and non-Catholics, and his concern for the independence of Greek Christians from Roman authority, suggested the same vision of a plurality of Christian Churches, which his history of the Council of Trent more subtly implied of the varieties of Christian belief and practice in Western Christendom since the time of Luther. But the vision of the Church in his public compositions, presented on request as opinions to the Venetian government, still saw the Church as an institution, in the medieval manner, embracing all believers in a state. The power of temporal government was asserted against a clericalization of the concept of the Church, which he believed he detected as a result of the Tridentine Council; but the right of individual subjects to their own faith, independent of state direction, was not asserted in these official opinions. The freedom of lay opinion on issues not strictly doctrinal was gradually asserted in Catholic society, despite the trial of Galileo, during the seventeenth century, until, with the eighteenth, the legal tradition, at Naples first of all, of asserting the rights of the secular state began to seek wider philosophical justification. The enlightened rationalism of the eighteenth century, in this case, owed as much to a tradition of legal antiquarianism, among regalian theorists, as to any interest in new scientific ideas. The advent of more mechanical ideas of matter and of mind, by the end of the seventeenth century, under the stimulus of the writings of Descartes as well as Locke, produced a claim to lay competence in the utilitarian pursuit of social improvement which was distinct from the concerns of the sixteenth century with human sin and eternal salvation. The area of secular rights to legislate for society, in economic terms not least, was thus extended. If the economy of Italy, and to some extent of the Iberian peninsula, remained relatively undeveloped in the eighteenth century, it was not for want of the assertion of secular authority over public behaviour, as over the property of religious orders.

Secular control over the work of the orders remained even more prominent in the overseas missions than in Europe. The original enthusiasm of the missionary friars from Spain, as well as the continued millenary expectations of Portuguese regulars, drew inspiration from late medieval forms of religious zeal, not always orthodox, connected especially with the Franciscans. The hopes entertained of the role of the Iberian monarchies in the subjugation of the world to Christianity, in a manner different from the arguments propounded by Lull, increased, almost as a response to the apparent failure of the European empire of Charles v and the disruption of divided Christendom by the new threat of Protestantism. But the work of the missionaries overseas was, from the start, controlled by the Iberian crowns. The presence of non-Portuguese, Italians and Spaniards, among the Jesuits in Japan did not lessen the fatal rivalry between the Jesuit mission in the island, under the auspices of the Portuguese *padroado*, and the Franciscans who arrived from the Spanish Philippines, during the union of the two crowns. The crown tribunal of the Inquisition had replaced episcopal activity in inquisitorial affairs in Peru as well as in Spanish Mexico by 1571. The control of an independent Index of Prohibited Books, in its effects on the Portuguese overseas territories, was made even more strict by the Portuguese crown tribunal than that of the Spanish tribunal and its Index. This was so despite the lack of a permanent tribunal in

Portuguese Brazil, as opposed to Goa. The relatively mild attitude taken by the crown Inquisition in Portugal itself and in the mixed society of Brazil to superstitious and magical practices at popular level raised questions about Catholic practice common in one way to both Europe and the missionfield. But in the Congo and other parts of Africa which came under Portuguese influence, Christianity remained distinctly a part of syncretic religious behaviour, combining with persistent folk ritual and pagan magic. The native marital customs, and Islamic ritual in certain areas, which survived the advent of Catholicism, reflected the superficial presence of Portugal as a trading power in Africa. The work of the Church, in Europe and overseas, was greatly affected by secular powers and policies: not least in the degree to which popular practice of religion could in fact be directed by ecclesiastics.

Questions of scripture and authority, as well as divisions between states and between religious orders, were involved in the crucial question of Catholic reaction to the new scientific theories and observations of Galileo. His circle of friends and contacts in Padua and at Venice included many who were not followers of Sarpi's opinions. The bibliophile Pinelli was equally a friend of the Jesuits, who were intent on promoting their own educational activities at Padua, before the Interdict. So too was the banker Welser, who continued to admire Galileo's scientific work, despite the latter's dispute with Jesuit theorists at an early stage in his career, and the suspicion that the banker was the author of the notorious anti-Venetian polemic, the *Squitinio*. Two Jesuits who were particularly involved in such issues, and contributed to the repeated papal refusal of a bishopric to Sarpi, were Achille Gagliardi and Antonio Possevino; both related to the episcopal activism of Charles Borromeo at Milan, whom Sarpi himself had briefly assisted. The subsequent Jesuit support for Galileo, led by Bellarmine despite continued reservations, was not merely a reaction to the attack of Dominicans on Galileo's views, in the wake of the dispute *De Auxiliis* between the two orders. Bellarmine was well aware of the necessity of avoiding a false reliance on biblical literalism, given his own involvement in the rectification of the unsatisfactory revision of the Vulgate by Sixtus v, and the Protestant criticism of such affairs, as in the work of Bodley's librarian, Thomas James. The decline of traditional cosmological or physical concepts, such as that of the Animal Spirits, which seemed to explain the process of diabolic possession, was not a sudden transformation, nor one confined to either Catholic or Protestant areas, in late sixteenth- and seventeenth-century Europe.

# CHAPTER 4

# NEW PROBLEMS OF
# CATHOLIC EXPANSION

DESPITE THE DOMINANCE of Catholic missionary work overseas by the patronage of the Iberian crowns, the French involvement in Catholic expansion outside Europe was in the end to prove determinative.[1] The opposition to Habsburg power within Europe might direct French Bourbon policy, as revived by Richelieu, to practical co-operation with Protestant powers, endangering in the end even the Catholic ally of France against the Habsburgs in the empire, the duke of Bavaria. But the Capuchin diplomatic agent and confidential adviser of the cardinal, Père Joseph, entertained at the same time dreams of reuniting Christendom for a final crusade against Islam. This object was still mentioned in papal diplomacy of the period, until the relief of Vienna in the reign of Louis XIV. The concept of action by force against non-Catholics was not in fact a Spanish or Habsburg preserve. The calls by a part of the French clergy for more determined action against the presence in France of the Huguenots led to the final Bourbon detachment from the original Protestant support for the new ruling house, as Lous XIV declared the privileges of the community to be no longer necessary, because of the supposed success of mass conversions to Catholicism. This final extension of royal authority and religious uniformity was of course comparable to that achieved by the Catholic monarchs in Spain at the end of the fifteenth century. But once again Catholic clergy faced the problem of free will and the value of forced conversion, topical as never before, in a France also debating the Jansenist and Jesuit views of divine grace and the nature of true religious persuasion. Some bishops, and the young Fénelon, not all of them Jansenist in their sympathies, had doubts about the draconian measures promoted by the royal government to force Huguenots into Catholic conformity. The approach to conversion by payment, and the question of the right to remove children from the care of heterodox parents – an issue already raised in England by government action against Catholic Recusants

– also involved measures as controversial as the alleged methods of the Jesuit missionaries in the Far East. Louis's revocation of the Edict of Nantes, while confirming English alarm at the supposed aim of royal policy evolving in England under James II, did little to win favour at Rome in fact. Papal reaction, in the previous century, to the Massacre of Saint Bartholomew, even if at first based on a misrepresentation of the events, had been more enthusiastic; but the diplomatic tempering of religious zeal at Rome, which was to be manifest in subsequent reception of news from the wars of James and William of Orange in Ireland, was already evident. Despite the intense diplomatic efforts of the papacy in creating the short-lived league against Islam, which led to victory at Lepanto, there had never been entire Roman trust in military efforts against enemies of Catholicism. The report of the Nuncio in Spain, on the failure of the Armada against England and Elizabeth, was appended to a more extended letter on jurisdictional problems of the Church under the Spanish crown, and was couched in terms which suggested the failure to be hardly unexpected.[2] The involvement of the Church in that enterprise, as in its projected sequel with a new fleet, was the financial contribution made by the Church in Spain; just as, in England, Anglican prelates continued to owe service to the crown for the raising of militia.

Catholic criticism of Louis XIV within France, however, as in Fénelon's writings, already made use of the literary device, to be extended in the eighteenth century, of contrasting native reality with exotic fantasy set in foreign parts. The transatlantic image of the American 'noble savage' was combined, in a way, with admiration for the sophisticated cultures being discovered in the East. The questions about the rights of native peoples, first examined by Las Casas, revived the use of the philosophical concept of a pristine state of existence. The Renaissance revival of Platonism, largely neo-Platonic in fact, had never eradicated the Aristotelian tradition in European learning, which included the defence of natural slavery. The tradition had indeed been reinvigorated by a part of the exodus of Greek scholars who reached Italy in the later fifteenth century. Although for Catholic contemporaries the reforms of the Council of Trent, including the Tridentine liturgy, represented innovations, and were resisted as dangerous novelties by Catholic governments in many instances, the religious revival of the fifteenth and sixteenth centuries also included a limited preservation of local antiquity. The privilege of older religious orders and of certain ancient episcopal sees, such as Milan, of retaining their own liturgical rite after the

Council, followed the revival by Cisneros of the Mozarabic rite at Toledo, to represent the historical richness of the Christian past in the diocese. In the Venetian empire in the Mediterranean, on the other hand, there was pressure to make Greek Christians conform more to the ways of the Latin Church, despite Republican exclusion of papal or Inquisitorial interference.[3] Such pressure often came, indeed, from the Venetian secular magistrates, chosen from the patrician families who maintained a conspicuous lay devotion, inherited from the religious revival of the early sixteenth century, and preceding decades, among Venetian and North Italian nobles and scholars. The carelessness, by Roman standards, with which Greek priests reserved the sacrament, and the laxity with which Greek prelates granted marriage annulments to the laity shocked pious Venetian nobles. Other causes of patrician complaint were the concubinage of Greek priests, as opposed to the legitimate wives allowed them by the Greek Church, and the tradition of hearing the confessions of married couples with both partners simultaneously present. Such questions of mixed import, touching on sacramental doctrine but also on social custom and popular behaviour, were the most problematic, as in the Catholic states of continental Europe after the Council of Trent too.

The jurisdiction of the Latin-rite bishops supported in the Mediterranean islands by the Republic was uncertain in practice, in such islands as Corfu or Zante, where cases, often matrimonial, involving Greeks were concerned.[4] The theory of the employment of a Greek episcopal vicar in the determination of such cases, if they were even brought before the bishop's court, was confused in practice by the presence of Greek prelates in these islands. Their presence in some islands was permitted by the Republic, intent on preventing candidates for holy orders in the Greek Church seeking contact with bishops on the mainland or at Constantinople, under Turkish rule. But in Crete, the most important island possession of Venice after the loss of Cyprus, the Republic rigorously excluded all Greek prelates, and maintained the authority, in theory at least, of the Latin-rite bishops over the whole population. The problems of this part of the Church overseas were largely financial. The ruin of cathedral buildings and churches in the remote, rural sees in Crete hardly encouraged residence. As in the case of dioceses on the Venetian mainland, in Istria or Dalmatia, there was a natural tendency for bishops to reside as absentees in Venice, comparable to the attraction of Naples for the bishops of small and impoverished sees in the Southern Kingdom. The maintenance of adequate

supplies of Latin-rite clergy, in number and quality sufficient
to serve the non-Greek population, was problematic; despite the
presence, for a while, of Jesuits in the island. The Venetian
or naturalized families of the capital, who put their daughters
in the convents of the city, resisted the enforcement of strict enclosure; for, in a small community, the control of conventual life by
the families of standing was more than ever a social and economic
necessity. In such ways, the Venetian Republic, in its small
and declining overseas empire, experienced the problems of practical Catholic reform which, though in a way common to the post-
Tridentine Church in continental Europe, were made more serious
by the special circumstances of territories beyond Catholic Europe
itself.

The criticism of Jesuit attempts to resolve the problems peculiar
to the Indian and Far Eastern civilizations, in the expansion of
Catholic missionary work, was not least a negative contribution of
France. Although French money and manpower increasingly supported the work of the papal missions in the Far East, under the
Roman Congregation *De Propaganda Fide*, the objections to Jesuit
attempts at cultural assimilation, as opposed to the *tabula rasa*
method of the early friars in Mexico, chiefly came from French
clerics serving in the East. The rivalry of the Jesuits and of the
products of the *Missions Etrangères* thus reflected the internal debate
in seventeenth- and eighteenth-century France over the power and
practices of the Society. The transformation of French Jansenism
from its pro-papal, *dévot* origins to a more Gallican and anti-papal
position was matched by the evolution of Jansenism in its original
Netherlandish home into a schismatic Church independent of Rome.
The schism of the Church of Utrecht arose from largely jurisdictional
questions, concerning the role of episcopal authority in the post-
Tridentine Church, and the rights of bishops in relation to papal
power, but also from the involvement of Jansenism with non-epis-
copal Gallicanism in France, England and the Netherlands. The
Richerism of the lower French clergy, in opposition to both papal
and episcopal claims, might seem parallel to the 'presbyterian'
disregard for bishops' rights alleged against the Jesuits. But at
Utrecht, the assertion of the rights of the chapter became the occasion for schism not least as a result of the intervention of a member
of the *Missions Etrangères*. Once again, the problems of the
Catholic Church in Europe and overseas combined, in an area of
home mission, where Catholicism was not the official religion,
such as the Dutch Netherlands; and Irish bishops, representing

the Catholic rigorism of another such area, were also suspected of involvement.

In the overseas missions under Spanish patronage, the problems confronting the Church were not confined to the resistance of regulars to episcopal authority among male missionaries. The intervention of royal authority in ecclesiastical disputes made resolution of another difficulty exported from Europe less easy: the control of female convents by bishops, in the interests of maintaining strict enclosure and observance of the regular life. Even a bishop with personal associations with royal authority, such as Palafox, found the imposing of high standards of Catholic practice problematic for such reasons. Just as pious Venetian magistrates in Crete feared that hostile rivalry between Greeks and Latins left the native population in a state of virtual paganism, so honest observers of the American missions under Spanish rule were aware of the often superficial nature of Catholic belief and practice. Such realism was far removed from the grandiose plans once entertained at the Spanish court for an alliance with the Persians, to surround the forces of Turkish Islam.[5] It was also in contrast with the imaginative optimism of the Spanish Jesuit, Gracián, who set his moralizing counterpart to European picaresque writing in the form of adventures by a 'noble savage' or *ingénu*, innocent of corrupting civilization. The possible theological overtones were suspect, however; and *El Criticón* was only continued in the face of disapproval by the Jesuit superiors, to echo, at a century's remove, the independence of mind shown by the Catholic humanist More, in his *Utopia*, rather than the contemporary magical interpretation of the contrast between New Worlds and European corruption in *The Tempest* of Shakespeare.

In the Spanish Philippines, the relatively idyllic conditions undermined the discipline of some of the regular missionaries, despite the royal aim of supporting papal policy, in the subjection of regular clergy there to episcopal authority. Jesuit antagonism to comparative religious toleration similarly disrupted the development of Catholicism in the English colony of Maryland, in North America, under the powers granted by the crown to Lord Baltimore. The good fortune of the Knights of Malta, in the mid-seventeenth century, however, laid the foundations of French possessions in the West Indies, where the crown established a *quasi-patronat* over the Church. The growth of the famous Jesuit reservations of Paraguay in the seventeenth century, on the other hand, was threatened by the attacks of Brazilian raiders from São Paulo, once the Portuguese had regained independence in mid-century especially. But in the older settlements of the Spanish crown, the Church, under the *patronato*, came to control a large proportion of land itself. The power of the Jesuits in the Reductions of Paraguay, contested by Portugal and Spain, in the eighteenth century, raised the further question of their relation to the Church hierarchy in Portugal itself, where the ceremonial concessions attached to the patriarchal title of Lisbon had not satisfied anti-Roman feeling. The suppression of the Jesuits within Portuguese territory, the work of Pombal, was thus part of the larger question of the relations in Catholic society between state, papacy and episcopate. The control of native converts in America by the secular clergy or regulars was also involved, while the reconciliation of Portugal with the papacy was only achieved with the Roman submission, finally, to the Bourbon states' demand for the suppression of the Society of Jesus. The Inquisition in Portugal, perfectly under crown control, was used against the Jesuits as once it had worked in Spain against them. The remaining pretensions of the Portuguese *padroado* in the Malabar, despite Dutch intervention, led to the perpetuation of division and schism in the Christian community of Saint Thomas, to the end of the eighteenth century, despite the efforts of the papacy and its Carmelite representatives to restore order.

The papacy had encouraged French intervention in the discovery of overseas territories, in the North Atlantic at first, from the early sixteenth century, despite the original terms of papal arbitration between the claims of Spain and Portugal. Similarly, royal authority in Spanish dominions had proved essential in religious questions as early as 1512, when the Laws of Burgos insisted on the theory of the American Indians being free men, to be converted by peaceful means only. The first bishop of Mexico, Juan de Zumárraga, appointed by Charles v in 1527, was a friar; so that at first the monopoly of the missionary friars in Mexico was undisputed, as careful catechizing of the Indians began. In Peru, on the other hand, conversion was less successful, at a time when the mendicant orders were divided over their attitude to native rights, in the face of their own rivalry with the new episcopal hierarchy overseas. In the Far East, under Portuguese protection and direction, the establishment of the Franciscans in Goa in 1517 had been followed by the creation of a bishopric in 1534 and the arrival of the Jesuit, Francis Xavier in 1542: so that, before the Council of Trent had begun in Europe, all the elements of future competition in the religious affairs of the East, among Catholics, had appeared. The Jesuit's arrival and work also confirmed the redirection of Christian attention in the East from the confrontation with Islam to the conversion of other non-Christians.

The dominance of the Church in Spanish America by European not native clerics, even where the former were of mixed blood or born overseas, was clear by the end of the sixteenth century. Universities were founded at Mexico and Lima in 1551, but the earlier college founded for Mexican Indians by the Franciscans declined. In the Philippines, the division of territory into separate spheres of missionary work for each religious order, according to linguistic boundaries, resolved much of the wasteful competition found elsewhere: a relative assimilation, rather than destruction of native tradition also followed. At the beginning of the seventeenth century the continued advance of the Franciscans in North America, reaching eventually the areas of later New Mexico and South Carolina, was paralleled by the advance of the Jesuits, who had now entered the field, along the Pacific coast, north from Mexico. Similarly, the Jesuits were active on the Pacific shore of Chile, as well as in Paraguay. But by this period there were increasing tensions among the clergy in both Mexico and Peru, between Europeans, those of European blood born overseas, and those of mixed blood, especially over the holding of office within the religious orders. The secular clergy claimed the tithes of Indians for its support, despite regular opposition; and the presence of the Jesuits increased tension between the regulars and the bishops, as in the case of Palafox. In the East, the Theatines joined the friars and Jesuits serving in India, by the end of the seventeenth century, and so did the Oratorians; but by the beginning of the next century the Dutch were attempting Protestant missionary work in their Eastern conquests, though religious activism remained subordinated to mercantile interests, by the Dutch East India Company's control of preachers, in a way comparable to the *patronato* of the Iberian crowns. The beginnings of French influence in Indo-China, however, were made by priests of the *Missions Etrangères* early in Louis XIV's reign. Other New Orders began work in new missionfields of the East, the Barnabites in Burma and the Theatines in Borneo.

Portuguese opposition to missionaries who were not subject to the crown *padroado*, not least for fear of French colonial rivalry, made the exercise of authority by the papal vicars apostolic in the East difficult, despite the papacy's determination to establish ecclesiastical jurisdiction there independent of Portugal, from the mid-seventeenth century. The regular clergy in the Philippines resisted the transfer of their converts to secular parishes; but the priests of the *Missions Etrangères* were elsewhere intent on encouraging a native priesthood, though non-Europeans in higher office in the Church were rare, and encountered general opposition. The regulars, or at least the friars, continued to oppose the admission of non-Europeans to their own ranks in the East. The Jesuits at the Chinese court survived the succession of the Manchu to the Ming empire, but the involvement of Jesuits in astronomical calculations which had astrological purposes there already caused doubt at Rome within the Society. By 1704 a papal representative had condemned Jesuit assimilative methods of missionary work in India, and he proceeded to condemn the disputed Chinese Rites in 1707. The papacy confirmed this French prelate's decision in 1715, despite continued debate and lobbying at Rome, and the large controversy over the Jesuit methods in France itself, fuelled by the Society's own published reports from abroad. A European debate, in one sense proper to Catholic Christendom, was thus influenced by questions arising from greater knowledge of non-Christian societies. The Dominicans had already revived their antagonism to Jesuit assimilation of Confucianism, by invoking in 1700 the authority of the Sorbonne, rather than that of the papacy, bringing European rivalries to bear on issues concerning non-European areas. For at Rome, despite the continued presence in the college of cardinals of prelates committed to the interests of ecclesiastical independence, rather than those of a particular state, the pressure of Catholic rulers to secure a pope in their favour, during conclaves, increased rather than diminished during the war of Spanish Succession, a colonial as much as a European struggle.

During the same period, of crisis in the Far East, Jesuit missionary expansion continued in America, both in Lower California and Arizona, and in the Amazon interior. But the latter advance caused Portuguese alarm at the extension of apparently Spanish claims. Jesuits and other New Orders continued to expand French Catholicism in North America, both by serving colonial settlements, and by missionary work with Indian tribes, despite the rivalry with the priests of the *Missions Etrangères*, who now joined in this too. The bishop of Quebec, supported by the French crown, excluded Jesuit missionaries from Louisiana, where a similar rivalry threatened, with unhappy results. The Portuguese in Brazil introduced Carmelite friars in the Northern Amazon interior, in place of the Jesuits. But the Society continued to favour the importation of African slaves, to reduce the necessity of Indian enslavement, despite the involvement of the Protestant Dutch and later the English in the Spanish slave trade. The opposition of independent Portugal and the Society, which produced Pombal's lead in Europe in attacking the Jesuits, had its origins overseas: once again the fortunes of the Church in

Catholic Europe were influenced by developments in European expansion abroad. With the eighteenth-century mining of gold in Portuguese Brazil, the strength of Portugal increased, together with a determination to defend her independence.

The limitations imposed on the Church by the Bourbon rulers of Spain, there and in the overseas empire, owed more, however, to the strengthening of native regalist practice by imported Gallican theory. The Bourbon claim to independent control of the overseas Church did not acknowledge the force of papal authority in the original grant of the *patronato*, and subjected Jesuit missionaries to closer royal supervision. Before the expulsion of the Society from Spanish territories in 1767, the Jesuits had, nevertheless, expanded their missionary work into Upper California, as did Franciscans in Texas and Capuchins in later Venezuela. In eighteenth-century China, on the other hand, the friars reaped the rewards of their attack on Jesuit missionary methods, when the emperor prohibited Christianity in the provinces of his realm. Chinese Christians could live openly only in the Philippines, despite Spanish racial and political antagonism there. The work of the religious orders overseas was not confined to active mission, however. The reassertion of contemplative values in the European Counter-Reformation included the reform, partly at papal instigation, of Benedictines in Portugal, and, before the end of the sixteenth century, such Benedictines had also been founded in Brazil.[6] At a time when the overseas expansion of Protestantism was still, for some period, to represent a concern for the salvation of emigrants' own souls, over and above political and economic considerations, the Catholic missionary expansion was decidedly intended for the salvation of others. Even among more 'Augustinian' critics of the Jesuit desire for accommodation with native tradition, in the *Missions Etrangères* above all, this altruistic concern was paramount, in contrast to the predominantly self-centred anxiety of the Jansenists in seventeenth-century France. To complement the export of contemplative foundations from Catholic Europe, the charitable work of specialized New Orders of the Counter-Reformation was also present, the Hospitallers of Saint John of God being in America by the end of the sixteenth century.

Spiritual provision for the American Indians nevertheless remained less certain, despite the missionary presence. In 1658 Pope Alexander VII still considered it necessary to condemn the restriction of access to the sacraments among the Indians, although by this time the original opposition to admission of Indians or *mestizos* to the priesthood, among the secular clergy at least, had faded. The early diocesan synods in Mexico had, by contrast, supported such opposition, which remained characteristic of the religious orders subsequently. But such early coincidence of views did not ease relations between regulars and bishops, even when, like Zumárraga and Las Casas, they were themselves religious. Las Casas, like Zumárraga, was officially Protector of the Indians too; but, at the end of his life, as bishop of Chiapa, in Southern Mexico, he encountered resistance from some diocesan clergy as well as the colonists for his defence of Indian rights. The position of the negro slaves in Spanish America was more neglected. Early missionary criticism of this aspect of the Spanish *patronato* there was repeated by Jesuit protest in the seventeenth century against such neglect, and the slave trade itself, in contrast to the views of some South American Jesuits in the next century. After the expulsion of the Jesuits from Spanish America, the crown ordered more Indians and *mestizos* to be trained as secular clergy. But though colonial-born Europeans eventually became bishops, the indigenous clergy naturally did not spread to the frontier mission stations, where the European regulars still served. As late as 1680, a diocesan synod in Cuba lamented the failure to baptize negro slaves: this contrasted with the early enthusiasm of the friars in Mexico, who brought together such large Indian congregations for catechism and worship as to necessitate the construction of the unusual open-roofed churches of the country, on an impressive scale. Aspects of the Aztec ritual indeed, as well as sacred representations and images, encouraged a degree of assimilation in practice, if not in theory; but the non-assimilative approach of the friars was clearer in moral and social questions, in the enforcement of monogamy, for example, on Indian society. There was thus a clear contrast with the later missionary problems in Confucian China, where there was a lack of possible convergence in ritual practice, except in the matter of veneration of ancestors, which remained precisely a contested issue in its interpretation by Christian observers. The lack of accommodation, more generally, to Indian tradition in Mexico, however, was shown relatively early, in the sixteenth century, when the crown Inquisition extended its competence in fact, whatever the theory, to execute a native product of the Franciscan college set up to educate Indian converts, who was convicted of heresy. The limitations of even Zumárraga, as bishop, regular, and Protector of the Indians, were demonstrated by such an event, despite his encouragement of a printing press, and of the new university in Mexico, with a missionary purpose. The friars' encouragement of popular religious festivals contrasted with the admiration of a seventeenth-century

Portuguese Jesuit for the sabbatarian observance of Cromwellian England; but conversion of native rites to Christian in the sixteenth-century Yucatan remained superficial, as outraged friars discovered.

The Franciscans of the sixteenth century nevertheless extended their missionary work into the Yucatan peninsula and defended the Mayas against exploitation, as well as gathering Mexican tribes in the north into mission settlements for conversion and defence. The later financing of missionary training and expansion came in fact from private bequests as well as state funds. Even with such settlement, the initial question involved in the missionary expansion remained – reflecting European debate between Catholics and Protestants, and among both Catholics and Protestants themselves – the efficacy of the sacrament of baptism in itself, or its proper dependence on the catechizing of adult converts. In Portuguese Brazil, the problems of the American missions were compounded by the particularly low quality of the secular clergy, the limited effect of episcopal authority until more than one bishopric was created, in the later seventeenth century, and the consequent conflicts between Jesuit missionaries among the Indian and negro population and colonial settlers. The prominence of the Jesuits made it more difficult for friars, Oratorians and other orders to replace them adequately after the expulsion of the Society. The Jesuit missionaries in French North America, in the first half of the seventeenth century, suffered from English attack on occasion; the creation of a bishopric at Quebec in the second half of the century represented an initial co-operation of papal and royal authority, Jesuit influence and that of the *Missions Etrangères*. The tribal wars of the North American Indians disrupted missionary efforts however, and in the 1760s the suppression of the Jesuits in France combined with the end of French rule in large areas of North America to reduce missionary effort vastly. The work of other New Orders, secular clergy and priests of the *Missions* instead was devoted successfully to maintaining Catholicism under British rule among the French population. The effect of Protestant government, as in Recusant England, was rather to increase loyalty to Rome, despite the local tradition of Gallicanism in the one case, as of the necessary independence of a proscribed community in the other. In the French West Indies, the presence of regular as well as secular clergy ensured that negro slaves were not entirely neglected. On the other hand, Protestant emigrants from Catholic as well as Protestant Europe helped to establish varieties of Protestantism in much of North America, so that once again the Counter-Reformation in Europe had a partly counter-productive effect overseas.

The presence of orders other than the Society of Jesus alone allowed Catholicism to survive in Portuguese Africa, in the Congo, Angola, and Mozambique, with varying degrees of superficiality, or geographical limitation. Italian Capuchins in the Congo and Angola of the seventeenth and eighteenth centuries acknowledged the authority of the Roman *Propaganda* as well as that of the Portuguese *padroado*; but these missions in Africa fell within the Portuguese trading-post empire, unlike the colonial settlements in Brazil, and their effects were accordingly limited. Thus early experiments in the creation of a native African clergy, in the Congo, did not lead to permanent results during the seventeenth and eighteenth centuries. In India, from the start of Xavier's mission, caste divisions proved an obstacle to missionary expansion, while the support of the Portuguese authorities encouraged mass conversions of a superficial rather than of a substantial nature. Jesuit hopes of an immediate conversion of the Mogul empire, starting with its ruler, proved false, especially in the light of Mogul fears about Portuguese expansion. The initial experiment of de Nobili in assimilating Brahmin culture and Catholicism aroused Portuguese resentment not least for the dissociation from their missions which the Italian Jesuit proclaimed; while, at this time, Roman support was eventually secured, to a degree, against such criticism. The post-Tridentine provincial council at Goa, in 1567, prohibited forced conversions, but in so doing implicitly accepted the permanence of the caste system which divided converts. The Theatines' presence in Portuguese India, at Goa itself, also reflected the internal divisions of Catholic missionary effort, since their acknowledgement of the Roman authority of the *Propaganda* supposedly outlawed them within the area of the *padroado*. Relations with the Malabar Christians were equally complicated by the competitive intervention of Portuguese and Roman authority; while the subsequent arrival of the Dutch on the Malabar coast at least reduced the possibility of Portuguese involvement. The opposition of the Malabar Christians to aspects of the Latinization of their Church, under Jesuit leadership, included objection to the enforcement of clerical celibacy on the model of the Western Church. Once again the question of European standards and native practice in religion thus arose. Even in the remaining enclaves of effective Portuguese presence, as at Goa, the standards in fact observed by the secular clergy declined, however; and the efforts of the regulars were hampered by divisions within religious orders, as by the objection of the friars to native reinforcements. Where the English replaced the Portuguese in India, in the eighteenth century, the presence of papal representatives was opposed as much as that of Portuguese clergy owing obedience to the *padroado*, though Italian missionaries themselves were allowed to continue their work. The Portuguese in Goa continued at the same time to assert their rights over the whole East, against the independence of the papal missions of the *Propaganda*, and used the crown Inquisition there in an effort to enforce this claim.

The recovery of Portuguese independence in the mid-seventeenth century, and the consequent tensions in relations with Rome were thus complicated by the appointment of vicars apostolic in the East, to supervise missions independent of the *padroado*. One result of this interaction of European and overseas difficulties was that even the see of Goa itself remained vacant for a prolonged period in the later seventeenth century. But the authority of the vicars apostolic in the East was no easier to establish than the theoretical jurisdiction of the archbishop of Goa, in fact, despite Rome's eventual confirmation of the *padroado* in territories controlled by the restored Portuguese crown. A racial distinction was also involved, in that the earliest vicars apostolic in India were not Europeans but Brahmin products of the New Orders' missionary work. English recognition, at the end of the eighteenth century, of the complicated relations between the Portuguese hierarchy and the papal representatives in Catholic India led to the alternation of Portuguese and non-Portuguese influence in the matter of archiepiscopal appointment which lasted even beyond the end of the British Empire in India. An oath of loyalty was exacted, however, from any non-Portuguese clergy within the territory still subject to the *padroado* in fact. The involvement of the French in the papal missions of the East produced, in a way, the most fatal division, with the complaints of French missionaries, Capuchins in the case of India, against Jesuit missionary methods of assimilation. The terms of the papal condemnation of the alleged assimilative rites in India, agreed before the arrival of the French representative in the East of the papacy, in the first years of the eighteenth century, touched on social and moral issues akin to those which proved problematic in the implementation of Tridentine reforms in Catholic Europe itself. Deviation from the Roman ritual in baptism was condemned, and child marriages prohibited. Certain practices which maintained caste distinctions were also proscribed, as was access to pagan books. The paradox of Portuguese resentment of papal intervention and French presence combining with Jesuit protest at the terms of the condemnation, despite the Society's supposedly absolute obedience to Rome, was a reminder of how far the Jesuits in the East had in fact become a part of the *padroado* missions. The subsequent competition of French and Portuguese claims did not prevent the ultimate confirmation at Rome of the condemnation, in 1744; though from the intermediate fluctuations in papal policy emerged, after nearly half a century of dispute, recognition of the ineradicable caste system. The Indian missions subsequently suffered the cumulative effects of war and Hindu expansion in the sub-continent, as well as Moslem aggression, against the background of Anglo-French competition, followed by the expulsion of the Jesuits from Portuguese and French possessions.

The *Missions Etrangères* were not able to replace the Society adequately; despite the work of other New Orders too, and an increase, in Goa as in America, of native secular clergy. Before the eighteenth century, the training of native clergy had begun, with both episcopal approval and the encouragement of New Orders. But once again the question of caste complicated a problem serious enough elsewhere in the overseas missions. The provincial council of Goa in 1592 opposed the ordination of those of low caste; but even upper-caste Indians were not respected by European clergy in fact. The objection to native membership of religious orders was most serious among the Franciscans, although Indians entered the Dominicans and Augustinians, as well as the Oratorians, from the upper castes. The Catholicism spread in India represented, in one way, that of post-Tridentine Europe: veneration was accorded to Saint Joseph as well as, obviously, to Francis Xavier, just as Venetian representatives in Crete, after the Council of Trent, reported the popularity of Saint Francis of Assisi among the Greek Christians of the island.[7] But the assimilative nature of Hinduism represented a more serious threat to Catholic identity of belief and practice. In Ceylon Portuguese authority was involved in the division of the island's mission between the competing forces of the Franciscans, Dominicans, Augustinians and Jesuits. The island population was also divided by internal political conflicts and by caste; and the Portuguese crown supported the jurisdiction of its bishops in Cochin over Ceylon, as well as expelling Moslems from the parts of the island directly under its control. The expulsion, in turn, of the Portuguese by the Dutch, by the second half of the seventeenth century, revived overseas the antagonism between Dutch Protestantism and Iberian Catholicism in Europe, even if without the tragic effects of Dutch encouragement of Japanese persecution of Catholicism in that century. The violent confrontation of the Reformation and Counter-Reformation was not confined to Europe, especially in the first half of the seventeenth century, before the final Spanish recognition of Dutch independence, at the very time of Portuguese recovery of independence from Spain. The subsequent confrontation of Dutch Protestants and Portuguese Catholics in the Far East showed that religious antagonism was stronger than any common opposition to Spanish rule. The limits of supposed Dutch toleration were shown, where commercial rivalry and colonial conflict were in question, in the second half of the century. Penal laws against Catholics were repeated in Dutch Ceylon in the mid-eighteenth century.

The survival of clandestine Catholicism in Ceylon, despite the destruction of Catholic shrines, represented another example of an island community which retained its traditional allegiance, as in England and Ireland, the Western isles of Scotland; and the rather different case of Japan. In Ceylon, as in England and Ireland, a clandestine priestly ministry was maintained by indigenous clerics. The Catholic faith was thus maintained in practice – as it could not be in Japan – into the eighteenth century, and survived Buddhist persecution as well, until Dutch restrictions were relaxed in the later century. The lack of Dutch ministers, by contrast, limited conversions to Protestantism, before the advent of British rule. In Indo-China Spanish penetration preceded the establishment of French influence, and from the later sixteenth century there was a Jesuit plan for the education of Indian Christians of St Thomas.[8] The expulsion of the Jesuits from Japan in the early seventeenth century, just as from Venice and, for a while, from parts of France, led to the presence of the Society, in Indo-China, after a brief expulsion from one area there too. The experiences of the Jesuit, Père de Rhodes, in the earlier seventeenth century, convinced him of the need for a native clergy, and missions independent of Iberian pretensions. He thus paved the way for the extension of papal missionary authority, and of French influence in Indo-China; though the appointment of French vicars apostolic, to represent the Roman *Propaganda*, and establishment in France of the *Missions Etrangères* were precisely at the origins of the dispute over Jesuit missionary methods in the East. The controversy over the Chinese Rites had repercussions in Indo-China in the eighteenth century; but the suppression of the Jesuits, later in the century, ended their assimilative methods in the latter area anyway. Other regulars, including Spaniards and other non-French groups, were already present in Indo-China to support the continued presence of Catholicism; though before the end of the eighteenth century, after the suppression of the Jesuits, the French crown unsuccessfully claimed from Rome recognition of a formal *patronat* in the area, to match its increasing involvement in political control. The particular connection of French, and subsequently American, government with the maintenance of Catholic rule in Vietnam was thus begun: a final transformation of the Counter-Reformation overseas.

In the East Indies, as in Japan, Portuguese and Spanish missions converged from East and West, and both Jesuits and other orders, old and new, began missions. By the end of the seventeenth century the papacy was represented by an Italian vicar apostolic in Borneo. But the relative lack of success in the East Indian islands, as opposed to Japan, of Catholic missionary work was less the result of internal divisions in the mission, than the consequence of Dutch and Islamic encroachment. Dutch Protestant ministers were left to face a debate, in the seventeenth and eighteenth centuries, over the reality of native conversion among baptized Christians and their admission to communion: this mirrored the double debate in Catholic Europe and the overseas missions over conversion and reception of the sacraments, among Europeans and non-Europeans. In Protestant Europe, however, by that date, excommunication had become a judicial rather than a religious issue, given the reductionism of Protestant sacramental theology; though in later seventeenth-century England the sacramental test was precisely the political weapon used against both Catholics and Protestant non-conformists. The spread of Islam in the Philippines, by contrast, was cut short by the arrival of Spanish rulers and missionaries. As elsewhere under Spanish rule, religious orders, old and new, were present side by side, and the first bishop of the see of Manila was himself a regular. So too, as in Spanish America, the colonial *encomienda* system was to support both the bishopric and the missionary work, which survived the eventual suppression of the Jesuits. Conflict between regulars and bishops, about the transfer of settled parishes to secular priests, and the exercise of episcopal authority over the pastoral work of the regulars, repeated, from the early seventeenth century, yet another aspect of the overseas export of problems internal to the Catholic Church of the Counter-Reformation.

In the eighteenth century, despite earlier royal support for the seculars, the regulars were still resisting episcopal authority and the transfer of parishes; while episcopal and royal encouragement of a native clergy further antagonized the European religious, after the suppression of the Jesuits. The island nature of the missions also increased regular independence of even the civil authorities, who did not in any case always support the hierarchy. Yet, in the seventeenth and eighteenth centuries, friars themselves complained of pagan survivals and the superficiality of much native Catholicism. The Dominican who was the first bishop and archbishop of Manila, in the sixteenth century, maintained the tradition of his order, and of the friars and missionaries more generally, of defending natives against exploitation and opposing their enslavement. The same tradition led to the promotion of lay education and the establishment of a printing press, as in Mexico. Eventually *mestizos* and Filipinos ascended the clerical hierarchy, in the eighteenth century; while the imposition of European Catholicism represented not only Baroque religion, including Jesuit foundation of flagellant devotion, but the attempted transformation of marital and family customs.

The Philippines thus represented both the strength and weakness of the Spanish *patronato* missions, almost to perfection, despite occasional papal interventions. Japan, by contrast, presented the results of the unreality of the Portuguese *padroado* in much of the East, the fatal clash of the two Iberian crown missions, despite the Spanish succession to the Portuguese crown, and the impotence of the papacy. In the recovery from the first wave of persecution, at the very end of the sixteenth century, the papacy recognized its inability to prevent not only Franciscan but other orders too from competing in the Japanese mission with the Jesuits. The attempt to bring all missionaries there under the Portuguese *padroado*, as opposed to the Spanish crown's authority, was as unsuccessful as the assertion of episcopal authority over the other orders by the Jesuit bishop in the island. The power of Spain, rather than of Portugal, was nevertheless feared by the new rulers of Japan, as a result of the conversions made by the Franciscans and other missionaries. The final exclusion, by 1640, of any Christian influence from outside Japan extended to the listing of prohibited books, in the Chinese characters which Japanese understood. The preservation of a clandestine faith by native laity could allow baptism in secret, but other sacraments and priestly ministration were impossible. The independence of China from Portuguese power, despite the theoretical jurisdiction of the crown's bishop in Macao, again revealed the limitations of unsupported missionary effort, beyond Iberian enclaves, as opposed to Francis Xavier's original hopes that the transmission of a Christianized Chinese culture would in turn lead to the conversion of Japan. Ricci, who began assimilative missionary work in China, had been educated in mathematics and astronomy. Jesuit correction of the Chinese calendar was indeed accepted at a time when Protestant and Greek Christendom still refused the revised papal calendar in

Europe. The Jesuit mission in Peking thus survived an expulsion in the early seventeenth century, at a time when the Society was expelled, for varying lengths of time, from so many European and overseas states. The position of the Jesuit Schall, despite criticism of his activities, ensured the favour of the new Manchu dynasty, when other Jesuits in China had supported the last of the Ming: this reflected the political divisions of other Jesuit provinces in the seventeenth century, such as that of France. The political as well as astronomical assistance given to the new dynasty by Schall was continued by Verbiest, so that Moslem competition in astronomical services to the emperor was still defeated. The arrival of papal representatives, with the French clergy of the *Missions Etrangères*, in the reign of Louis XIV, was followed by that of French Jesuits, distinct from the existing Jesuit mission at Peking, owing theoretical obedience to the Portuguese *padroado*. The provincial missions of the friars were also joined by Italian Franciscans owing allegiance not to the Spanish *patronato*, like the existing friars from the Philippines, but to the Roman *Propaganda*.

The divisions of Catholic missionary effort overseas in the Counter-Reformation were well represented in China: the Portuguese and the rival Spanish, the French, the papacy, friars, and Jesuits who were themselves divided. No native hierarchy was permanently created, as opposed to those European rivalries. By the end of the seventeenth century, the papacy was forced to recognize new Portuguese bishoprics in Peking and Nanking, as well as its own apostolic vicariates in China. The diplomatic and cartographic services of the Jesuits to the emperor won official toleration for Christianity; but missionaries of the *Propaganda*, who wished to avoid the crown routes to the missionfield, via Lisbon or the Philippines, were forced to travel by laborious ways overland to China. The total number of missionaries in China was tiny compared to the size of the population. The original Dominican attack on the assimilative missionary methods of the Jesuits was complicated, in the last decade of the seventeenth century, after delphic pronouncements from Rome at an earlier date, by the condemnation expressed by a French vicar apostolic, a member of the *Missions Etrangères*, and the resistance of Jesuits owing allegiance to the Portuguese *padroado*. The European debate on the subject enlarged to include Leibniz himself. But a further conflict of authority was fatally involved: that between imperial declaration of the nature of traditional Rites, and papal condemnation which rejected this interpretation from distant Rome. The dispute between the French representative of Rome, subsequently Cardinal Tournon, and the Portuguese prelates of Goa and Macao, over the enforcement of the papal condemnation, was, by contrast, relatively an affair of European jurisdictional controversy. The authority of the Roman Holy Office was similarly added in support of the papal decision, as opposed to the use made of the crown Inquisition in the East by the Portuguese, in defence of the *padroado*. The legation of Mezzabarba, after the death of Tournon, thus managed to reconcile some of the European jurisdictional difficulties, involving the Portuguese, but not the fundamental opposition of imperial authority and papal claims in China. By the middle of the eighteenth century the Roman condemnation of the disputed Rites was confirmed, and in the second half of the century the suppression of the Jesuits in Europe had its effects in China.

The French Revolution and its aftermath adversely affected the work continued at Peking by former Jesuits and other French ecclesiastics, despite the maintenance of clandestine missions in the provinces too. French orders at work in China at the beginning of the nineteenth century included Portuguese members; and in eighteenth-century Naples a college was founded to train clergy for the Chinese mission. By then the European fashion for chinoiserie had begun, both in northern and southern Europe. This was at the very time when the failure of any major conversion of Chinese society to Catholicism had been made certain, by the refusal to allow assimilation of native practice to the Catholic faith, not least in response to controversies internal to European Catholicism itself. Jansenist criticism of Jesuit methods, however, gave way to rationalist use of the Jesuits' own reports of Chinese culture, as proof of the superiority of natural religion to alleged revelation. The adjustment of Catholic ritual to Chinese attitudes was barely tolerated by Rome, and the imposition of the liturgical use of Latin, as reasserted at Trent, created another barrier, as in the Japanese mission, to the creation of a native priesthood on a large scale. In Japan, as in China and the American missionfields, even the term for the Christian Deity proved problematic, unless European terms, Latin or vernacular, were introduced. The original design of the independent papal missionary effort, the *Propaganda*, to create a native priesthood in areas outside Europe seems, by contrast with such a crucial question, even more ambitious, though the aim was repeated by the French *Missions Etrangères*. The final papal confirmation, in the mid-eighteenth century, of the condemnation of the contested native rites in both India and China, was made by Benedict XIV, within Europe regarded as the most enlightened of popes. The problems of accommodation of non-European societies and Catholicism were represented by the positive effects of the use of native catechists, in the American and Eastern missions, and the negative deductions drawn by natives from the practice of baptism *in articulo mortis*, which seemed to suggest that missionaries caused death.

The relative distinction between the missionary history of America and the Far East and that of Africa, in the Counter-Reformation, is a reminder of the vital importance of European colonial expansion and political presence: the Iberian and French settlement in America, the competition of European powers in the East, led to support of missionary activity, however uncertain and divided, which was lacking in the African interior. The distinction of China and Japan, in the East, from territories in fact under European control suggested the difficulties of the Catholic missions where such support could not be given. In China, however, the Confucianism of the Mandarin class was not the only alternative to Catholicism. The Buddhism of the uneducated faced missionaries in the provinces, just as militant Buddhist monasticism did in Japan. In the case of China, the Counter-Reformation attention to exorcism of those suffering from demonic possession proved a useful export, for this reason.

In India, the assimilation of Hindu and Catholic practices, at least attempted by Jesuit missionaries, contrasted with later Protestant opposition in the sub-continent to what was seen in either case as pagan ritual; while the Malabar Christians, as a people apart, had never attempted missionary work, and had originally rejected sacred images, other than the cross, in their distinction from Hindus. The introduction of Catholic sacramental doctrine and practice among the Malabar Christians, at the end of the sixteenth century, led to misunderstandings among the Indians, not least because of fear of subjection to Portuguese authority. But the free provision of the sacraments by missionary priests contrasted favourably with the necessary dependence of the Malabar priests on fees. The profession of faith eventually imposed by the archbishop of Goa on the Malabar clergy was essentially the Tridentine, and Marian devotion was enhanced to accord with Roman tradition. The decrees of the Council of Trent were indeed declared to be binding on the Malabar Church, and it was supposedly subjected to the crown Inquisition at Goa. The prohibition of beliefs and practices suggestive of Hindu influence, including ceremonies at marriages and the music of Hindu musicians at mass, on the other hand, represented a complete contrast to the assimilative methods being practised by the Jesuits from the same period. The visitations personally conducted by the archbishop, among the Malabar Christians, promoted the practice of confession, in the face of popular fear of a rite associated with the dying. Exorcism was also employed in response to the use of dramatic propaganda by the opponents of the archbishop's policy of reducing Malabar practice to Roman standards. The Jesuit bishop, subsequently archbishop, who was provided for the Malabar Christians from the beginning of the seventeenth century, remained at odds with the Portuguese bishop of Cochin until the native archdeacon of the Christians, previously the head of his Church in all but liturgical functions, disappointed of his earlier promise of episcopal office, revolted against the Jesuit: in this he was encouraged by friars who opposed, as in Japan, the combination of Jesuit and episcopal authority. The Jesuit seminary for priests of the Church did not prevent schism, complicated by the Portuguese patronage of the new archbishopric, and the papal attempt to intervene and end the schism by means of Italian Carmelites and subsequently vicars apostolic.

The original justification advanced by Spaniards for the use of force in the conquest of pagan lands in America included the Augustinian concept of just war leading to the establishment of peace. But in Portugal, after the recovery of independence in the mid-seventeenth century, messianic expectations, associated with both the old and the restored royal line, urged renewed belligerency; and this in turn lay at the root of Portuguese Jesuit involvement in overseas commercial investment. Such involvements and Jesuit defence of Indians and negro slaves in Brazil from the start aroused the opposition of the friars and crown Inquisition, as well as the colonists. In seventeenth-century Mexico City the civil authorities and ecclesiastics sometimes aroused popular demonstrations in their conflicts with one another, but could co-operate in the face of serious riot. The organization of religious festivals in Brazil was particularly the work of lay confraternities; but the Portuguese segregation of women, intense even by Mediterranean or Hispanic standards, limited opportunities for the education and catechizing of girls there, among both the upper and lower orders of society. The Jesuits staged religious drama in Brazil as in Europe, Japan and Indo-China, however. The initial involvement of Inquisitorial authority, in Mexico, with Indians was the work of Zumárraga, despite his role as Protector of the Indians, though he acted by virtue of his powers as ordinary; for the corollary of asserting Indian rationality was the liability of the natives to conscious heresy. The crown tribunal of the Inquisition in Mexico was erected only in 1571; but even after this, episcopal authority in Inquisition matters was claimed over the Indians, while the crown tribunal was supposed not to concern itself with the natives. Competing jurisdiction in fact continued to be at issue, especially as Inquisitorial matters, after the Council of Trent, included offences against ecclesiastical marriage regulations, as well as proceedings against Indians for pagan practices which represented the pervasive syncretism of Mexican religion.

The racial confusion between Indians and *mestizos* was also a cause of conflict. Evidence of native paganism continued into the eighteenth century, when moral irregularities among the Indians were placed under the crown tribunal by the Bourbons. But at an earlier date, in the Yucatan, early in the second half of the sixteenth century, episcopal authority had restrained the Inquisitorial activities of friars against Indians who were only supposedly, it is clear, converted to Christianity. The use of torture was thought to have encouraged false confessions too. Episcopal authority also represented the original form of Inquisition in Portuguese Brazil. But after the succession of Spain to the Portuguese crown, the cardinal archduke, Albert, as viceroy and Inquisitor General in Portugal, extended Inquisitorial activity in Brazil, where its object was chiefly alleged Judaizing among New Christians. The Spanish connection brought a general search for Judaizers among Portuguese in Peru and elsewhere in Spanish America. But, by the end of the eighteenth century, the Spanish Inquisition in Mexico was rather used in defence of the Bourbon monarchy, with the prohibiting of English books, including those of the Catholic, Alexander Pope, as well as Protestant writers. Episcopal authority, outside Inquisitorial matters, was limited in Spanish America, as in Castile and elsewhere in Spain itself, by the possibility of clerical appeal against the orders of bishops and their courts: in America the *recursos de fuerza* were directed to the secular *audiencias*. Royal, and later viceregal, permission was necessary for diocesan synods in the Spanish overseas empire, which were held in the presence of the viceroy, or sent their decrees for his approval and that of the king. The royal decision of 1574 to support episcopal authority against regulars was never fully implemented. The sale of the *cruzada* indulgence also undermined episcopal authority, as it did in Spain itself. In the early years of the seventeenth century, however, the friar Garcia Guerra combined the offices of archbishop of Mexico and viceroy.

The integration of religious and civil life was predictably clearest in the case of female convents in Mexico, where, by the eighteenth century, nuns retained personal incomes, and convents employed lay agents to manage their property and made loans at interest; a return to truly communal living was resisted. By contrast, female convents were few in the Portuguese East, at Goa and Macao; but conventual life in eighteenth-century Brazil resembled that in Spanish America. In Latin America, it is clear, the problems experienced by the Church after the Council of Trent were to a considerable extent those of the European Church, even if the peculiar conditions of royal patronage prevented the solutions attempted at least in parts of Catholic Europe. On the other hand, the problems of converting a non-Christian society to Catholic belief and practice were present beyond doubt in America, if in a less dramatic way than in the civilizations of the Far East. The limited development of the secular clergy in America, in the face of successful regular independence, contributed to the surviving superficiality of much Catholicism in the Iberian possessions, quite apart from the allegedly lower quality of the seculars' life, compared with that even of the European secular clergy. In French North America, though, the work of both seculars and regulars, notably New Orders, consolidated colonial Catholicism, which survived under Protestant rule, even if the success of Indian missions was limited.

Friars in Mexico acted as Inquisitors from the start of the missionary presence, even before the establishment of an episcopate. The trials of settlers for blasphemy are indicative of the friars' attempt to impose higher standards of Catholic practice on the European colony, in the face of their example in fact to the natives, as well as reflecting political tensions within the colony. Regulars who became bishops, however, could use their Inquisitorial powers as ordinary against other religious who were resisting episcopal authority, while also attempting to eradicate immorality among the secular clergy. Archbishop Montúfar of Mexico also tried to use his Inquisitorial authority to support his ordinary jurisdiction over the dean and archdeacon of the city, Molina, in a case which coincided with the last years of the Council of Trent, and which had political ramifications, as well as touching on the relations of bishops and regulars. Such questions reflected European problems; but the inclusion in the end of natives in Inquisitorial processes demonstrated the ill-resolved difficulties of Catholic missions among non-Christians, just as did the more dramatic disputes in the Far East. The French Jansenists made use of the attack by a Dominican on the Jesuit missionary methods in China. But the papal condemnation of those methods, in the early eighteenth century, was followed by the condemnation of the Jansenists, by the bull *Unigenitus*, in 1713. The Jesuits had nevertheless offended the opinion of French Catholics, including apostolic visitors, by seemingly applying a lax moralism to definition of native Chinese practices, as well as by their independence of papal authority in the Far East missions. The argument of some Jesuits, that the Chinese had implicitly received Christian theism in antiquity, independent of the special revelation of Christ himself, was seen as particularly dangerous in an age of advancing rationalism and scepticism: it touched directly on the disputed questions of grace and salvation, quite apart from that of biblical authority. The Jansenist protagonist Arnauld extended his criticism of the Jesuits to include their arguments about Chinese religion. The final condemnation of the tolerance of native rites in India, by Benedict XIV in 1744, cited Augustine as authority for the rigorist approach; while the apparent disobedience of Jesuit missionaries contributed to the final suppression of the Society itself. The legacy of the Jesuit mission in China and the European dispute over the 'Chinese Rites' was more secular than religious, however, in one sense. The interest taken by Leibniz in Chinese achievements, as reported by the Jesuits, stimulated his own calculations; while Ricci's translation of Greek texts on mathematics and astronomy represented the beginnings of Western intellectual influence on Chinese thought, however subordinate to native tradition. By contrast, the Inquisition in Portuguese India had been occupied from the mid-sixteenth century, not only with the crowds of European clerics in Goa, but also with Hindus accused of magical practices: the European preoccupation with pagan and demonic superstitions accompanied the missionary presence, as in America.

In Japan, the social divisions between the converts of the Jesuits and those of the Franciscans were in the end overcome by the similar constancy shown under persecution; the Jesuits' encouragement of flagellant devotion had already proved popular, as elsewhere in overseas missions. The sufferings of the English Recusants were compared to those of the Japanese missionaries and their converts by a Jesuit in Japan; though the preceding attacks of secular authority in Japan on the militant and independent Buddhist and sectarian monks had proved a period of toleration for the foreign missionaries, seen as allies in the ruler's cause, unlike the prelude of the English Dissolution. The Spanish nationality of the Franciscans proved fatal, however, at a time of Spanish conquest in the neighbouring Philippines; and the respite in persecution of Japanese Christianity, at the beginning of the seventeenth century, corresponded with a brief interlude of good relations, established by a new ruler in Japan, with the Spanish government there. By contrast, Ricci had won approval in China as an Italian not an Iberian; and, despite the change of dynasty, China did not suffer the internal and external divisions and apparent threats which Japan experienced. The establishment of the Tokugawa regime in Japan began with the power of Ieyasu, as shogun from about 1615, intent on extending his authority through-out Japan, at the time when in Europe the assertion of authority by conflicting states was about to result in the quasi-religious Thirty Years' War. In Japan the last stand of a peasant revolt in 1638, which included Christian converts, led to the closure of the country, to a large extent, to outside influence from about 1640; at that time in Europe Portugal was attempting to win independence from Spain, reflecting the tragic rivalry of Spanish Franciscans and Portuguese Jesuits in Japan. From 1640 a state tribunal for the 'examination of sects', designed to root out Christianity as well, was created in Japan, and native monasteries were required to register the faithful in their area, true to the national religion: the methods, in Catholic Europe and Protestant countries such as England, of control of dissent were thus precisely parallel. In Japan the hunting of clan-destine Christians among the lay population continued to the end of the eighteenth century, and into the nineteenth, outlasting the similar policies adopted in Europe, reciprocally in the struggles between Catholicism and Protestant nationalism.

The long-term difficulties of the Catholic overseas missions, not least in the Iberian empires, and under Habsburg rule, even before Portuguese and Bourbon succession, contrasted with the great suc-cess of the European Counter-Reformation in Poland. Habsburg support for a Jesuit mission to Russia in the late seventeenth century admittedly produced no more substantial gains than the earlier in-volvement of Polish regulars in the claims of the 'False Dmitri' to the Russian throne. The alliance of the Catholic Vasa crown, in Poland itself, at the end of the sixteenth and into the seventeenth century, with the Habsburgs, by the typical marriage policy of the latter family, after the transitory involvement of the Valois in Polish affairs, established a Catholic axis: its operation against the Turks was eventually symbolized by Sobieski's relief of Vienna, despite a cooling of personal relations, accompanying the decline of the Turk-ish threat in fact by this time already. But the relative success of the Polish acquisition of the Eastern-rite Christians who adhered to the Union of 1596 suggested a model for similar expansion of Roman allegiance among such Christians in Habsburg lands. By the end of the seventeenth century a Uniate Church had been established in Hungary, though the Serbian Uniates in Croatia had a less certain existence. From the very end of the century, Romanians were becoming Uniates in the parts of Transylvania taken by the Habsburgs, following the Union there of Armenian Christians. In Eastern-central Europe, however, the progress of Catholic reform was long delayed, by the size of dioceses, and periods of prolonged vacancy or non-residence. Many Hungarian prelates were of necessity titular, until the Habsburg recovery of Turkish conquests, from the last two decades of the seventeenth century. This was nearly two centuries after the Turkish defeat of independent Christian Hungary in 1526, one year before the sack of Rome itself, at the hands of an army supposedly in the pay of the Catholic Emperor, Charles v.

The more striking, therefore, was the relatively early and largely peaceful recovery of Poland for Catholicism, the work not least of Hosius, who presided at Trent, before the Conciliar decrees were accepted by the Polish episcopate with royal encouragement. Hosius introduced the Jesuits into Poland at the very end of the Council, and their educational influence on laity as well as clergy was followed by the creation not only of diocesan seminaries, but also of specialist seminaries, on the Roman or Milanese model, to train clergy specifically for work among Protestants. The ideal of Charles Borromeo as a reforming bishop, and attention to the continued example of the Milanese Church, were explicitly avowed in Poland after Borromeo's diplomatic understanding of the need for care and caution in any Catholic restoration there. Hosius and Borromeo indeed extended their attentions to episcopal provision and monastic reform in the Habsburg territories of Austria, Hungary and Bohemia, as well as in Poland. The Polish crown was allowed by Rome to benefit from a further secularization of Baltic lands belonging to a military order, lest they should follow the earlier transfer to Protestant dynastic foundation in Prussia. The gradual reduction of the tolerance allowed to non-Catholics by the crown was evident by the end of the sixteenth century, and the internal divisions of the variety of Protestants found in Poland were used to advantage by Jesuit writers and the itinerant preachers of the Franciscan Observants. It seemed as though the relative unity of Catholic powers in the face of the Turkish danger, and the relative co-operation of Catholic missionaries against Protestantism – in Poland if not in England – were as contrasted with the conditions in the overseas missions as were the very different results of these aspects of the Counter-Reformation.

# CHAPTER 5

# RELIGIOUS DIVISIONS AND POLITICAL SIMILARITIES

CERTAIN PARALLELS in the evolution of Church–state relations, in Catholic and Protestant areas of Western Europe after the Reformation, have already been noted; as also the lack of any clear distinction of economic development between one area and another, according to religious allegiance. At the beginning of the seventeenth century, at the time of the English reception of Sarpi's attack on the development of papal power in the Catholic Church, crosscurrents, overriding denominational divisions, seemed stronger than ever in political relations between Catholic and Protestant states. The antagonism of James I, as king of England, to those English Protestants whom he believed to be favourably disposed towards a Presbyterian reorganization of the English Church, led to disappointment, just as his policy towards English Catholic Recusants produced notorious examples of disillusioned despair. The ruler brought up as a Calvinist king of Scotland was opposed to the restrictions on royal authority which he believed both Jesuits and Presbyterians to advocate. The continued division in fact of English Catholics, not least over the related questions of hierarchical authority within their own community and political obedience to the English crown, represented in part a further difference between Jesuits, and others. The Jesuits and their supporters accepted the inevitable patronage of Spain, especially financial support of clerical training abroad, while others, especially some secular priests, hoped to find a more disinterested link with Rome, by means of contact with French Catholicism. The policy of Richelieu, to try to impose effective episcopal leadership on the English Catholics, was thus, in part, an anti-Jesuit and ultimately anti-Spanish move, in the Bourbon plan for resisting Habsburg hegemony in Europe. But at an early stage, before *dévot* criticism of Richelieu's policies became marked, Bérulle, cardinal and founder of the French Oratory, was also in favour of this aim, since episcopal authority seemed the key, throughout Catholic Europe, to the implementation of Tridentine reform.

The opposition to Jesuits and their supposed anti-monarchism had been felt in the France of Henri IV, despite the reconciliation of the first Bourbon king to Rome; for the prolonged papal support of the anti-Bourbon alternative of a Spanish succession in France had not been forgotten, but had revived legal and even clerical Gallicanism. James I of England thus sympathized with Henri IV, not least in his support of the Venetian Republic against the effects of the papal Interdict of 1606–7, during which the Jesuits had been expelled from Venetian territory. Bourbon kingdom and Catholic republic had a common interest in resisting what was seen as Spanish pressure on their territories, though Spain's attitude during the Interdict in fact wavered between armed threats against Venice and tacit support for the Republic's defence of state rights against the papacy's claims. Yet the peace by which James I concluded the long hostilities between Spain and Elizabethan England did not, in this case, lead to English sympathy with Spanish concerns. The danger of division in Europe reverting to avowedly religious lines was still imminent at the beginning of the seventeenth century, not least because of the proximate expiry of the Twelve Years' Truce in the Netherlands, which would raise the question of Spain's attempted recovery of an area in which both England and France had interests which were economic or strategic, rather than strictly religious. In the event, revolt in Bohemia encouraged by German Calvinist leadership was to mean, indirectly, the loss of the Palatinate by the daughter and son-in-law of James, largely by virtue of Spanish military action on the land route to the Netherlands; while economic rivalry between states contesting Baltic littoral areas of expansion and the revenues from European shipping through the Sound was to promote war in central Germany conducted in part on lines of religious allegiance, despite the common Protestantism of some at least of the Baltic kingdoms. The effective suppression of Calvinism in France, though begun in a military and political sense by Richelieu, was thus to be delayed, by the demands of foreign war, until the second stage of contest between Habsburgs and Bourbons, under Louis XIV, after the reconciliation of the two Catholic powers of France and Spain by Mazarin in 1659. By that date Spain had failed to recover the Dutch Netherlands from the hands of Calvinist republicans; but in England Presbyterian and other anti-episcopal Protestant attacks on royal policy and authority had eventually led to a Protestant republic.

The presence of Calvinism thus seemed to contemporary rulers, until the mid-seventeenth century, to threaten legitimate authority in the state, Catholic or not. In sixteenth-century France and Scotland, in the Netherlands too, and in seventeenth-century central Europe the demands of Calvinist nobles and town oligarchs had apparently led to the disruption of government. With the necessary subordination of the French Huguenots to the new Bourbon line, debate within Catholic France, as opposed to the Protestant community, came to turn increasingly on the relations between the crown and Rome, from the Estates General summoned in the wake of the assassination of Henri IV onwards. The moderate episcopal Gallicanism – typified perhaps by Bossuet – present among the upper clergy was supremely revealed after the threat to French royal authority represented by the Frondes: an episode in which French Protestants as such took no coherent part, in contrast to contemporary events in England. To that extent the mid-century revolts in France were certainly more comparable with the revolts in the entirely Catholic societies of Naples and Sicily, Portugal and Catalonia. The recovery of royal power by Louis XIV was demonstrated by his armed threats against the papacy, and its territorial enclave at Avignon, in pursuit of his increased economic and general control over the French bishops and clergy. The theoretic advance of royal claims was separately allowed by the clerical leadership, as far as relations with Rome were concerned, in the adoption of the 'Gallican Articles' by the assembly of the clergy, which restated Conciliarist claims against papal supremacy. But the demand that these articles be required teaching in the French seminaries was tacitly withdrawn in the fluctuations of Louis's foreign policy. The need for European allies in the terrible wars of the last decades of his reign, so criticized by Fénelon, produced a division between royal Gallicanism and the Gallicanism of the lawyers who had from the start supported the Bourbon succession. The desire of Louis to eradicate the Jansenists in France meant a co-operation between royal and papal authority, which left the would-be loyalists who revered the memory of Jansenius, while seeking to remain in obedience to Rome, with no alternative but to seek Gallican protection. Despite the sympathy of some French bishops, who respected the rigorist standards of the Jansenists and disliked Jesuit influence at the royal court, the only sure support was from the last defenders of the supposed Gallican liberties of the French Church, among the secular lawyers of the parlements. The independence of mind demonstrated by some lower clergy in Paris, caught up in the convulsionary manifestations of early eighteenth-century Jansenism, was not however to the taste of the Gallican bishops. For, from the Gallican revival of the late sixteenth century onwards, the advocacy of the rights of the clergy, as opposed to bishops, suggested that this Richerism was too akin to the Presbyterianism of the Calvinists or the quasi-Presbyterian disregard for episcopal authority of which the Jesuits were accused. Yet whereas the Jesuits of the early seventeenth century, in England, France and Venice, were accused of a subversion of legitimate government similar to that caused or threatened by Calvinism, the critics of Jesuit influence at the courts of Louis xiv and James ii objected rather to the apparently excessive support provided by the Society for unrestrained royal absolutism.

The Spanish Habsburg view of ecclesiastical authority and the rights of secular government revealed similar complexities. The interest of Philip ii in defending papal supremacy against Conciliarist claims at the Council of Trent was clear, given the importance of Spanish influence in papal conclaves, and the danger of nationalism further dividing the remaining Catholic part of Europe. Yet Philip's reserve of his royal rights, in accepting the decrees of the Council, proved no theoretical gesture. The king was supposedly critical of the reduction of episcopal powers in relation to those of Rome which some observers detected in the Conciliar decrees. But the independence of bishops in post-Tridentine Spain and its dominions remained rigorously restricted by royal authority. In Spain itself, the king regulated the dress of bishops and their social standing, just as Elizabeth of England did. The visitation of convents, entrusted to certain bishops by the Nuncio in Spain, was allowed only on condition that the visitations were regarded as royal inspections, and reports made to the court. Visitation of churches and abbeys in Sicily was indeed a royal activity, over which Rome had no effective control. Spanish bishops and canons were employed as royal visitors within the Spanish system of secular government, or retained at court to preside over royal councils: the Nuncio's protests about the duty of residence were of no more effect than similar protests at the royal obstruction of episcopal visits to Rome, required at stated intervals by the post-Tridentine papacy. Lawyers in Spanish service elaborated theories about episcopal subjection to the authority of royal councils or viceroys, though these theories were more easily put into practice in the kingdom of Naples than in Spanish-ruled Lombardy. The union of the crowns of Castile and Portugal in 1580 was immediately followed by the careful control of both Church and state in the latter kingdom, by means of the papal grant of legatine status to the cardinal archduke who governed there.[1] The papal Nuncio in Spain was thus left without a means of defending episcopal independence in Portugal, and such independence was attempted only by the bravest souls, such as the archbishop of Evora, who was from the family of Braganza.[2] When this family eventually supplied an independent line for the Portuguese throne once more, after 1640, some measure of local reaction against the period of papal co-operation with Spanish hegemony was natural. Although the papacy had resisted some of Philip II's schemes for the virtual subordination of Portuguese provinces of different religious orders to Castilian superiors, the culmination of difficulties between Portugal and Rome emerged in the eighteenth century, over both colonial and dynastic questions of independence.

The restored independence of Portugal in the later seventeenth century, however, allowed Catherine of Braganza, wife of Charles II of England, to patronize English Catholics, at least to the extent of presenting a silver crozier, symbol of episcopal office, to one of the vicars apostolic who sought to bring order and organization to the confused Recusant community. In Restoration England, the return of royal rule was in the end followed by the re-establishment of the Anglican Church on its pre-revolutionary episcopal model, since Presbyterian and other anti-episcopal forms of Protestantism were considered responsible for regicide and anarchy. But while the ordinary Church courts were restored, the most effective grant of royal authority, exercised by means of the High Commission, was not allowed in religious affairs, especially as Parliament now maintained its own more elaborate system of policing non-conformity. Only in the peculiar conditions of James II's reign did the question of royal prerogative and ecclesiastical commission arise again, while the king's attempts to introduce Catholics to Oxford colleges were seen as a dangerous attack on clerical education. The role of the Seven Bishops in maintaining eventual, if reluctant, resistance to James was arguably as important as the inclusion of Compton's name among the signatories of the contrived summons to William of Orange to protect English Protestantism. The idiosyncratic result, however, was the schism of Anglican bishops and clergy, as Non-Jurors, at the end of the seventeenth and into the eighteenth century, in England and Scotland; while in the equally peculiar conditions of the Dutch Netherlands in the early eighteenth century the schism of Utrecht involved Catholic clergy and, in the end, bishops. Both the Anglican and the Jansenist schisms in fact turned on questions of authority and obedience, rather than on any properly theological issues.

During the course of the eighteenth century, Catholic states moved towards the reduction of ecclesiastical privileges, and pursued a

policy of expelling Jesuits from their territories. The example of
Portugal and Spain was also followed elsewhere in Catholic Europe,
in the confiscation of other monastic property, to a certain extent,
and limitation of any further extension of ecclesiastical mortmain.
In Austrian Habsburg territory control by the state of clerical education was attempted by Joseph II, following the end of Jesuit dominance of lay education. In the related state of Tuscany the reduction
of religious festivals was attempted, whatever the subsequent signs
of popular resistance to such changes. Josephinism in Austria proper
and the Netherlands also met popular opposition, in the attempt to
modify popular devotion and the local practice of Catholicism. Although Josephine reform gave way to a large degree, in Revolutionary Europe, to political reaction, elsewhere in Catholic Europe
the revolutionary era and Napoleonic sequel saw the destruction of
the Inquisition. The security of state police systems and government
censorship finally replaced the old organs of ecclesiastical supervision
of society. Such jurisdictional developments from the limited defence
of state rights in Catholic territories after the Council of Trent
represented a transformation of the older assumption of a balanced
division between Church and secular authority, contested in practical
interpretation, but drawing on a tradition variously expressed by
Dante or Marsiglio of Padua. The sovereignty of the state was not
achieved in fact during the Reformation and Counter-Reformation
– the period of religious warfare, when governments attempted to
coerce the minds and souls of their subjects – but rather in the
century following the last wars of religion. The economic consequences of attempting to assert absolute control over the belief of
subjects had proved, in many cases, counter-productive. The unpaid
armies of Spain which mutinied in the Netherlands, for example, did
much to destroy any chances of reimposing finally Spanish rule and
the Catholic faith. The increasing cost of war in the seventeenth
century, felt so clearly by France, as well as by Habsburg Spain, led
to a belated but consequent attempt to maximize the revenues of
secular government, while extending political control of society.
Economic redistribution during the Protestant reformation had allowed an earlier chance for such gains by Protestant states, even if
rulers were not always able to benefit as much as lay subjects, as, in
different ways, the results of monastic dissolution in England and
Scotland showed.

The relations of secular and ecclesiastical authority were not, despite that, to be easily and immediately settled in Protestant states:
this was demonstrated in Calvin's own Geneva, or later in the dis-

agreements between Presbyterian clerics and lay leaders in Scotland or mid-seventeenth-century England, or the Dutch Netherlands. The wars of religion of Western Europe, in the sixteenth and early seventeenth century, nevertheless had the effect of strengthening the claims of the state, in both Catholic and Protestant areas, over the Church. The need to assert internal authority in the face of revolt, or to meet external commitments, led to the use of ecclesiastical resources, as has been noted in the case of Spain and Venice for example. The employment of clerics as civil servants in post-Tridentine Spain, or their role as ministers of the crown in France, represented in one way a survival in Catholic Europe of the medieval world, with its ambiguous clerks, at once clergy and clerical staff. But after the Council of Trent this distinctive feature of Catholic as opposed to Protestant areas was balanced by the desire in Catholic states to resist the Church's reassertion of clerical immunities, fiscal and legal, called for at Trent. The Conciliar insistence on the powers of the priesthood, in the face of Protestant attack which was theological but carried with it socio-economic consequences for the clerical profession, was not in question; but the economic and political strengths of a celibate hierarchy were in practice challenged. Erastianism was not a preserve of Protestant Europe, even if the full evolution of Catholic erastianism, following precocious leads from seventeenth-century Venice and Naples, supported by French and Spanish experience, was not clear until the eighteenth century. This later development was not least a secular reaction against doctrinal quarrels which had largely jurisdictional implications: the Jansenist-Jesuit controversy, above all, in Catholic Europe itself. The clash between royal Gallicanism and the Gallican *parlementaires* over Jansenism, from the early eighteenth century onwards, showed the way in this respect.

The disruptive effects in Catholic society of rivalry between Jesuits and their opponents suggested the desirability of state supervision of education, even if the crucial occasion for attack on the Society was finally provided by its financial involvement in enterprises that were colonial rather than simply missionary. To this extent the early aim of reformers within the late medieval and Renaissance Western Church had only been ambiguously achieved. The ideal of improving the education of the common clergy, and of introducing a scriptural and theological basis in place of a canonistic dominance among educated clerics, was shared by Cisneros in Spain, episcopal and regular reformers in early sixteenth-century France, Colet and even Wolsey in England. But while such Christian humanism and evangelicism had been soon distracted, in many parts of Europe, by debate over the rights of mendicants and the authority of their teaching, the serious study of doctrinal questions in the face of Protestant challenge had produced the paradoxical result of continued theological controversy and religious rivalry within the Catholic Church. The ideal of a priesthood free of secular duties to rulers or lay patrons was not achieved entirely, despite the new standards for clerical education and behaviour laid down at Trent. The awareness of Cardinal Pole, as legate in England, that only a newly formed clergy could recover lasting allegiance to the true faith led to his seminal plan for specialist institutions for vocational training, which was adopted not in England, nor even in Allen's original idea of Catholic scholarship in exile, but elsewhere in Catholic Europe, in the Tridentine diocesan seminaries. The Anglican clergy instead remained an increasingly graduate profession, educated at the existing universities of England, which lay patrons, at the end of the sixteenth century, were themselves frequenting, even if combining their studies with those continued at the Inns of Court, where a largely secular law was taught. Early seventeenth-century Spain, as well as England, in fact saw increasing competition between secular lawyers and ecclesiastical authorities.

It was in Protestant Europe that the political theory of the state, especially in its relations with the Church, was fully evolved on independent lines. The views of Hobbes represented an abrupt departure from the patriarchal argument belatedly published by Filmer, even before Locke's subordination of other rights to the priority of property. Hobbes's strict subordination of the claims of religion was equally a far cry from the pragmatic eclecticism of the apologia put forward by Hooker for English Church and state in the sixteenth century. But the interlude of the Interregnum, in mid-seventeenth-century England, raised acutely in practice as well as theory the question of religious enthusiasm, inspiration and authority, in relation to the peaceful organizing of a stable civil society. Luther's pragmatic evolution of the doctrine that the godly prince should rule his subjects' religion had been complicated by the later sixteenth-century development, by Calvinists if not by Calvin himself, of a theory of just revolt against an ungodly prince, provided such revolt followed the legitimate command of intermediate authority.[3] The right of resistance to 'tyrants' was thus enunciated, even if the later sixteenth-century assassinations of rulers in Western Europe did more to create belief in Jesuit responsibility for regicide. The public political theory of Sarpi, in Catholic Venice, as has been seen, remained by contrast more antiquarian, in its reflection of Gerson and Gallican opinion. For the Gallican revival in early Bourbon France claimed precisely that ancient liberties of France and its Church were to be protected under the new royal line against papal or other innovation. The royal lawyers of Spain and Naples were obviously unwilling to question papal supremacy openly, in the face of Protestant attack; but, in resisting change in the post-Tridentine Church, wherever that suggested a threat to existing royal rights, they resorted to the obstinate recital of past history, or of supposed factual evidence at least.

This antiquarian regalism nevertheless produced, in early eighteenth-century Naples, the historical relativism of Vico, of a more speculative kind, which encouraged the extension of state rights claimed in the theories of Giannone for the secular sphere. It was this Neapolitan evolution, as much as the historically inspired considerations of Muratori about Church and state in earlier times, which had an effect on Lombard and Austrian Josephinism and late Jansenism. For here Count Firmian acted as an intermediary, even if there were also independent contacts, as at Salzburg, or as in Joseph's own admiration for Catholic erastianism continued at Venice from Sarpi's day to his own. Venetian Catholic erastianism after the Council of Trent, however, had shared with Spanish policy precisely the limited resistance to practical change, the aim of maintaining pre-Tridentine practice, whatever the wider considerations put forward by Sarpi in his opinions as jurist and theologian of the Republic. In Sicily, within the European as opposed to missionary territories, Spain most successfully preserved medieval conditions in the direction of ecclesiastical affairs. For the exclusion of appeals to Rome as of Roman representatives, the nomination of bishops, and their subjection to the viceregal court of the *Monarchia* all contributed to the isolation of the island Church, further enforced by the presence of the Crown Inquisition of Spain. Catholic Sicily thus strangely resembled the insular isolation of the Anglican episcopal Church, under royal government, in Elizabethan England, where again a substantial part of the medieval organization of the Western Church was maintained, after the failure of Pole's proposed Catholic reforms, and the resistance of the new queen to calls for a further Protestant reformation.

The presence, outside Sicily, of papal representatives in Catholic states, after the Council of Trent, was reorganized by the papacy as permanent diplomatic representation. The system of Nuncios was thus, in a way, a tribute to the continued power of Catholic rulers

over the Church in their territories, despite the resistance at Trent
to dangers of a division into national 'Catholic' Churches. The Nuncios of the immediately post-Conciliar decades were, however, also
a symbol of the papal determination to enforce application of the
Tridentine reforms, as far as possible, on a uniform basis. The choice
of diocesan bishops, seconded for brief periods to such diplomatic
duty, not only avoided the charge of resisting the clear Conciliar call
for an end to non-residence, but enabled the papacy to solve the
consequent financial problem of funding Curial administration. The
gain was that such bishops, from their own experience of practical
obstacles to diocesan reform, were able to try at least to support the
work of reforming bishops against secular opposition. This they did,
in Spain, Naples and Venice, for example, as well as elsewhere, as,
to a degree at any rate, at Florence and Turin, with persistence if not
always with success. The financial and diplomatic complications of
their work were never absent, whether with the question of Church
funds and Sicilian grain, in the Venetian or Spanish Nunciatures, or
with those of dynastic struggle and international conflict, in the
French and German lands. But the rise of the great European continental war of the first half of the seventeenth century, from about
1620 onwards, led to a transformation of the papal diplomatic service. Career diplomats who were primarily Curialists, not diocesan
bishops, came to serve as Nuncios for longer tours of duty, with
certain advantages, as political questions dominated the reports from
Nunciatures, to the gradual exclusion of questions of ecclesiastical
reform. The papacy indeed had resisted policies which might lead to
such a conflict, not least because of the danger of further division in
Catholic Europe, and because of an accurate fear that war might
spread south into the Italian peninsula, with the attendant dangers
of foreign troop movements and the spread of heretical ideas. The
Spanish hesitation about war in the peninsula, at the time of the
papal Interdict of Venice, in 1606–7, was thus replaced by 1618 at
the Viennese court, by an advocacy of the benefits of war; while papal
diplomacy at this later date advocated peace, but was defeated, with
the imprisonment of Cardinal Khlesl. The continued hostility to
Venice of Spanish viceroys in Naples and governors in Milan, and
the danger of the encirclement of Venice by Habsburgs or those
they protected on three land frontiers and on the Adriatic, meant
continued reserve in the Republic for papal claims, even after the
Interdict, and the ambiguous solution advocated by France, where
Henri IV suffered a similar sense of Habsburg encirclement. In the
Thirty Years' War in Germany, the papacy's contribution to the

Habsburg cause – distinct as it was from that of Catholic Bavaria – was limited to the financial. However the imperial victory over Bohemian rebels and heretics, at the Battle of the White Mountain, was to be celebrated in the Roman church of Our Lady of Victory, in which Bernini's celebration of the contemplative ecstasy and mystical penetration of Saint Teresa was eventually to find a place, in a chapel commemorating a family of Venetian origin.

The disjunction of avowed religious conflict from international war in Western Europe after the Peace of Westphalia in 1648 led, in the long run, to greater freedom for papal diplomacy. The Baltic wars which continued in the later seventeenth century, and into the eighteenth, saw a final identification of Catholic and national unity, as Poland resisted Swedish invasion. But the abdication of Christina of Sweden had been a separate issue from that of her subsequent reception in the Church and city of Rome. By the beginning of the eighteenth century the conversion to Catholicism of individual German princes could be contemplated without the certainty of major war as a result. After the continental and colonial wars of the eighteenth century, the progressive reduction of papal diplomatic strength culminated in the impotence of papal policy in the face of revolutionary attack on the Church in France. But the escape of the papacy from its Revolutionary and then Napoleonic captivity, which followed, and the paradoxical security which Venice afforded for the conclave which alone guaranteed the Roman apostolic succession, led to the romantic approval of Protestant England for the pope, as much as for French clerical émigrés, and to the revival of diplomatic relations between Rome and England, for the first time since the interludes of the early and later Stuart period. The last of the Stuart line, Cardinal Henry Duke of York, maintained the presence of the exiled House at Rome still, but was himself in receipt of a Hanoverian pension. Before the dangers of the Revolutionary era and triumphs of the Napoleonic years, however, the papacy had been reduced to subservience already to Catholic rulers. The policies of Joseph II created sufficient alarm to necessitate a papal journey to Vienna, productive of popular rather than of substantial triumph. The realism of Benedict XIV, as a rational reformer, experienced in the continuing work of reforming the Church in Bologna, before he became pope, attempted to avoid unproductive conflict with Catholic states. But the papal acquiescence in the final dissolution of the Society of Jesus represented not only a blow to papal prestige, but the major loss of educational influence in society by the Church more generally. In Protestant Europe, credal conformity might still be demanded in institutions of higher education, above all the traditional universities, but in England, for example, the eighteenth century also saw the development of sectarian diversity in education, through the non-conformist academies.

The failure, during the Marian restoration, of any projects for major re-establishment of monastic institutions in England, at the expense of new lay owners of ex-monastic property, represented the permanence of economic transfer of resources, matched certainly in the differing circumstances of the Lutheran states and of Scotland. As has been seen, the continued use of monastic and other ecclesiastical wealth to support lay society indirectly, through the selection of bishops, canons and commendatory abbots, combined, in Catholic states in Italy, Spain and France, as well as in German lands, the traditions of Catholicism and the advantage of secular society: and this was in a way even clearer in the case of female convents. The erosion of ecclesiastical immunity and reduction of ecclesiastical property in the eighteenth century, at the hands of Catholic states, thus represented a belated adjustment of the traditional system, in a direction more akin to certain earlier Protestant developments. But whereas, in England and Scotland at least, monastic dissolution had ultimately benefited individual landowners, rather than the ruler, the strengthening of the state in eighteenth-century Catholic Europe ensured that gains made at the expense of the Church would remain in central control. Individual patronage remained a means of lay subjects' involvement in clerical life, just as such patronage, even without the further complication of overt Puritanism, obstructed in Anglican England the limited reform of the parochial clergy promoted by the official hierarchy, before and during the Laudian regime. The triumph of erastianism in Western Christendom was thus in some ways a continuous process, from at least the beginning of the fifteenth century onwards, quite apart from possible Norman, Carolingian or even Constantinian precedents. This long process continued until the disruption of the French Revolution, but by very different means and at different speeds, in Catholic states and in various Protestant areas. By the later eighteenth century, lay speculative study of civil rights at Milan, on such topics as penal reform, encountered limitation from the Austrian government: no longer from the Church, in a city where once the Borromean Counter-Reformation had produced an unusual degree of subjection of secular society to ecclesiastical authority, within post-Tridentine Catholic Europe.

The Protestant criticism, in seventeenth-century Europe, of supposed Jesuit casuistry, in the sense of equivocation, was ironic in the light of the development of political theory in Protestant areas. The sophistication of concepts of evidence, at judicial level, was slow to occur anywhere, as was demonstrated by the Popish Plot scare of later Stuart England, as much as by heresy trials, witch-trials, or the prosecutions of English Recusants, in sixteenth-century Europe. The practical extension of the state's powers, ending 'liberties' of which the Church of Western Europe within England was only the greatest, was attempted under Henry VIII by the work and projects of Thomas Cromwell. The foundations of this aspect of Tudor policy included considerations drawn from the assertion of state rights by Marsiglio of Padua. The ecclesiastical wealth released by monastic dissolution in England was not in the end directed on any equivalent scale to the promotion of clerical education, as envisaged by Wolsey, or to the endowment of new dioceses which might make episcopal supervision of over-large sees less of a problem. The proceeds were rather intended, however unsuccessfully in the end, for the support of the crown's general finances. In his dangerous refusal to accept the new order of his royal relation in English Church and state, Cardinal Pole identified the new teachings of Machiavelli as a cause of disruption of the old order of Western Christendom. The Paduan education of Pole allowed him to take seriously the implied criticism of Christianity in *The Prince*, as but one of the systems by which social legislators might hope to control the obedience of subjects. The works of Machiavelli were later to be found on the Roman Index, and conservative distrust of the lessons which the author appeared to teach remained dominant in Catholic and Protestant Europe until the shocking 'atheism' of Hobbes appeared in England. For the argument for Gardiner's authorship of *A Machiavellian Treatise*, supposedly matching his prolonged acceptance of jurisdictional, though not doctrinal innovation in early Tudor England, has still not won universal acceptance. The identification of 'Jesuitical' and Machiavellian equivocation nevertheless became a stock image in Protestant England, even outside circles where political theory was limited to a literal belief that the papacy, or subsequently episcopacy, represented Antichrist. Yet criticism of Jesuit alleged practice stressed the danger to legitimate state authority, while Machiavelli seemed to justify and demonstrate the absolute powers of the ruler more successfully than Botero, who was better appreciated by the Spanish monarch than by Cardinal Borromeo.[4]

The English penal laws against Recusants were in one sense as productive of Catholic profession as, in reverse, the draconian policies of Spain were of Calvinist commitment increasingly in the Netherlands. The Marian restoration in England involved no new organs of repression, no Inquisition, Roman or Spanish. The return, by the crown in Parliament – by means of a royal supremacy which could not in fact be ended over the English Church – to the Roman obedience involved the reversal of the Edwardian abolition of the old heresy laws, which had been applied in the fifteenth century and in the reign of Henry VIII. The return to persecution, by the co-operation of Church courts and secular authority, was however unproductive, in so far as a wider degree of heterodoxy, in parts of the country at least, had resulted from the Edwardian interlude and spread of continental Protestant ideas. In the politically sensitive capital and south-east, execution of heretics seemed to involve substantial numbers of respected laity – not members of a minority who could be safely despised by the majority – quite apart from the ejection of clergy who had married, legitimately by Edwardian standards, and the unpopular association of Spain with the new régime, by virtue of the queen's marriage. Obedience to Rome was logical for a queen whose legitimate succession had been accepted by her subjects, despite an attempt, at Edward's death, to place religious continuity before dynastic continuity. In precisely the same way, the legitimacy of Elizabeth as Mary's successor depended on rejection of Roman authority, unless the royal title were to be made dependent on papal legitimization. But the evolution of Elizabethan penal laws against Recusants, promoted by royal proclamation, as well as parliamentary statute, was modified, not begun, by the subsequent, and much delayed, papal bull denouncing the queen as unlawful ruler, and not entitled to the obedience of true Catholics. The increasing specification, in the penal laws, of religious acts as worthy of punishment, for their supposedly axiomatic treasonable quality, replaced the original and negative proscription of non-attendance at parish churches: Catholic Recusants, as opposed to recusants in general, were identified by governmental decision, rather than by the actions of Catholics themselves. The attempts of Jesuit and other missionary priests to end all 'occasional conformity' by Catholics, by which heads or male members, most often, of a family attended the established church at intervals, were never entirely successful.

The long-term economic pressures of Tudor, Stuart and Interregnum governments were to prove more effective, in destroying lay allegiance to Catholic separatism in England, than the most savage periods in the intermittent application of the penal laws against laity. Despite frequent historical assertions to the contrary, contemporary minds, in sixteenth-century England, were capable of distinguishing between political obedience and religious allegiance, even before the late Elizabethan attempts of Cecil to play on such a distinction for the internal division of the Catholic community. Apart from the famous episode of the Armada threat and the attempt of Catholics to prove their loyalty to the queen, against Spain, on that occasion, the reluctance of Justices of the Peace, frequently and in many areas, to act against fellow members of the gentry, or even of the Bench, for alleged Catholic Recusancy, did not end in 1570. The ability to detect political loyalty or disloyalty was believed, at local level, to involve no necessary persecution of religious differences. Such differences could provide a motivation, on the other hand, for action to promote personal or family rivalry, even if such competition for economic and social advantage did not reach the bloody levels of continued war within divided France in the later sixteenth century. In the seventeenth century, English sovereigns were on occasion served by ministers reliably believed to be crypto-Catholics; but the century in France saw the transformation of service to the crown, after the reign of Henri IV, into a Catholic preserve, aided by a few acclaimed conversions of leading figures. Despite the Popish Plot and Exclusion Crisis, the failure of the latter, and subsequently of Monmouth's Rebellion, allowed James II of England to succeed to the throne with considerably strengthened authority, for all his known Catholicism. While the possibility of a continued Catholic succession, on the birth of a male heir, arguably raised much greater difficulties, not least for the Anglican hierarchy of the state Church, only the policies actively pursued by the monarch, against papal advice, brought disaster for the House of Stuart and, for a while at least, to the English Catholic community, momentarily relieved from its political disabilities.

By contrast the beginning of Elizabeth's reign had seen, in Lancashire at least, parochial clergy maintaining much of the old religion, despite a tacit acceptance, apparently, of royal supremacy. The leading clergy who, throughout the country, were examined, after the queen's succession, as to their obedience to the royal government of the Church and to the articles of religion which clarified, in outline at least, a Protestant religious policy, on occasion agreed to accept the one but not the other: jurisdiction and doctrine were again distinguished, as earlier, if belatedly, by Gardiner, although refusal of either meant deprivation. Such English examples are instructive, however, chiefly for indicating a difference of outlook between government concerns, common to European states whether Catholic or Protestant, and a more refined awareness of political reality and religious conviction among subjects, in England at least. The Spanish belief that political resistance – even when originally led by native nobles of the Netherlands who were moderate Catholics – sheltered and even promoted heresy became a self-fulfilling view. The evolution of Calvinist leadership in the northern Netherlands, in a struggle for independence from aspects of Spanish rule, was not merely an accident of geographical and military logistics; while for some time Catholics remained prominent in the northern states, despite official policies, not least in commerce, as a reminder that the north had not been the original source of Protestant ideas in the Netherlands. The attempts, in France and the Empire, to guarantee equality of justice for Catholics and Protestants after the sixteenth-century wars of religion, suggested a concept of natural or civic rights which might extend even to 'heretics'. Yet such attempts were to be qualified severely in practice, firstly by Richelieu's reduction of Huguenot privileges previously granted by the Edict of Nantes, and, in the second case, by the strengthening of princely autocracy within the Empire, by the terms of the Peace of Westphalia. The hopes of eirenic thinkers, by the early seventeenth century, were often confined to the world of 'enlightened' believers in mysteries such as those of the Rosicrucians, as both Catholic and Calvinist Churches sought ever more fiercely to define their own orthodoxies, and eradicate all opinion which might seem to suggest the opposing doctrines, Arminian or Jansenist. The supposedly eirenic views of Sarpi, if not of all his correspondents, turned rather on hopes of political and religious intransigence which might counter all accommodation with the power of Habsburg Spain. Only by the end of the seventeenth century were eirenic schemes among rational thinkers more realistic than enthusiastic: and within Catholic Europe doctrinal battles internal to Catholic society, by a paradox, became more purely jurisdictional. In Protestant England, however, after parliamentary reversal of the relation of the monarch's religion to that of the state, by the events of 1688–9 and subsequent adjustment of the royal succession, the removal of political and educational disabilities from Catholics was to prove a much longer affair; so too in Scotland, and even more so in Ireland.

In most of Catholic Europe, the complete replacement of religious by civic tests of allegiance, in such issues, awaited the Revolutionary and Napoleonic era. The Swiss cities and cantons provided an alternative solution, of federal diversity in religion, after the internal religious struggles of the early sixteenth century. But such a solution led to the dangerous possibility of international intervention to alter the local religious dominance: the history of the Grisons and the Catholics of the Valtelline, on the edge of the Swiss world, demonstrated that clearly. Yet the Spanish activity which, from the base of Lombardy, was related to attack in the early seventeenth century on the Protestant population of the Valtelline, did not represent the only approach, even of the Catholic monarchy, to such an anomalous area. The Spanish had reached agreement with the Alpine communities – despite papal and Inquisitorial protests – over the freedom of Protestant merchants to trade in Milan, at the heart of the Borromean Counter-Reformation, provided stringent conditions to guard against all offence to Catholicism were observed.[5] By contrast, the papal and Inquisitorial attempts in Northern Italy, to prevent Venetian diplomatic links with non-Catholic powers, or to prevent Catholics from residing in Protestant areas for purposes of trade were a failure. Even before the later seventeenth century, it was possible for Protestants who were careful in their behaviour to visit Catholic Italy, and not only Venice, but even Milan, as the cases of Coryat, Fynes Moryson and John Evelyn indicate. At that date, however, any intention of leaving Catholic Italy for a Protestant area abroad, in the mind of a native of the peninsula, unless for temporary commercial purposes, was regarded as evidence of heretical leanings: a noble from Vicenza, in Venetian territory, was noted by Church and state alike as entertaining such a plan. But the Republic was careful to limit the pressure which Inquisitorial authority might bring to bear on subjects who were of good birth, or of advanced years, or of simple mind.

The impossibility of separating authority from doctrine in the Church had already been realized in England by Thomas More, in the face of the evolving claims of Henry VIII over the English Church. The reduction of the English universities, following that of the Church, to dependence ultimately on the crown and the governmental watch on lower levels of education, left the later Catholic Recusants, in Elizabeth's reign, with little alternative but to develop educational institutions outside the realm. This education of boys not necessarily destined to become priests at the Catholic schools in exile became a chief preservative of the old religion in English society, despite government attempts to exercise a monopoly in the control of education, as in that of official doctrine in England. The work of the schools abroad was never ended, although boys from Recusant families might also, for a while, attend schools, universities or Inns of Court in England as well. The recourse of female members of English Recusant families to convents abroad also represented a special case of the use of such institutions as social benefits by Catholics still, after the Council of Trent. The English convents abroad were able to provide for those who were unable to marry, but the complications of clandestine or schismatic marriage in England itself made the problem of matrimony greater for English Catholic gentlewomen. In such ways the English Catholic Recusants demonstrated a precocious ability to regard themselves as simultaneously loyal subjects of the crown, despite breach of clear legislation, and as persons withdrawn from the natural jurisdiction of their ruler in the spheres of religion and education. The systematic provision of voluntary, denominational education, specifically designed to resist the ideology supported by the state, was thus, by a paradox, begun by Englishmen in exile. By contrast, the following century in France saw the extension of theoretic claims by a Catholic ruler, which were increasingly self-justifying, and had in the end little relation to religious ideals; the practical powers of Louis XIV over different areas of France was in any case a distinct question. In the attempt of Louis XIV to make supplementary provision for the succession to his throne, as the prospect of a minority and regency became clearer, the questions of natural law and positive law were raised, because of the design to legitimize the royal bastards. Opposition to such a move suggested again the prevalence of a concept of ultimate limitations to the powers of the ruler, even in a kingdom where the independence of the Gallican realm from any superior jurisdiction, that of the pope especially, had been assiduously asserted.

Appeal to some form of recognized natural law, above the interests of individual states, was again implicit in the attempt of Louis XIV to justify to European public opinion his reassertion of the contingent claim to the French throne of the new Bourbon king of Spain, in admittedly difficult circumstances. The fear of the papacy, at the end of the sixteenth century, that a Habsburg succession in France might leave no alternative Catholic power in Europe for support against the dominance of a single House, already predominant in the Italian peninsula itself, was replaced, a century later, by the difficulty of avoiding offence to either the Habsburg or the Bourbon side in the struggle over the Spanish succession. The eventual replacement of the former Spanish Habsburgs by the Austrian Habsburgs in Northern and Southern Italy did nothing to relieve the sensation of the papal states being held between these two blocks. The ultimate succession of a Bourbon line in the south produced no improvement in the jurisdictional conflicts between Naples and Rome, and the escalation of campaigns at Naples designed to reduce the powers and wealth of the Church in the kingdom. The borders of the kingdom still lay near to Rome, on the south and east, as in the days of Philip II; then the massing of troops on the frontier could be used to encourage a conclave to take note of the royal exclusion of candidates for the papal throne unacceptable at the Spanish court, pronounced by Spanish cardinals.[6] The independent policy of the popes of the later sixteenth and early seventeenth century was all the more remarkable, especially when this involved conflict openly with Spain, as in the kingdom of Naples. Even the timing of such moves as the pronouncement of excommunication against Elizabeth of England was a matter for disagreement with Spain; while other, equally counter-productive strokes of papal diplomacy, such as the Interdict against Venice, were decided on by the pope alone. The quality of papal diplomatic policy was not always high, despite the relatively hard-working ability of many cardinal nephews of the period. The policy of the Aldobrandini towards Venice, for example, avoided the open conflict produced by Borghese policy, but not the general worsening of relations with the Republic, despite the reconciliation with the new Bourbon line in France.

Religious division in England, which in fact Tudor and early Stuart rulers proved as unable to prevent as the early Bourbons in France, continued a distinction between Catholic Recusant attitudes and those of Protestant dissidents from the official religious settlement. The eclectic origins of doctrinal Anglicanism allowed the reception of a strand of continental Protestant thought characterized as Adiaphorism. The advantage of this view of human works, if not essential for salvation, as matters of indifference, was that it provided a further argument for the authority of the secular ruler in the ordering of religion within the state. For the very reason that it undermined much opposition to state regulation, however, it could be seen as encouraging Nicodemism, which was denounced by militant Protestants led by Calvin; just as the Catholic priests on mission in England attempted to exclude occasional conformity with state religion from Catholic lay practice. But the question of what was essential for salvation naturally raised again the relationship of doctrine and authority, as from the start of the Lutheran development. In England, Protestant precisians regarded questions of clerical dress and ceremonial rubric as essential, not inessential, and so were led to resistance to state policy. But the Catholic Recusant tradition inevitably regarded works, if commanded by the true Church, as essential for salvation: hence the retention of pre-Tridentine forms of fasting and household devotion, on traditional and new imported models. Despite the practice of occasional conformity, there could properly be no area of things indifferent, in the sphere of religion. The clerical leadership of the English Catholics thus came, also, to consider questions of authority in a more radical light earlier than the biblical literalists among the Puritans. The Jesuit Persons, representing one extreme of clerical attitudes among English Catholics, in his pursuit of a political solution to the fate of the Catholic faith in England, had to address himself not only to the purely 'Recusant' question, of Catholics' refusal to attend the parish churches of their land; but also to the question of the succession, by which the religion of the state might legitimately be altered. His published polemics on these subjects thus complemented his involvement in political plotting. But the confusion of missionary or political purpose could thus never be perfectly resolved, as Jesuit martyrs and their judges equally found.

The case of the English mission, once proscribed in English law for its very existence and purest purpose of reconverting the queen's subjects to the old religion, was an excellent illustration of the impossibility, in Western Europe of the sixteenth or early seventeenth century, of distinguishing perfectly between a Counter-Reformation, of largely political and military nature, and a Catholic missionary endeavour. In the extra-European missionfield of Japan the same problem eventually arose, once secular authority had proscribed the presence and purpose of the Catholic mission there, on the grounds that the missionary presence represented a danger to the independence of the state. The necessary self-help which the English lay community of Catholic Recusants had evolved, both before the arrival of the new missionary priests, and afterwards, in educational organization above all, enabled shelter for priests to survive even the worst periods of persecution. So that the essential provision of the sacraments, for all the jurisdictional anarchy which attended the impossibility of maintaining an episcopal hierarchy comparable to that elsewhere in the post-Tridentine Church, was continued; while the Japanese Catholic community was ultimately deprived for centuries of that essential of Catholic religion. Such questions are obviously distinct from any supposedly anti-Catholic attitude among the erastian rulers and statesmen of eighteenth-century Catholic Europe. The aristocratic anti-Curialism of the Febronian bishops of the Empire, in that century, might in the end seem to verge on contemplation of doctrinal compromise, in an area still divided in religion. But the devout Catholicism of Maria Theresa was merely more demonstrative than the religious beliefs of her son: it has been shown that

Joseph II never indulged in plans to attack Catholicism as such, whatever the views spuriously attributed to him. The authoritarian regimes of the eighteenth century in the Italian and Iberian peninsulas, or in the German and Habsburg lands, were far from ready to accept the attack on religion suggested by a few of the French *philosophes*. There were indeed connections between the traditions of Louvain and Febronian views, as between the declarations of the Synod of Pistoia and the Gallican Articles of France; but the policies of Joseph II were distinct from those of Leopold of Tuscany, before Leopold succeeded to the Austrian throne. In non-Protestant Western Europe, between the Council of Trent and the Napoleonic Captivity, the practical power of the papacy was certainly reduced; but that did not necessarily imply an attack on Catholic belief and practice, any more than it did in early seventeenth-century Venice, or in the accident of the imperial troops' Sack of Rome in 1527.

The problem of distinguishing doctrinal compromise from jurisdictional issues, so evident in the whole evolution of Jansenism within Catholic Europe, was never absent for the papacy of the sixteenth and seventeenth century. The papal condemnation of the proposed oath to be taken by Catholic subjects of James I of England served only to deepen the divisions within the English Catholic community. In the later sixteenth century, the attempts of Gregory XIII to bring some clarification to the confused conditions in the Scandinavian kingdoms turned in the end on proposals made, for his realm, by John III of Sweden. An oath of allegiance to be taken to the king, by bishops who could be recognised as orthodox at Rome, was not ruled out by the papacy. But marriage to be allowed for the secular clergy, liturgical use of the vernacular, and communion of the laity in two kinds were as impossible to concede as, ultimately, in the German lands, because of the doctrinal implications which such strictly disciplinary concessions had inevitably acquired. Such considerations overrode any further issues, such as the problem of former Church lands, which arose equally in England and the Empire. The failure of negotiations with the Swedish king raised for Catholic missionary priests the same problems as faced those in England, of clandestine activity but eventual acknowledgement of their status and purpose. But, by contrast, tensions between papal and secular claims to authority remained precise in detail but vaguer in theoretical outline, within the Catholic world in and after the Counter-Reformation. Sarpi's use of the caesaro-papist tradition of the Byzantine emperors was limited to the assertion of the supreme headship of the Venetian Republic over its Greek subjects, in the Venetian Mediterranean empire; though, in practice, after the Peace of Westphalia, the papacy was increasingly disregarded as a political force in Europe, even where the succession to areas over which it claimed suzerainty, Naples and Sicily, was at stake.[7] The contrast of Orthodox Russia is also suggested, by the abolition, under Peter the Great, of the Moscow patriarchate, and the substitution of a Holy Synod at the head of the Church, under government control. Such change, however, was too late to prevent the enthusiasm of the Old Believers – in their reaction to the ecclesiastical reforms of the patriarch Nikon – from producing schism. The direction of religious practice and the problem of authority in the Church could not be separated in Russia, any more than in Western Europe.

In the West a reliance on Old Testament support for the powers of the ruler immediately under God marked Protestant rather than Catholic political theory, however, until the mid-seventeenth century. The decisive shift in the attitude of Henry VIII towards papal authority over matrimonial questions came over the issue of the absolute impediment of scripture, by the word of the Old Testament, which the king persuaded himself it was beyond papal power to remove, against marriages such as his own with his deceased brother's wife, Catharine of Aragon. Such an attitude was fundamentally different from the long-standing involvement of rulers in Christian Spain in religious questions, even in the Visigothic Councils which treated matters as much doctrinal as disciplinary, under royal leadership. The effect of the Reconquest certainly strengthened royal authority in ecclesiastical affairs in the Iberian peninsula, not only in the special privileges involved in the kingdom of Granada, or the genesis of the Crown Inquisition, but in the direction of monastic reform and improvement of clerical education undertaken by Cisneros and other clerical servants of the crown, acting at once by royal and papal authority. The retirement of the Emperor Charles V, after his abdication, to the Spanish monastery of Juste, and the design by Philip II of the Escorial as a royal convent which might house the court, demonstrate the continuing regard in Spain for the traditional doctrines of the Church, whatever the practical limitations imposed on papal power within the Iberian kingdoms. From his youth, Charles had been educated by Christian humanists in the hope of a reform Council of the Church, to do what the Fifth Lateran Council had so failed to do effectively. But although this hope led to an initial misunderstanding of Luther's demand for a free Council, and to the unrealistic imperial view that concessions such as communion for the laity in both kinds might reunite German Christians, Charles never seriously considered an assault on the office and authority of the papacy as such. His own relationship with Rome was entirely different from the later posture of Napoleon, crowning himself emperor in the presence of an effectively captive pope. The views of Charles v about the needs of Christendom, in the aftermath of the final loss of the Eastern Christian empire, were more realistic in considering the necessity of both papal and Conciliar authority.

Such problems as the relations of bishops and regulars were not new in the Western late Medieval Church, but went back to the earliest days of Eastern monasticism, and the involvement of bishops and monks in the doctrinal controversies of the East, where imperial authority was exerted over such issues as the veneration of sacred images, or the titles of the Mother of God. In the West, in the fifteenth century, reform Councils had proved ultimately impotent, in the reaction of papal authority in alliance with secular rulers. The Conciliar ideal after Trent could only remain suspect, as well as unrealistic. Saint Cyran was notorious for his criticism of Tridentine decisions, even in France, where the disciplinary decrees remained in contest. The early eighteenth-century appeal of French prelates and clergy against papal condemnation of Jansenism represented a Gallican assertion of the superiority of General Councils, but was ineffective in its results. There was an obvious antiquarianism, in the Jansenist search for Augustinian Christian practice – as well as in the historical work of Tillemont, an associate of Port-Royal – just as in the whole programme of Gallicanism. As a leader of the *politiques*, the earlier historian de Thou shared Sarpi's opposition to the results of the Council of Trent, which had in the end produced some reforms, by the difficult assimilation of papal, episcopal and secular authority. The avowedly mystical nature of Quietism in the later seventeenth century, by contrast, whether in the French circles of Mme Guyon and Fénelon, or in the Italian centres of such ideas, dependent, like Queen Christina in Rome, on Molinos, or independent of him, was innocent of any intentional challenge to constituted authority in one sense; though the implications of its reliance on personal experience as opposed to hierarchical ministration obviously led to its condemnation. Italian Quietism in places represented the anti-Jesuit rivalry of secular and regular clergy, despite the antagonism between Jansenists and Quietists in France.

The relations between states were even less susceptible to papal direction than those between orders and movements within the Catholic Church. The papal award of new territories to be discovered to the Iberian powers was effectively disregarded, not only by

English and Dutch intervention in America and the Far East, but by the entry of Catholic France into colonial rivalry. The identity of national and religious sentiment begun, in a way, in Marian England as a result of opposition to the Spanish marriage, was not immediately advanced at Elizabeth's accession. For the contingencies of international relations led Spain at first to court the favour of England, as opposed to that of France; and the old Franco-Scottish danger remained a real alternative for Catholic hopes of a change of ruler and religion in England, until the execution of Mary Queen of Scots. The papal attempt to prevent Venetian recognition of Henri of Navarre as legitimate king of France, after his conversion to Catholicism, but before his reconciliation with Rome, showed the difficulty of avoiding an alliance between the independent Catholicism of the Republic and that of Gallican France.[8] Papal disapproval of diplomatic contacts between Venice and Protestant England was equally unavailing; while during the Interdict, other Catholic states proved reluctant to exclude Venetian representatives from the ceremonies of court chapels.[9] The eternal questions of diplomatic precedence, not least between France and Spain, threatened at all times: at the Council of Trent, as much as at the papal court. The sensitivity of lesser states, the Republic of Venice or the grand-duchy of Tuscany, was acute, not least in questions of material interest, like the nomination of bishops. After the Council of Trent the papacy experienced immediately and continually the concern of Venice that the privileges still maintained, despite Conciliar decrees, by Spain and France were to be denied to the Republic.

Diplomatic contacts which crossed denominational divisions could nevertheless hold out some hope of the amelioration of the lot of Catholics under Protestant rule. Negotiations over the proposed marriage of Charles, heir to the English throne, and the Spanish Infanta, in the reign of James I, could not avoid the subject. The court of Charles's eventual queen, Henrietta Maria of France, provided marginal encouragement to Catholics within the royal circuit; but the anti-Spanish interests of France also brought Puritan sympathizers, from among the peers, during Charles's years of rule without parliament, to pay court to a queen later denounced by parliamentary supporters as a source of evil advice to the king. In exile, the queen's failure to interest Catholic rulers in the fate of a monarch who was not, in the end, of their faith, produced her strengthened conviction that only a Catholic could hope successfully to defend his throne and an episcopal Church against attack. Her views were resisted by her son, until his restoration as Charles II, already crowned in Scotland by Presbyterian rites. But both he and his brother, in the case of the latter's second marriage, took wives from ruling houses which were Catholic, though not Spanish. The relations of the later Stuarts with Catholic France, however, were not productive of any permanent change in the religious allegiance of England, nor of any permanent improvement in the conditions of the English Catholics. The anti-popery politics of later Stuart England did not arise from any growth in the size or strength of the Catholic community, which remained a divided movement, further enfeebled by the fiscal policies of the Interregnum.

Formal diplomacy, in sixteenth- and seventeenth-century Europe, often seemed less productive than espionage; and the Venetian Republic markedly developed its own secret service within the organs of government themselves, the Inquisitors of State, even after an apparent reduction of the role of the Council of Ten and its Heads, in the constitution.[10] The dangers of such developments were already clear in the reign of Philip II, with the flight of the royal confidential servant, Pérez, to England – a fruitful source of material to feed anti-Spanish feeling.[11] The self-defence attempted in Aragon by Pérez had involved local opposition to the overriding authority of the crown Inquisition; but Aragonese liberties were in the end reduced by Philip. Yet the state in Catholic Europe continued to assert its rights over the individual liberty of subjects more generally: Richelieu's campaign against duels was not simply the result of the cardinal's response to the Tridentine condemnation of them. In the literature of the Spanish Golden Age, the conflict of external law and religious restraints with the demands of personal honour was dramatized; but in France the demands of personal conscience exemplified in Racine's plays reflected rather a Jansenist resistance to royal policy. The failure of Spanish hostilities against Elizabethan England, reflected in the Jacobean peace of 1604, left Ireland, the scene of Spanish action at the very end of the queen's reign, to the continued English policy of Protestant settlement as a means of subduing native Catholic resistance; this was reinforced, under James VI and I, by Presbyterian plantation of Ulster from Scotland. The later seventeenth-century intervention in Ireland by James II, supported by Catholic France against the new ruler of the English and the Dutch, William of Orange, was equally a failure, in terms of relieving the pressure of Protestant government on the Catholic society of Ireland, which had already suffered the heavier hand of Cromwell, during the union of the kingdoms without a king. The Iberian kingdoms' claims to their overseas empires were defended by royal lawyers on grounds

distinct from the papal award of new territories. The fortunes of
Catholic rule were decided elsewhere in practice equally without
reference to Rome. At the end of the sixteenth century the duke of
Savoy took Saluzzo from French possession, which was to lead to
the persecution of Calvinists there who had benefited from French
support and protection. But Savoy could never be entirely free of
competing pressure applied by France and by Spain, intent on control of the land route from Genoa to the Franche Comté, throughout
the seventeenth century; even if that did not alter subsequent ducal
persecution of the Piedmontese Waldensian Protestants.

The eradication of Protestantism in the Austrian lands of the
Tyrol, Styria, Carinthia and Carniola, depended on the policies of
individual archdukes and their political strength at the end of the
sixteenth century, though Cardinal Khlesl led the restoration of
Catholicism in Austria proper, in the bishoprics of Passau and
Vienna. The imperial lands of Germany in the second half of the
sixteenth century, between the Peace of Augsburg and the outbreak
of the Thirty Years War, were confused by the dynastic politics of
prince-bishops, elected by mercenary chapters, and contending with
divisions in religion among canons, city authorities, and subjects.
The elective monarchy of Poland might remain in Catholic hands,
during the same period, but the international considerations of policy
which led to the election of Henri of Valois, subsequently king of
France, as a counterbalance to Habsburg pressures, were not calcu-
lated to advance the cause of Catholicism specifically. The internal
political importance of the upper clergy, the aristocratic prelates
headed by the primate, allowed them to begin the implementation of
Tridentine reforms, however. But the Uniate status accepted by
many of the Eastern-rite Christians of the kingdom, in 1596, was not
a complete Roman triumph: a minority of Orthodox believers refused
obedience to Rome, seeking rather the protection of Protestant
princes in Poland. Italian influence, not least Venetian, in Poland
encouraged nevertheless the early opera of the royal court, and its
pious works, symptomatic of Counter-Reformation devotion, as in
*The Story of Joseph*. But royal courts, as with that of Henri III in
France, were never wholly satisfactory as instruments for the promotion of Catholicism, for all the splendours of the Bavarian ducal
court and the music which Lassus composed for its chapel. The
aura of orthodox piety fostered at the French court by Louis XIV in
old age, under the influence of Mme de Maintenon, gave way, by
a natural reaction, to the licence of the Regency, the cynicism of
Dubois; and the political manœuvrings of Fleury, in international

relations as in the approach to internal divisions within French
Catholicism, recalled those of Mazarin, the earlier cardinal statesman. Political considerations had already complicated the relations
between early Bourbon France and Jacobean England, for, despite
common cause made on occasion, the compositions issued in the
name of King James opposed the views not only of Cardinal Bellarmine, but also of Cardinal du Perron. The French cardinal acted as
intermediary between Henri of France and Rome; as Cardinal Joy-
euse later did between Venice and Rome, at the end of the Interdict.

Justification of royal power by image and masque nevertheless
crossed the lines of religious division. The terms and symbols in
which Elizabeth of England was celebrated as Astraea were akin to
those by which Henri IV was acclaimed as the Gallic Hercules and,
later, as Father of his Country. The theoretical celebration of absolutism by French writers, such as Le Bret, du Chesne and Loyseau,
went beyond the literary if not the dramatic bounds of Stuart claims.
But Charles I commissioned Rubens to depict on the ceiling of the
new Banqueting House of Inigo Jones, at Whitehall, the apotheosis
of his father, James; and the thaumaturgic touch of English monarchs
was continued throughout the Stuart period. The eventual interjec-
tion of the House of Orange, in the Stuart succession, was ironic not
only because of the family relationship between the two houses, but
because the fortunes of the princes of Orange, within the Dutch
Netherlands, had been supported by the strict Calvinists, triumphant
at all moments of crisis since the Synod of Dort; while the disciplinary, if not equally the doctrinal, aspects of anti-Arminianism had
caused concern to the first two Stuart kings of England. Religious
ideals could not be entirely separated from political conclusions at
any time in the seventeenth century. Even the Jewish diaspora was
affected by the call of the 'Mystical Messiah', Sabbatai Zevi, for a
return to the Holy Land. The effective pragmatism of Richelieu's
*Political Testament* nevertheless included claims for the moral
character of sound government. The continued search of the papacy
for independence within Catholic Europe led to the difficulties encountered by the Barberini pope, Urban VIII, in the mid-seventeenth
century, not only in the exhaustion of papal finances, further depleted
by the patronage of the arts on a grandiose scale in Rome itself, but
in the apparent necessity of favouring French aspirations as a
counterbalance to Habsburg dominance. The condemnation of the
terms of the Peace of Westphalia by his successor, Innocent X, included the resentment of the pope at the imperial addition of a new
elector to the imperial college which elected the emperor, without

reference to Rome; although the retention of a Bavarian electorate favoured a Catholic majority in the imperial college, and rewarded a Catholic state which for periods of the Thirty Years War had in fact been the ally of France.

Habsburg power, on occasion at least, continued to promote the restoration of Catholicism, in Transylvania at the very end of the seventeenth century, as in Moravia and Silesia earlier. But within the Polish kingdom, in the first half of the century, the Orthodox who resisted union with Rome looked to Russian protection, in their search for perpetuation of their own hierarchy. In the Ottoman Mediterranean empire, on the other hand, the gradual and spasmodic decline of Venetian power, and the advent of French interests in the Eastern Mediterranean, allowed the papacy to assert the authority of the Congregation of the Propaganda in the area, despite Venetian protests that this sphere of influence could not be regarded as being *in partibus infidelium*.[12] But the work of Capuchins and Jesuits, supported by France and the Austrian Habsburgs, faced antagonism from the Orthodox Greek Christians, encouraged by the representatives of Protestant powers, which led to the confused doctrinal positions of the Patriarch Lukaris. The Catholic clergy of Crete were to demonstrate brave commitment to the defence of the island against the Turks, but they could not prevent the final Islamic conquest. Crete, as well as other islands, like Chios, were lost to Christian Europe. In Spain itself, the change of ruling house, after the long war of the Spanish Succession, did not at first mean a challenge to Catholicism or the Church, at the beginning of the eighteenth century; though the lingering reign of Charles II, the last Habsburg ruler, had been marked by some limitation of ecclesiastical power, after the failure of proposed reforms under Philip IV. The new Bourbon court was perhaps no more free than that of the long-suffering Charles from the intrigues of other Catholic states and their representatives. But the interlude of Cardinal Alberoni's power led to the brief prospect of Hispano-Italian dominance in the Western Mediterranean. Jesuit influence in Venetian territory, on the other hand, was only restored with the belated readmission of the Society to Republican dominions in 1657.

In the Dutch Netherlands, Catholic emancipation in the eastern provinces was aided, not by Spanish power, but by the invasion of Louis XIV in 1672, supported by the North German prince-bishops. The struggle of continental land-powers and maritime states in the European and colonial wars from that time onwards had its effect on Catholic fortunes within Europe and overseas alike. In the wake of the accession of William of Orange to the English throne, the Catholic enclave of Maryland, in North America, was brought under royal control, as opposed to the family possession of the Baltimores; and while the residual political powers of Anglican bishops, in the House of Lords if not otherwise, remained in England, episcopacy was officially abandoned in Protestant Scotland. Scotland indeed proved a last retreat for non-Jurors, after the effective lapse of the clergy's own assembly, Convocation, in eighteenth-century England. In Portugal, after the restoration of an independent line, the native hierarchy achieved prominence, especially while Rome delayed diplomatic recognition. In the later seventeenth and in the eighteenth century, the relative isolation of late Habsburg and early Bourbon Spain did not prevent the Church feeling the repercussions of Quietism; while Jansenism was known even among the Catholics of the peninsula.

The evolution of the papal court itself was naturally fundamental to the development of Catholic Europe. This was especially true after the Council of Trent, with the effective reduction of the independent power of cardinals, even in the formulation of diplomatic policy, despite the continued nomination of cardinals by rulers. The choice of a pope at conclaves thus became more important than ever, as did the role of the chief ministers of the popes, the cardinal nephews, subsequently acknowledged as cardinal secretaries of state. The influence of Charles Borromeo, as papal nephew, on the proceedings of the final stages of the Council of Trent was important, for encouraging the presiding legates in their conclusion of business. The later example of Paul V in deciding on his action with respect to Venice against the moderating advice of cardinals was less happy. The great power exerted by Charles Borromeo, subsequently archbishop of Milan and legate in Italy, under his uncle, Pius IV, marked the 'new' nepotism of able and conscientious ecclesiastics which contrasted with the 'old' nepotism which had disgraced the pontificate of Caraffa. Borromeo had undergone a personal conversion of life, to an extreme asceticism, despite residence in Rome; while Paleotti was similarly persuaded of the new ideals of episcopal reform set forth at Trent, despite having attended the Council to represent the vested interests of the Roman Curia. Charles Borromeo was hardly less powerful under his uncle's successor, Pius V, since observers concluded that the new pope wished to be thought as pure a guardian of reform as his predecessor.[13] The pope's zeal against heresy was equally noted by contemporaries, but the departure from Rome of Borromeo, to reside in his archiepiscopal see of Milan, left the direction of papal policy for a while in a state of relative uncertainty. The consolidation of hierarchical authority in the post-Tridentine Church was nevertheless clearly demonstrated by Gregory XIII, pope from 1572, by his publication of the code of canon law in 1582. Spanish expectations of his successor, Sixtus V, were disappointed, since his supposedly pro-Spanish leanings did not preclude his vigorous defence of the independence of the Church, not least in the kingdom of Naples. His past career as a friar placed him among the most zealous in the watch for heresy, on the other hand. The brief pontificate of Gregory XIV, in which his nephews controlled policy, represented the weakest point in papal resistance to Spanish pressure, before the diplomatic volte-face of Clement VIII.

Sfondrato had pastoral experience as bishop of Cremona, and virtual leader of the Milanese ecclesiastical province, after the death of Charles Borromeo in 1584, in the attempt to maintain the high standards of episcopal reform begun under the archbishop of Milan, in the face of secular opposition.[14] But his concessions as pope to the demands of secular powers were as evident in Northern Italy as in his support for the League in France. With the arrival of Aldobrandini on the papal throne, from 1592, decisive diplomatic ability was evident, in the pope himself, if less so among his competing nephews. His experience of the Nunciature in Poland was crowned by the achievement of the Union, during his pontificate, with Eastern-rite Christians in that kingdom. Although the final persuasion to reconcile Henri of Navarre to the Church was only achieved by the serious pressure brought to bear by Baronius and others in the circle of the Roman Oratory, the potential freedom from Spanish dominance thereby achieved was Clement's reward; even if the initial result was the increased obstinacy of Spain in all jurisdictional negotiations, in response to what was considered papal injustice to the rightful claims of Spain to the French throne.[15] The attempts of Clement VIII to settle the doctrinal controversy *de Auxiliis*, begun in Spain, were less successful in the event, as were those of Paul V. Under his government, Scipio Borghese's search for funds to support his art patronage represented a retreat to something more like the 'old' nepotism. By contrast, the influence of the able Cardinal Ludovisi, during the brief pontificate of his uncle as Gregory XV, revived the attempt to defend the interests of ecclesiastical independence against political, not least Spanish pressure. The creation during the pontificate of the Congregation of the Propaganda, as an instrument to promote missions under papal not Iberian control, was a vital extension of this policy. The policy of Urban VIII in the same direction of securing papal independence, during the Thirty Years War, was less successful; and it was not accidental that after the pope's death his nephews fled to France. The Barberini period of power in Rome had not been one only of display and the celebration of papal authority, however, for one nephew, though a cardinal, was a member of the austere Capuchins. The ability of Clement VIII was less certainly shown in the doctrinal issues involved in condemnation of the *Augustinus* of Jansenius. The subsequent involvement of the Pamfili pope, Innocent X, in the question was equally unhappy; while his own independence was in question, as a result of the dominance of his sister-in-law. The apparent impotence of the papacy, demonstrated by his condemnation of the terms of the Peace of Westphalia, was counterbalanced, to a degree at least, by the able energy shown by his successor, Alexander VII, who had experienced the Westphalia negotiations as papal representative. But the new danger of French dominance, already apparent under the Barberini, was clear from the resentment of Mazarin at Gondi's reception at Rome, and the humiliation exacted from the pope by Louis XIV at the start of his personal rule.

In the subsequent deterioration of relations between the papacy and the French king, it was not unnatural that Louis XIV should regard Clement X and his nephew, Cardinal Altieri, as pro-Spanish. Papal independence was pursued by Innocent XI, who succeeded in 1676, by means of restoring papal finance, which involved an abandonment of the nepotism of some preceding pontificates. The further decline of relations with France was nevertheless marked by the interdict of the French church in Rome, San Luigi, and the French attack on Avignon. The danger of a revival of Richelieu's dream of a patriarchate of the Gauls, independent in effect of Rome, also threatened; while the Franco-papal contest over the election of the archbishop of Cologne was not without repercussions on Orange's plans to invade England. French hopes of a more concessionary attitude from Cardinal Pignatelli, elected pope in 1691, as Innocent XII, were only moderately fulfilled. More useful was the support of the Albani pope, Clement XI, in the war of Spanish Succession, until military and political pressure forced the reversal of papal policy, in favour of the Habsburgs. The eventual gain, from the Peace of Utrecht and its subsequent revisions, of the kingdom of Sardinia by Piedmont, paved the way for the later rise of the Savoyard monarchy as the power which could claim a leading role in the destiny of the Italian peninsula, at the expense of papal temporal power. Parma and Piacenza, in the early eighteenth century, were equally disposed of, already, without reference to the claims of papal suzerainty, after the period of power of Cardinal Alberoni, a Piacentine. In the growing threat from Bourbon attacks on the rights of the Church in Spain and Naples, Benedict XIV was able to reach some agreement by concessions made in 1753 to Spain, and similar concordats were made with Portugal and Savoy, while the fiscal immunity of the clergy in the kingdom of Naples was reduced.

Such concessions, however, were not sufficient to prevent papal acquiescence, in the pontificate of Clement XIV, in the demands of Catholic rulers for the suppression of the Society of Jesus. The impotence of his predecessor, Clement XIII, in the face of the Jesuits' expulsion from Catholic states had arguably left little alternative. In Portugal the earlier European accusations of Jesuit complicity in attempted regicide were revived, and the issue raised of Jesuit involvement in commercial profit and loss, at stake too in France. The Spanish accusation of Jesuit treasonable conspiracy produced the suppression of the Society not only in Spain but at Naples and Parma too; and Malta followed suit. Bourbon solidarity, and the revival of the threat to Avignon, defeated the papacy's last attempt at resistance, in the case of Parma. This attempt, like the much more long-standing contest in Catholic Europe, over the post-Tridentine form of the bull *In Coena Domini*, had to be abandoned at the beginning of Clement XIV's pontificate. But in the pope's mind, sympathy with anti-Jesuit theological traditions, and the persistent criticisms by rival orders of the Society's missionary activities, contributed to political pressure in determining the fate of the Jesuits. While the struggle of Rome with the Bourbons, dating from the personal rule of Louis XIV rather than from the succession of Henri IV, had in a sense concluded with the defeat of papal independence by Catholic erastianism, the papacy, after the suppression of the Society in 1773, still had to face the intransigence of Habsburg power in the person of Joseph II. The education of Joseph had been entrusted by the devout Maria Theresa to tutors who were chosen so as to temper Catholic piety by a just appreciation of secular rights. The jurisdictional implications of late Jansenism in the Austrian lands were clear, not least with regard to the position of bishops and regulars, at issue in Catholic Europe and overseas ever since the Council of Trent.

Pius VI, on the eve of the Revolution, faced the independent actions against papal power of Joseph, of Leopold of Tuscany, and of the prince-bishops of the Empire. The relative weakness of Clement XIII, the Venetian Cardinal Rezzonico, allowed him little gain from the improved relations of Rome with his native Republic, where the established tradition of Catholic erastianism had produced new encroachments on ecclesiastical immunities under Benedict XIV. For the Braschi family of Pius VI was reserved the final honour of erecting the last papal family palace in Rome. The decline of papal political power outside the city was however clear by the early eighteenth century. While the Tridentine papacy had sent Cardinal Morone to settle the dangerous internal unrest at Genoa, in the interests of maintaining the stability of the Italian peninsula in divided Europe,[16] the attempt of the over-active Cardinal Alberoni to take the Republic of San Marino for the papal states, in 1739, was a failure. The eighteenth-century papacy suffered from the dominance of the Bourbons as much as the late sixteenth-century popes had experienced Spanish Habsburg pressure. Charles III of Spain was confirmed in his regalist policies by his previous experience as ruler of Naples, where the regalist tradition was ancient and still active in the eighteenth century. The missionary work of the Church overseas suffered from the expulsion of the Jesuits from all the territories of the Spanish crown. Even the Spanish Inquisition had its power reduced by Charles III. The inevitable failure of the Council of Trent to change the system of episcopal appointments in the major Catholic states of Europe led to the impotence of the papacy in the face of secular opposition, just as much as at the time of French episcopal compliance in the Gallican Assembly of Louis XIV. The eventual sympathy of many of the lower clergy of France with the early stages of revolutionary activity by the representatives of the Third Estate, on the other hand, represents a Richerist revenge on the economic exploitation which they had long experienced at the hands of the upper clergy and of monastic institutions.

In eighteenth-century Spain, the Benedictine Feijoo, from Galicia, published works designed to spread the ideas of the enlightenment in a form compatible with Catholicism. But in Maria Theresa's Austrian lands active policy against the Jews was revived, as under earlier Austrian rulers; while in the prince-archbishopric of Salzburg, anti-Protestant policy was reactivated in the early eighteenth century. Joseph II and Kaunitz may not have considered seriously the plan for the dismemberment of the Venetian state, but in the Austrian lands the papal suppression of the Jesuits took effect under Maria Theresa: the Venetian Republic was to outlive the Society, in its first period of existence, but not for long. The reduction of the numbers and property of the regular orders, and the subjection of regulars to episcopal authority, in Joseph's ecclesiastical changes, were a final, pre-Revolutionary stage in the conflict of bishops and regulars in post-Tridentine Catholic Europe. The creation of new dioceses in the Austrian lands, as well as the redrawing of parochial boundaries, were at once a response to episcopal demands, in eighteenth-century Jansenism, for the effective realization of episcopal authority in the Church, and a revival of the original aims of the Council of Trent itself to promote diocesan and parochial reform. The last pre-Revolutionary attempts at reform of Catholic practice were made in the name of an Austrian emperor: at the end of a programme originally adopted by the papacy, with initial seriousness, in the pontificate of Hadrian VI, tutor of the Emperor Charles V. For if Hadrian's short pontificate saw little achieved by way of practical reform, the pope's commitment was more certain than that of Paul III, who received the celebrated plan of the reforming cardinals and prelates *de emendanda Ecclesia*, but was reduced to pursuing papal political independence by means of promoting the advantage of the Farnese family.

The Sack of Rome did more than any programme of reform to introduce prelates in Italy to the realities of episcopal residence and the problems of Church government. But despite the dispersal of previous residents at the Curia which the Sack produced, the implementation of the decrees of the Council of Trent depended from the first not only on episcopal action but also on papal support. From the time of the Council itself the dominance of the Italian peninsula by foreign powers, originally the Habsburgs of Spain, was established: so that even the restoration of Medici rule in Florence and the alliance of Medici and papal policy could not alter the effects of Spanish pressure, represented also by the Spanish control of bases on the Tuscan coast; while the results of this in turn made Venice the more suspicious of papal policy. The later Medici might carefully control university education in the grand-duchy, but the post-Tridentine papacy never had uncontested control over the Western Church, in the face of opposition from secular rulers of Catholic states. Even the intense zeal of the aged Caraffa pope, Paul IV, for ecclesiastical reform was compromised in fact by his breach with the Spanish rulers of his native Naples. The search of the papacy for political independence by means of territorial extension or military action was to remain illusory from the sixteenth century until the French Revolution, and indeed beyond, to the loss of the papal states at the time of the declaration of papal infallibility. The lack of papal freedom from political constraint nevertheless had its effect on religious developments, as in the results of the inability of Clement VII to annul the marriage of Henry VIII with Catharine of Aragon, given his own relations with the Emperor Charles V. Whereas the fiscal concessions made by Hadrian VI to the dukes of Bavaria led the way to the promotion of the Catholic interest in the duchy and more widely in the German lands thereafter, independently of imperial policy, under ducal authority. The creation of the Inquisition in Portugal, which was allegedly designed to counter the Judaizing tendencies of New Christians, preserved Catholic orthodoxy in the kingdom, in the same way, but was the result of the fiscal needs of the crown, rather than of papal concern for any danger to the faith there. Above all, the suppression of any serious danger of revolt as a result of the radical reformers' millenarianism in sixteenth-century Western Europe was the result of firm action by Catholic rulers and magisterial Protestants alike. The imperial coronation of Charles V by Clement VII, in 1530, in the papal city of Bologna, and in the Italian peninsula over which the long medieval contests of Guelf and Ghibelline, representing the claims of papacy and emperors to leadership and dominance of the Italian states, had been fought, marked in fact the end of any decisive power, of either authority, in the determination of the religious allegiance of the states of Western Christendom. The papal states were enlarged under Clement VIII, by the incorporation of Ferrara, with French support; and the last successful extension of temporal rule, to include Urbino, under Urban VIII, was followed by the failure to take Castro at the end of his pontificate. Even the papal grant of the grand-ducal title to the restored Medici in Tuscany, to reinforce the working alliance of Florence and Rome against foreign dominance, proved little more than the theoretical freedom of the papacy after Trent from the last vestiges of imperial authority in Italy.[17]

Although the imperial claims of the Habsburgs in Italy lasted into the eighteenth century, and Giannone found shelter at the imperial court, the role of the Habsburgs in promoting the Counter-Reformation within the Holy Roman Empire as a whole was limited. Until the reign of Maria Theresa, the Habsburg emperors continued to exert some theoretical powers of censorship within the Empire, exercised on behalf of the Roman religion; though the operation of any Index of prohibited books within German lands was more practically determined by local ecclesiastical and secular authority, often, of course, one and the same. More generally, imperial authority continued to encourage Catholic states and the conversion of rulers, from the Northern neighbour of Poland, from an early date, to the later conversion of Augustus the Strong, which fitted the Elector of Saxony to become king of Poland. This process was not interrupted by the terms of the Peace of Westphalia, but continued, in a sense, until the invasion of Silesia by Frederick the Great. Despite the failure of the grandiose plans for religious reconciliation, devised by the Habsburg clerical servant, friar and bishop, Rojas y Spinola, in concert with Leibniz, even North German states continued to harbour enclaves of Catholicism. Habsburg encouragement of such survivals was not defeated by the French courting of German princes after 1648, for even the Palatinate was eventually provided with a Catholic Elector, in the second half of the seventeenth century, under imperial aegis; while some of the Winter Queen's children ended their lives as Catholics. The French interest in the great electoral sees of the Rhine frontier, in the same period, was in conflict with imperial intervention in elections to bishoprics within the Empire. But the interests of Catholicism were rather protected by the alternative axis of France and Bavaria. Cologne was held by Wittelsbach prelates from the late sixteenth to the eighteenth century. The independence of Mainz, after the Peace of Westphalia under the electoral archbishop, von Schönborn, resisted Habsburg influence, but confirmed Catholicism in the first see of the Empire. But further south, the family status and possessions of prince-archbishops of Salzburg, in the seventeenth and eighteenth centuries, linked them to the surrounding Habsburg territories, from Marcus Sitticus von Hohenems II, through Paris Lodron, Graf von Thun, to Mozart's sometime master, Colloredo.

The Counter-Reformation in the personal territories of the Habsburgs, by contrast, was promoted more by the dynasty than by bishops. Indeed it has recently been argued that the consolidation of a Habsburg monarchy, in the Austrian lands and related kingdoms, was substantially based on the reassertion of Catholicism, beginning from the end of the sixteenth century, and not merely after 1648. The possible activity of post-Tridentine bishops in much of this area was certainly limited. In the Austrian provinces and Tyrol, many of the diocesans were bishops of extraneous sees, lying beyond the confines of the Habsburg holdings. In Hungary, until the collapse of Turkish rule and Habsburg exploitation of this, from the later seventeenth century, many of the bishops were necessarily titular, their sees still lying *in partibus infidelium*. The prolonged independence of Transylvania prevented the establishment of a resident episcopate. Only in Bohemia and Moravia was the episcopate arguably more important in the reassertion of Catholicism, during the seventeenth century, and even there, in the case of Olomouc in Moravia, Habsburg prelates themselves occupied the sees in the mid-century. The religious orders, by contrast, provided a force for the re-establishment of Catholicism which overrode the divisions of the Habsburgs' personal territories. This was true not only of the highly centralized Society of Jesus, but also of the provincial organization of older orders, like the Premonstratensians, or of orders bridging the traditional and the new, like the Capuchins. The rivalry of older orders, in the face of Jesuit competition, not least in educational enterprise, could on occasion support the independence of prelates, as in the archbishopric of Prague in the Catholic restoration after the Battle of the White Mountain. But the leader of the Hungarian Counter-Reformation, Pázmány, rose to be cardinal and archbishop from within the Society of Jesus. The triumphant rebuilding and redecoration of monasteries in the Baroque style, within the Danubian monarchy, included the provision of imperial halls, designed for the reception of the ruler; just as the earliest entry of the young Mozart to Italian musical circles was supported by the close links between the monarch and the Augustinian order. By contrast, despite the presence of papal Nuncios at Vienna, the specifically Roman authority of the Inquisition or Index was little felt within the monarchy. There was thus some parallel to the early influence of the Jesuit Canisius on the Counter-Reformation in Bavaria and beyond, followed by the later protest of German bishops at the stationing of a papal Nuncio at the Bavarian court.

Even the rivalry of religious orders, old and new, Jesuits and Capuchins, could not weaken the effect of renewed Catholic devotion in promoting some sense of unity within the Habsburg monarchy. This was obviously true of Marian devotion, as the seventeenth century saw the revival of pilgrimage churches and erection of monuments throughout the Habsburg lands. But it was also true of the crowning symbol of the Trinity, mysteriously surmounting both high altars and imperial columns; and also of the cult of St Joseph, fostered in the Counter-Reformation as patron of the Church Militant. While the victorious statue of the Child Jesus, protecting Catholicism at Prague, was of Spanish origin, Bohemia exported the cult of certain other saints to the rest of the monarchy. Devotion to St Vitus, as to St Norbert, was characteristic of Baroque piety in Tyrol, as much as in Bohemia itself; and the fame of St Florian was similarly spread from the Danube to the Inn. Saint Stephen contributed to the delicate relationship between Hungary and the Austrian monarchy; but the Bohemian re-establishment of Catholicism eventually produced the triumphant figure of St John Nepomuk, martyr for the priestly privilege in the sacrament of confession, in artistic symbolism if more contestedly in historical fact. The pervasive presence of Nepomuk, in painting and sculpture, carried the Counter-Reformation into the eighteenth century, as his canonization spread his cult from Prague to remote Tyrolean valleys. The continued stress, in the Habsburg monarchy, on the physical presence and power of the saints, through their relics, possibly as a counter to popular magic and charms, was part of a more general enthusiasm, in the South German world, for the corporal body of the saints in the Baroque age. In many churches rebuilt or redecorated in the Baroque or Rococo style, place of honour under side-altars was reserved for the entire skeletons of saints, joyfully received from the Roman catacombs where the supply of presumed saints or martyrs seemed limitless, as exploration continued. The influence of Rome was, in this way at least, exerted in the South German Counter-Reformation, even if the subterranean studies of the Jesuit Kircher – resident in Rome but patronized by the Habsburgs – suggested a more hermetic than truly archaeological interpretation of antiquity and Christian revelation.

The consolidation of an indisputably Catholic monarchy in the Habsburg lands, however, was also dependent on more obviously human support. The profuse conversions of nobles, from families which had adopted varieties of Protestantism, were the crucial decisions in each province and kingdom, so that the reidentification of nobility and Catholicism, to a very large degree, during the seventeenth century, corresponded to a similar process in France. In both areas, indeed, the relation of the extensive properties of the Church to the prosperity of the nobility was evident, even if the importance of religious orders rather than directly of bishops in parts of the Habsburg territories allowed the occasional rise of more humble clerics to prominence. In Hungary, indeed, signs of independence remained among prelates, as among lay nobles; and it was precisely in the areas of Hungary belatedly won back from the Turks that symptoms of a more draconian approach to the lower orders, including the persistence of witch-persecution in an area only uncertainly reconverted, were manifest into the eighteenth century, after the age of the French dragonnades.

In the positive restoration of Catholicism in the Habsburg lands, even the smaller orders could thus contribute to the promotion of major forms of devotion. The Servites, spreading from Tyrol into other parts of the monarchy, were characterized by the Marian piety which their official title denoted, despite the obscuring of this by Sarpi's notoriety. While the Piarists, as elsewhere in Catholic

Europe, eventually became a major force in more popular education, the Jesuits in the Habsburg monarchy, not least in terms of manpower and intellectual gifts, were rich enough to indulge in scientific experiment, as well as more traditional forms of philosophy. The range of interests within the Society, in these territories, embraced even a revival of Lullist methodology. The state of the secular parochial clergy, where indeed parochial duties were not performed by regulars, remained less impressive, throughout the Catholic restoration in the Habsburg monarchy, despite the creation of seminaries. Under the Emperor Leopold I, originally trained for the priesthood,[18] as under Joseph II, with his attention to the sacristy minutiae of parish life, it was the dynasty rather than the clergy whose essential sanctity and piety were fulsomely advertised or even self-advertised. Although episcopal synods, according to the Tridentine prescription, continued in Hungary, the decrees of a Prague synod, held in 1605, were reprinted at intervals into the eighteenth century. The precocious origins of the Counter-Reformation in the Habsburg lands had indeed owed more to leading prelates. But the tensions between the Habsburg rulers and the partly ultramontane standards of the bishops, until the arrest of Khlesl and the outbreak of the Thirty Years War, represented a wasting of energies.[19] The dynastic repression of Protestantism, on the other hand, beginning in Styria and Tyrol, was to prove in the end more lasting, even allowing for the varieties of local conditions still allowed in fact, even after 1620 or 1648, in parts of the personal territories, not least Hungary. In Bohemia, the decades after 1620 were not in effect as destructive of linguistic or cultural diversity as of religious pluralism, but the cultural transformation effected in the monarchy as a whole by dynastic Catholicism represented an end to uncertainty and the proclamation of confidence, which has been characterized as the transformation of the Mannerist into the Baroque. The parallel of dynastic rather than hierarchical Catholicism is striking in the very different conditions of the Iberian kingdoms, under Spanish Habsburg rule. But the fortunes of Catholicism, in the sixteenth, seventeenth and eighteenth centuries, in Habsburg or Bourbon territories, France, Spain or Austria, were clearly dependent on the decisions of secular rulers rather than of popes. To that extent, the evolution of Catholic and Protestant Europe was a single history.

# CHAPTER 6

# CATHOLIC REFORM AND
# AUGUSTINIANISM

THE BEGINNINGS of reform within the Western Church at the end of the fifteenth and beginning of the sixteenth century were associated above all with bishops and with regulars. In both cases the model of Saint Augustine was influential. The depiction of Saint Augustine as the perfect diocesan bishop, scourge of heretics, reached its sixteenth-century triumph in El Greco's painting of the miraculous *Burial of the Count of Orgaz*, in Toledo, the see where Carranza had briefly begun his reforming work. The various religious orders which followed versions of the supposed rule of Saint Augustine included many branches which were attempting to return to a purer observance of the rule at the end of the fifteenth century. The power of the papacy in these developments was more indirectly exerted. The work of Nicholas of Cusa in the German lands represented an attempt to impose higher standards of clerical life by delegated Roman authority. The cardinal protector of each religious order could intervene in the life of the religious to promote reformed standards of observance, as Giles of Viterbo did as general in the Italian and other provinces of the Austin friars. The disputes of conventual and observant houses within an order also, however, led to appeals to Rome; not always with happy results. Luther's experience of the city of Rome, which he visited on business concerning the reform within the German province of the Austin friars and opposition within that province, was a contributory cause of his anti-Romanism. The papacy remained at the same time the guardian of the privileges and exemptions which it had previously dispensed to religious orders. With the exception of the canons of Windesheim and those of San Giorgio in Alga, a part of the early sixteenth-century and earlier Venetian religious revival, the canons regular of the Church, who owed obedience to the supposed rule of Saint Augustine, remained conspicuously unreformed. At the same time, the Venetian ideals, represented in one way by Tomaso

Giustiniani and Querini, with their calls for a general reform of the Western Church and reunion with the Eastern Church, were most continuously pursued in writings on the duties of diocesan bishops.

The patristic model, and above all that of Saint Augustine as bishop, was naturally decisive here. Before the Council of Trent, Giberti, as bishop of Verona, in Venetian territory, began work as a resident diocesan intent on reforming the life of both clerics and laity in his see, continuing a much earlier tradition in Venetian dominions, shown forth by Lorenzo Giustiniani. Giberti experienced the need for special papal powers, however, to reinforce his ordinary authority, in the face of opposition to practical reform; especially when such opposition received support from secular authority, for Giberti was not himself a patrician of Venice. His diocesan constitutions, and his tentative experiments in clerical education, were to prove influential, not only for his eventual successor in the same see, Agostino Valier, but for Charles Borromeo too, as archbishop of Milan. In Southern France, Sadoleto attempted a similar reform of clerical and lay life in his diocese, but experienced the opposition of secular authority, which in this case was that of the papal temporal government. An ironical prelude to Paleotti's post-Conciliar experiences at Bologna was thus established. Independently, in Portugal, Bartholomew de Martyribus, archbishop of Braga, was attempting to revive Church life in the ancient primatial see of the Western Iberian peninsula. His influence, in personal meetings with other leading prelates, and through the written word, exemplifying his activity, was great. Despite the problems of political developments in Spain and Portugal in the later sixteenth century, his ideal was later pursued by Archbishop Braganza of Evora. The plans of Cardinal Pole, as legate in Marian England, for the true revival of religion in England, which had proved so weak in the face of the attack of schismatic erastianism under Henry VIII and heresy under Edward VI, included the catechizing of the people: this was to lead to the subsequent prosecution of his Spanish collaborator, Carranza, by the crown Inquisition of Spain, for the supposedly heretical overtones of the very catechism prepared.

But Pole also tackled the two weakest spots, not only of the Church in England, but of the Western Church of the late Middle Ages and Renaissance in general: the financial structure of Church organization, and clerical education. While the reactivation of the Church courts against heresy, under Mary, not least in the areas of Pole's and Bonner's activity, in London above all, was on entirely tradi-

tional, and, in the literal sense, reactionary lines, the royal campaign
to return lost lands and revenues to the Church was a discriminating
process, using royal patronage to redirect loyal and enthusiastic
clergy to important posts. The refusal of the Marian episcopate to
accept the return to Protestantism under Elizabeth was in great
contrast to the behaviour of the old episcopate in the reigns of Henry
and Edward. Only the question of monastic revival had to be treated
with caution, and limited to royal foundations which did not affect
lay rights to former monastic lands. Pole's plan to provide, for the
lower clergy especially, some form of professional and indeed vocational training was, however, innovatory. This plan was to prove
decisive in the later stages of the Council of Trent, when clerical
formation in the Church was reconsidered. But in England the reform
of the existing universities, where clerical graduates were educated,
a reform in which Carranza was again involved, proved short-lived,
in that such reform could be reversed as easily as the changes enforced, even against resistance, at Oxford and Cambridge, during
the reigns of Henry and especially of Edward. The exhumation of
the bones of Peter Martyr's wife, which had been intentionally
approximated to those of Saint Frideswide at Oxford, merely contributed to English unease at Spanish collaboration in such work. The
transmission of Pole's decrees and example from England, where the
legate died just as the queen's reign ended, to the Tridentine Church
was the work of Ormaneto, a follower of Giberti. He was to prove a
key figure in the formation of the post-Tridentine Church, even
before his own reforming work as bishop of Padua in Venetian
territory, and his knowledge of obstacles there, such as obstinate
nuns refusing reform and strict enclosure, when he went to support
similar episcopal attempts in Spain, as papal Nuncio. Ormaneto was
assistant to Pole in England, and friend of the legate and of Carranza:
as such he was suspect in ultra-zealous Spanish circles, as were other
reformers, in fact loyal to the Church, such as Priuli. But his knowledge of diocesan reform in practice led to his employment, in the
years after Pole's death in 1558, in the reform of the pope's own see
of Rome. He was also sent by Charles Borromeo, about to go to
reside in Milan as archbishop, to that city, to prepare the way for
similar reform, in a see which had been without a resident bishop for
many decades. In Milan, as in Pole's England, the chosen beginnings
of such work were provincial and diocesan synods, by which decrees
precisely answering to local needs might be passed, and articles for
investigation during episcopal visitation prepared. The articles prepared by Pole, and imitated by Carranza in his brief beginning of

work in the Spanish primatial see of Toledo, were closely followed by Ormaneto, in his work in Italy.

The work of Charles Borromeo himself at Milan rapidly established itself as a model for other resident bishops, after the Council of Trent. Both before and especially after his canonization in 1610, his example was copied elsewhere in Italy, in Spain[1] and France, in the Austrian lands and in Poland. The identification of Charles, whose confrontation with secular authority was not unknown to contemporaries, with Saint Ambrose, who had opposed the illegitimate claims of secular power, was natural within the Milanese Church. Elsewhere in Catholic Europe, the figure of the new saint was depicted most often in cardinal's choir dress, rather as Saint Jerome commonly appeared after the Council of Trent. But any suggestion that the papacy was thus reducing reference to the undoubted independence of Charles, once he had become metropolitan archbishop of the Ambrosian Church, loyal nevertheless to Rome, by insisting on his status as a cardinal of the Holy Roman Church rather, overlooks the realities of individual commissions for paintings, and the absence of any central artistic censorship in the post-Conciliar Church. In the Milanese province, Charles was most commonly shown in archiepiscopal liturgical dress, in the favoured posture for Saint Ambrose. The Borromean revival of Ambrosian chant, as opposed to the Gregorian chant of the Roman Church, and defence of the ancient Ambrosian rite, at the very time that, with Charles's support, Rome was enforcing the uniform Tridentine rite on other dioceses and on many religious orders, was natural, in the light of Milanese history.

But the continued tradition of Saint Ambrose did not mean neglect of Saint Augustine's memory: that would have been to overlook the events of Augustine's own life, and the intervention of Ambrose in it. So that the choice of Pavia for the college founded by Borromeo to educate young men of good birth for both clerical and lay life reflected not only the city's ancient status as the Lombard university town, but also the fact that it was in a special sense the 'City of God', in which the reputed tomb of Saint Augustine was to be found, just as that of Saint Ambrose was venerated in the basilica of Sant'Ambrogio at Milan. In Venetian territory, by contrast, where the presence of Greeks from the Mediterranean empire was a continued element in the life of post-Tridentine Padua, the episcopal practice of residence and pursuit of reform maintained the pre-Tridentine tradition in the Republic of seeking inspiration from the Greek as well as Latin Fathers. The active bishop of Belluno, Lollin,

of an old Cretan family, helped Baronius in his work on the Greek
side of the early Church's history. But at Rome the Eastern tradition,
in its later manifestations too, was not forgotten. The Roman publication of the Greek *Acta* of the Council of Florence, at the beginning of the seventeenth century, was intended to help attempts at
reconciling the Greek Christians with Rome, against infidel and
heretical dangers, fruitless though this proved in fact. Morone's
reforms at Modena, on the other hand, and his patronage of evan-
gelical preachers, not all of subsequently proved orthodoxy, as the
early Jesuits suspected, showed dangers of heresy at the heart of
mid-sixteenth-century Italy.

Despite the enhanced authority with which the papacy emerged
from the Council of Trent, the role of the hierarchy in general was
made in a sense more important in the Church by post-Tridentine
reform in practice. The residence of cardinals in their dioceses, where
they still held sees, was a major consideration for those – whether
recalcitrant canons, regulars, nuns, or laity – who wished to oppose
the imposition of reform in their own lives. Cardinals were more
particularly fortified with Roman authority, against possible appeal
to Rome in defence of previous privileges: this was so not least in the
appointment to clerical benefices of a certain value, where ordinary
bishops found continuing Curial patronage after the Council still a
disruptive influence in the selection of suitable parochial clergy.[2]
Charles Borromeo, on his arrival at Milan, was further enhanced in
authority, by being papal legate in Italy. But his subsequent role as
apostolic visitor of other sees, within the Milanese ecclesiastical
province, but outside Spanish Lombardy, in the case of Bergamo
and Brescia in Venetian territory, or of areas in sensitive Alpine
territory, was more important in practice, in the spread of his own
high standards of ecclesiastical life, outside his own diocese. For
the Council of Trent reinforced the ordinary authority of diocesan
bishops against previously exempt bodies and persons, canons of
cathedrals above all, and to a limited extent regulars, but also against
possible interference from metropolitan archbishops of a province.
A powerful person, such as Charles Borromeo, could use the rede-
fined powers of the metropolitan, to convene provincial synods, exact
observance of their decrees, as laid down at Trent, and supervise in
general the work of the diocesan bishops of the province. But the
Council ended the metropolitan's right of visitation in the other
dioceses of his province, whereas the Laudian period in Anglican England was to see an attempt to reactivate just that metropolitical power
of the pre-Tridentine Western Church, as employed by Pole as legate.

The reinsertion of papal authority in the working of the Church and its hierarchy, at the Council, was the compromise solution of the tense debates on the effective relation of episcopal and papal power in the last sessions. This took two forms. One form was the employment of prelates as apostolic visitors, which left even archiepiscopal sees, like Borromeo's own diocese of Milan, open to inspection by a specially appointed bishop, acting by Roman authority. The other was the direction, in the Conciliar decrees, of episcopal action in many spheres, against those previously enjoying the papal grant of exemption, in the name of papal authority itself: by the order that bishops take such action in their sees not by virtue of their own ordinary powers, but as delegates of the Holy See. This seemed to compromise the insistence on the independent apostolic authority of all bishops, but, by saving the form of Roman authority as previously exerted, it in fact gave some greater chance of successful episcopal intervention against canons and regulars, by reducing the *prima facie* grounds for appeal to Rome by such persons. It was by such complex ways that Charles Borromeo, having influenced the wording of the Conciliar decrees by his letters from Rome to the legates presiding at Trent, came himself to represent the exemplary model of a metropolitan archbishop and diocesan reformer, loyal to Rome, but ready at all times to remind the Roman court of his own independent rights, and to seek support for his action against those who opposed reform. The distinction increasingly applied by the papacy after the Council between cardinals who were mainly to reside in their sees as diocesan bishops and those who were rather to reside in Curia or at the courts of secular rulers, as statesmen, meant, on the other hand, that not all cardinals by any means followed the Borromean path in the post-Tridentine Church. The employment of cardinals, Spanish, like Zapata, or in Spanish service, like Granvelle, as viceroys, at Naples for example, led to clashes with both episcopal and papal authority in practice, which were not edifying.[3]

The career of Cardinal Doria, a Genoese in Spanish service, like so many of his family, in the early seventeenth century, was a good example of the continuing complications of Catholic life. Doria was archbishop of Palermo, and a resident pastor, who defended his metropolitan and ordinary authority against secular attack, within bounds, even if the isolation of the island Church of Sicily, by virtue of the royal *Monarchia*, left him little contact with Roman authority. But he served as interim viceroy, between the periods of office of Spanish nobles who held that office ordinarily, and led the clerical estate, in the Sicilian parliament, in granting regular supply to the crown. As interim viceroy, he found himself in the position of banning the works of Cardinal Baronius, as ordered by Spain, because of the Oratorian's attack on the *Monarchia*. Yet papal approval of Baronius's attack, in his Church history, was based on precisely the isolation and subordination of the Sicilian Church, which Doria at times, at least, objected to himself. The Spanish view, however, was that Sicilian bishops, who were usually Spaniards, only complained of that position when a particular decision had gone against them in the royal *Monarchia* court, which alone heard appeals from the metropolitan's tribunal. At any rate the sending of papal agents, visitors or vicars apostolic, to Sicilian sees was an impossibility, even when prolonged vacancy in a see, or marked incapacity in the bishop, suggested this. Doria was left in no doubt of papal displeasure; but cardinals in Spanish service could hardly be made more amenable to papal wishes in practice. The position of Paleotti as bishop, subsequently archbishop of Bologna, free from the metropolitan authority of Ravenna, was hardly easier. Before he retired to Rome, as a Curial cardinal and episcopal reformer in the nearby suburbicarian sees of Albano and Sabina, his confrontations with cardinals and prelates acting as temporal governors of the city, as papal legates and vice-legates in Bologna, over the direction of ecclesiastical and religious life, had hardly ended to his advantage.

The successor of Charles Borromeo in the archbishopric of Milan, Gaspare Visconti, experienced the relative weakness of an archbishop, not himself a cardinal, in relations with the papacy, secular authority, and the diocesan bishops of the province. The cardinals within the ranks of the diocesan bishops, in fact, rather took the lead in the ecclesiastical affairs of that province. Yet even such complications, in one way, represented an advance on the isolation of resident bishops attempting even limited reform of their dioceses before the Council, whether Fregoso, once a figure of literary rather than apostolic fame, or Caraffa at Chieti. The influence of the New Order which the latter helped to form, the Theatines, was crucial in the formation of a greater number of bishops of the new, active style. For many of the Theatines, a somewhat exclusive order socially, accepted sees, including less remunerative dioceses in Italy and the Mediterranean coasts, with a view to residing and bringing reform to their charges. The result was clear from the generic use of the term 'Theatine', in late sixteenth- and early seventeenth-century Catholic Europe, to refer not only to members of the Theatines specifically, or to Jesuits, by an interesting cross-reference, but to any secular cleric or prelate who conspicuously followed the ideals of post-Tridentine duty and personal life: so that the prelates associated with Neri's Roman Oratory, though not themselves members of that institution, received the appellation frequently. Such association also represented undoubted doctrinal orthodoxy, whereas episcopal reform in pre-Tridentine France, as at Meaux, had not been entirely free from suspicion of an evangelicism which went beyond the Catholic Erasmianism of reformers loyal to Rome: just as Pole and Carranza, like Morone and Priuli, had to face suspicion of heterodoxy, despite association with anti-heretical campaigns or the promotion of internal reform of the Church.

Apart from Carranza, however, Spanish activists among diocesan bishops did not incur such suspicion, but rather practical limitation of their independence, as a result of royal policy and conciliar government, despite the veneration of symbols of episcopal authority, like Saint Ildefonso. Spain indeed remained devoted to the tradition of the independent apostolic origins of the Spanish Church, through the supposed presence of Saint James, whose tomb in Galicia remained the place of pilgrimage for many in post-Tridentine Catholic Europe. The Spanish outrage at Baronius's implicit attack on the historicity of this presence in early Spanish Christianity was to be compared only with the perpetual defence at Venice of the legend of Saint Mark's comparable role in the apostolic origins of the Venetian Church, independent of Rome and its Petrine authority.[4] The Spanish dispute over the recognition of Saint Teresa as a co-patron of the country weakened the assertion of Saint James's unique role. But the Spanish crown, in the period of the disputes with the papacy of Philip II and Philip III, made much of pious places, in Rome itself[5] and in Assisi, associated with Saint Peter and Saint Francis, but in royal patronage or protection, and less dependent on the papacy for that reason. The preparation of many Italian prelates for episcopal office, like that of Gaspare Visconti himself at Milan, remained the legal experience of a Curialist; and some Curial cardinals, from Spanish-ruled Italy for example, never had pastoral experience at any time in their careers. But the previous service of some bishops nominated by Spain to sees in Southern Italy or to ecclesiastical office in Sicily was rather the purely civil work of judicial or fiscal tribunals in the Spanish governmental system. The creation of Jesuit and other colleges in Italy, from the later sixteenth century, above all the Collegio Borromeo at Pavia, nevertheless allowed many nobly born prelates to undergo an element of vocational training or at least spiritual formation, throughout the seventeenth and eighteenth centuries, during their education. The diocesan seminaries might remain, when eventually created, rather the training-place of the less well-born; but in Borromean Milan it was eventually true that the canons of the collegiate churches of the city had mostly received at least part of their education at a seminary, even if separately from clerics of common origin.[6] The emphasis on casuistic rather than patristic learning was characteristic of seminary education in Italy, from the start; but the libraries of individual clerics as well as of ecclesiastical institutions continued to contain patristic works or selections. Even in eighteenth-century Piedmont, more open to French intellectual influence than other parts of the peninsula, despite government control of intellectual life, the book collections of parish priests appeared to contain no serious element of Jansenist writings. The Jansenism of Savoy remained, as further south in Italy, much more a jurisdictional affirmation of Catholic erastianism by secular authority, or the assertion of aristocratic episcopal independence of Roman authority.

Greater uniformity in the post-Tridentine Church was not merely the result of papal imposition of a standard revised liturgy and breviary. The spread of devotion to the new saints of the Counter-Reformation itself, canonized soon after their death, was not confined by state frontiers. At Venice the cult of Charles Borromeo was popular, and his Catholic rigorism was attractive to the lay rigorists of the state who increasingly proved influential in the direction of state policy, not least in relations with Rome, in the decades leading up to the Interdict, such as Nicolò Contarini. But the spread of common inspiration to active bishops, by the diffusion of biographies of the Saint, and of editions of Borromeo's synodal decrees and acts of episcopal government, produced a similar cross-reference in secular opposition. The leader of opposition to the independent assertion of archiepiscopal authority in the Milan of Federico Borromeo, archbishop from 1595 to 1631, in succession to Visconti, was at first the lawyer in government service, Menocchio. As Sarpi makes clear, in his account of the papal Interdict of the early seventeenth century, the Venetian Republic consulted the counsel of Spanish government in Lombardy, in preparation of its own defensive measures against Rome; while Menocchio left at his death, for posthumous publication under Spanish authority, his considerations on the powers of the Church and of the Spanish crown more generally.[7] The Tridentine plan to reform the abuses of the religious orders by the radical reduction of all regulars to a single monastic order of the Western Church, rather like the Eastern Basilians, had been abandoned, realistically. But the attack of the assembled bishops of the Church on the regulars was not forgotten within the orders, who saw their special links with Rome undermined by the device of apostolic delegation and the extension of episcopal authority over pastoral activity by regulars in the Conciliar decrees. Just as a concerted attack on the new Society of Jesus and its close relationship in the end with the papacy was evident among mendicants, on occasion within the post-Tridentine Church, so the resistance to episcopal extension of control over the religious and their lives, monks, nuns and friars, was often manifest. The substantial proportion of questions arising for Roman decision from contested application of the Conciliar decrees which reflected such tensions led to the creation of the Curial Congregation of bishops and regulars, distinct from the general work of the Congregation of the Council. The intervention of secular authorities, after the Council of Trent, in the life and organization of religious orders reduced episcopal influence over regulars still further. The views of Spanish government in Lombardy, of the Venetian Republic and of the duke of Savoy determined the redrawing of the boundaries of the Franciscan and Capuchin provinces in Northern Italy: states disliked the headship of convents remaining in the hands of those who were not subjects.[8]

By contrast, it fell to the bishops to try to implement the Tridentine ban on new mendicant houses being created within too close a distance of one another, where competition for alms could only place unrealistic burdens on lay charity. Bishops intent on directing lay devotion by their own authority after the Council were in any case anxious to limit the number of those licensed to seek alms within their jurisdiction: this was as true of Borromean Milan after the Council of Trent as of other Italian dioceses in the eighteenth century.[9] Apostolic visitation was also contested by governments other than that of Spain, in the case of Sicily. The Venetian Republic was alarmed at the prospect of Borromeo's visitation of sees within the Republic, fearing the alteration of its own privileged control of clerical life and, to an extent, finance; and the modification of aspects of religious life, such as the supervision of female convents and lay confraternities, or charitable institutions, which affected the laity and their property. The prelates native to the state who were diocesans were expected to temper the effect of decrees left by Charles Borromeo as a result of his visitation; though Domenico Bollani won the praise of Borromeo, as bishop of Brescia, despite his previous experience, typical enough of Venetian noble careers, as secular governor of the city. The intervention of an apostolic visitor also raised the questions of the post-Tridentine form of the bull *In Coena*

*Domini*, by which the papacy was attempting to limit secular interference in Church affairs and its application within a state. At Venice
itself, the Republic persisted in maintaining that clerical life needed
no reform, in the face of papal demands for the admission of an
apostolic visitor to the diocese of the city. But the most crucial
objection was in fact to papal intrusion into the life and funds of the
female convents of the city and lagoon, and of the rich major confraternities, the *Scuole*. A compromise involved Valier, in the end, as
a visitor known to the Venetian authorities, and coming from the
nobility of the state himself, acting, as he often did, as a mediating
influence between Venice and Rome. But his association with the
diocesan, the patriarch of Venice, in the visitation, was at odds with
the whole concept of an ordinary's subjection to apostolic visitation,
and the convents and confraternities were excluded from the scope
of their investigation. The Republic's concern to maintain its right
of nomination of the patriarch prevented acquiescence, however, in
any examination of patriarchs themselves, whether in Rome or at
Venice.[10]

   The pre-Tridentine reform internal to certain religious orders was
continued more generally in the post-Conciliar Church. While the
earlier reforms had on occasion invoked papal support, to determine
the rights of conventuals and observants in the orders of friars, for
example, royal authority had also been involved in monastic reform
in Spain. But after the Council of Trent, despite continued Spanish
governmental intervention in places, the influence of Rome was felt
in the direction of promoting centralization within even ancient
orders. The most primitive form of monasticism surviving in the
Western Church after Trent certainly experienced this. The Basilians, or monks of the Eastern rite, found in central and Southern
Italy, Sicily and Spain, were brought under a general; but this was
the result of papal defence of their rite against Spanish attempts to
impose the Latin rite and Benedictine rule on the Sicilian houses.
The papacy urged the separation of the financial benefits of the
commendatory abbots of these houses from the jurisdiction of the
claustral superior and the general, in the interests of maintaining
discipline.[11] The Benedictines had experienced pre-Conciliar reform
in many countries, within which the reformed houses tended to
group themselves together, with a greater degree of common organization than was otherwise traditional. This was true of the Italian
congregation, later called the Cassinese, based on Santa Giustina in
Padua, where monks were professed in the congregation, not to a
particular house. The Venetian impetus for austere and regular prac-

tice of the monastic life, in the early sixteenth century, was also seen in the Benedictine offshoot, the Camaldolese. In Spain reformed Benedictine houses grouped themselves together by the early century, and San Benito in Valladolid was the centre of the famous Spanish congregation, which later inspired the English Benedictines in exile to claim the right to independent status, on the same model of organization. In the German lands the reformed congregation of Bursfeld was encouraged by the post-Tridentine papacy to continue its work.

In France, by the seventeenth century, two congregations of reformed Benedictines had formed some organizational links between houses, and the more famous, in a way, was that based on Saint Maur, where the Maurists devoted special attention to the Benedictine duty of study. The Cistercians in seventeenth-century France also showed evidence of reform, both in the common and in the strict observance. The Trappist offshoot of the reformed Cistercians led by Rancé, and effectively though not strictly founded by him, became the last word in ascetic mortification. Female reformed Cistercian houses followed, under Rancé's influence; whereas in Spain the royal and powerful female foundations of Las Huelgas, owing obedience in theory to the Cistercian rule, proved resistant to the strenuous efforts of papal Nuncios to introduce a more reformed way of life.[12] The abbess of the Burgos convent was in any case fortified by her quasi-episcopal jurisdiction, and continued to enjoy the use of episcopal crozier and ring. The Carthusians, throughout Catholic Europe, continued to demonstrate the vitality and purity of observance which had marked them out as exceptional in the late medieval and Renaissance Church. The admiration which the London Charterhouse had inspired in Thomas More was matched by the fortitude of those members of the house who resisted the Henrician schism, in a rare display of monastic opposition to royal policy then. The Carthusian paradox remained even more evident in the seventeenth century than in the sixteenth, as the tradition of accepting royal and noble patronage on a lavish scale, for the building and decoration of conventual churches and houses, continued, in Italy and Spain above all. There the Charterhouses remained more splendid than almost any other major monasteries, in physical appearance. Yet the lives of the community were seemingly never corrupted, possibly because of the eremitic basis of the Carthusian rule. The canons regular, until after the Council of Trent, represented the reverse of this picture. The various families of canons regular, owing allegiance to the supposed rule of Saint Augustine, were, with exceptions in the

Netherlands and at Venice, among the least impressive parts of the later medieval and Renaissance Church. After the Council of Trent, reform was imposed, with Roman support; and the Premonstratensians, in particular, recovered their vigour, after surviving an early seventeenth-century crisis over the issue of the order's ancient rite, and the new Tridentine rite in use elsewhere in the Western Church. In the end the distinction of their rite, like that of the Dominicans and those of the Carthusians and Cistercians, was preserved in some measure, and this branch of the canons regular became active in the support of restored Catholicism in German and Austrian lands. The pre-Tridentine reform of the Venetian canons of San Giorgio in Alga had by the end of the sixteenth century lapsed into disorder, however, and continuous papal intervention was necessary to restore reformed standards.[13] The circles in which Peter Martyr Vermigli had moved in Italy, at Lucca and Naples, suggested, furthermore, that the canons regular had included, in the early sixteenth century, some whose Augustinianism leaned rather towards the Lutheran interpretation of doctrinal questions.

The orders of friars presented the spectacle of pre-Tridentine internal reform, which had created almost as many problems as it solved. The dispute between conventuals and observants was almost as old as the order, in the case of the Franciscans, and had contributed to the conflicts over poverty, and orthodox and heterodox views of that virtue, in the later Middle Ages in Western Christendom. The reform of the observants in fifteenth-century Spain, under royal supervision, led to the vitality which Franciscans showed in the early American missions, as well as the internal confrontation with Moorish subjects of the crown made Christian. The reformed observants were found in the sixteenth and seventeenth century in Italy too; but throughout the Mediterranean world, and eventually throughout the Catholic world, the new offshoot, the Capuchins, came to represent the most zealous following of the Franciscan ideal. Not that other Franciscan branches accepted this view; the older dispute between observant and conventual houses, over novices in particular, which the post-Tridentine papacy tried in vain to resolve finally, was repeated, with even greater bitterness, in the Franciscan attempts to prevent recognition of the Capuchins as a distinct branch. The long battles and temporary victories of the older branches ended with final papal recognition of the Capuchins, despite the damage to their image as enthusiastic and devoted preachers to the poor caused by the flight of Ochino, their fourth vicar general, to Protestantism. The heroism of the Capuchins, in treating the poor and sick, especially in epidemics, thereafter made them perhaps the most popular of the mendicant orders in the post-Tridentine Catholic world, despite the presence of members of their order at the courts of rulers and among international statesmen.

The Minims represented a pre-Tridentine offshoot of the Franciscan movement, and had originally been characterized by a late medieval emphasis on extreme asceticism, distinct from any intellectual inspiration. But by the seventeenth century, the French province, and its Rome house, included some of the leading scientific minds of Catholic Europe. The Dominicans also showed intellectual vigour, in the defence, largely, of their own traditional teaching, both at the Council of Trent, and in the Church of the late sixteenth and early seventeenth century more generally. This was not least the result of earlier reform, conducted in Spain within the order itself, and the order had weathered disputes between conventuals and observants. The Austin friars showed resilience, in outliving the reputation of having harboured Luther, in the German province divided between conventual houses and reformed groups of houses, to which he had belonged. Their theologians proved influential at Trent, and in subsequent doctrinal disputes in Catholic Europe, despite the defeat of Seripando's personal views at Trent. His Augustinian theology was in no way the same as Luther's, which he was careful to reject; and the Austin friars, like the Dominicans, showed a practical concern for converting all men, in the missionfields overseas, while the Dominicans, with the Franciscans, remained powerful in the Inquisitorial suppression of heresy.

The orders of friars, and the Augustinian offshoot, the Hieronymites, found in Italy and Spain, were particularly influential in Spain in the universities, and above all, especially in the last case, at the royal court. The Hieronymites, with the Escorial library collected by Philip II, continued a live scholarship, after the end of Erasmian influence in Spain, which, when enhanced by personal rivalry, led to internal Inquisitorial investigation. Such personal rivalry also played a powerful part in promoting the persecution of Carranza, pursued by both rival Dominicans and Franciscan opponents. Spain also witnessed the later sixteenth-century reform of the Carmelites, male and female, the work associated with Saint Teresa of Avila and Saint John of the Cross, sharing a mystical experience which crowned the reassertion of purely contemplative and ascetic values in the Church, among the friars as much as among some of the orders of monks. After suspicion of heterodox 'enlightenment' had been painfully overcome, both reforms in the end received the belated support of

pope and king. The Servite friars continued a less prominent existence, before and after the Council of Trent, and overcame the adverse
publicity which Sarpi's membership of their order brought in the
early seventeenth century. After this, indeed, they became rather
more prominent in helping the Catholic restoration in Austrian and
South-German lands, not least by their particular association with
Marian devotion. The Trinitarians and other smaller orders of mendicants, devoted to collecting funds for the ransom of prisoners taken
captive by Turks and Barbary Moors, were still allowed to pursue
their work, in the Western Mediterranean especially. The Trinitarians were reformed, and restored to strict observance of their rule,
under their cardinal protector, Federico Borromeo, at the end of the
sixteenth century.[14] By contrast, Charles Borromeo, in the later
sixteenth century, used his powers as cardinal protector of the
Umiliati, in Lombardy and Venice, in the total suppression of the
order, with papal support, when reform proved impossible to impose
successfully. Their property was reallocated to other orders, after
Charles had survived an attack on his life by an outraged member of
the wealthy community, which led to the papal suppression.

Zealous cardinals and protectors, such as the Borromeo archbishops of Milan, also used their position as commendatory abbots
to impose reform on monastic communities, and, on occasion, to eject
monks who refused reform, in order to introduce a more ascetic
order, usually Capuchins. The combination of medieval heights of
asceticism and poverty with an activism which went beyond even the
original purpose of the friar preachers and Franciscans made the
Capuchins a link between the old orders and the New Orders of
the Counter-Reformation. Jealousy between old and new certainly
existed, not least over property and benefactions, as well as over ecclesiastical privilege and educational and pastoral influence. The
attempt by the mendicant orders to encourage the papacy to refuse
recognition to the Society of Jesus, denying it the privileges of the
religious orders, failed in the end, given the Society's final privileges,
arguably going beyond the extensive exemptions of the monks and
later great privileges of the mendicants. But the failure of the New
Orders, as they are known traditionally in English historiography, to
exhibit the characteristics of existing orders, especially the recitation
of the choir office in common, was precisely what made such attack
possible; though such flexibility and freedom in the use of time and
energy, which distinguished the New Orders – which should in
origin be distinguished as societies, congregations and institutions
– marked the difference between their activism and that of the men-

dicants. The Theatines provided, in a way, the model for subsequent New Orders, by being a group of clerics devoted to pastoral work as missioners and parish priests, eventually as bishops, yet following a common rule: clerks regular. The influence of the Theatines was thus more extensive than the results of their pastoral work in Italy and Bavaria, for example, alone. The generic use of the term 'Theatine' in contemporary society showed their identification with reformed standards of clerical life in Catholic society by the end of the sixteenth century. Their numbers remained relatively limited, by their exacting social and educational requirements; but this élite of clergy, which received considerable lay patronage, led the way in insisting that perfection of life should characterize the secular as well as the regular clergy.

The confraternities of parish priests, in various dioceses of post-Tridentine Europe, which had only a guild rule, under episcopal control, represented a simpler version of the same ideal; and an attempt to use such an ideal for the creation of secular clergy to serve in the overseas missions under papal, not Iberian crown direction, preceded the papal creation of the seminary to provide priests for the missions of the Propaganda and the founding of the French Seminary of the *Missions Etrangères*. The ideal represented by these developments also found earlier expression in Northern Italy, where so much early sixteenth-century Catholic reform began, in the Barnabites and Somaschi. These were, by their activism, New-Orders, of clerks regular in effect, yet they still exhibited, like the Capuchins, a late medieval devotion to extreme asceticism in their personal and communal lives. The internal missionary work of these groups, later spreading outside Northern Italy, prepared the way in Milan for the episcopal direction of clerical life and lay devotion by Charles Borromeo. Other smaller New Orders limited their activities to some specific work, charitable or educational. They thus replaced some of the smaller orders of friars and hospitallers, which the papacy suppressed in the seventeenth century. Those New Orders which devoted heroic attention to the sick, the terminally ill or the syphilitic, were founded by Saint John of God and Saint Camillo de Lellis. Only the pastoral activity of the latter's followers could, in places, pose problems in relation to diocesan authority.

All these movements sprang, in one way, from the early sixteenth-century revival of clerical and lay piety, in Northern Italy first of all, which found expression in the Oratories of Divine Love, first in Genoa, and later in Rome as well as elsewhere, after the new initiatives of the Brethren of the Common Life in the Netherlands.

Such mixed groups of laity and clergy differed from traditional confraternities chiefly by being free of any even remote associations with specific crafts or skills, and by devoting practical charity to society at large, or sectors in need, not to members of their own institution alone. The Oratory founded in Rome by Philip Neri started as a similar group of helpers, clerical and lay, of his unusual catechetical work with Roman city children. Only gradually did the Roman Oratory become an institution, with secular priests becoming permanent members, acquiring a church of their own, and rebuilding it as the headquarters of the institution. An essential part of this was the adjacent oratory in which non-liturgical presentation of doctrine, by the arts of music and scenic effect, could take place. The Oratory thus remained carefully free of organization, allowing each member to pursue his own talents; and the same freedom was accorded to houses founded elsewhere in Italy in imitation of the Roman Oratory. The first established house, at Naples, indeed paradoxically used its freedom to become totally distinct, in pursuit of a more regular life and even habit. The French Oratory of Bérulle, equally, was founded in the seventeenth century on the model of the Roman Oratory, but independent of it; and other French houses were offshoots of Bérulle's foundation, not Neri's.

To some extent, the work of the Theatines, Oratorians, and, to a lesser degree, the Jesuits, was devoted to the same ends: missionary work, preaching, catechizing, and providing an example to the secular clergy. The learned and artistic work of the Roman Oratory was only a particular form of this, and, in early days, the Roman Theatines on occasion co-operated in such activity.[15] In the same way, for the archdiocese of Milan, Charles Borromeo founded his own special force, the Oblates of Saint Ambrose, who were a New Order akin to the Jesuits, but bound by their special vow of obedience to the archbishop of Milan instead of the pope. The Jesuits were unusually replaced, to a large degree, in such work as the direction of seminary education at Milan, by the Oblates; and the latter provided an example to the parish clergy, when they acted as parochial clergy themselves or supervised others as rural deans in the diocese. The Oblates remained influential in the Milanese archdiocese, despite the greater use of Jesuits made by Gaspare Visconti, after Charles Borromeo's death, and the reaction of the Oblates against him as a result.[16] They rarely worked outside the diocese, except at their Roman house, unless seconded as temporary helpers to friends of the Borromeo archbishops, such as Archbishop Tarugi at Avignon.[17] France in the seventeenth century similarly saw the creation of New Orders with fairly specified roles. The followers of Saint John Eudes led the Catholic restoration in Normandy, by their missionary work, and became influential as staff of the first French diocesan seminaries. The greatest influence in French seminary education in the seventeenth century became that of Saint-Sulpice, however, founded by Olier. This was a part of the more ultramontane reaction of the early century to the Gallican revival of the new Bourbon regime, and led the way in educating parochial clergy for their duties in France. The staff of later seminaries were often the products of Saint-Sulpice themselves. This clerical formation thus complemented the missionary and charitable work among the laity promoted by Vincent de Paul, who also cared for clerical formation himself. The pro-papal atmosphere of Olier's original foundation was nevertheless diluted with expansion, as the overwhelmingly Gallican complexion of the French clergy in the later century demonstrated; while the noble composition of the upper clergy was never much susceptible to the influence of seminaries.

The Jesuits in seventeenth-century France revealed the paradox of the rapid growth of the Society during its first century. The original constitution, finally accepted by the papacy after much debate and the opposition of the Society's opponents, was the antithesis of the freedom which characterized the Roman Oratory. The long years of rigorous training, including charitable work in hospitals as well as intellectual formation and vocational testing, which prepared Jesuits to approach the inner or outer circles of membership with their different vows, were only the basis on which the powers of the central congregation and the large authority of the general were erected. The patronage of noble and royal families in Catholic Europe, the demand for educational establishments under Jesuit direction, the geographical dispersion of the Society's forces, and the rapid growth of membership, led to strains in an organization which had expanded more, and more rapidly, than had been anticipated. By the end of the sixteenth century there were signs of this, in the belated recognition at the centre of the Society that lay education was to be one of the proper, and most important, sectors of activity, and in the difficulty, already, of controlling the individual initiatives, not least political, of members. A revision of the constitution eventually proved necessary, to give greater independence, and therefore a more realistic chance of control over members, to provincial authorities within the Society; but this was not accomplished without much difficulty and tension. The result was that large provinces, like that of France, in turn became divided: in that case, because of those who favoured collaboration with royal power, through influence at the court of Louis XIV, rather than the assertion of papal authority in French ecclesiastical policy, for which the Jesuits had originally suffered so much hostility in early Bourbon times. The division of Jesuit policy was similarly revealed in the Peking mission, after the papal condemnation of the Chinese Rites, and missionary methods of assimilation. In the agonized debates as to whether or not to 'receive' the papal ruling and observe it, the Jesuit mission was divided by the presence of Portuguese and others, owing obedience to the crown, and the fathers, largely French, who owed obedience instead to the papal Congregation *de Propaganda Fide*. The supposed influence of the Jesuits at the papal court was often overestimated, even if partly as a result of Jesuit skill in advertising the achievements of the Society. Different popes took more or less note of Jesuit views, but the final condemnation of the 'Eastern Rites' was a triumph for critics of Jesuit missionary methods, even before the suppression of the Society later in the eighteenth century. The most dramatic alteration in papal diplomatic policy, by which Clement VIII recognized a Bourbon Catholic France, independent of Spain, was effected under the influence, dominant at Clement's court, of Neri, Baronius and friends of the Roman Oratory.

The fortunes of the female helpers of Saint Vincent de Paul, and of the followers of the English Catholic Mary Ward, demonstrated the difficulty of maintaining female activism in the post-Tridentine Church. The papacy and bishops were so intent on trying to impose a reasonably ascetic life and strict enclosure on the existing female orders, that they opposed the extension of new, unenclosed activity, by female religious. The charitable work of Vincent de Paul's followers persisted in fact, and the peculiar isolation of England allowed Mary Ward to establish educational work, even in clandestine conditions, which was impossible on the continent of Catholic Europe. The Ursulines founded by Angela Merici in early sixteenth-century Northern Italy continued their educational work with Catholic girls, in Italy and France, but North Italian houses were brought into stricter enclosure by the Borromeo archbishops of Milan, despite the resistance of their members. The followers of Mary Ward took the Society of Jesus as their model, including the number of vows, but the New Orders were always anxious to avoid any responsibility for directing female convents and any of the suspicion which attached to the older orders as a result of such involvement. The opposition of monks and friars to being removed from control of female convents by bishops was supported by lay opinion; and not all those female convents which were already, before Trent, under episcopal not male regulars' supervision had maintained higher standards of religious life. The reform of female orders was nevertheless promoted by Nuncios and bishops, despite fierce resistance to enclosure from nuns and their relatives.

In places rural nunneries were brought for safety within town walls; but the fusion of two communities rarely proved successful. The social exclusiveness of many female convents, as far as choir sisters were concerned, survived into the eighteenth century, in Spain, France, Italy and elsewhere. The austerity of the Discalced Carmelites, and of the Second Order of Saint Francis, the Poor Clares, was undoubted, however; and other nuns, following the traditions of mendicant orders, were gradually or partially reformed. The often rich and powerful convents owing allegiance to the supposed rule of Saint Augustine were more problematic, and were hardly noted for ascetic living. The power of abbesses, especially if related to royal or great noble families, or controlling ecclesiastical patronage, in Spain or France, was considerable. The papal campaigns for greater uniformity in the organization of religious orders, after the Council of Trent, favoured the triennial election of abbesses, to reduce this power; but the administration of substantial property and extensive revenues proved an obstacle in Spain and France.[18] The post-Tridentine campaign to reduce female tertiaries to either purely confraternity status or the strict enclosure of true nuns was more successful.[19] The Franciscan male tertiaries included, by contrast, a fully conventual branch, which was conspicuous in early seventeenth-century Venetian territory at least for organized crime rather than for piety however.[20] The work of nuns in the missions overseas remained largely that of enclosed prayer and contemplation in support of the activities of the friars, Franciscan, Dominican and Augustinian, on mission, though charitable and educational work was also undertaken. The French Catholic revival of the earlier seventeenth century, which led to the original direction of the nuns of Port-Royal by pro-papal *dévots*, also led to an elaboration of penitential and contemplative female religious life. The honour accorded to such communities by the attentions of Anne of Austria or by membership which included the cast-off mistress of Louis xiv was a mixed blessing; but Père Joseph, the Capuchin adviser of Richelieu, also promoted female conventual life of a reformed standard.

The direction of female religious by male regulars was not the only cause of conflict with bishops in the post-Tridentine Church, however. The involvement of some male and female regulars in charitable

works – in hospitals, or the running of institutions for girls in moral
danger, in Italy and Spain especially – led to the double demand for
episcopal intervention by the terms of the Tridentine decrees, since
charitable foundations were to be open to episcopal inspection and
supervision according to the Council fathers.[21] More common was
the problem of enforcing regulars' obedience to the Tridentine provision that the pastoral work of the regular clergy, preaching and the
hearing of confessions especially, was to be subject to episcopal
examination, licence and regulation. The authority of episcopal synodal decrees which explicitly included the regular clergy in their
scope on these grounds was contested by appeal to Rome, though
powerfully connected prelates like the Borromeo archbishops of
Milan could win substantial victory in the end.[22] The Council had
also allowed for the visitation by diocesans of churches in regular
hands, if these were open to the faithful; but enforcement of diocesan
regulations in such churches was still problematic. Competition for
benefactions and the lucrative rights in funerals, between secular and
regular clergy, still disfigured death beds and disturbed obsequies in
the post-Conciliar Catholic Church. Public processions, apart from
burials, were also occasions of friction between secular and regular
clergy. The papal condemnation of bull-fights, after the Council,
was ignored by bishops, seculars and regulars in Spain; only the
Jesuits, as Clarendon noted in mid-seventeenth-century Madrid,
demonstrated a conspicuous loyalty to Rome by absence from the
*plaza* and the simultaneous celebration of public devotions.[23]

The clergy of Spain continued to be present at public dramatic
performances, to the horror of the papal Nuncio, reflecting the
opposition of Italian reforming bishops to the rather different traditions of Italian popular drama.[24] For some of the Spanish plays,
not least the Baroque mysteries of Calderón, were composed for
performance at religious feasts, especially that of Corpus Domini. In
Italy the private theatres of cardinals, spectacularly that of the Barberini, were a different question too, as were the musical representations of religious themes in Neri's Roman Oratory. At a popular
level, Italian piety, in the eighteenth century, was encouraged by
internal missions still, and the devotions promoted above all by Saint
Alfonso Liguori, which seemed to critics to threaten once again the
late medieval dangers of an unbalanced emphasis on the physical
sufferings of Christ and physical attributes of his human body. The
cult of the Sacred Heart of Jesus was opposed by Jansenists in
eighteenth-century France and Italy, without final success; and in
Italy the opposition of Jansenist bishops to the devotional and pro-

papal traditions of Liguori were hardly more successful in the end. Even more influential in the eighteenth century, in Catholic Europe, was the extension of education at a simple level, and even in technical skills, to boys destined for lay careers, from social strata below those for whom the Jesuit colleges provided. This was the work of the Pious Schools, and the New Order which ran them gradually spread these institutions to many towns and cities in Catholic Europe before the French Revolution. Their influence was arguably more rationalistic than that of Liguori, who promoted doctrines of the Immaculate Conception of Mary, and of papal infallibility, which had not been officially defined, and argued for papal supremacy over Councils of the Church. His casuistic teaching was disliked by Italian Jansenists, not least for its appearance of going beyond the probabiliorism of some Jesuits, to outright probabilism; yet his influence, in Italy at least, outlived the suppression of the Society of Jesus.

The opposition, to the Redemptorist popular missionary influence, of Muratori and Italian Jansenists thus touched on questions of doctrine as well as discipline. Yet the élitist approach to religion of Muratori, or of the Synod of Pistoia, was at odds with the populism of this mission, while both nevertheless shared a rigorism in respect to social and moral behaviour quite distinct from the supposed laxism of Jesuit spiritual direction. Jurisdictional questions, reflecting the old division between pope and bishops, were ultimately more crucial in this opposition: just as the 'Presbyterianism' for which Jesuits had once been criticized by Catholic bishops came to be associated rather with the Richerist lower secular clergy of eighteenth-century France, or the self-proclaimed authority of the Old Chapter among the secular priests of the eighteenth-century English Catholic community. The Redemptorist missioners took up the cause of frequent lay communion, in eighteenth-century Italy, formerly attacked by the French Jansenists of the seventeenth century; yet the older élitism of the religious orders, in parts of Catholic Europe in the eighteenth century, such as France, showed some signs of decline, in terms of numbers entering the regular life at least. Secularization of monasteries began before the Revolution, in the second half of the eighteenth century, in German lands as well as in France, and in places represented a triumph of long-standing episcopal objection to monastic exemption, or provided financial benefit to a diocesan see. But Innocent x had already made revision of monastic houses, closing some which were very small, in the second half of the previous century, in Italy. The Tuscan reform of ecclesiastical affairs in the reign of Leopold ii sought to reduce regulars in the state to dependence on local authority, echoing again episcopal feeling about regular exemption from the period of the Council of Trent and before. At the end of the seventeenth century, the Jesuits, through the more critical hagiography undertaken by their scholars in the Netherlands, the Bollandists, added the Carmelites to the list of their enemies among the mendicant orders, by attacking the alleged origins of the Carmelites in the epoch of the Old Testament. Despite the support of the leader of the French Benedictines of Saint-Maur, who pursued a more critical approach to ecclesiastical history, the Jesuit attack remained for a while under papal censure; but the question of the nature and purpose of the religious orders could not be suppressed in the following century. Secular or non-conventual membership of Third Orders by lay persons, rather as in a confraternity, continued, but the golden age of such piety was the seventeenth rather than the eighteenth century. The noble rather than religious quality of the Knights of Malta became ever more apparent. At the time of internal conflict in the order, over the powers and policies of the Grand Master, in the later sixteenth century, the papacy had intervened to some effect. But the direction of religious life in Malta itself, among the lay population, was contested by the Grand Master, the Inquisitor and the bishop. During the period of Spanish rule in Sicily, the Inquisitor was an official of the crown tribunal of Spain, and the bishop was appointed by a process involving the crown, the order, and the papacy. Popular religion nevertheless manifested its strength in the building and decoration of churches, and in processions, into and beyond the eighteenth century, despite Anglo-French maritime rivalry in connection with the island.[25]

The creation of New Orders in Catholic Europe did not cease in the later seventeenth and in the eighteenth century. Many, though not all, had a practical purpose, charitable or educational, and often were limited in numbers or in the geographical location of their houses. But the popular missions conducted in Italy by the Redemptorists had their equivalent in eighteenth-century France, the work of the priests of the Mission, founded by Vincent de Paul, and of later foundations. The results were seen in the popular Catholic reaction in parts of Western France to the development of the French Revolution. In the same way, the division between regalists and papalists among the Redemptorists in Southern Italy did not prevent the popular Catholic reaction of the end of the century, there and in other parts of the peninsula, against both Jansenist reforms and Revolutionary changes. Similar missionary work, internal to Catholic Europe, was undertaken by the Passionists in eighteenth-century

Italy and elsewhere. The French foundation of the Christian Schools, for education in the vernacular among boys of more modest social background, proved influential in France, in the way that the Pious Schools were in other parts of Catholic Europe. These and smaller orders for educating boys and girls at simple levels continued the work of Catholic education after the suppression of the Jesuits. By contrast, the foundation in the second half of the seventeenth century, of a congregation of secular priests to work in the overseas missions under papal, not Iberian patronage, the *Missions Etrangères*, was originally the work of a Jesuit, Père de Rhodes, whose experiences led him to urge the necessity of vicars apostolic, in the East especially, under the Roman Congregation of the Propaganda: an ironic initiative, in the light of the subsequent attack on Jesuit missionary methods in the East, led by representatives, not least French, of the *Missions*.

The restoration of Catholicism in Europe remained as much dependent on the activity of diocesan bishops as on the initiatives of religious orders, old and new. The importance of episcopal residence and reform was already clear in Italy, before the end of the Council of Trent, where the eradication of abuses in clerical and lay life was more an answer to long-standing plans for internal reform than a reaction to specific Protestant danger. In several of the sees of the Venetian mainland the work of resident bishops proved effective, on the model of Giberti's work at Verona; Brescia, Bergamo, Belluno, Treviso were also involved.[26] The necessity of enforcing residence on Venetian bishops was still experienced after the Council of Trent by papal Nuncios, since many patrician pastors were used to spending part of the year in Venice itself. But more problematic was the promotion of residence in Istrian and Dalmatian sees under Venetian rule, and in the smaller and less wealthy island dioceses, especially in Crete. In the south of Italy a similar problem – of small and impoverished sees in many cases – encouraged the absence of bishops, at the viceregal court in Naples or at the papal court, despite the continued efforts of the Nuncios after the Council to ensure the residence of bishops in the Kingdom.[27] The active episcopal government of Aleander at Brindisi set an early example in the South; while the Istrian and Dalmatian sees of the Venetian Adriatic littoral were investigated by Valier, as apostolic visitor, whose work produced some improvements in Church life in the area.[28] Seripando was most active as reforming general of the Augustinian friars, but he also had episcopal experience as archbishop of Salerno; while the work of Caraffa as archbishop of Naples was later continued by the zealous archbishops Gesualdo and Acquaviva, at the end of the sixteenth and beginning of the seventeenth century, and by Archbishop Filomarino later in the seventeenth century.

The later century did not see the end of active episcopal reform either at Milan, as the work of Cesare Monti and, less successfully, Archbishop Litta showed, or in the Venetian Republic, as was demonstrated by Saint Gregory Barbarigo. In the empire, in the wake of religious warfare in the mid-sixteenth century, Augsburg became a leading centre of the Catholic restoration, under the patronage of Cardinal Otto Truchsess, aided by the Jesuit Canisius. A friend of the cardinal's, as of Pole's, was Hosius, legate at the Council of Trent, who worked for the restoration of the Catholic faith not only in his own diocese of Chelmno, but more widely in Poland, where Canisius also prepared the way for Jesuit missionary work. In Eastern Europe the lack of able, resident bishops was more widely to be felt for some time, however, despite such work. In sixteenth-century France, the political involvements of the Cardinal of Lorraine and the Cardinal de Guise represented rather the militant aspects of the Counter-Reformation Church, despite the importance in the end of Lorraine's presence at the final stages of the Council of Trent. Reform based on ascetic observance of a regular life had reached Paris and certain other parts of France by the early sixteenth century, partly under Netherlandish influence, but co-existed uneasily with the Catholic humanism of other reformers inside the Church, and was limited in its effect by monastic and jurisdictional disputes. In the diocese of Meaux, Briçonnet attempted to reconcile some of these influences, under episcopal authority, in the interests of reform. But the evolution of elements in Christian humanism into Lutheranism was to disrupt the work begun there. Provincial councils to promote clerical reform were held at Sens and Bourges, two decades before the Council of Trent, but the authority to impose the suppression of clerical abuses was more in doubt, even before the outbreak of civil war in France, let alone the abuses of lay confraternities, before the advent of Calvinism. In sixteenth-century Vienna and Passau, on the other hand, episcopal activity led the Catholic restoration, and in Hungary it was promoted by the primate, Cardinal Pázmány, in the early seventeenth century.

In the later seventeenth century and the first half of the eighteenth century, Italian bishops continued to improve clerical life, not least by encouraging seminaries, and popular missions were conducted by many orders and individuals, such as Saint Leonard of Port Maurice. This work was maintained despite such conflicts between Church and state as those over the plans of Innocent x to benefit diocesan revenues by the grant of proceeds from the suppression of small religious houses, and the Interdict imposed on Sicily during the period of Piedmontese rule in the island, in the early eighteenth century, when Venetian compositions of the Sarpian era were re-employed. In late Habsburg and in Bourbon Spain, resident and zealous bishops were found, but conflicts with cathedral chapters still continued, after the Council of Trent, over the imposition of reform. The growth of seminaries was often delayed until the later eighteenth century, when some benefited from ex-Jesuit property. The decline of provincial synods after the reign of Philip II was never fully reversed, however. In the France of Louis xiv, Catholic rigorism on the Borromean model was maintained by Le Camus, bishop of Grenoble, who nevertheless disapproved of the royal policy of attempting to force the conversion of Huguenots by violent measures. Le Camus was rewarded by the papacy, being made a cardinal despite royal displeasure, while the flight of French Protestants led to the reopening of the question of the ruler's right over his subjects' religion, in the writings of the exile Jurieu, as well as in the mind of the Catholic critic, Vauban. Catholic comparison of authoritarian measures against heretics with those used against Donatists in patristic North Africa was nevertheless an explicit form of apologia. A revision of opinion among the majority of French clergy followed the enforcement of the policies connected with the revocation of the Edict of Nantes, as the presence of forced conversions continued to be felt. The role of the successive diocesans of Paris in the Gallican and Jansenist disputes of Louis's reign and of the early eighteenth century revealed their weakness and compliance; but the promotion of episcopal Gallicanism by the French bishops, against the exemptions of regulars and the indiscipline of the lower clergy, was rewarded by royal authority, at the end of the seventeenth century, to support diocesans' rights, in return for co-operation in the disputes with Rome.

The revival of the struggle over Jansenism in eighteenth-century France, not least in Paris itself, largely a jurisdictional contest, by virtue of the intervention of the Paris *parlement*, nevertheless turned once again on the pastoral practice of confession and lay access to the sacraments, because of the refusal of the Last Rites to unreconciled Jansenists. The subsequent suppression of the Jesuits by the *parlement* could be seen as a final move in a long jurisdictional struggle, but the negotiations of the eighteenth century between some Gallicans and some Anglicans suggested rather a compromise in areas which ultimately concerned the doctrine of the Church. The state intervention which followed, to reduce the numbers, houses and property of other religious orders in France, arose on the occasion of a protest from within the Maurist congregation of the Benedictines about aspects of their rule, raising clearly questions about erastian involvement in the matter of monastic vows. The episcopate belatedly revised its favourable view of such reduction of regular exemption, at first seen as being to the advantage of episcopal authority. Both French Jansenists and English Catholic leaders in the eighteenth century, however, sought to revivify lay participation in the mass by liturgical variation or the promotion of para-liturgical devotions. Despite the conscientious administration of many, though not all, French bishops in the later seventeenth and in the eighteenth century, non-residence remained prevalent, and the creation of diocesan seminaries still proceeded slowly. As in Italy, the discipline of the lower clergy, and the enforcement of correct clerical dress required constant intervention. But in France the cult of the reserved Sacrament, among the faithful, survived the suppression of the *Compagnie du Saint-Sacrement*, and both Saint Francis de Sales and Le Camus advocated relatively frequent lay communion. The discipline of Saint-Sulpice was undermined by fashionable clerics in the eighteenth century, despite the strength which was to emerge from the institution, in defence of the Church, after the outbreak of the Revolution. Practical charity among the clergy could reach heroic levels still, as was shown by the bishop of Marseille, in the epidemic of 1720, reflecting the role of some bishops in Northern Italy in the epidemics of the late sixteenth century and of 1630–1.[29] More frequent lay communion was encouraged in eighteenth-century Italy and Spain, but Roman approval of the cult of the Sacred Heart of Jesus was delayed until the very period of the European attack on the Society of Jesus, after concern in Italy about the possibly Quietist overtones of the cult.

In the Netherlands, the south, under Spanish and then Austrian rule, afforded a retreat for French Jansenist leaders, as well as harbouring native Jansenists who nevertheless avoided the schismatic outcome of Utrecht. The religious orders, including the Jesuits, also flourished, however, until the period of Josephine reform, though bishops found unreconciled Jansenists among other orders, both there and in Liège. Catholic scholarship at Louvain was maintained in the eighteenth century, despite the difficulties caused by Jansenism. The French invasion of the Northern Netherlands under Louis xiv provoked an anti-Catholic reaction in places, but the semi-clandestine Catholic life of the United Provinces was otherwise more troubled by questions natural in such a community, as also in England, concerning the valid conditions for marriage for example. The fusion of doctrinal and jurisdictional issues which produced the schism of Utrecht led to the much more serious, and permanent, division of the former Catholic community in the Dutch Netherlands, to which the antagonism of the secular and regular clergy, not least the Jesuits, had also contributed. In Sweden an anti-Catholic reaction followed the conversion of Christina, despite her previous abdication and self-exile, and the effects of this were only mitigated in the late eighteenth century. By contrast Irish bishops maintained an effective presence in the island, despite persecution, as in the extreme case of Oliver Plunket, and the complications of association with the fortunes of the Stuarts in exile. The English Catholic leadership in the eighteenth century managed, on the other hand, to overcome accusations of association with Jacobitism arguably better than did the Non-Jurors in England, who were far from solidly Jacobite.

In the empire of the late seventeenth and eighteenth centuries, Catholic reform or missionary effort was promoted by some aristocratic prelates, such as Fürstenberg, bishop of Paderborn, and Schönborn, prince-bishop of Würzburg. The expansion of the religious orders in Bavaria, at the end of the seventeenth century, was obstructed in the following century, but seminaries in German dioceses continued to be established, if not without difficulty. Popular devotion, especially Marian, remained prominent in Southern Germany despite episcopal opposition, increasingly, to the disorders associated with popular pilgrimage. In Catholic Switzerland, in the same period, expansion of the religious orders, as well as popular piety and pilgrimage continued, despite political tensions. After the suppression of the Society of Jesus, some ex-Jesuits continued to find shelter for their activity in places, as also in places in England: the absence of absolute Catholic governments could be an advantage. In the Austrian lands and in Hungary, in the period before Joseph II, clerical education and popular religion were encouraged, and Uniates of the Eastern rite were also found in the Habsburg lands. In the prince-archbishopric of Salzburg, expulsion of Protestants was revived in the mid-eighteenth century. Benedictine scholarship remained evident there, as also at Melk, on the Austrian Danube, though other religious orders divided over the doctrine of the Immaculate Conception. The Uniate monks in Poland, on the other hand, suffered some Latinization of their traditional rule. The Northern War of the early eighteenth century more generally troubled Polish Catholicism

and the Uniates, by virtue of contested election to the throne, and
Russian invasion; while subsequently tension remained between
Latin-rite Catholics and Uniates, fostered in part by social and
geographical distinctions. This prepared the way for the disruption
caused by the eighteenth-century partitions of Poland. The suppression of the Jesuits altered the forces of Polish Catholicism, while the
Russian gains at Polish expense harmed the Uniates. Uniates of the
various Eastern Churches were found in other parts of Eastern
Europe, including Romania, and the Eastern Mediterranean in the
eighteenth century; and the Greeks and Albanians in Southern Italy
and Sicily continued relatively undisturbed in their rights, under the
eighteenth-century papacy.

The presence of the Stuart court in exile, in eighteenth-century
Rome, however, encouraged not only political intrigue, sometimes
under cover of art-dealers, but the spread of freemasonry in Catholic
society, in its early forms of Franco-Scottish celebration of romantic
antiquarianism and the occult. Such enthusiasm thus spread in Catholic Europe at the very time that the reaction of enlightened rationalism against the continued doctrinal disputes within the Church,
and within Western European Christendom more generally, resulted
not only in the jurisdictional attack of eighteenth-century states on
the remaining exemptions and independence of the Church, but also
in the challenge to Christian teaching itself. The pastoral repercussions of political relations could never be avoided. While Bavaria had
remained prominently Catholic, after the Thirty Years War, under
ducal supervision, the absence of a see proper to Munich – where
the court chapel and the New Orders exerted their influence – produced increasing discontent in the eighteenth-century opposition
between Bavaria and the prince-archbishops of Salzburg. The papal
Nunciature at Munich, created at the end of the century, did not
resolve the problem caused by Roman concern at the prospect of
altering the balance of power in the empire, and the Febronian opposition of the imperial bishops to any such alteration. The Bavarian
reaction nevertheless represented a form of state limitation of ecclesiastical rights which foreshadowed the policies of Joseph II in Austrian
lands; while it was under Russian government that the Jesuits found
shelter for a continued existence, after their suppression.

The contrasts within the application of practical reform by bishops
in Catholic Europe after the Council of Trent were already apparent
in the Italian peninsula, at the end of the sixteenth century and the
beginning of the seventeenth. Diocesan officials who had served
under Charles Borromeo, or his immediate successors, at Milan, and

even canons of the cathedral chapter, after the inspiration of reform by archiepiscopal authority, became in turn bishops of sees elsewhere in Italy. The most active of the vicars general who served the Borromeo archbishops, Seneca, was particularly detested by Spanish authority for his resolute defence of ecclesiastical independence.[30] He subsequently found it possible to implement reform of the clergy and laity in the smaller diocese of Anagni, near to Rome, of which he became bishop, without experiencing serious difficulty with the temporal government of the papal states, and in a see which was immediately subject to the papacy, not to an intermediate metropolitan. One of the British Catholic exiles connected with Borromean Milan, Owen Lewis, also served as vicar general and won the approval of the archbishops. But his association with the assertion of ecclesiastical rights there almost prevented the Spanish crown accepting his nomination as bishop in a Neapolitan see. Paleotti found the depressed condition of the peasants in the central papal states, in the suburbicarian sees of Albano and Sabina, and the failings in the Christian life which this encouraged, similar to that of the inhabitants of his former diocese of Bologna, also under papal government: so much so that the same pastoral directions proved valuable in both cases.[31] At Bologna, however, enclaves of temporal jurisdiction belonging to other secular rulers lay within the diocese, and complicated the work of the bishops.

A similar problem confronted the patriarchs of Aquileia, at the head of the Adriatic, from the time of the Council of Trent to the eighteenth-century solution, finally, of dividing the patriarchate.[32] The jurisdiction, both spiritual and temporal, of the patriarchs extended across the frontiers of Venetian and Austrian archducal territory. The desire of the Venetian Republic to ensure a succession of patriarchs from Venetian noble families produced complicated devices for appointing coadjutors with the right of succession, and any papal acquiescence in such policies produced difficulties with the Austrian Habsburgs. The chapter of Aquileia was more dominated by canons devoted to Austrian interests, so that the seat of diocesan administration increasingly was Udine. But Venetian patricians who became patriarchs were limited in their practical power to enforce reformed behaviour on clergy and laity, even when they themselves sought to do this directly, rather than remaining permanently in Venice, by the opposition of the Austrian authorities to what was seen as Venetian interference; while Venetian secular magistrates, as elsewhere in the Republic, refused to allow ecclesiastical intervention in conventual or confraternity affairs. The undoubted

spread of heresy in popular forms in sixteenth-century Friuli was
thus partly the result of such conflicts, at least until the suppression
of Protestantism by Austrian authority within the territory of the
archdukes. Similar divisions of temporal rule and ecclesiastical organization complicated the promotion of diocesan reform at Trieste.
Among the prelates normally residing at Venice, between the end of
the Council of Trent and the late eighteenth century, was the bishop
of Torcello, whose tiny and impoverished islands in the lagoon were
increasingly depopulated. The discipline of female convents in these
islands remained poor, despite the intervention of diocesan, patriarchal and above all Republican authority.[33] But even where episcopal
action was not contested by the state, as in the design to create a
seminary, the poverty of the see and sparse number of clergy prevented such a thing. The bishop of Torcello at the end of the sixteenth
century, a Venetian noble, was able to publish diocesan decrees of
the most stringent sort, concerning the life of the laity, the observance
of religious feasts, the deployment and defence of Church property,
and the legal immunity of the clergy, on the very edge of the city and
patriarchate of Venice itself. Yet the Republic, which was so vigorous
in limiting such assertions of episcopal independence, either by the
patriarchs of Venice, or by bishops elsewhere in its dominions, could
afford to overlook such a display, in so small and impoverished a see.
The government's attitude to this loyal noble certainly contrasted
with the draconian suppression of any such sign of episcopal assertion
of authority by the non-noble bishops of Istria and the Dalmatian
sees in the same period.[34]

Even in Crete, because of its political sensitivity within the Venetian Mediterranean empire, the noble archbishops of the island,
despite the greater degree of Republican influence in their selection
than in any other see in the dominions, bar the Venetian patriarchate,
found their independence carefully restricted: not least in respect of
convents and relations with the Greek clergy and laity.[35] The episcopal activity of the bishops of Ceneda, on the other hand, on the
Venetian mainland, was distracted by their claims, largely supported
by Rome, to be temporal subjects of the papacy, not of the Republic,
as allegedly enjoying both temporal and spiritual jurisdiction in their
diocese.[36] Political conflict also interrupted at times, in the Tridentine Church in Italy, the work of episcopal government at Florence
and Lucca, with the exclusion of prelates from their sees. In Siena,
reforming bishops like Tarugi tried to impose reform on female
convents, for example, despite the background of political conflict
between the Medici rulers of Tuscany, and the subjects of Siena,

who had sought independence under French protection, earlier in the sixteenth century.[37] In Venetian territory, the operation of the Roman Inquisition, after the Council of Trent, and even before the Interdict, was circumscribed not only by the enforced participation in the tribunal's work of secular magistrates, both in the city of Venice and in its mainland territories, but also by the claims of some cities to be represented by their own lawyers on the local tribunal.[38] The Republic insisted that the records of the Holy Office in its territories should be kept by the bishops, at a time when the papacy supported the claim of the friars appointed at Rome as Inquisitors to control these. The Roman Inquisition attempted to avoid the suspicion of financial gain which attached to the Spanish crown tribunal, by virtue of the latter's procedure, which began with the confiscation of a suspect's property. But this raised problems in the disposal of the property of the condemned in Venetian territory; while in Spanish-ruled Milan the confiscations were handled by the representatives of the secular authority on the local tribunal of the Holy Office.[39] The papacy, at the time of the Council of Trent, had eventually accepted episcopal and popular resistance in Milan and Naples to the introduction of the Spanish Inquisition in the former, and a reorganized Roman tribunal in the latter. Bishops at Trent feared, in the light of the Carranza case, the further reduction of ecclesiastical independence under Spanish rule in Italy. The eradication of Protestantism in the Italian peninsula, both north and south, was nevertheless virtually complete by the end of the sixteenth century.

The poverty of sees in Sardinia limited the power of post-Tridentine bishops to found seminaries, for example, and recourse to Rome against recalcitrant canons was limited in practice by viceregal intervention.[40] The Medici rulers of Florence tended to support lay resistance to confraternity reform or conventual reform even when attempted by an archbishop of the ruling family; and the papal Nuncio did not always support Tuscan bishops against such secular opposition. But in the decades after the Council of Trent or in the first half of the seventeenth century, episcopal reform, even against local opposition, was pursued in sees such as Alessandria, Crema, Cremona, Piacenza; or Novara, where the outstanding follower of Charles Borromeo, Bascapè, was bishop.[41] The activity of seventeenth- and eighteenth-century bishops in Italy, and in other areas of Catholic Europe – Spain, France, the German and Austrian lands, Switzerland and Eastern Europe – is still being revealed, diocese by diocese, and period by period, in the works of historians. The assessment of popular piety and the parochial practice of religion in the Counter-Reformation Church, between the Council of Trent and the French Revolution, is equally the object of careful but necessarily slow study, as wills and bequests are examined, for example, to reveal the attitude of the faithful to the teachings of the Church and the devotional life of the laity. Such research involves co-operative effort and complex calculation, but a beginning has been made, not least in France. Another vital source of evidence for the state of the Catholic Church, area by area, and year by year, during this period, is the material contained in the records of episcopal visitation, few of which have been published. Even for a diocese as remarkable as that of Milan under Charles Borromeo the whole picture is far from clear.[42] From the personal visitations of his cousin, Federico Borromeo, throughout the diocese, during his archiepiscopate, from 1595 to 1631, a picture emerges of a laity faithful to the sacraments, but not always fulfilling the terms of pious bequests of their ancestors; attentive to the catechetical Schools of Christian Doctrine, in urban centres, but not always so in rural areas.

The clergy at parochial level were certainly not always perfect in their lives, though their failures were more often at the level of not maintaining correct clerical dress or the correct fittings of the church, than at that of criminal activity; their level of education on the other hand was clearly improving, not least as a result of compulsory attendance at organized classes to discuss pastoral, especially casuistic, questions. The Borromean organization of the Milanese diocese was criticized even by the zealous Paleotti, for the centralized control which denied initiative to the clergy; but the results seemed in the end to show what determined bishops could achieve, despite opposition, in the Counter-Reformation. Charles Borromeo in particular has been seen, both by contemporaries and subsequently by historians, as the model bishop, in the implementation of the Tridentine decrees, reforming Catholic clerical and lay practice. But his singularity, and that of the tradition which was maintained at Milan by his successors, lies not in the absence of obstacles to be encountered – which indeed were those faced by bishops generally in the post-Conciliar Church, whether financial, political, or ecclesiastical – but in his unusual ability, by personal energy and determination, and fortunate aspects of his relations with Rome or the accidents of Spanish power in Lombardy, to overcome such obstacles. Such an example, in its very singularity, the degree of success established, and maintained, with variations, from the 1560s into the second half of the seventeenth century at least, demonstrated precisely what the reforms within the Church intended by the Council of Trent might finally achieve. The opposition which Catholic reforming bishops faced rarely demanded the most extreme sacrifices from them, despite the internal persecution, within the Church, which Carranza, Pole and Morone encountered.

But, before the Council of Trent, a conscientious diocesan bishop in one of the smaller English sees, John Fisher of Rochester, found himself, though only marginally and inadvertently involved in political questions, in the position of resisting royal policy. This concerned not so much the question of Henry VIII's marriage, as that of the king's claims to supremacy over the English Church and episcopate. Similarly Pole's career was to move from the possibility of his perpetuating a Catholic line on the English throne, by marriage to Mary, to the ironic defence of his legatine powers by the queen, against the papal attack of Caraffa, at the end of the English restoration of the old religion. The papal creation of Fisher as cardinal, in the face of Henry's action against him, arguably only brought the prelate to a swifter execution. But the memory of Fisher, as also of the layman, More, was venerated by continental reforming bishops after the Council of Trent, even though neither was at that time canonized.[43] The English example – as with Pole's seminal reform decrees from the Marian restoration – thus proved important once more, despite the end of a Catholic hierarchy properly constituted in England, which left the shelter of priests on mission, like Campion, and the clandestine printing press of the Catholic Recusants, to the responsibility of lay households, like that of Stonor. On the continent of Europe, though, the English example could still be followed by conscientious leaders of episcopal reform in the Church, alongside continued Catholic veneration of the memory of Savonarola, in an unofficial tradition among reformers.

The unusual degree to which archiepiscopal authority was successfully asserted at Milan was not least the result of the personal visitations conducted by the archbishops after the Council of Trent. Even a collegiate church which claimed exemption, as a royal peculiar, that of Santa Maria della Scala at Milan, was in the end subjected to such visitation in fact, despite resistance, and a continued debate at theoretical level about the Tridentine reservation of rights to such foundations.[44] The chapter and the minor canons of the cathedral were brought to obey rules of life laid down by the archbishops with papal support.[45] The canons of other collegiate churches in the city and diocese were similarly made to observe a reformed style of life and strict performance of their duties, even where such intervention

by the archbishops was made as delegates of the holy see, as at the
ancient basilica of Sant'Ambrogio, Milan, with the complication of
its two chapters, of canons and of monks.[46] The local superiors of
the city clergy were responsible to the vicar general of the diocese,
for the parish priests in each sector of the city. In the diocese the
precedence of the rural deans, at the most ancient or eminent church
in each area, was reduced to a matter of ceremony alone; and a new
style of rural dean, appointed at the will of the archbishop, controlled
the secular clergy in fact, reporting frequently to the vicar general
and meeting at stated intervals with the archbishop. As well as this
disciplinary system, a further provision was made, for senior and
experienced clergy to act as deans in another sense, as sources of
advice and encouragement to younger clerics.[47] The seminaries, despite financial difficulties and, in the case of the Swiss seminary at
Milan, political complications, were maintained in good order; and,
after long struggles, strict discipline was imposed on female convents.[48] Although the older male religious orders retained a considerable independence in fact, for a long time, the peculiar circumstances
of the epidemic of 1630–1 necessitated some single control of spiritual and charitable activity at Milan, and the papacy gave Archbishop
Federico Borromeo, at the end of his life, the unusual power of
absolute control of all regulars, as of secular priests, for the duration
of the epidemic.[49] The laity were successfully encouraged to frequent
the Schools of Christian Doctrine, as teachers or pupils, until the
epidemic again caused the disruption of these meetings.[50] The building, rebuilding and redecoration of churches in the city and diocese
represented a substantial investment of income, not least from the
laity, and provided a more lasting memorial to the exemplary implementation of Catholic reform in Borromean Milan.

Even at Milan, however, 'foreign' clergy, from outside the diocese,
retained as private tutors, could threaten native clerical discipline,
by setting a poor example of behaviour. The control exercised over
clerics from Borromean Milan studying at Bologna by the archbishop there, Paleotti, on behalf of the Milanese diocesan was a rare
arrangement between friends. At Venice, after the Council of Trent,
male regulars, also employed as private tutors, continued to wander
about the city, free from conventual discipline.[51] At the Venetian
state university of Padua, the reform of monastic communities was
much complicated by the involvement of the secular magistracies
charged with supervision of the university, as a result of the appointment of religious to professorial chairs.[52] Lay confraternities and
parochial communities, in Italy and Spain, continued to hold con-

vivial celebrations in church buildings into the seventeenth century or beyond, despite episcopal disapproval. The co-operation of ecclesiastical superiors with secular health authorities, at times of epidemic, in regulating the gathering of crowds for devotional intercession and procession, could not be guaranteed; and the control exercised by such superiors over local clergy and communities, in these circumstances, was often insufficient to prevent a challenge to secular orders for isolation, which conflicted with economic interests as much as with the demands of popular religion. Secular standards, in a different sense, were still evident in the cathedral chapters of Spain and Portugal, after the Council of Trent, despite episcopal intervention, in a long tradition of Iberian confrontation between bishops and canons.[53] Married men, or those with illegitimate children, or those who indulged in secular games or duels were still present in Spanish and Portuguese cathedrals immediately after Trent, despite the theoretical demands of residence, less relaxed than elsewhere. In Portugal, as in Spain, clerics could appeal to secular tribunals against their ecclesiastical superiors, and in both countries such tribunals regarded themselves as empowered to order bishops to lift spiritual penalties imposed on the disobedient. The application of recovered Church property was contested in the German and Habsburg lands between the Jesuits and older monastic orders.

The realities of life in Catholic Church and society after the Council represent the limitations in effect of the Counter-Reformation as a reassertion of pristine purity in the face of Protestantism. But the ideal of Catholic reform, under episcopal direction, in the revived patristic tradition, was acknowledged not only in Catholic Europe, but in missionary areas too, where the cult of Saint Charles Borromeo reached the Netherlands and the English Recusant community.[54] This cult, favoured at Venice especially by the association of Saint Charles with protection against plague, did not necessarily mean the observance of ascetic standards of behaviour however. In that city the celebration of carnival, despite momentary efforts by secular and ecclesiastical authority to restrain its licence, became famous for its extended relaxation of social constraints, and eventually attracted visitors anxious to benefit from the prolonged season which linked one festival to another. Venice thus developed not only opera houses, of a public nature, in the seventeenth century, but the performances of the female conservatories too, for sacred music even in the seasons when opera was prohibited. Despite the immediately post-Tridentine attempts to restrict the music of these chapels to chant with organ accompaniment, the elaboration of figurative settings and instrumentation was apparent already in the earlier seventeenth century. Yet, by the end of the eighteenth century, as the spectacle of the Venetian carnival reached its greatest international renown, the financial burden of maintaining the notable example of Catholic charity and piety which the Venetian female conservatories represented caused the silencing of their famous choirs. The variety of conditions in different dioceses of Catholic Europe, in the period between the Council of Trent and the French Revolution, still remains to be examined in detail, not least by the study of Nuncios' reports on various dioceses at intervals, and the periodic reports *ad limina*, presented by bishops at Rome: work which remains as yet incomplete.

# CHAPTER 7

# PURITANISM OF THE RIGHT AND BAROQUE EFFECT

IT HAS BEEN NOTED by historians that the austerity which characterized Catholic reform, at the end of the sixteenth and beginning of
the seventeenth century, prevents the easy identification of the Baroque style with the art of the Counter-Reformation. To an extent
this is true, but there is equally a danger of assuming an identity
between Mannerism, which was often a consciously élitist and sometimes an obscure form of representation, and the Tridentine ideal of
religious art which would educate and inspire the faithful. Firstly,
the distinction between religious painting and sculpture, intended
for ecclesiastical use, and the visual arts as patronized by private
patrons for non-ecclesiastical locations, needs to be observed; quite
apart from the separate problems of terminology and periodization
in the literary and musical arts. Secondly, the varieties of development embraced by such terms as Mannerism and Baroque have to
be remembered. Thirdly, the clear proof of the dominance of private
patronage in the evolution of even religious art, from the mid-sixteenth century onwards, in Catholic countries, has to be accepted.
The exceptional case of Veronese's examination by the Inquisition
in Venice, for the supposed irreverence of his painting of a religious
subject, is an indication of the absence, otherwise, of any central
control in the Counter-Reformation over the content of the visual
arts. Certain buildings or decorative schemes were specifically subject to ecclesiastical oversight. The completion of Saint Peter's,
Rome, during the sixteenth and seventeenth centuries and the continued decoration of its interior by painting and sculpture were
controlled by a papal commission. The groundplans at least of Jesuit
churches, in the same period, were referred to the central authorities
of the Society for approval; and the similarity of such groundplans,
and the influence of that of the main Jesuit church in Rome, Il Gesù,
are thus not surprising. But though the Jesuits themselves built
churches, as a New Order, throughout Catholic Europe and overseas,

there was hardly a 'Jesuit style', and certainly not one found in non-
Jesuit churches of the Counter-Reformation or Baroque. The patronage of individual families altered the original decorative scheme
for Il Gesù itself; and only perhaps in the Jesuit church at Antwerp,
with Rubens's famous cycle of paintings, did the whole scheme of
decoration in a Jesuit church represent the perfect model of the
Society's design. The unusual degree of control established over the
Jesuits in Milan by the Borromeo archbishops, on the other hand,
led to archiepiscopal control even of the building of the Jesuit church
of San Fedele there; for which the Mannerist architect, Tibaldi,
favoured by Charles Borromeo, produced a characteristic design of
ponderous monumentality.

In parts of Europe, the Jesuit churches seemed the most spectac-
ular in Baroque display, however: as at Venice, where the relatively
late decoration of the Jesuit church creates the impression of conspicuous extravagance. The Society in Rome possessed eventually
several churches, as well as Il Gesù, and some of these others acted
as chapels for the students, clerical or otherwise, educated by the
Jesuits. The genius of the papal architect Bernini was to create the
oval, yet Baroque rather than classical perfection of the noviciate
church of Sant' Andrea al Quirinale, in the seventeenth century; and
in the subsequent period the *trompe-l'œil* ceiling and dome of Sant'
Ignazio, by the Jesuit brother, Pozzo, was to represent the climax of
Baroque illusionistic art, and the culmination of the Italian evolution
of the decorated and painted ceiling, from the sixteenth century
onwards. But some of the older churches adapted by the Society as
chapels for their students were meticulously decorated, at the end of
the sixteenth century, with cycles of martyrdoms explicitly showing,
with Mannerist contortion, the tortures which those going on mission to non-Catholic lands might expect themselves. The scenes of
male and female martyrdom so laboriously and extensively displayed,
in Santo Stefano Rotondo, for example, were intended to familiarize
the future mission priest with such terrors.[1] The exquisite torture
and crucifixion prepared for the Jesuits, and Franciscans, in Japan
saw remarkable constancy in fact among the missionaries and their
native converts, with but a few exceptions; the tortures and prolonged methods of execution suffered by Jesuit and other priests in
Recusant England, though not including crucifixion, equally produced constancy and a few apostasies.

The rivalry of the Jesuits and Franciscans in Japan produced its
tragic effects even in the visual representation of the martyrdoms
there, which were circulated in Europe to encourage the support of

the faithful and advertise the heroism of the missionaries. Although Japanese converts of the Jesuits and Franciscans were in fact martyred together, and in the same place, on the most famous occasion of mass execution, the rival orders circulated prints which showed only the martyrs of their own suffering. The singularity of Jesuit architecture, on the other hand, in Catholic Europe, was not necessarily marked, in relation to the new or rebuilt churches of other orders, or the redecoration of churches and cathedrals more generally. Outside Rome, the Society's church in a city often served both the faithful, and the students of the Jesuit college in the place. The careful segregation of even lay students, from the temptations of society, which was the characteristic of the Society's colleges which so appealed to the Catholic parents of good families, led frequently to the prominence of galleries in such churches, in which the students might worship apart from the ordinary congregation. But in Spain there was an older tradition, among many religious orders, both monastic and mendicant, male and female, of substantial choir galleries at the west end of the church, separated from the nave below, opened to the faithful at large. This plan was reproduced indeed at the royal basilica of the Escorial, built for the court and the Hieronymites by Philip ii. So too at Salzburg, the later university church there, in a subdued Baroque style, reproduced the prominent gallery for the members of the Benedictine university. The Mannerist design, of a cold monumentality approaching the sepulchral, by Herrera of the Escorial, and of the cathedral at Valladolid founded by Philip ii, in that alternative capital, was devoid of any sign of flamboyance or of conspicuous display, unless in the sheer size of the buildings.[2]

There was thus, in Philip's enclosed Spain, a reaction after the late medieval profusion of detail in Iberian architecture and sculptural detail, embellished under Charles v by the external influence of Flemish painting and sculpture, in all its meticulous elaboration. The influence of Italian Renaissance architecture and sculpture, of a classical restraint, fused with this rich tradition, rather as in the work patronized by the early Tudor kings and Wolsey in contemporary England. In Spain, however, the multiplication of chantry chapels, other than those of the Catholic monarchs themselves, was less distinct architecturally: tombs were placed before the altars of existing chancels and chapels to a greater extent than in England, in the last days of the old religion there. But whereas in Protestant England the tombs of nobles and gentry, rather than the traditional brasses of knights, clerics, or substantial laity, came to dominate the interior of churches, in Catholic Spain and other areas of Spanish rule, such as Southern Italy, the façade of the church sometimes consisted of a giant celebration of the founder's or patron's munificence, by virtue of a *blasón* occupying the whole surface. In Italy and elsewhere in Catholic Europe of the Counter-Reformation, new churches, whether built by the New Orders or not, most commonly allowed a clear view of the high altar, by providing a wide nave, and often dramatic illumination of the sanctuary by means of a dome over the crossing or over the chancel itself, as in Saint Jacob at Innsbruck. The New Orders, in any case, did not require the massive choir stalls of the monastic and mendicant orders, since their celebration of the mass, often with special liturgical splendour, was not complemented by regular solemn recitation of the choir office in common. The choir screens which obstructed the view of the high altar in many Spanish cathedrals, dividing the laity from the sanctuary by the solid impediment of the canons' choir, were in places moved, at different dates after the Council of Trent, to allow greater access for the faithful, between the altar and choir; the same was eventually true in some cathedrals in the Southern Netherlands. Pilgrimage churches, or churches which combined a nave for the laity and an enclosed choir for the nuns of a convent, retained idiosyncratic plans in the post-Tridentine Church. But otherwise, in new churches built in the sixteenth and seventeenth century, a groundplan on the Latin cross became most common. Side-altars, for the reasserted cult of the saints and the celebration of private masses, both attacked by Protestant reformers, were now subordinated to the main sanctuary. This reflected the design by Vignola of Il Gesù, but was not the result of any Jesuit direction of church building outside the Society, rather of liturgical fashion.

The visual evidence of the physical state of churches in the post-Tridentine Catholic world needs to be considered with special care. In parish, as opposed to cathedral churches, after Trent, the reserved sacrament was increasingly ordered to be kept on the main altar, in a tabernacle, as opposed to the varieties of location for sacramental reservation found in the pre-Tridentine Church. The cult of the Sacrament was certainly promoted by the New Orders, not least the Jesuits, and the original design of the high altar at Il Gesù included a prominent tabernacle. Yet the large tabernacle which dominates the high altar there at present is not the original one, which was at some stage replaced, and found its way, in pieces, to Tipperary. More generally, the rich décor of marble and stucco, fresco and gilded plaster, in the interior of Il Gesù, represents an alteration of the original design, which contrasted a simple and unadorned interior with the conspicuous colour and grandeur of the high altar. The erection of the altar to Saint Ignatius, after the canonization of the Society's founder, however, encouraged the elaboration of Baroque decoration of all parts of the church, by the Roman families who patronized the Jesuits. The original plans of the Society, for their main church just as for their educational involvements, were thus altered by the intervention of lay patrons.

The neighbouring churches of the other major New Orders in Rome, the Theatines' church of Sant' Andrea della Valle, and the Oratorians' new church of the Chiesa Nuova, similarly display a Latin-cross plan, wide naves and an unimpeded view of the high altar.[3] But while the wealth of patronage of the Theatines produced the golden frescoes of their church, the interior of the Chiesa Nuova, one of the most sumptuous in Rome, represents the effects of similar patronage and the complete reversal of the original design, of the age of Neri and the foundation of the Roman Oratory. Borromini's exotic and clever design for the Oratory itself, next to the church, and the Oratorians' library above, organized first by Baronius, was a different matter from the pristine plan for the décor of the church. It was intended, before Neri's death, canonization and entombment in the church, that the interior should be unadorned, whitewashed even, to dramatize the colour and richness of the high altar and chancel. The bequests made by Henri IV of France – grateful for Oratorian promotion of his reconciliation and for Baronius's dedication of a volume of the *Annales* to the French rather than to the Spanish monarch – and by the friend of the Oratory, also in the end involved in the reconciliation, Federico Borromeo, for the decoration and furnishing of the high altar, were made on this assumption. The Oratorians' appreciation of the visual arts, as of music and scholarship, led to the commission to Rubens to paint the altarpiece, which, for liturgical and devotional reasons, had to embrace the existing, primitive depiction of the Madonna, from the old church on the site. The miraculous quality of the representation had thus to be preserved, even by a great master of European painting and diplomacy. Pastoral considerations similarly led to the commission of a second altarpiece, to replace Rubens's first painting. The first, on canvas, reflected the light to such an extent, from its location above the altar, that it proved invisible to the faithful. It was therefore repeated on slate, to reduce the reflection. Such considerations are a reminder of the dominance, often, of non-aesthetic criteria, in the patronage of religious art in the Counter-Reformation; though the influence of individual or family patronage in altering schemes originally drawn up with pastoral or liturgical aims in mind is also increasingly evident, in the seventeenth and eighteenth centuries. In either case, such questions are totally distinct from that of the stylistic influence exerted by one artist on another, as in the case of those who claimed to follow the manner of the late Michelangelo. The religious paintings of Vasari, art critic and disciple of Michelangelo, who virtually ensured the respect subsequently shown to the memory of the great architect, painter and sculptor, provided many altarpieces for churches in sixteenth-century Tuscany and other parts of Italy. Yet the dark palette adopted, and the confusion, very often, of the design of the canvas, while demonstrating certain qualities of Mannerist art all too well, do not in fact represent the Tridentine ideal, of a religious art of didactic clarity, establishing the truth of Catholic doctrine and the inspiring example of Christian virtue by simple realism, which the faithful could not mistake. The realism of Caravaggio's religious painting, on occasion, was to prove unacceptable in turn, however, to the original ecclesiastic commissioning patrons.

In Tuscan painting an artificiality of design, not least in the unrealistic colour and finish of canvases, survived in religious art into the seventeenth century. But not all the works of Dolci, for example, were intended for ecclesiastical locations, by any means: some religious paintings were for private piety, for the devotions of the ducal and other patrons who commissioned them. By contrast, the realism of the models chosen, from lower levels of society often, in the religious canvases of Caravaggio was followed elsewhere in Catholic Europe, in the tenebrist works of la Tour and others working to the same style, for example, in France. Yet the pervasive style associated with Caravaggio, in Italy, France and elsewhere, was marked rather by the dramatic use of chiaroscuro, particularly hidden or artificial sources of lighting. This dramatic use of light effects was different both from the dark palette of Tuscan painters and from the sombre scenes, illuminated by high points, of Ribera and other religious painters in Spain and Naples. The influence of Netherlandish artists was felt in Italy, at Genoa for example, as well as at Rome; while residence and study in Italy marked the development of many Netherlandish artists, not least through membership of the Roman Academy of Saint Luke. The eclectic style which characterized Bolognese artists in the later sixteenth century and afterwards, not only the Carracci, but Reni too, whether working at Bologna or in Rome, demonstrated the attraction necessarily asserted in the Italian peninsula by the papal court and the opportunities in Rome for commissions from individual and institutional patrons, in the creation and rebuilding of palaces and public monuments, as well as of churches and convents. The series of young boys, posed as saints, which Caravaggio provided for Cardinal del Monte, represented one facet of clerical patronage; while the arrival of Christina of Sweden in Rome provided the opportunity for decoration of the city and Vatican palace, in part of which she was briefly received. The varieties of art-collecting were demonstrated not only by her taste for the erotic or suggestive in Renaissance painting, but in the appreciation of the purity of some earlier painters, such as Luini, by the art collector, Federico Borromeo, who regarded the art gallery at his foundation of the Ambrosiana, in Milan, as an essential adjunct to the library, itself decorated – in the style of the time, as at the seventeenth-century Bodleian – by figures of past fame, literary and other. His own taste for still-life, including the work of Caravaggio, and landscape was at the time unusual in Italy, as opposed to the Netherlands. But he appreciated the paintings of certain Netherlandish artists anyway, such as Brill, Rottenhammer and Jan Bruegel. Such a taste was very different from that shown by Philip II for the bizarre and obsessive schemes of Bosch, or the more suggestive works of Titian. The distinction of Philip's collecting from the discrimination of Federico Borromeo is in any case apparent from Philip's commissions, in the artist's later life, for quantities of Titian's work, unspecified as to subject or manner.

The difference between secular art and religious was what concerned Borromeo, however: hence his training of young artists at Milan, in schools of design also attached to the Ambrosiana originally, in the distinct requirements of ecclesiastical as opposed to secular painting and architecture.[4] Rome remained the source of inspiration, nevertheless: so that chosen artists were sent to study classical and Renaissance works of art there, after working from copies at Milan. But the speed with which fashion changed could vary from one part of the peninsula to another. One artist sent to Rome by the cardinal complained from there that Milanese taste still wanted a degree of extravagance in gesture and placing of figures which Roman fashion no longer accepted as reasonable. The cardinal's personal admiration for the Zuccari, and the choice of Barocci – also connected with the Roman Oratory – for works at Milan to celebrate the life of Charles Borromeo, suggested his own appreciation of proto-Baroque qualities however. The Milanese ecclesiastical architecture of Ricchino, whom he patronized, also showed a modified and early Baroque display, very different from the lack of any

exuberance in the stately, and often heavy, work of Tibaldi for
Charles Borromeo, as inside the cathedral at Milan. The eclecticism
of style demonstrated in the careers of some Italian painters was still
evident in Guercino, but the altarpieces of the Bolognese school were
often similar – in their clear layout, dramatic lighting of the principal
figure or scene, and a measure of Baroque convolution of form – to
those produced in Milan by the artists patronized by Federico Borromeo: they were very different, in either case, from the distorted
and elongated figures of earlier Mannerist painters in Rome, Florence and elsewhere, who did not even bring the main figure or scene
clearly to the foreground in all their religious paintings. The distinct
development of Venetian painting was encouraged by the commissions of the state, for the redecoration of the doge's palace, and of
the *Scuole*.

The Council of Trent, contrary to what is sometimes believed or
suggested, made little reference to either the visual arts or music of
a religious nature. As an assembly of bishops, not specialists, the
Council naturally produced statements which were general rather
than specific, negative rather than positive, and confined to the religious as opposed to the secular arts. The Council wished the paintings and other decorations of the church to be free of anything which
might corrupt faith or morals. It urged the abandonment of secular
themes in religious compositions which might suggest the original
connotations of the music. The desire to eradicate any visual representation which might produce heretical misunderstanding was more
important in theory than in practice perhaps. Those bishops who
wrote, after the Council, on ecclesiastical art, like Paleotti of Bologna
and the two Borromeo archbishops of Milan, stressed the importance
of not misrepresenting the Trinity, for example, or the Madonna.
Moral puritanism was shown in the disapproval of the formerly
common depiction of the Madonna breast-feeding the Infant, which
also seemed to suggest an unbalanced view of the humanity, as
opposed to the divinity, of Christ. Paleotti urged the omission of any
pagan details, such as grotesques, from ecclesiastical decoration. A
theme like the Madonna feeding the holy child did indeed become
less common in the religious art of the post-Tridentine Church, after
its Renaissance and medieval popularity. The moral rigour which
the papacy briefly demonstrated threatened the destruction of Michelangelo's *Last Judgement*, commissioned by an earlier pope, after
the Sack of Rome and disruption of the papal court. But this threat
arose not from the circumstances of the original commission, but
because the scene which dominated papal conclaves in the Sistine

Chapel included the pagan figure of Charon, ferryman to the underworld, and many figures in the nude, which papal prudery insisted should be clothed by inferior craftsmanship. The fresco was not particularly admired by Federico Borromeo, who showed no great appreciation of Michelangelo, and approved the covering of the lowest part of the work by the canopy over the altar of the chapel. His own concern for religious decorum and moral decency suggested the alteration of copies of classical works of art, intended for study by artists training at Milan, so that they represented saints and virtues, rather than pagan figures and heroic themes; but he was not suggesting any alteration to original works of art. Indeed his concern for the preservation of earlier art extended to the first, unfruitful attempts to preserve Leonardo's *Last Supper* at Milan – already showing signs of decay – and an appreciation of drawings and studies by artists, Leonardo above all, as guides to identification and interpretation. With Baronius and the Barberini he also cared for the recording and restoration of the early churches of Rome, even while they were being transformed by Baroque alterations and additions.[5]

Such concerns were very different from those of Charles Borromeo, in his work on ecclesiastical art, which earned him the title of 'cardinal sacristan' among fellow cardinals, for its devotion to detailed regulation of the design of church furniture and equipment. Bernini's later achievements, in the seventeenth century, included the expansive conception of the papal altar and baldacchino, in Saint Peter's, Rome, for the Barberini, the *Cathedra Petri* in the same basilica, to symbolize and assert the claims of papal authority, apostolic tradition and patristic support, Eastern and Western, the monumental tabernacle there too, in the Blessed Sacrament chapel, and the colonnade of the piazza, surmounted by the Saints of East and West, embracing the crowds gathered to receive the papal blessing to the city and the world. But Charles Borromeo attempted to regulate the visible Church by minute orders about the cut of vestments and shape of candlesticks. The pastoral considerations behind his regulations were paramount. The blocking of side doors at Milan cathedral prevented the casual passage through the building which characterized the great churches of Europe, including St Paul's, before Wren's new cathedral for London in later seventeenth-century England. The call for all churches of any size to have two separate doors in the main façade, at Milan and elsewhere, encouraged the spread of the three-door façade, which was not the result of Jesuit influence. For Borromeo's concern was that male and female worshippers should enter the church by separate doors, to avoid any

occasion of contact, taking their places either side of the barrier
which he erected in the main churches of the city, dividing the nave
lengthways.⁶ The exclusion of the laity from the chancel, and from
the side-altars, by means of altar-rails was as much a Borromean
preoccupation as, in Protestant England, a Laudian aim; though in
Milan cathedral long disputes followed as a result, over the placing
of the Spanish governor's throne, which the successive governors
wished to see as prominent as those of the viceroys at Naples and
above all Palermo.⁷

The relationship of Charles Borromeo to Palestrina, in the development of the Church music of the Tridentine period, has also
been the subject of mythical interpretation. The nineteenth-century
opera, *Palestrina*, by Pfitzner, contains brilliant examples of pastiche
of the earlier composer's work, even if the devotion of the second act
to the debates of the Council of Trent has limited its box-office
appeal. But the Council of Trent did not decide on the prohibition
of polyphony, in fact; while Charles Borromeo, as cardinal archpriest
of Santa Maria Maggiore in Rome, presided over the papal basilica
for which some of Palestrina's most emotive and elaborate compositions were written. In Milan, the distinct Ambrosian chant was
revived together with the Ambrosian liturgy by Borromeo, whose
regulations tended to the prohibition, there alone, of all other religious music;⁸ but that was not related to the rest of the Church in
Catholic Europe, where the new Tridentine liturgy was imposed
gradually, accompanied both by the ancient Gregorian chant, in
forms modified by centuries of use, and by the compositions of
polyphonic writers, who sometimes alternated verses in plainsong
and verses in polyphony. After the Council, the Roman Curia urged
the employment of clerics alone, not lay musicians, as singers; and
the use of the organ alone, as opposed to other instruments whose
amorous or martial associations were unsuited to accompanying
Church music.⁹ Such restrictions did not find universal application,
however; though at the papal basilicas in Rome *a cappella* singing
survived unadulterated to a large degree. Vittoria, from Spain, as
well as Palestrina and others composed masses for Roman use, at
Saint Peter's, and elsewhere, as at the Roman Oratory or the chapel
of the Collegio Romano, which preserved a musical counterpoint,
while re-establishing a single line in the setting of the words: so that
the Curial concern that the faithful should be able to hear the words
of the Proper and Ordinary of the mass clearly was met, as had not
been the case in much late medieval and Renaissance Church music.
The distinct text was thus sung in concentrated sequence; for the

imposition, in most dioceses and all the more recent religious orders, of the standard Tridentine liturgy, as a result of the revision of the missal left to the papacy by the decision of the Council, also brought about the end of other earlier musical practices, like the troping of parts of the Ordinary of the mass by the intrusion of other texts.

The use of orchestral instruments in Church music, over and above the organ, was maintained in the non-liturgical devotions of the Roman oratory as well as in the elaborate compositions for the ducal chapel of Saint Mark's at Venice, in the period of the Gabrieli and Monteverdi. The design of the chapel encouraged a dramatic contrast in the use of antiphonal choirs of voices, as well as instruments, which went beyond the conventions of choral practice elsewhere, and achieved a declamatory effect which might be called Baroque. The local traditions of Venetian Church music were maintained in the churches and convents of the city, into the eighteenth century, by the work of Vivaldi, Marcello, and Galuppi, for example. The foundations for educating girls in conventual surroundings led to the spectacle of female choirs and orchestras at Venice in fact, whatever the designed seclusion of the girls' galleries. Outside Italy, the ducal court of Bavaria, in the Catholic restoration of the late sixteenth century, provided employment for the talents of Lassus, whose rich and dramatic settings of liturgical texts, and of devotional matter, as in the *Seven Penitential Psalms*, foreshadowed in a way the dramatic effects, achieved by technically simple means, of Allegri, whose *Miserere* became the monopoly of the Sistine Choir. The use of orchestral forces, supplementing chorus, soloists and organ, culminated in the masses of Mozart and Haydn, in the later eighteenth century, performed at cathedrals and court chapels in the German-speaking lands, or in the princely chapel at Esterháza in Hungary.

The royal family's courts under Louis XIV had already provided a setting for Church music, such as that of Charpentier, which used orchestral as well as choral or organ effects. The compositions for convents, in France of the seventeenth and eighteenth century, combined variety of tone and colour with the deployment of limited resources: and the organ interlude, to mark moments of the mass, such as the silent consecration and elevation, was specifically developed in France, while preparing the way for orchestral interludes in later masses. The disposition of voices, in choral and solo passages, nevertheless remained the essential of mass settings in the Catholic Church, as in the celebratory devotion of the *Benedictus* in later works, whose length came to place that movement of the setting after the consecration, during the silent second part of the canon, said by the priest at the altar. The patronage of commissioning clerics and princely employers remained as vital as in the visual arts, however, in Catholic Europe just as much as in the English employment by Elizabeth I of the Catholic composer, Byrd, at the royal chapels. The English composer Philips learned from Frescobaldi, organist of St Peter's, Rome, the art of organ interludes for the moments of the mass.

The papal choir maintained into modern times its distinctive use of *castrati* singers. But compositions intended only for male voices included those elsewhere where the leading line was written for adult *castrati* voices, not trebles, as in eighteenth-century Spain for example.[10] The didactic religious oratorios of Neri's Roman Oratory established the genre of non-liturgical religious music, reflecting Neri's Florentine background. The first opera in a theatre north of the Alps was staged at the archiepiscopal court of Salzburg, following the quasi-operatic performance of a religious work, the *Representation of the Body and Soul* by Cavalieri at the Roman Oratory. The patronage of music, drama, and opera at Catholic courts, whether in the theatre of the Palazzo Barberini, in Bernini's Rome, or in the Paris of Richelieu and Mazarin, led to the subsequent adoption of the oratorio as a sacred work, in distinction to the profane opera, in Protestant countries especially. But accusations of theatricality, applied to the visual and musical religious art of the Catholic states, between the late sixteenth and late eighteenth century, represent a chronological inversion: the restored splendour of liturgical and non-liturgical religious ceremonies after Trent, not least in Rome itself, above all at the Roman Oratory, provided the model for the seventeenth-century employment of scenic and musical effect in the evolving masque, opera and related court ballet. The celebration of royal authority at the English court of Charles I and the French courts of Louis XIII and Louis XIV followed the same path as the separate monumental celebration of papal authority, in the fountains, obelisks and palaces of late sixteenth-century and later Rome, and the dramatic splendour of the Barberini palace, with its main ceiling by Pietro da Cortona allegorizing the family's triumph. The royal basilica and mausoleum of the Escorial was at the centre of the gridiron plan; and the papal rebuilding of La Sapienza, the Roman university, in the seventeenth century, took as its focus the brilliant exercise in Trinitarian symbolism of Borromini's Sant'Ivo.

The complete plan of Charles I's reign for the rebuilding of the royal palace at Whitehall, of which Inigo Jones's Banqueting House provided the backdrop in the end for the staging of the king's execution, may have included a chapel at the centre, of a greater splendour than that provided by Jones for Henrietta Maria. But the final plan of Versailles, as elaborated by Louis XIV, after the rejection of Bernini's plans for the rebuilding of the Louvre, added the chapel as a side-effect. Despite the devotional display of Louis's later years, court ceremonial still revolved around the daily cycle of the king's rising and retiring: the palace remained unquestionably heliocentric. There was some accidental sense in the objections of English Puritans to the art collection of Charles I, on the grounds of association with Catholic idolatry, though the sales of the king's paintings in the Interregnum most benefited other rulers in Catholic Europe. But the prominence, in the Catholic areas of continental Europe, of certain religious subjects rather than others, after the Council of Trent, demonstrated the complex effect of official patronage and consequent popular devotion. Marian themes remained as popular as in medieval and Renaissance art, though the Spanish devotion to the Immaculate Conception, as in Murillo's decorative paintings, represented a doctrine which neither the Council of Trent nor the papacy had officially promulgated. The physical sufferings of Christ remained a constant theme, supported by the varieties of martyrdom which emphasized sometimes the realism of pain, more often the triumph of faith. The thaumaturgic saints, like Saint Roch, remained popular in many areas of Catholic Europe, despite the challenge of Protestantism. In the face of Protestant attack certain doctrines were reasserted visually: the holy souls in purgatory, and, associated with them, the holy guardian angels. The new representation of Saint Peter, in tearful penitence for his denial of Christ, asserted the doctrine of sacramental confession, at the risk of suggesting the human failings of the Petrine office. St Mary Magdalene in penitence became more popular, avoiding such a suggestion, and allowing depiction of a beautiful female in tears. The anatomic perfection of Saint Sebastian remained almost as choice a theme as in the Renaissance displays of mastery of the human body, while his sufferings became if anything even more convincing. The secrecy of the confessional was asserted in Bohemia, after the Catholic reconquest, by the canonization of a supposedly earlier martyr, Saint John Nepomuk, whose cult then spread, by sculpture and painting, to the other lands of the Habsburg crown in the eighteenth century. The doctrine of the Eucharistic Real Presence was asserted by the adoption of the scene of the breaking of the bread at the Last Supper, rather than that of the apostles' question as to the betrayer, or the washing of feet; and the Supper at Emmaus entered the canon of painting in the same cause, offering possibilities for *Caravaggisti* of portraying a tavern interior, just as the stress on Saint Joseph, as guardian of the Church militant, provided opportunities for realistic treatment of the venerable carpenter.

Jansenist illustration of sacramental occasions naturally suggested greater reserve. The approach to the visual arts of Jansenist circles was generally restrained, as the quiet grace of the paintings of Philippe de Champaigne reveal. The classicizing restraint of Baroque display more generally, in the work of French artists, Poussin and Dughet, as well as Claude Lorrain, brought to seventeenth-century France a concept of grandeur and good taste which could not fully appreciate Bernini's sculptures of Louis XIV; this was despite the honour paid to the artist, as to the subject, by the papal permission for Bernini to undertake such work, so sought after by Charles I of England. The influence of the major French artists who worked in Rome also made itself felt in the changing taste of Roman collectors and patrons themselves, as landscape came to be appreciated, even if still populated by Poussin's classical figures and vestigial architectural remains. The evolution of secular painting, sculpture and architecture, in Italy as in France, is however a distinct history. From the qualified splendour of French 'classicism' in the seventeenth century, though, the Baroque elaboration of more temporary works of art, even there, stands out. The triumphal exoticism of funerary décor in seventeenth-century France showed little restraint. The royal and princely catafalques were but the centre-pieces of dramatic scenes, in which the whole interior of the cathedral of Notre Dame could be transformed, to celebrate the achievements of the deceased, rather than to inspire consideration of the rigours of death. In this the French temporary cenotaphs contrasted with the papal tombs of seventeenth- and early eighteenth-century Rome, erected in St Peter's and other papal basilicas, which often combined the macabre or grotesque with the assertion, even from beyond the grave, of papal authority. The papal tombs were, in this way, more akin to Bernini's representation in marble of the ecstasy of Saint Teresa, with its realistic interpretation of mystical experience, reflecting the literary imagery of Catholic mystical and poetic writing at the end of the sixteenth century and the beginning of the seventeenth.

The images so carefully dissected in the iconological treatises of the sixteenth century, which guided artists through the intricacies of pagan and Christian symbolism, and helped standardize both religious and secular art to some extent, were an Italian achievement more succinct than the enthusiastic compilation of German and

Dutch emblem books of the same period, some of which verged on the occult sciences. But the images given life in the Catholic poetry of Saint John of the Cross, in the vernacular, of the Catholic English exile Crashaw, who hymned Saint Teresa, or in the Holy Sonnets of John Donne in Jacobean England, who was brought up a Catholic before becoming Anglican Dean of Saint Paul's, where Charles I, Laud and Inigo Jones were to provide the last great addition to the old cathedral, shared a common identity. The influences of both continental Catholic writing and English native developments, as in the Mannerist devices of euphuism, were arguably already evident in the devotional work of the Catholic Southwell. But the French funerary style, in visual representation rather than literary panegyric, was more similar to the typographic experiments of poetic letterpress, representing a physical image in its setting, found both in the Anglican writer Herbert, and in some continental printing of the period. Literary art was in any case less clearly distinguished by Catholic or Protestant allegiance than the visual arts, in the period of the Counter-Reformation, given Protestant exaltation of the Word, sometimes to the despair of the illiterate in Protestant society. The Italianate classicism of Milton suggests this, although the architectural and sculptural celebration of royal and Marian splendour, in Laud's additions to Saint John's College and the university church at Oxford, survived Puritan attack. The Protestant rejection of the visual arts, in religious contexts, was never absolute. In the Northern Netherlands Rembrandt came to provide illustration of biblical themes, alongside the pervasive popularity of secular genres in Dutch painting, just as Dürer and Cranach had once illustrated the biblical and apocalyptic message of the early Lutheran reformers. The pompous display of court decoration at Versailles or of funerary art suggesting a Pelagian theology was perhaps not to the taste of the Jansenists in France; but the greater informality of French architecture, painting and sculpture, after the death of Louis XIV, produced in the eighteenth century the Rococo, which was so much admired by German princes wishing to imitate what Voltaire described, by a strange revision of history, as the great era of the sun-king. Quite apart from the palaces of prince-bishops, like that superbly adorned at Würzburg by the Venetian Tiepolo, before his retreat to Spain and replacement in European esteem by the neo-classical Mengs, the Rococo style was adopted in German-speaking lands for churches and convents.

The advent of war and epidemic in seventeenth-century Italy reduced the artistic leadership of the peninsula in Europe, despite the fame of Bernini, and the splendour of Baroque Rome under the Barberini and in the immediately succeeding pontificates. At Rome architecture, painting and sculpture pursued modifications of the Baroque style until the arrival of neo-classicism at the end of the eighteenth century, as at the last papal palace, built by the Braschi. To some degree this was true elsewhere in Italy, though Venetian architecture and painting remained distinctive, as at earlier periods: the Baroque of Longhena, in his church of Santa Maria della Salute, built to mark the end of the seventeenth-century epidemic in the city, was as different from the more solid Baroque of Roman architects as Palladio's modified classicism, at San Giorgio Maggiore, Venice, or Il Redentore, built at the end of an earlier epidemic, was from Vignola's evolution of a late Mannerist and proto-Baroque style in Rome. The fears of Federico Borromeo, forced to divert funds destined for the Ambrosiana to the relief of food shortage and subsequent plague in Milan, that the arts would flee Italy, invaded by war and disaster, proved to a degree true.[11] The French lead in the visual and literary arts of Western Europe became clear by the end of the seventeenth century, while Italy became the object of the Grand Tour rather than of pilgrimage, where sightseers looked for classical remains as much as for the work of Renaissance or subsequent artists. The Baroque, as a style of ecclesiastical architecture above all, had already spread however to Spain, Portugal and their overseas territories, from Italy. The reimportation of influences from the foreign missionfields was once again evident in the Iberian peninsula, though, in the arguable inclusion of American Indian devices in the elaborate sculptural decoration of Churriguera and other Spanish architects, into the eighteenth century; though only in Portugal did the massive devastation caused by the Lisbon earthquake of the century allow the rebuilding of churches, palaces, and a whole city on an entirely new scale of grandeur, while Brazilian bullion could support its decoration.

The Baroque, as a style of church building and decoration, began to spread from Italy into Austria and Southern Germany, even to Poland, to Bohemia and Hungary, as well as to the Swiss cantons. The Tyrolean abbey of Stams showed an early reception of the Baroque, in its high altar reredos. The prince-archbishop of Salzburg, Marcus Sitticus von Hohenems II, rebuilt his cathedral and parts of the medieval city in the style of the Italian Baroque, borrowing workmen from his relation, the art patron and archbishop of Milan, Federico Borromeo. At Graz the archduke Ferdinand prepared his burial-place, at the centre of his Catholic reconquests, by securing Italian workmanship for the rebuilding of the city, where the Jesuits had established their educational presence under the Archduke Charles. Austrian, Bavarian and South German Baroque thereafter evolved independently to a large degree, despite Italian influence on certain ecclesiastical buildings, as at Wilten, on the edge of Innsbruck. The late Baroque in the German lands closely resembled aspects of the Rococo style, to which it became assimilated. The lightness of interior decoration in conventual, pilgrimage and other churches did not mean a reduction of scale, however. The wealth and power of abbeys in particular were demonstrated by the vast monastic buildings planned, and often built, as at Melk or Saint Florian. The new churches were also on an expansive scale often, as with the Theatines' church at Munich, or the church of Saint Charles Borromeo, on a triumphal imperial model, at Vienna. The elaboration of buildings in eighteenth-century Vienna continued until the advent of neo-classicism, both in the visual arts, and in the literary influence of Italians and others at the Habsburg court. The work, in the Austrian lands, of Prandtauer complemented that of Fischer von Erlach, the more successful follower of Borromini, as a commoner ennobled for his architectural virtuosity, von Hildebrandt and the Asam brothers or Neumann, also in German lands. The late Baroque and Rococo thus became, in much of Europe, the art of the Catholic Church in fact, though not exclusively an ecclesiastical style, before the development of buildings in the same style in areas of more mixed religious allegiance, as at Dresden. The distinction of the arts in German lands had never followed religious divisions completely in any case. The music of Bach for Lutheran worship was not entirely dissociated from compositions for Catholic use, and the Italian influence of the Venetian and Bolognese developments of choral and orchestral music reached Germany – whether in the religious music of Schütz or Buxtehude, or the development of the Baroque concerto – from the instrumental interludes at mass, perfected in the basilica of San Petronio at Bologna, which allowed for displays of virtuosity like the Mannheim crescendo. Classical myth, in any case, remained the favourite theme of the secular visual and literary arts in Catholic Europe.

Despite the appearance of neo-classicism in the visual arts of Catholic Europe, for ecclesiastical building or religious painting, by the end of the eighteenth century, the independent evolution of that style represented much more a secular reaction against the late Rococo of both Church and princely courts. The fluctuations of fortune, as of style, in the career of the French painter David did not prevent his survival of the Revolution, and of the Napoleonic rise to power. The moment of Napoleon crowning himself emperor, in the presence of the pope, was painted by David in the splendid yet realistic manner of his later style, and seemed to symbolize the independent development of the arts in Catholic Europe after the Council of Trent. The Council had not dictated a particular style for the use of the Catholic Church, but the Church had certainly not, as an institution, maintained control of the arts in Catholic Europe. There had indeed been a limited attempt to purify the arts in the service of the Church, but such rigorism had never been opposed to all display, despite the French opposition – of Jansenist and other rigorist clerics – to theatre in the seventeenth century. A selective employment of visual and musical art was rather reasserted against Protestant criticism, especially in the Calvinist, rather than Lutheran, stripping of ancient churches and simple singing of vernacular psalms, sometimes without even organ accompaniment. The Catholic ideal, on the other hand, found expression after the Council of Trent even in the penal conditions of Elizabethan England, where most masses had to be said clandestinely. Despite the slow adoption of the new Tridentine rite by the English mission priests, the splendour of the Catholic liturgy was represented by solemn masses, sung to complete settings, within the relative security of the noble household at Battle Abbey. The restrained yet dramatic realism of Crespi's portrait of Charles Borromeo, at his solitary meal in Milan, was very different from the heightened colour and dazzling shift of perspectives in the miraculous scenes painted at Venice by Tintoretto; yet both attempted to express aspects of the Catholic religious revival of the Counter-Reformation.

While secular art made its own independent development, as with the eighteenth-century growth of genre painting with classical overtones, in place of some direct depictions of classical myth, the religious art of a popular nature encouraged or permitted by the Catholic Church evolved much more slowly: its continuity was represented not only by the preservation of venerated and miraculous images of earlier periods, but by elaborate scenic devices, such as those at the Sacro Monte of Varese, in the chain of chapels patronized by Charles Borromeo on pilgrimage.[12] The final assertion of the sacred status of miraculous representation, as opposed to human art, indeed, came with the pilgrimage made by Charles Borromeo to venerate the Holy Shroud, brought to Turin for him, and thereafter preserved in the ducal and royal chapel, after this public act of recognition by a leading prelate of the Church.[13] Even chivalric fancy, in vernacular literature, was brought back to a Christian point of reference, in the rhetorical language of Tasso's *Gerusalemme Liberata*, after the freer inspiration of Ariosto's *Orlando Furioso*, before the preciosity of later Spanish and Italian religious poetry. Such fusion of the traditional and the new was also to be found in the Jesuit oratory attached to Sant'Ignazio in Rome, where the pre-Tridentine discipline of the flagellant confraternities was transformed by the addition of sacred music and verse, as an aid to meditation. In the life of the Neapolitan prince, Gesualdo, Mannerist composer and relation of the Borromeos, the conventions of honour and the conspicuous piety of the Counter-Reformation clashed in a way reminiscent of the Spanish plays of the period: nature imitating art. While the dramatic dissonances in his compositions were professedly in accord with the Borromean attitude to ecclesiastical music, his personal revenge on his wife and her lover led to his own retirement to a country retreat.

Despite such an episode, Italian culture, in the visual arts at least, remained intensively creative, until the later seventeenth century, not least in Barberini Rome: so that the apparent decline of intellectual originality in Baroque Italy has been seen, in one view, as but a shift to representational creativity. Even in the second half of the century, in Naples, where the elaboration of Baroque architecture was not least an ecclesiastical and conventual affair, a romantic individuality was shown in the paintings on secular themes of Salvator Rosa. In Spain Valdés Leal, in the period after the death of Velasquez, arguably showed even greater religious intensity in his painting than had been demonstrated by the great artist and portraitist. In eighteenth-century Sicily and Piedmont the architectural invention of Juvara continued the idiosyncratic Baroque of the Theatine Guarini in late seventeenth-century Piedmont. Sensitivity to earlier styles of ecclesiastical architecture, and the 'medievalism' of aspects of the Catholic revival and Baroque period, led to the contemplation of 'Gothic' designs for uncompleted façades, such as those of Milan cathedral and San Petronio, Bologna. While mathematical calculation supported the designs of Guarini and von Erlach, Herrera, at the Escorial, had still been influenced rather by occult symbolism, for all the severity of his style.

Unlike the monumental quality of German Baroque architecture, as epitomized by the work of Pöppelmann, the new churches of the Catholic Netherlands, after the Council of Trent, revealed the strong continuing local influence of surface ornament: a sort of northern Mannerist detail. Such architectural freedom was very different from

the original severity of Tridentine Spain, where critics among the
canons of Toledo cathedral had wished to reject El Greco's *Stripping
of Christ*, because his startling perspective allowed the heads of other
figures to appear above that of Christ on the canvas. The architectural
highpoint of Spanish Baroque was possibly the *Trasparente* altar at
the same cathedral, whose originality of design and lighting depended on pastoral concern for reverence to the reserved sacrament.
By contrast, Louis XIV's court, at least before the devotional rigour
of the king's last years, protected the anti-clerical humour of Boileau,
and, less certainly, the attack of Molière on false *dévots*. Jansenist as
well as rationalist publication, by the end of the reign, however, had
to seek the security of the Netherlands; while the schismatic non-
Jurors in England turned productively to antiquarian and historical
study. The antiquarian exoticism of Piranesi's Roman priory for the
Knights of Malta, though, is in an idiosyncratic form of late Baroque,
rather than truly neo-classical; and attempts to detect masonic symbols in the ornaments, as more properly in Mozart's popular opera,
*The Magic Flute*, are a reminder of the complications of patronage
in the Catholic world by the later eighteenth century. Such influences, however, were very different from that of Augustine, on the
sixteenth-century confessional writing of Saint Teresa, or the Milanese promotion, at the end of the century, of the Forty Hours
Devotion to the reserved sacrament, which represented a climax in
the devotion of the visual arts to the reasserted doctrine of the
Church, with the elaborate décor for the exposition of the sacrament.
The meditative devotion acquired in old age by Michelangelo, associate of Vittoria Colonna and the Italian Catholic reforming circles of
the *spirituali*, complemented the medieval influence reasserted in his
design for the dome of Saint Peter's, as completed by della Porta.
But whereas the extension of the nave of Saint Peter's, to form a
Latin cross plan, in place of a centrally planned structure, led to the
disappointment of the façade by Carlo Maderna and the failure of
the bell towers, Michelangelo's genius had still been visible in the
transformation, which he began, of the Roman Baths of Diocletian
into the monumental church of Santa Maria degli Angeli, next to the
Rome Charterhouse.

The dramatic immediacy of Counter-Reformation piety, typified
in this respect by the Jesuit *Spiritual Exercises*, continued to inspire
other artists' efforts at heightened realism, even after the death of
Michelangelo, at the end of the Council of Trent. The periodic
exposition of the most prized relics of the Roman church in St Peter's
led to the creation of the four tribunals of the crossing by Bernini,

and the necessity of a defence of his memory against allegations that he had weakened the strength of the central piers supporting the dome. The personal piety, of a spontaneous sort, revealed in Mozart's letters was represented not only in his perfection of the post-Tridentine motet, in his *Ave Verum*, but in the agonized conflict between hope and despair of his *Requiem*, all but finished on his death, at the very end of the eighteenth century. The Good Friday Catholic tradition of the Three Hours Devotion, for which Haydn wrote his orchestral interludes, *The Seven Words of Christ from the Cross*, was, like the oratorio, to become, at a later date, a favourite form of Protestant piety, in England; while in the eighteenth century, the English Catholic Alexander Pope had seen the rational sentiment and humanism of his poetry applauded by the literary world. In continental Catholic Europe the external cult of the reserved sacrament represented, in one sense, the reverse of Jansenist moderation; though the development of the popular ceremonies of children's first communion represented, in its own way, an assertion of the pastoral care necessary in preparing the faithful for the sacraments of the Church. The Marian devotion of the rosary achieved a popularity even greater than in medieval religious practice, while the enthusiasm for relics from the catacombs provided altars in the German lands, after the Council of Trent, with their exposed bodies of ancient saints. While in Bavaria Jesuit influence spread from Ingolstadt, the Society naturally remained strong in reconquered Bohemia; but in the seventeenth century episcopal authority was reasserted there by the creation of two new sees. The Baroque architecture of the Jesuit college in Prague was the work of an Italian; but native architects and sculptors developed a local Baroque style for churches in the city and the decoration of the Charles Bridge. Columns in honour of the Immaculate Conception were erected in the Austrian Habsburg lands, like that erected in the nineteenth century by Pius IX, in the Piazza di Spagna in Rome; while in German-speaking Europe votive plague-columns marked the end of epidemics, without the polemic overtones which came to mark the Monument after the Great Fire of London. The communal vows made in plagues led to a flourishing of religious drama of a popular nature too, of which the most famous became the Bavarian Passion Play of Oberammergau. The doctrine of the Immaculate Conception however was espoused by the Sorbonne, as well as by revived Austrian imperialism at the end of Louis XIV's reign.

In the city of Rome itself, the Renaissance spectacles of bull-fights and races run in the nude gave way to theatrical displays of originally religious inspiration: as with the early seventeenth-century music drama *Sant'Alessio* by Landi. Elsewhere instrumental music was stimulated in its development by the liturgical fashion for 'supplying the verse', or producing an organ interlude between verses of canticles such as the *Magnificat* at Vespers, sung by the choir: the organ interludes of Pachelbel, who began his career in the second half of the seventeenth century at the Catholic centres of Ratisbon and Vienna, illustrate this. Venice maintained its lead in the establishment of secular opera-houses, and Naples too continued to represent Italian operatic tradition. The introduction of dramatic rhythm and tonal colour achieved by successions of chords, in place of true counterpoint, became evident in ecclesiastical music in seventeenth-century Italy – as in the compositions of Carissimi – in contrast to the greater reserve shown even in solo writing, in the verse anthems for Protestant use of composers in England. The liturgy of Holy Week in the Catholic Church precluded vernacular settings and elaborations of the Passion, like those of Bach; though the greatest of his mass settings, that in B minor, was finally completed in a form suitable for Catholic worship. By contrast the Church music of Soler, composed at and for the abbey of Montserrat in the mid-eighteenth century, showed the harmonious traditionalism of the Benedictine liturgy performed there. Handel's work had Roman origins too, demonstrated in his early setting of *Dixit Dominus*, the psalm sung at Sunday Vespers, composed in the city; just as Mozart's early Italian experience proved influential in his own development. The tradition of orchestral accompaniment of masses was interrupted, however, at the end of the eighteenth century, by the liturgical reforms imposed by Joseph II, another example of the ironic revival of certain immediately post-Tridentine issues by the erastian interventions of the emperor.

The organ, as the most common instrument in Church music, was developed on individual lines in Germany and France, by the eighteenth century; while the Iberian peninsula preserved the dramatic musical effect of horizontal 'royal trumpets' in addition to vertical pipes. Throughout Catholic Europe, the organ case offered possibilities for Baroque display, as much as did confessional boxes or pulpits. The development of Catholic devotional art was not always, however, from the simple to the more elaborate, after the Council of Trent. The Tridentine rebuilding of Santo Spirito in Sassia, Rome, by the younger Sangallo represented an early restraint. But in the papal basilica of Santa Maria Maggiore, Sixtus V employed Domenico Fontana to create the grandiose Cappella Sistina, to rehouse the sacred crib of Christ, object of pilgrimage veneration. The same pope and architect were responsible at the same period, the mid-1580s, for the rebuilding of the Scala Santa, at the Lateran, which pilgrims ascended on their knees, in memory of Christ's judgement in Pilate's palace. The new roads, which led to the seven basilicas, begun by the pope, were followed not only by humble pilgrims but by leading prelates, like Charles Borromeo, who made the circuit of the churches on foot.[14] The Jubilee of 1600, however, was followed by the placing of Caravaggio's picture of the *Madonna of the Pilgrims* in the church of Sant'Agostino, which was a simple exercise in realistic description, and soon acquired great popularity. Bernini's baldacchino for Saint Peter's, Rome, in the seventeenth century fixed in bronze the image of the canopy carried in processions over the reserved Sacrament. Yet in Spain the painted saints of Zurbarán revealed a dramatic immediacy nevertheless sombre and meditative. The greater restraint of most French religious art was clear in Poussin's second series of *The Seven Sacraments*, even after his return from Paris to Rome. But the moral rigour suggested by his art was, in turn, in contrast to the hedonism of the last Medici court at Florence, in the mid-eighteenth century, at a time when French political and artistic influences were beginning to be felt at the courts of the Italian peninsula. The papal court and the city of Rome, from the end of the sixteenth century to the eighteenth century, continued to represent a life of splendour and conspicuous display, rather than austerity. The households of cardinals remained princely; and even those who led austere lives in their sees, as did Charles and Federico Borromeo at Milan, conformed with this pattern of life to a degree at least when in Rome. The scholarly Cardinal Baronius moved, at the end of his life, in the early seventeenth century, from the Roman Oratory to the neighbouring Piazza Navona, which Bernini was to make another public monument to papal authority, in the hopes that the relative elevation of Federico Borromeo's Roman house would improve his declining health.[15] But cardinals' households were also centres of learning, as well as of patronage of the visual and performing arts. Charles Borromeo, while still in Rome, encouraged the studies of other prelates, by his academic *Noctes Vaticanae*; and the young Federico, while at Rome and as a Curial cardinal, devoted himself to patristic as well as canonistic study, under tutors who included a Catholic priest in exile from Britain. At the end of his life, in 1631, however, a papal ruling had just elevated cardinals to the style of *Eminenza*, in place of mere *Illustrissimo*.

The interior spirituality of the post-Tridentine Church showed the same variety of development as did the exterior institutional forms, or the architectural and artistic manifestations. Even in the unpromising conditions of later sixteenth-century France, amid the anarchic conflict of Catholics and Huguenots, the beginnings of the interior revival which was to advance the institutional restoration of Bourbon France were apparent. In Provence, the influence of Tarugi, archbishop of Avignon, from Neri's Roman Oratory, spread the example of his friend, Charles Borromeo. Tarugi also encouraged the formation of a Provençal Oratory, on the model of the Roman, which was later made part of Bérulle's French Oratory. In the last three decades of the sixteenth century the Feuillant branch of reformed Cistercians was formed in France; while Henri III brought the Hieronymites to France, not from Spain but from Poland. Despite Gallican opposition to the Jesuits in France, the influence of the Society was felt on royal policy from the beginning of the Bourbon regime, with Père Coton in the later reign of Henri IV, and the Jesuit confessors of Louis XIII and Louis XIV. Enthusiasm for the mystical and miraculous was at the heart of early seventeenth-century French spirituality, whatever the reserve of the late century, in this matching the mood of the early century in Italy, where episcopal investigation of asserted miracles proved necessary at times. But a love of the ecstatic, admired in Neri's life, for example, contrasted with rigorist condemnation of games of football or snowball fights among the human diversions of seminarians in Italy, though Neri himself approved of children's games. The miraculous in lives of saints, as written in both Italy and France in this period, contrasted with the earlier, physical fantasies of Rabelais. Yet Père Coton, as much as Francis de Sales, tried to create a form of spiritual direction for those immersed in public life, in contrast to the Jansenist theory of the necessity of retreat from society in order to secure salvation.

But in the early seventeenth-century revival of French Catholicism there was as yet no distinction between *dévots* and Jansenists, while Jesuits and Oratorians were not yet rivals but collaborators. The Capuchins, whose arrival in France at the time of the religious wars led to their initial involvement in the politics of the League, produced a more mystical influence on the seventeenth-century revival of Catholic religion in France, represented not so much by Père Joseph as by the English-born Benet of Canfield. The mysticism of the early seventeenth century was, by the end of the century, regarded in certain cases with distrust, on account of supposed leanings towards a proto-Quietism. This was as true of Benet of Canfield's views as of the devotional writings of Federico Borromeo, whose spirituality, with its emphasis on peace and joy, rather than on penance and sorrow, was in fact formed under the realistic influence of the cheerful Neri. The spiritual standards held out to laity as well as ecclesiastics, in the world of the French *dévots*, like Marillac, increased the danger of denunciation of directors: as criticism, in different ways, of both Jesuit confessors and Fénelon was later to show. The contemplative and the active, within the regular life, however, were both encouraged in the French Catholic revival, by the efforts of Madame Acarie on behalf of both the Carmelites and the Ursulines: she, indeed, shared the common sense of Teresa of Avila. With Teresa too she shared a rare concern that entrance to conventual life should be the result of vocation, not merely of social pressure; the publication of Teresa's works diffused knowledge of her example outside Spain. Madame Acarie was also familiar with the difficulties of females living as tertiaries of a religious order, but still in society, which concerned the post-Tridentine Church.

In Venetian territory, after the Council of Trent, the secular magistrates still ordered female convents on occasion to receive noble married women, whose marriages were temporarily in difficulty, despite protests from the nuns that the presence of such matrons could only disturb the regular life, and was indeed against their rule: convents were persistently seen as the preservative of noble reputation.[16] In the France of Richelieu, the Carmelite nuns, formed under Spanish tuition but placed under French superiors, moved in the atmosphere of the cardinal and Père Joseph, as well as of Bérulle: devotion to the Sacrament, and prayers for the fortune of French arms. On the other hand, in older established convents, the noble birth or family connections of abbesses sometimes helped them to impose strict enclosure and a common life on nuns who had become used to less austere ways in the confusion of late sixteenth-century France. For in France, as at Venice, personal property had been effectively reintroduced into female conventual life, in contradiction to the monastic rule. Such conditions nevertheless existed side by side – in the first half of the seventeenth century in France – with ecstatic experiences by nuns which, on occasion, left permanent physical marks; in the same way the ecstatic yet realistic Philip Neri was regarded as having been permanently affected by his mystical experiences. Francis de Sales praised to Jeanne de Chantal the compliance of the austere Charles Borromeo with Swiss drinking habits, in the interests of winning Swiss allegiance to Catholicism: rigorism and Jansenism were distinct.

The political involvements of Bérulle's life caused his occupation with the marriage of Henrietta Maria to the Protestant Charles I of England, the fortunes of English Catholics, and even the ambitions of the duke of Buckingham. But, at the same time, he and the Oratorians promoted one of the most popular and human forms of post-Tridentine devotion, to the Infant Christ, which was also taken up in reconquered Prague. Yet again, Bérulle had a certain influence on Descartes's mental development. But the later Jansenist opposition to aspects of devotion to Christ's humanity does not alter the evolution of rivalry between the French Oratorians and the Jesuits, over seminary and educational influence, as over the direction of the French Carmelite nuns. Despite such divisions, and the distractions of the Frondes, some improvement in the life of the secular clergy, as a result of the influence of the Oratory, Saint-Sulpice and the other New Orders in France, was evident by the beginning of Louis XIV's reign. Even noble canons of Notre Dame, Paris, were performing their duties in person, according to Vincent de Paul. The effusive piety of Bérulle and his followers nevertheless found pictorial expression in the more restrained, classicizing form of painting favoured in France, as opposed to the splendour of Italian Baroque. Olier, founder of Saint-Sulpice, commissioned Le Brun to decorate the seminary chapel, and followers of Condren, who represented the link between Bérulle's original plan for the French Oratory and the seminary work of Saint-Sulpice, appreciated Poussin's depiction of the Seven Sacraments. But devotional statuary, as of the Child Jesus, was attended, at the same period in the circles of the French Catholic revival, with all the signs of popular attachment to be found in Italian piety: robes of precious material and jewelled gold and silverwork. Jean Eudes was also formed in the French Oratory, but his religious enthusiasm embraced the work of exorcism, to relieve a possessed woman of the effects of witchcraft, as well as the promotion of the cult of the Sacred Heart of Jesus. The Sacred Heart also appeared as a Jesuit emblem, at a time when European medicine was making important advances in knowledge of the circulation of the blood. But the *putti* of Baroque painting and stucco work represent an idealization of childhood purity, associated with angels, in place of the disturbing neo-platonism of Michelangelo's wingless, sinless, but more distinctly pubescent angels: only Bernini revived the adolescent charm of the winged seraph for his three-dimensional representation of the climax of mystical experience, in Saint Teresa's ecstasy at the hands of a sacred cupid.

Visual as well as literary representation was essential in the Cath-

olic world after the Council of Trent: not only the Jesuits' *Imago* of
the Society's first century of existence, but the Venetian Republic's
adoption of a grander form of official dress for its magistrates, in
addition to promotion of an official history.[17] Even in France, the
fusion of all the arts, which has been seen as a characteristic of the
Baroque, was represented by the compositions of Charpentier for
sacred dramas at the Jesuit college in Paris. While the development
of the non-literary arts in France on the grandiose scale was arguably
delayed until the seventeenth century, compared to later sixteenth-
century Italy, by the interruption of the civil wars, the patronage of
the royal court and statesmen, on the basis of the state's accumulation
of national resources, not all spent on war, provided stimulating
patronage; though monotony can be detected in the literary and even
visual celebration of royal authority under Louis xiv. In German-
speaking Europe the flourishing of the visual arts followed the disruption of the Thirty Years War; and Vienna was transformed after
the relief of the Turkish siege, in the late seventeenth century, to
reach its full splendour in the eighteenth, as the Austrian Habsburg
lands were made relatively more subject to Viennese control. But a
German vernacular literature did not so easily flourish, in the age of
French literary dominance. Spanish literature from the later sixteenth century onwards received Italian influence, and exerted a
reciprocal effect; while direct Italian architectural transmission in
Spain occurred not only at Jesuit churches but at the University of
Salamanca too. Certain themes became as popular in devotional
literature after Trent, with examples in both Italian and English
Recusant literature, as in the visual arts: the tears of Saint Peter, the
penitence of the Magdalene, the humble glory of the Infant Christ.
But by the end of the seventeenth century and the early years of the
eighteenth, in Italy itself, a rationalist approach to religious as to
social questions was apparent, in works published at Venice and
Naples, for example, even if still at times with false imprints. Naples
produced Valletta and the jurisprudence of Gravina, Verona, in
Venetian territory, the antiquarian but critical insights of Maffei.
Vico followed Gravina in giving a social value to the purpose of
religion, but went on to suggest a relativity in the concept of truth.
In eighteenth-century Italy, the historical researches of Muratori
represented a critical approach to the ecclesiastical as well as secular
past, without the design of Baronius to defend the development of
the hierarchical Church. The concept of 'natural' man appeared, as
in Neapolitan thought, in Muratori's consideration of Christianity
in the Reductions of Paraguay. The devotional tradition in Italy had

not prevented the evolution of such radical thought, treating the will in a Cartesian rather than Jansenist manner.

In any assessment of the effect of Tridentine reforming rigour and Baroque triumphalism in the Catholic Church of the sixteenth, seventeenth and eighteenth centuries, the case of Ireland is particularly interesting. Unlike Italy, Ireland could obviously not display the outward signs of the Catholic cult on a grand scale; nor were the financial resources of the Church in the island those of the Roman court, where the older departments of the Curia, despite Tridentine reforms, continued to extract substantial sums from parts of Catholic Europe, in the administration of provision to benefices and succession to sees.[18] The conflicts between bishops and regulars existed in Ireland, just as within continental Europe, the English mission, and the Catholic overseas missions. Added to this was the division between the 'Old English', of the Catholic community in Ireland, and the 'native' Irish Catholics, both resident and established groups, but racially and socially divided to an extent. There was also the effect, at different times, of Spanish and French political involvement in Ireland; and the complication of continental developments, not least Jansenism, affecting Irish colleges in continental Europe. The moral rigorism of the Tridentine Church was certainly apparent in the attempts of the hierarchy in Ireland to equate a standard of social and moral behaviour accepted, in theory at any rate, in England and continental Europe, with the true practice of Christianity; but native adherence to rituals better suited to a partly clandestine Catholicism was not in fact eradicated. The refinements of ecclesiastical legislation on baptism and marriage, and the Tridentine attempt to eradicate personal vendetta, met with some of the popular resistance which Catholic reforming bishops in continental Europe experienced; the wake however chiefly defied Irish episcopal attempts to restrict social celebrations surrounding the religious observances of death and burial. The successful defence and preservation of Catholicism, despite penal legislation, were undoubted in Ireland, yet this remained more than anything a popular and social triumph, rather than the work of the hierarchy. Catholicism and Irish birth remained closely linked, though there were none of the artistic celebrations of Catholic recovery found in Poland or Prague, or the monuments to Catholic expansion found from North and South America to Goa.

Similarly, in Scotland, in the period after the Council of Trent, the persistence of at least a vestigial Catholicism was arguably strongest in the Celtic society of the north-west and the Isles. The institutional collapse of one of the most unreformed parts of the late medieval Western Church otherwise led to the necessary leadership of nobles, and dependence on the fortunes of clan and family allegiances for the survival of Catholicism. In the north-east and southern parts of the kingdom the importance of the household was evident, as in Recusant England: at Blairs, for example. The political complications of French and Spanish interests could not be avoided by the priests trained in the Scots colleges abroad; and the importance of capturing the king's person, in the Scotland of James VI's youth, as in France of the later sixteenth century, represented the dominance of political considerations in religious rivalries. In Ireland too the influence of the Catholic noble leaders was crucial, in relation to financial support for bishops, who were at odds with the regular missionaries who had kept Catholicism alive under Elizabeth. The conflicts of bishops and regulars, and divisions within each group, reflected not only the competition for limited resources, but also the tensions, found elsewhere in the European and overseas Catholic Church after Trent, over parochial responsibility and obedience to the episcopate. These internal confrontations divided Catholic action in the face of changing Stuart policy, and the disruptions which followed Strafford's government, in the Cromwellian reaction, and the international interventions of the late seventeenth century. But, despite Protestant attack, continuity of Catholic practice was arguably represented by popular pilgrimage, a survival of medieval and even Celtic traditions in Irish religion. The survival of a vestigial form of the 'old religion' in England and even in Wales, after the Reformation, was also apparent at popular level, not least in the north of England, in veneration of certain holy places, wells, or even former monastic sites, like Mount Grace, before the antiquarian and romantic rediscovery of a monastic past in eighteenth- and nineteenth-century England. The Borromean control of popular religion in Lombardy took over and incorporated popular pilgrimage to the *Sacro Monte* at Varese or Varallo; and German bishops attempted to impose order on traditional pilgrimages. But, in the largely clandestine practice of Catholicism in post-Tridentine Ireland, such lay devotion represented a determination to continue ancient religious practice, independent of either the rigorism or the triumphalism of the institutional Church after the Council. The independence of regulars from episcopal control in Ireland might possibly represent local reinforcement of a more common problem, by virtue of the traditions of the Celtic Church, but lay maintenance of ancient rituals certainly secured the continuity of Irish Catholicism after Trent.

The contrast, within continental Catholic Europe, between the Society of Jesus and the Roman Oratory again underlined the differences in doctrinal outlook and pastoral practice which marked the evolution of Catholicism after the Council of Trent. Both groups, as New Orders, though with antithetic constitutions, represented in one way the concern to use conspicuous grandeur in Church building and liturgical or devotional celebration to reassert the truth of Catholic teaching and revive loyalty to the authority of the Church. Yet the Oratory of Philip Neri itself, at once following and departing from his concept of freedom for members and any new houses of his movement, was divided at an early stage by the desire of the Neapolitan Oratorians for a more monastic rule, demonstrating a more traditional austerity and poverty. But the opposition of the most prominent of the Oratorians, after Neri's death, his successor Baronius, to aspects of contemporary Jesuit development was more marked than his sympathy for both traditions within the Oratory and his sadness at the Neapolitan division. To Baronius, a Church historian rather than a theologian, the 'new' pastoral morality of the Jesuit school represented by Molina was a distortion of apostolic and patristic tradition in the Church. To the 'Pelagianism' of Molina he opposed the 'Augustinianism' of the true Church, free from the innovations of Protestant heresy. The Augustinian division of the secular and divine order, as in the *City of God*, also supported the argument of Baronius, as confessor of Clement VIII, for the necessary independence of the Catholic Church from the demands of Catholic Spain. By contrast, the Jesuit general at the beginning of the seventeenth century, Acquaviva, faced with the tensions within his own Society which rapid numerical and geographical expansion caused, in a highly centralized constitution, proved compliant, to a degree, to Spanish royal wishes, as over the policies to be followed in the overseas missions; even if this was an attempt to deflect the attempts of Spanish members of the Society to produce a clearer dominance of national interests, in the international body.[19]

To Baronius and the Oratorians, like Tarugi, the Church was the community of the faithful, under its universal hierarchy: friends, like the Bozio brothers and Federico Borromeo, asserted the authority of bishops, in theory and in practice, against all secular claims. The sacraments were the means of salvation, as defined at Trent, and as the later Jansenist opponents of the Jesuits were to stress, by their concern for careful and less frequent reception. The Jesuit insistence on human education and social control, by contrast, was seen by Baronius as 'Pelagian', because over-reliant on human, not divine aid. This 'humanism' of the pastoral practice suggested by Molina was thus regarded as pessimistic, not allowing for the power of divine grace to create the Christian peace and joy which Neri and his followers valued, with their spiritual optimism, and Neri's own libertarian regard for individual potential under God. The pontificate of Clement VIII thus anticipated the debate between Jansenist 'pessimism' and Jesuit 'optimism', but in a reverse sense, in the climate of the search, by Oratorians and their friends, for greater ecclesiastical independence, before the later seventeenth century. The Jesuit rigorism of the earlier period was demonstrated by the restrictive view of the Society's theologians, in the German lands, towards the use of interest. This was combined with a censorious intervention in book collections held by Catholics in the empire, even at the cost of discomfort to a leading patron of the Society there, like Marx Fugger, of the great banking family of that name. The mixed religious composition of German cities such as Augsburg in any case created social as much as ecclesiastical problems, when the Catholic authorities adopted the reformed papal calendar, in the face of Protestant civic opposition. Even in Poland Catholic apologists could claim that toleration of Protestantism weakened royal authority, with some degree of plausibility. But, by the eighteenth century, the Oratorians were as important as the Jesuits and Piarists in maintaining Catholicism in Poland by educational activity. The stress on obedience, of Baronius if not of Neri, left an aura of Christian neo-stoicism, found among other Catholic associates of the Oratory in the seventeenth century too,[20] which may help to explain the tempered sympathy of the eighteenth-century Oratory, French and Roman, for Jansenist opposition to Jesuit teaching and practice, already opposed by Baronius himself. Yet this 'liberal' concept of obedience was even then at odds with the human regulation of Catholic society represented not so much, perhaps, by the Ignatian *Exercises*, as by the promotion by Acquaviva of the detailed educational regulations for the Society of Jesus, the *Ratio Studiorum*.

The Society of Jesus nevertheless made use of the historical work of Baronius, the *Annales* designed to counter Protestant attack on the Catholic Church, in their own anti-Protestant polemic; and they honoured the memory of the Oratorian at his death. Opposition to 'Machiavellian' reason of state among both Jesuits and writers in the circle of the Oratory equally involved denunciation of the French *politiques*, despite belated papal recognition of Henri IV, at Oratorian instigation to a large degree. The Roman Oratorian, as at first the French Oratorian tradition, asserted episcopal and clerical independence against Gallican claims. It was hardly surprising that Sarpi in the end was so dismissive of Baronius's views, after the Oratorian had attacked Venetian as well as Spanish interference in ecclesiastical affairs. Catholic erastian criticism of such views, in Naples and elsewhere in Italy, continued into the eighteenth century, in writers as different as Muratori and Giannone, despite the evolution of the eighteenth-century Oratory in a pro-Jansenist and anti-Jesuit direction. The more erastian and the more papalist Venetians and Paduan scholars who shared Galileo's intellectual interests alike were, however, distinct from his care to avoid the jurisdictional disputes of Catholic Europe, in his attempt to prove the true wonder of the cosmic creation. Even if Sarpi, the dissident friar, remained a protected, if less often consulted figure, except perhaps in questions concerning the Inquisition, at Venice, he finally found himself as opposed to the person of Henri iv as to the policy of James i. The Venetian painter, Lorenzo Lotto, ended his life at the Holy House of Loreto, a Marian shrine particularly venerated, by pilgrims from all parts of Catholic Europe, in the Counter-Reformation, as a symbol of the visible Church on earth.

But, by the eighteenth century, Catholic society in Europe was showing some decline in vocations to the clerical and regular life, as well as in lay devotion as represented by the confraternities. The popular practice of religion was apparently in decline, in parts of France at least, in the second half of the eighteenth century, before the Revolution; and this can arguably be seen in the failure of lay charity, too, in these circumstances, to keep pace with accelerating poverty and social dislocation. The involvement of some French bishops, at the end of the seventeenth century, in promoting charitable institutions, on the other hand, was more evidently in the tradition of Borromean provision at Milan, in the epidemics of the sixteenth and early seventeenth century. The social welfare included in the internal missions in France, in the Catholic revival of the first half of the century, was complementary to the religious purpose of the priests of the Mission, founded by St Vincent de Paul: an internal missionary model, once again, for the later French work in the overseas missions. Such altruistic concern was akin to the public denunciations of lay failure to help the poor and invest in declining sources of industrial employment, pronounced by Federico Borromeo in the Milanese epidemic of 1630-1. This contrasted with the admission of parish priests, in the mountainous regions of the pre-Borromean diocese, that they cast magic spells but failed to maintain the reserved sacrament in their churches. Individual episcopal charity continued to be demonstrated into the eighteenth century, in France and Spain, though both areas also continued to show great disparities in the allocation of resources between the higher and lower clergy and among even the upper clergy. In both areas, too, a failure to revise parochial and diocesan boundaries, and the consequently over-large parishes in some parts, left parishes without the means to support a resident priest for periods in the eighteenth century. The century thus saw, arguably, a reassertion in places of a popular lay religion more devotional than sacramental. Yet, in the diocese of Rome itself, severe reform of court, city clergy, regulars and laity, was imposed in the later seventeenth century by Innocent XI and in the early eighteenth century, by Benedict XIII; this was before the pontificate of Benedict XIV, who continued in Rome his reforming policies – if of a more relaxed variety – begun during his pastoral experience as archbishop of Bologna.

Elsewhere in eighteenth-century Italy, the expansion in the number of clergy and regulars of the first half of the century gave way to an absolute decline in the later part. Continued episcopal attempts to control confraternities and the manifestations of popular religion still met serious resistance. While newly promoted cults, such as that of the Stations of the Cross, allowed regulars to channel popular piety, clerical formation in seminaries remained often rudimentary. The episcopate contained those who had risen from non-noble society, and others from religious orders, so that its composition was at least more varied than in some other parts of Catholic Europe at this date. In Portugal, by the eighteenth century, nobles, both ecclesiastic and lay, were dominant in the episcopate and even in the management of the richest confraternities or charitable institutions, which claimed to be under royal patronage.[21] The unequal distribution of clerical revenue and of parochial clergy left the South of the country, as in Spain, without adequate pastoral care. The distinction between Old Christians, and the New Christians of Jewish origin, was finally abolished during the century, but in the first half of the century, at any rate, the Inquisition was still busily occupied with superstitious or diabolic practices, while bishops still struggled, as in seventeenth-century Spain, to overcome the exemption from their authority claimed by the numerous familiars of the Inquisition.[22] The economic dominance of the military orders in Portugal, controlling much of the total of ecclesiastical wealth, continued from the sixteenth to the eighteenth century.[23] The large proportion of clergy and regulars in the population was limited by state intervention before the end of the eighteenth century, but not before some advance had been made by charitable and educational orders. The lay confraternities showed vitality into the later years of the century, while in the Azores episcopal attempts, from the sixteenth and seventeenth century onwards, to control popular festivals, of supposedly religious aspect, had clearly failed by then.

By the end of the eighteenth century, Italian confraternities were in a relative decline, though the failure to follow up the immediate post-Tridentine attempts to rationalize parochial boundaries in parts of Italy left a very inadequate distribution of pastoral provision.[24] New developments of the Marian cult were fostered by the orders, not least those involved in rural missions. Yet, although the papacy was responsible for unleashing the expansion of the religious orders' membership, after the careful restrictions of the second half of the seventeenth century, the most striking characteristic of the eighteenth-century papacy was its doctrinal restraint, resisting not only the calls to approve assimilative methods in overseas missions but also the pressures to adopt and promulgate the doctrine of the Immaculate Conception or the devotion to the Sacred Heart of Jesus. After the pontificate of Gregory xv, earlier in the seventeenth century, short but seminal for artistic patronage and sympathy with both scientific work and Jesuit ideals, the height of artistic display in Baroque Rome, under Urban viii, led to the end of major commissions for Bernini, after the death of Alexander vii. The pontificates of the last decades of the century saw already a concentration on the austere defence of remaining papal authority, a suspicion of Jesuit laxism, supposedly present in Europe and overseas, and a susceptibility to renewed calls for patristic standards, under the inspiration of French clerics at Rome who, while not necessarily Jansenist, were consciously favourable to the tradition of Augustine and Charles Borromeo.

In Poland, the eighteenth-century extension of Catholic education was interrupted by the suppression of the Jesuits and the successive partitions of the state. But by that date the Piarists had established their own educational establishments, while the Jesuit influence on education had never been without challenge, even at the heart of Polish Catholicism, as at Cracow university. The Polish crown had indeed already defended the Piarists in their conflict with the Jesuits. Jesuits and other clergy were aware of the importance of using the vernacular in non-liturgical contexts, as indeed was true in Bohemia too. The extension of the Marian cult in Poland, from the seventeenth century, not least at the great pilgrimage centres, was accompanied, in the same period, by a growth of monastic institutions, especially important in the eastern provinces, where bishoprics and parishes covered even larger areas than elsewhere.[25] The combination of popular devotion and pilgrimage, not least Marian, with ecclesiastical initiatives in education and charity was found in German-speaking Europe of the eighteenth century too: both in the Empire and in the Habsburg lands. Although in Hungary episcopal leadership continued to represent often a support of national rather than dynastic loyalties, this was balanced to a degree by the crown's claim to legatine control over the episcopate, reinforced at the end of the century by Joseph II's interventions in the Hungarian just as in the Austrian Church. The education of the secular clergy in such areas advanced slowly in the eighteenth century, before the Josephine reforms, and bishops were still often obliged to employ regulars, including Jesuits until their suppression, to staff diocesan seminaries. The redistribution of ecclesiastical wealth in Hungary and the Austrian lands attempted by Joseph and his predecessors was designed to benefit the relatively impoverished parochial clergy, at the expense of the upper and regular clergy. But in Hungary at least part of the funds found their way to the state, not to the parish priests, and throughout the Austrian Habsburg lands the shortage of secular priests and size of parishes or even of dioceses in many areas left the regulars in a necessarily dominant position.

The noble dominance of cathedral chapters and episcopates in German-speaking Catholic Europe and adjacent lands was, if anything, made more secure in the eighteenth century, though lay appropriation of tithes and Church lands in many areas meant that such ecclesiastical support for the aristocracy was both direct and indirect. Austrian charity, in the eighteenth century, under both ecclesiastical and secular direction, demonstrated the increased specialization which had characterized earlier Italian initiatives in charitable provision. Prelates in the Austrian lands were still integrated to a degree in secular administration, in fact, but by the second half of the century Italian influence represented, in doctrinal and pastoral terms, a *via media*, between the extremes of Jesuit and Jansenist party positions. By the middle of the century, too, the Jesuits lost their control, exercised for more than a century, over book censorship. Popular religion, on the other hand, was not merely devotional, to the exclusion of the sacramental: Jesuit emphasis on frequent communion had obviously had effects, and, in Poland too, eighteenth-century Jesuit missions saw a stress on confession and communion. Eighteenth-century European Catholicism has sometimes been represented as a moribund force, lacking the reforming zeal of the original Counter-Reformation. Yet many areas in fact

demonstrated vitality, at popular level as well as in pastoral or jurisdictional polemic. The second wave of Catholic reform, typified by
rural missions as much as by rational and noble prelates, arguably
followed the revival of reformed standards at Rome itself at the end
of the seventeenth and beginning of the eighteenth century. The
growth, in this period, in the Italian peninsula and elsewhere in
Catholic Europe, of the numbers of clerics and of ecclesiastical wealth
was followed, after the early eighteenth century, by a renewal of
internal reform as well as by increased erastian intervention.

Ecclesiastical involvement, in Italy and elsewhere in Catholic
Europe, in the funding and direction of charity remained marked,
into the eighteenth century, despite the counter-productive conflicts
over clerical supervision of philanthropy and confraternities after the
Council of Trent. The ecclesiastical initiatives were not confined to
provision for the poor or disadvantaged at times of specific emergency, in plagues or wars or famines. Although clerical criticism of
Catholic social divisions rarely went beyond a call for greater charity
towards the less fortunate, or occasionally an exhortation to reinvest-
ment in declining sectors of employment, after some economic crisis,
the Counter-Reformation saw the expansion of provision for the
poor and sick, as a permanent part of life, along new lines, under
clerical as well as lay leadership. The immediately pre-Reformation
period had seen, in the relatively well-provided Italian peninsula, an
assumption, in places, of secular responsibility for social welfare. But
the New Orders of the sixteenth century and the bishops of the post-
Tridentine Church, both immediately and into later centuries, represented by their activity a counterbalance of planned as well as
casual relief. Even in the eighteenth century there was no clear and
simple takeover of responsibility for charitable provision by secular
authority, in Italy at least. The care for souls as well as bodies was
axiomatic in Catholic welfare, yet rarely confined to any purpose as
specific as the foundation for catechumens, usually converts from
Judaism, to be found at Venice. Foundations for this purpose were
also found at Rome, and a few other Italian cities, from the later
sixteenth century onwards; but they were not as numerous as the
institutions designed to convert prostitutes, found at Venice and in
many other cities of the peninsula. In provision for such groups, as
in the preventive care of houses designed to save poor girls from
becoming prostitutes, any earlier concept of the absolute virtue of
poverty in itself had certainly been abandoned. Post-Tridentine
episcopal concern to limit unauthorized begging represented the
same transformation of attitudes.

During the seventeenth and eighteenth centuries, moreover, secular authority in many parts of Italy was intent on removing beggars from public places and confining the poor to purpose-built institutions, where, in some cases at least, a more productive life could be imposed on the able-bodied among them. The attitude to gypsies similarly became less sympathetic, so that they were distinguished from genuine pilgrims on the road to Rome. Despite the economic difficulties and famines of late sixteenth-century Rome and the central papal states, means were found in the same period to establish new institutions in the city to cope with those in need. In the necessity of providing also for the pilgrims entering Rome for the Jubilee of 1600, some resort was made, in addressing the local poor, to stressing again the spiritual benefits to be derived from suffering; but an attempt was also made to reorganize small-scale charity at parochial level in the city. Lay confraternities under regular direction, founded in the same immediately post-Conciliar decades within the city, equally had charitable purposes, limited to specific classes of need, but directed outwards, not confined to members of the confraternity.

At Florence, before the end of the sixteenth century, the secular control of the Medici over charitable provision was reasserted, even in cases where ecclesiastics had been involved in the foundation of institutions originally. Dominican initiative was still apparent in the creation of an enclosed house for women in moral danger; but in the food shortage of the last decade of the century the *Monti di Pietà* proved insufficient as a palliative. Church and state were involved in coordinating urban grain distribution and rural hand-outs of rice, while regulating begging more strictly. The epidemics of the second and third decades of the seventeenth century brought further secular control of health regulations, and a new lay initiative to enclose beggars in an institution specifically founded for them. These epidemics accelerated the decline of industry within the city of Florence, evident from the 1560s and 1570s, and the associated increase in the number of poor in permanent need of relief. The continued problem of rural poverty in Tuscany, already remarked by ecclesiastics in the later sixteenth century, prolonged the presence of vagabonds, while in the 1640s a cleric tried to create a house of correction for teenage boys, in the absence of adequate opportunities for apprenticeship. By the 1670s ecclesiastical attempts to resurrect the failing provision for adult beggars in the city were obstructed by papal and grand-ducal opposition to the diversion of funds from monastic establishments. In the last decade of the century, however, Medici co-operation with Jesuit plans inspired by French initiatives in charity provided a new model for licensed begging and productive work imposed on the able-bodied; and this model was adopted in Rome, in the first half of the next century, as part of the continuing papal reform of Benedict XIII's pontificate. In the same way, at Siena, archiepiscopal activity, at the end of the seventeenth century, to reorganize parochial charity and improve the care of poor children, followed French Jesuit ideas, and was related also to the work of Pope Innocent XII.

At Genoa, in contrast to Venice, state control of charitable provision remained partial, even after the creation of new magistracies at the end of the sixteenth century. The archiepiscopal supervision of a major board for the provision of charity from testamentary bequests led to counter-productive jurisdictional conflicts between Church and state. Institutional care remained conservative, in the sense of being provided within a single building for different categories of need, with secular oversight. The epidemic of 1580 however naturally produced more specific measures for institutional isolation, as in other Italian ports; and post-Tridentine synodal prohibitions of begging in churches of the city coincided with stricter secular controls on the entry of non-citizens into Genoa. By the 1660s and 1670s, in a development more akin to Venetian experience, the Inquisitors of State were enforcing the control of residence in the city originally evolved in the epidemics of the sixteenth and seventeenth century. By a similar connection, the lazzaretto was used, outside times of plague, as a poor-house. At Rome, the number and equipment of charitable institutions, with general or specific purpose, excited the admiration of observers from the end of the sixteenth century onwards, even from backgrounds unsympathetic to Roman Catholicism, such as Protestant England; and this praise was sometimes extended to the foundations of other cities, such as Florence, Venice, Milan and Naples. The landed endowment of the major foundations helped to preserve their income during the relative difficulties of the Italian economy in the seventeenth century indeed. By the later eighteenth century, an English scientific observer could even praise the hospitals of Catholic Spain in the same way as those of Italy. In seventeenth-century Piedmont prolonged periods of war, and increasing tax exemption among the privileged, produced greater numbers of debtors and poor, with abandonment of the land in some rural areas by the 1660s and 1670s. While social control was attempted by state regulations, the Church participated in charitable relief, as in the Jesuit direction of a lay confraternity with a philanthropic purpose, alongside new provision for medical care of the poor.

Even in the eighteenth century, new forms of institutional housing for the poor, under secular control, showed a reliance still on the inspiration of the Counter-Reformation, in Italy at least. In the mid-century, at Milan, the design of a new, major poor-house, under Austrian rule, was based not only on utilitarian considerations, but also on the specifications of Charles Borromeo for the planning of convents. Borromeo had himself intervened in the regulation of begging in the city, licensing only those attached to a particular confraternity, and requiring parish clergy to certify the genuine state and need of the poor: measures apparently acceptable to the secular authorities as a basis for social control. The plans for a major poor-house in eighteenth-century Milan were also originally inspired by the model of similar institutions not only at Genoa but also at Madrid. Ecclesiastical inspiration in and after the Counter-Reformation, in the sphere of charity, thus seems to be more lasting than the instances of the abandonment of responsibility by religious bodies to secular authorities during the fifteenth century, not only in Northern Europe and subsequently Protestant areas, but in Italian cities such as Mantua and Reggio Emilia. In sixteenth-century Mantua, the famine of the last decades, following the epidemic of the 1570s, severely damaged the industrial expansion of the earlier part of the century, creating an evident problem of poverty among the marginal workers. The secular levy of a poor-rate, in these circumstances, is in one way reminiscent of later Tudor England; but is also, in another way, parallel to the archiepiscopal visitation of Federico Borromeo, in early seventeenth-century Lombardy, where the articles of inquiry required, among other things, the recording of those parishioners capable of themselves making charitable provision for others. For, precisely in 1594, Francesco Gonzaga, bishop of Mantua, instituted a lay congregation to supervise poor relief; while he also concerned himself with the care of women in moral danger, from economic want or otherwise. Begging by the unauthorized, even clerics and regulars, was thus once again prohibited by a post-Tridentine diocesan. The house for girls in danger was expanded in 1607 and, under the supervision of subsequent bishops, continued to provide education for the inmates, including writing as well as the more common skill of reading, until the secular reorganization of charitable institutions and their endowments, common to many parts of Italy in the second half of the eighteenth century. Yet even in the very last years of that century, at Bologna, after the end of papal rule, reference was still made, in the organization of charitable assistance, to the need for education and Catholic catechism as a part of such provision, as originally demanded by Charles Borromeo. So too in the enlightened reforms of charity by Leopold, in later eighteenth-century Tuscany, placed under strain by the food shortage of the 1760s, archiepiscopal authority could still prove useful to disperse a crowd besieging a grain distribution centre, by handing out alms.

Under Spanish rule, in Sicily of the second half of the sixteenth century, viceregal initiatives promoted charitable foundations, alongside existing ecclesiastical and lay activity. By contrast, in the same period, viceregal authority at Naples was attempting to limit begging by insisting on government licence. Charitable provision remained conservative, linked to the guilds of the city and their members, even in such matters as the provision of dowries for the female dependants of their families. Despite the eventual appearance of major institutions at Naples, the multiplicity of confraternities with a charitable function was commented on by Archbishop Gesualdo in 1599: this was the background to the Neapolitan disputes after Trent over episcopal supervision of lay confraternities and their funds.[26] Secular government at Naples, on the other hand, continued to abstain from positive involvement in charitable provision, even after the epidemic of 1656, for the most part. But foundations of the later sixteenth century, designed to provide relief or financial aid on a wider basis in the city, strongly asserted their independence of episcopal jurisdiction, and such contests continued into the seventeenth century. Similarly, from the beginning of that century, a large number of *Monti* were created, for the financial needs of specific groups, to supplement, on an extensive scale, the Neapolitan *Monte di Pietà*, founded in the early sixteenth century. From these later *Monti* also evolved forms of institutional care, but still for the benefit of a confined circle of families in effect. On the other hand, spiritual care was reorganized, in the face of such traditional lay management, by Archbishop Gesualdo's revision of parochial boundaries from 1596, which resulted in the creation of many new parishes in the city. A further increase in the presence of the secular clergy was achieved in 1606; quite apart from the economic support provided by the vast numbers of crowded male and female convents. From the early seventeenth century, the presence of the New Orders of the Counter-Reformation began to produce new foundations, of a charitable and educational purpose, at Naples, more directly under ecclesiastical control; as well as the teaching of the catechism. Individual bequests remained important, for the funding of charities, both before and after the mid-century revolt. But, by comparison with the creation of new major institutions for the poor – to be found elsewhere in Italy from the later sixteenth century onwards – innovation on any scale was delayed at Naples until after that challenge to Spanish government, and the subsequent epidemic of 1656.[27]

In the last decade of the eighteenth century, in Bourbon Sicily, female orphans above a certain age were still regarded as the responsibility of diocesan bishops, and institutions for the protection or recovery of girls in moral danger were still an important part of charitable provision in eighteenth-century Palermo. *Monti di Pietà* were in use by the end of the sixteenth century at Palermo and Messina, to be followed elsewhere in the island in the next two centuries. But the *Monte* of Palermo was diverted in its purpose, after 1731, to the economic support of the upper classes. Similarly in the kingdom of Naples, from the later sixteenth century, as the level of marriage dowries rose, the extension of funds for the provision of dowries was at first still limited to members of a particular family, establishing trusts for this purpose. Only later did the bequests for providing dowries to the deserving poor, common from before the Counter-Reformation in central and Northern Italy, appear in the kingdom, following initiatives in certain cities there. In Bourbon Sicily the supervision of confraternities by bishops was in any case limited to the spiritual, as opposed to the economic sphere, as in immediately post-Tridentine Naples. But the eighteenth-century confiscation and reapplication of confraternity funds by the secular authority in the island represented the end result of state 'protection' of lay interests; and it was an ironic sequel to the efforts of Clement VIII, at the beginning of the seventeenth century, to enforce the Tridentine provision for ecclesiastical control. The eighteenth century in Sicily witnessed the continued dependence in fact of the laity on the self-help organized by confraternities. In that century, in Catholic Europe more generally a reassertion of noble privilege and consolidation of the fiscal exemptions of the propertied classes has been detected by many historians examining different areas. But the extension of secular authority over charitable activity, during the century, was not necessarily an adequate recompense for the poor and less privileged. Such development certainly contrasts with the mid-seventeenth century provision of medical care for the poor of Rome by Cardinal Francesco Barberini, on a scale proportionate to the elaborate embellishment of the city by that papal family of the high Baroque.

# CHAPTER 8

# CONCLUSION

THE COUNTER-REFORMATION has been regarded by historians not only as a period of differing character but also as one of varying duration. The political Counter-Reformation was commonly seen as ending with the Peace of Westphalia and the final recognition of the interests of states rather than religions in Europe, despite the belated activities of Louis XIV and James II. Such a view could safely date the beginnings of the Counter-Reformation from the reaction of pope and emperor to the challenge of Luther. As soon as a less partial definition of the Catholic Reformation was adopted, incorporating the political history of reaction and repression but not confined to it, the chronology became less simple. The undoubted attempts at internal reform of the Western medieval Church could mean the unlimited extension in retrospect of the beginnings of Catholic reform. The arguments for regarding the mid-fifteenth century as a new beginning have been outlined here: it was just when the old methods of attempting reform of the Western Church and reunion with the Eastern Church, by means of Councils, finally proved the failure of institutional reform imposed from above that the crisis occurred. The reaction of the papacy against Conciliarism, and papal alliance with the growing power of national states in Western Europe, which together combined to defeat Conciliar reform, led to a more profound consideration of the nature of the Church, but above all of the individual believer's fate: salvation or damnation. If there was little hope from the institutional Church the more important became the individual's understanding of the means of salvation. The revival of reform, at the level of monastic orders and single dioceses, which followed the failure of Conciliarism, in the later fifteenth century and the first decades of the sixteenth, owed little to the papacy, more in places to the secular authority of the ruler, but was above all an interior revival. This was as true of communal activity, as with the

Brethren of the Common Life or the Paduan Benedictines, as of the individual stance of Savonarola or of Luther.

The limitations of even monastic reform and return to observance were understood: hence the personal spiritual crisis of so many of the *spirituali* or 'evangelicals' who emerged from the Christian humanist movement, in its Italian or Northern European forms; not just Luther, but Contarini and Pole too. The failure of the papal Council, the Fifth Lateran Council, to impose any of its agreed reforms in fact to any degree, under the post-Conciliar papacy, did nothing to disturb this return to individualism. Ignatius Loyola's own personal conversion is the type of this interior crisis, even though in his case it led to a design to reduce the will of his companions, and his own, to absolute obedience to the papacy. The inspiration of such collective and individual conversion in the age of Christian humanism was first of all the scriptures, and then the early Fathers of the Church. For, so it seemed, only by study of such sources could the true form of Christian life be recaptured and revived. In the concern to trace the possibility and nature of the individual's salvation, almost independent of the visible, institutional Church of the day, which so clearly departed from the patristic model in many ways, the most inspiring and demanding author seemed to be Augustine, who had precisely considered the individual's salvation at a time when the institutions of his world seemed to be in disorder and decay. From the later fifteenth century, then, in Western Christendom, a new form of Catholic revival may be detected, one in which even traditional attempts at monastic observance or diocesan reform were fired by a new, interiorized devotion and theological preoccupation. The attempts to educate the secular clergy are as symptomatic as the popularity of written devotions among the laity: a purely ritual administration by the clergy was not adequate for laity devoted to the 'Imitation of Christ'. The appeals to a General Council are in fact less characteristic, made by the French crown in a political confrontation with the papacy, by Savonarola and Luther, two friars whose plans for institutional and personal reformation of life seemed doomed by the opposition of the papacy. Luther's success in the German world lay rather in his vernacular appeals to the laity.

If the origins of the Counter-Reformation are thus reasonably clear, its immediate transformation from a movement of internal reform within the existing Church, to a continuation of that search inextricably mixed with reaction against separatist reform is also easy enough to comprehend in outline, though confused by the intricacy of political events. The *de facto* separation of Luther's reform movement from the previously existing Church, whatever his own original intentions, became clear not only because of the rebellion of princely rulers against both papal and imperial authority, but also because of Luther's own theological evolution. The doctrine which the Protestants came to stand for was not, in the end, that of the Western Church of the preceding centuries: Luther was brought to shocked personal recognition of this, in his enforced reappraisal of Hus. Few contemporaries had the theological awareness to see this so clearly at once, especially as they had sometimes shared the same initial crisis of belief for reasons just considered. But Contarini was aware of the genuine gulf between Catholic and Protestant theology, by the time of Regensburg, and Seripando by the time of the Tridentine debates on Justification. An examination of the doctrinal reaffirmations of the Council of Trent, in relation to the teachings of Protestantism at the time, may thus attempt to demonstrate the degree to which the Tridentine decrees were conservative, rather than innovatory: reaction was the hallmark of the political Counter-Reformation, but not necessarily of the whole movement. The clear distinction between Catholic and Protestant doctrine, by the mid-sixteenth century, during the suspension of the Council of Trent, did not prevent continued attempts, by political leaders in France and the empire, to impose theological compromise; but this was understandably unsuccessful. Nor did it prevent the incongruous persecution of some Catholic reformers by others, where the latter suspected the former of theological deviation from the reaffirmed orthodoxy of the traditional Church.

The Counter-Reformation did not, however, undergo some dramatic change in the hands of Caraffa: to contrast his spirit and that of Pole is to overlook precisely those activities of Pole as Legate in England which were repressive not reformatory, and which led to the unpopularity of the Marian restoration, without redeeming Pole's reputation in the eyes of the pope. So too with Carranza, whose activity in England, immediately before his arrest in Spain on suspicion of heresy, was as much repressive as reforming. The remarkable insight of Thomas More had already allowed him to see the nature of the doctrinal division between the orthodox and Protestants, even when to most ecclesiastics the changes of Henry VIII's reign affected only jurisdiction, without endangering the faith. For More, in his own opposition to Protestants, by the pen and the sword, detected the crucial question to be one of authority in religion: secular or ecclesiastical, that of the Church or that of the scriptures individually interpreted. So too in Spain of the Catholic Monarchs, where the new forms of monastic revival and clerical education were originally based on Christian humanist concern, as much as on the conflation of papal and royal authority, the distinction between reform and repression was not a later development. The early overtaking of Talavera's patient attitude towards the Moorish population of Granada by the action of the Inquisition followed the fifteenth-century activation of the crown tribunal against Jewish believers, whether in fact *conversos* or not. The search for Catholic purity had from the start a double aspect: the revival of patristic standards of Christian practice, and the external compulsion of those who stood apart from this revival; or, in Spain, those who had the misfortune to be racially distinct. The Counter-Reformation was from the start repressive as well as reformatory, but what was at issue, rather, was the question of authority. The papacy of the sixteenth century feared to summon another General Council after the virtual inefficacy of the Fifth Lateran; but also found the danger of revolt against its own authority to come ever more strongly from Christian rulers. This was true not only of the English king, of the emperor, or the German princes who embraced Lutheranism; but also of the French crown and the Spanish monarchy. The survival of even a part of the traditional Western Church was endangered as much by the independent activities of rulers as by the disagreements of theologians: it was here that the distinctive development of a political Counter-Reformation was felt.

The confusion of policy and authority in the Counter-Reformation was well demonstrated by the developments of the later sixteenth century. The policy adopted towards the German Protestants by the emperor had rarely been in accord with papal views: the imperial search for compromise had been pursued beyond the bounds of realistic identification of Protestant theology; papal concern to attempt Conciliar discussion, nevertheless, with Lutheran representatives was complicated by the armed contests between the emperor and the rebellious princes. Spanish policies were similarly out of sequence with those of the papacy: in regard to both England and the Netherlands, the papacy at first urged firmer action on a cautious king, and then objected to counter-productive repression in the Netherlands, while retreating to a reserved watch on Spanish attempts against England, after the failure of the independent papal policy of pronouncing the excommunication of Elizabeth. The papacy and Spain remained at odds from the end of Caraffa's pontificate, with the Marian defence of Pole against the pope, and papal protest against the Spanish arrest of Carranza, despite momentary agreements then and subsequently. The history of the Spanish attacks on Protestant areas of Europe became increasingly distinct from that of the ecclesiastical reform movement, especially after Spain had failed to succeed to the French throne, not least as a result of the belated papal recognition that an independent Catholic France was necessary if the Habsburg dominance of Rome was ever to be shaken. The Counter-Reformation, as opposed to the history of Spanish policy, or the independent course of civil disorder and war in late Valois France, thus became in part an ecclesiastical movement opposed to secular dominance in Catholic Europe: the consideration, at least, given at the Council of Trent to the possibility of reducing the powers of secular rulers over the religious life of their states makes this clear.

The distinction of such ecclesiastical history from the political involvements which produced the alliances of the Thirty Years War, and the continuing Habsburg–Bourbon struggle after that, is clear, not least from the case of Poland. There the success achieved in reconverting areas lost, in whole or in part, to Protestantism, magisterial or radical, by the religious means of preaching, catechizing and education, was the more evident, for lack of a central royal authority capable of making serious attacks on the independence of the noble landlords. The Catholic missions in England and Ireland, similarly, were failures, if the Counter-Reformation is seen essentially as a history of political revolt in the name of Catholicism, and an attempt to defeat Protestantism by military means. But if the missions are considered, as some though not all the clerical participants and their lay flocks understood them, to be rather the means of perpetuating the traditional faith and religious practice, at all costs, they were undoubtedly successful. The continuity of the old religion, in either case, was preserved, and, because of the peculiar circumstances of a religion under proscription, this was achieved with relatively little reference to the internal reforms made in the Catholic Church on the continent of Europe by the Council of Trent. The continued reform of the remaining parts of the traditional Church on the continent was not abandoned after the pontificate of Caraffa, any more than was the Council of Trent. The remarkable reassertion of papal authority in the remaining institutional Church, in the face of episcopal and secular assertion of independent rights, was one important result of revived papal perseverance with the work of the Council. The other major achievement of the Council was to establish a renewed potential authority for diocesan bishops, in the interests of seeing the proposed reforms subsequently enforced, and not neglected like those of the Fifth Lateran Council. If the authority of bishops within the Church was in one way reduced, in relation to papal authority, it was potentially increased, by alliance with the papal office, against the exemption of secular and regular clergy, and the interference of secular rulers. The control of Church life by the laity nevertheless remained undoubted, after the Council of Trent, not only at the level of clerical taxation or the punishment of criminal clergy, the supervision of convents and of confraternities, but at the crucial level of appointments to bishoprics, as well as benefices, and of nominations to the dignity of cardinal. In such respects the Council of Trent represented, not the revolutionary changes denounced by Sarpi, but an arrested revolution: one not wholly carried through. The remaining parts of Catholic Europe, in one respect, represented continuity more than innovation, with respect to medieval Western Christendom, despite the Counter-Reformation.

The Council of Trent, then, represented both the crucial consolidation of Catholic reassertion of doctrine and reform of religious practice, and, simultaneously, the failure of a complete transformation of the remaining parts of the pre-Lutheran Church. Neither the Sarpian denunciation of innovation, nor the Protestant attack on the supposed reaffirmation of unchanged abuses was accurate. The individuality of the Catholic Church within Western Europe, however, was asserted not only by means of the Tridentine doctrinal and disciplinary decrees, but also by the accidents of political developments in Europe. The *de facto* establishment of other Churches, alongside the remains of the traditional institution, had begun, despite himself, with Luther, and had been consciously promoted, in different ways, by Zwingli and Calvin, by the English and Scandinavian kings. The Peace of Westphalia, in the mid-seventeenth century, marked not so much the end of the Counter-Reformation, as the *de jure* recognition, by all except the papacy, of this new development in Western Europe, a result of certain developments in medieval Western Christendom. For though the caesaro-papism of the Byzantine empire had never been fully paralleled in the West, the tradition of erastianism had never been without practical or even theoretical support in the Western medieval Church. The outcome was seen, in different ways, in newly divided Europe, at the time of the papal Schism, and later, in the regalism of Philip II and his successors, the Gallicanism of Bourbon France, as well as in the conversion to Protestantism and married foundation of secular dynasties of North German prince-bishops and the Grand Master of the Teutonic Knights. To this extent, once again, the question of authority in religion was crucial in the development of both the Protestant Reformation and the Counter-Reformation. Whatever Luther owed to economic grievance or the fortunes of the printing press, the establishment of Lutheranism as a distinct Church owed much to the assertion of princely independence by secular rulers, as its success in German and Scandinavian lands, but failure in France, demonstrated.

The failure of Protestantism, in any form, to take root in the end in either Spain or the Italian peninsula also owed much to the independent action of state authorities: the Republic of Venice as much as the crown Inquisition in the Iberian peninsula. In this case, the distinction between the consolidated royal authority of one area and the disparate rule of individual states in the other seemed to make little difference, even allowing for the increasing dominance of Italy by the Spanish Habsburgs in the sixteenth century. Yet the assumption, by both Catholic and Protestant rulers in sixteenth- and early seventeenth-century Europe, that obedience in religion must accompany obedience in all else was in any case the common legacy of medieval erastian traditions. The distinction of Catholic Europe from Protestant states was thus not to be detected by examination of assertions of secular authority, any more than by a clear and lasting difference in the economic progress or lack of development in areas characterized by one religious allegiance rather than another. The Counter-Reformation remained distinctive only inasmuch as the pursuit of Catholic reform was still continued, and this largely by ecclesiastics, not secular rulers, with obvious exceptions in Bavaria, the Austrian lands, and the German prince-bishoprics which remained Catholic. The consolidation of Catholic orthodoxy and reformed practice of religion thus remains the crucial test for the nature, duration and success of the Counter-Reformation. For the political aspects, as has been seen, represented a continuing convergence, not divergence, between Catholic and Protestant states: so much so that by the eighteenth century, the papacy, now under Bourbon rather than Habsburg dominance, witnessed in Catholic Europe the delayed imposition by secular authority of social and economic changes which had been enforced in Protestant states in the sixteenth. Thus monastic property was confiscated, contemplative orders dissolved, ecclesiastical possessions limited, clerical education controlled, legal immunities of the Church attacked, and lay observance of religious feasts by abstention from work reduced. That this did not, nevertheless, bring about a change of doctrine, despite the threats implicit in Jansenism and explicit in Febronianism, was arguably the mark of the Counter-Reformation in its true achievement: the progressive inculcation, among the clergy and faithful, of a new comprehension of Catholic doctrine, in place, at least in part, of a system of ritual performed without theological comprehension. The Counter-Reformation is therefore best assessed in the long term, rather than in relation to purely political developments in the balance of power in Europe down to 1648.

Some modern histories of the Counter-Reformation have shown with care and exactitude the influence of political developments on different stages, either of the Council of Trent, or of papal attempts to implement the Tridentine decrees. The value of such detailed study is self-evident. The relations of the papacy with both Spain and Venice for example, after the Council, cannot otherwise be understood. But there is, perhaps, still a danger, in historical writing in English at least, of assessing the Counter-Reformation only on its hopes and promises: of analysing the decrees of the Council of Trent, as though the mere passage of the decrees produced instantaneous adoption of orthodox uniformity of belief and systematic universality of reform in practice. Of course historians have been aware that the triumphs of Trent were triumphs on paper only, and that from the very end of the Council, even in Spain, the enforcement of the Tridentine decrees proved problematic in fact. The study of the early implementation of post-Conciliar reform has nevertheless proved too partial, to date, to reawaken English historians at least to the real effects of the Counter-Reformation within the Catholic Church. For example, in English historical writing, and in American, the relations of Rome and Venice after the Council of Trent can still be found described with the false perspective of comparison with Protestant Europe. As has been seen, there were indeed similarities of political attitude, not so much in the distinct personal world of Sarpi, but in the common erastianism of both Catholic and Protestant states after the early sixteenth century. Yet the closest parallels, despite Venetian political alliance with Protestant England as well as Catholic, if Gallican France, are with Spanish practices after the Council of Trent, despite the political confrontation between Venice and the Habsburgs. The political history of sixteenth-century Western Europe will produce many similarities between Catholic and Protestant states: not surprisingly, as has been suggested.

But to understand the Counter-Reformation, it is necessary to know two apparently simple things, peculiar to the Catholic states of Europe rather than common to all states of Western Europe. The first question arises from the doctrinal decrees of the Council of

Trent: was the recovery of Catholicism in much of Europe in fact the result of the reassertion of clear orthodoxy? The second concerns the Conciliar disciplinary decrees: was the original inspiration of the Catholic reformation, before Luther, finally achieved, of a return to a pristine observance of religious practice? To understand the achievements and failures of the Counter-Reformation it is thus no longer sufficient to chart the course of reaction, from Spanish attack on Jewish believers in the fifteenth century, supposedly guilty of Judaizing in their religious practices, to the plots against Protestant rulers or military campaigns against Protestant states. So much is now commonly accepted. But it is still not sufficient to recite the decrees of the Council which finally, and unexpectedly, produced co-operation between papal and episcopal authority, to a degree arguably unknown for centuries, despite the brief interlude of the Fifth Lateran Council. The achievement of the Catholic Reformation can only be fully and adequately measured by studying also the degree to which uniformity of belief and practice was recovered in those parts of the Western Church which still remained in formal obedience to Rome. Such uniformity is not the same as the supremacy of Roman authority, necessarily, for the doctrinal decrees of the Council were above all the work of bishops and theologians; while the disciplinary decrees represented, as has been suggested, a compromise between the two ideals found in early sixteenth-century Southern Europe: reform to be achieved by the continued operation of renewed episcopal direction, or reform to be imposed by a recovery of papal authority, the lack of which had left the decrees of the Lateran largely a dead letter. The reform programme, *De emendanda ecclesia*, submitted to the papacy in the first half of the sixteenth century, saw the necessary co-operation of both aspects of the hierarchy, equally challenged by Protestant attack on the institutional claims of the traditional Church. The authority of the papacy had to be devoted to serious pursuit of reform, but the bishops had to be free to act in their own dioceses against the abuses which were too well known: both parts of the hierarchy had failed in their duties, and both parts had to recover their proper vocation. The reform of the Catholic Church was not called forth by the Protestant Reformation but continued to be pursued, not least in response to the criticism of practical abuses which were already acknowledged.

Whether considered as a continuous attempt at reform and restoration of orthodoxy, or as a reaction to the challenge of Protestant separation, the Counter-Reformation can thus be identified only by its achievements, not by its aims and proposals alone. To study the immediate problems which arose in enforcing reform in Italy itself and Spain, after the Council of Trent, is obviously the first step; and even here too much remains unknown or obscure, again not least for those whose access to historical scholarship is limited by linguistic boundaries. The political developments of the later sixteenth and early seventeenth century in France and Germany, as well as further East in Europe, necessitate a prolonged study of the delayed beginnings of Catholic restoration and revival in these areas. Much valuable work has been published on this precise topic, and rather awaits assimilation in historical accounts within the English-speaking world. To limit the Counter-Reformation chronologically, so that it ends in about 1600, is to rule out consideration of any attempts to implement the decisions of the Council of Trent in much of Europe, despite the brave beginnings of Nuncios and some bishops in the empire, for example, in the immediately post-Conciliar decades. Even in Italy and Spain the success and failure of the Tridentine transformation of the remaining parts of the traditional Church can only be truly evaluated by looking into the seventeenth century and beyond. It would be, for example, misleading to describe the singular triumph of reform in the Milan of Charles Borromeo, if research on later episcopates proved that this had been a personal achievement only, rather than the foundation of a tradition continued, though with difficulty, into the seventeenth century. The question of the relation between Tridentine ideals of ecclesiastical reform and the most visible remains of Catholic restoration, the Baroque churches, paintings and monuments of seventeenth-century Rome, Spain, France, Germany and areas still further from Italy, cannot even be considered, if the Counter-Reformation is viewed only as the search for reform in the sixteenth century, and the beginnings of implementation at the very end of that century. To understand what the Counter-Reformation attempted and what it achieved, it is necessary to study Western Christendom from the mid-fifteenth century into the eighteenth century.

The necessity of studying Western Christendom, rather than just Catholic Europe, to a degree at least, is also clear from any examination of the history of Catholic doctrine after Trent. The supposed orthodoxy which was the Council's greatest achievement, the uniformity of belief in all non-Protestant areas of Western Europe, proved to be both true and false simultaneously. It is true that the internal missionary work, the catechizing and educational work pursued from Italy to Poland, from the mid-sixteenth century into the eighteenth, represents perhaps the single most important factor in the consolidation of lay belief: whether in the rural missions and catechetical classes, at popular level, or in the colleges and schools run by Jesuits and other orders at a more advanced level. But it would be surprising if the crisis of individual belief, the search for certainty in personal salvation, which the failure of earlier attempts to reform the visible and acknowledged failings of the medieval and Renaissance Church helped to create, had been easily and suddenly ended, by the doctrinal definitions of the Council of Trent. The inspiration sought, in that crisis, not only from the scriptures, but from the interpretative authority of the Fathers of the Church, of Saint Augustine above all, could not be summarily reduced. This was obvious enough in Protestant Europe, where the ideal of individual interpretation of the scriptures, the magisterial demands of Church and state for uniformity of belief and practice in fact, and the inevitable problem of diversity of individual interpretation, combined to prolong doctrinal dispute into the seventeenth century and beyond. The wish to confront the apparent solidity of Catholic doctrine reasserted at Trent encouraged the denunciation of rival schools of thought within Protestant Europe, not only as between Lutherans and Calvinists, for example, but within the doctrinal world of Calvinism itself. But it is not surprising that the questions raised by study of Augustine, by the mid-sixteenth century, were not resolved or suppressed by the decrees of Trent, which sought to reconcile different theological traditions within the general bounds of orthodoxy as previously, if less clearly, understood. The theological controversy within the Catholic Church continued, just as much as that within Protestant Europe, from the later sixteenth century onwards, and from the very end of the Council; the desire for unity against Protestantism equally fuelled accusations of deviation from newly established orthodoxy.

The continuation of such, largely learned, debates within Catholic Europe is arguably a refutation of the view that the Counter-Reformation meant the end of Christian humanism in Catholic Europe: at least inasmuch as Catholic Augustinianism, as has been suggested here, was never synonymous with Jansenism, in any of the manifestations which the latter took. Catholic rigorists among reforming bishops and monastic reformers were not necessarily Jansenists, while the adherents of Jansenist theological or jurisdictional positions were hardly motivated by humanist opposition to ecclesiastical authority. Catholic Augustinianism, as continued after the Council of Trent, represented a Puritanism of the Right, to a large degree, not Erasmian expansiveness; but the Jansenists themselves, by the

time of the transformation of their movement into a largely jurisdictional rather than theological affair, were the victors not the van-
quished, in the Catholic Church of the eighteenth century. Theological, pastoral and jurisdictional questions all have to be considered
distinctly in fact. The final defeat of later Jansenist episcopal reforms
came rather at the hands of popular reaction, from the faithful who
had never been much disturbed by the original theological propositions of Jansenism. The later Jansenist bishops, in eighteenth-century Italy or Germany, sought a pastoral ideal which would bring
religion as they conceived it to the people: only to be defeated by the
forces of a popular religion largely formed by the regular orders.
Jurisdictional Jansenism had defeated the Jesuits, as theological Jansenism had not; but pastoral Jansenism was in turn defeated by a
popular reaction which owed much to the surviving strength of old
and new religious orders after the Council of Trent. To understand
such complications, the original development of the Catholic Church
after the Council of Trent has to be clearly examined: bishops who
attempted a reform inspired, perhaps, by Catholic moral rigorism,
but not by Jansenist theology necessarily, found themselves at odds
with regulars as well as secular authorities. The effects of the
Counter-Reformation in practice were determined by the interaction
of continued episcopal reform, since Trent had left so much initiative
intentionally to diocesan bishops, with papal authority, Curial practice, and the work of the religious orders. But all this, even papal
policy, was limited by the ultimate determination of local issues by
secular governments. To this extent erastianism remained the key to
the practical effects of the Counter-Reformation, as much as to the
evolution of Protestantism in different states. Since the development
of Catholic erastianism only realized its full effects in eighteenth-
century Europe, despite precocious advances at an earlier date, in
Venice and Naples above all, the Counter-Reformation can again
only be understood in such a longer perspective.

The necessity of such a long-term analysis, and the identification
of a common element in the transformation of both Catholic and
Protestant religion in and after the sixteenth century in Europe, have
been admirably demonstrated by the French historian Jean Delumeau, in works at least partly available in English translation. The
competitive imposition of comprehended credal systems, by ecclesiastical élites, on the less educated mass of the laity in Europe, both
Catholic and Protestant, has been seen as the crucial element in this
transformation. Such an aim has been detected too in common
attacks on popular practices redesignated as superstitious, not

religious, in both parts of Western Christendom, and on the supposedly popular resort to an alternative religious practice, by the demonic pact alleged to characterize witchcraft. To a degree this picture seems true enough for Europe itself, if perhaps overlooking the complex nature of credal and ritual attachments which inspired popular Catholic resistance to Enlightened reforms and Revolutionary changes in parts of Italy, France and Austria, at the end of the eighteenth century and beyond. The question of the supposed transformation from a merely ritual Christianity at popular level in the Middle Ages is also worthy of further consideration: but there a medieval expertise is more necessary. The Erasmian and Lutheran objection to the theological confusion demonstrated by much popular religion in their day is certain; but study of late medieval confession, for example, does not necessarily suggest a popular religion confined to blind ritual observance of half-Christian practices. The approach of Delumeau, however, possibly implies a coherence and unity in the doctrinal position of the Catholic leadership which, while certainly existing as far as catechetical teaching was concerned, was not in fact assured within the élite: some of whom, indeed, began by doubting the possibility of salvation for the many.

Thus there was, arguably, a contradiction between the élitism of the original, theological Jansenists, who doubted the application of saving grace to all but a few; and the élitism of later, pastoral Jansenists, who wished to revive a purified popular religion, as they themselves conceived it. The distinction has perhaps not been clearly noticed, despite the common element of debate over approach to the sacraments. Nevertheless, it seems an undoubted key to the development of Catholicism after the Council of Trent, as a religious revival and reform confined to a few or successfully brought to the mass of the faithful. On that, any evaluation of the Counter-Reformation, as more than a history of clerical reform programmes, must surely be based. The essential goal of the Counter-Reformation, as of any religious revival, was the conversion of the people to the true religion, as then conceived. The chief aspect of the Catholic restoration was its devotion to embracing the many, not the few; despite the preciosity of Port-Royal and Jansenist *salons*, it took its part here with Wesley, not with the Countess of Huntingdon. Nowhere is this clearer than in the history of the overseas missions which, like internal Catholic reform, began before the challenge of Protestantism and continued after it. The original design to reunite Eastern and Western Christendom largely failed, despite the continued threat of Islam to Western Europe. The recovery of all Protestant areas by political and military means was certainly unsuccessful. The extension of Christianity, then of Catholicism as opposed to Protestantism, to non-Christian peoples outside Europe was both a great if superficial success, and a great failure. The conversion, after a fashion, of large parts of the central and South American population was achieved by a mixture of mass evangelism and more careful instruction; but the civilized cultures of the Far East presented a greater challenge. What has perhaps not been sufficiently understood, in identifying the nature and achievements, even the chronological duration, of the Counter-Reformation, is the vital interaction of missionary experience overseas, and the doctrinal and practical evolution of Catholicism in Europe itself. The missionary work outside Europe, conducted by the religious orders, if not directly under ecclesiastical control, committed the Catholic Church to defence of a theology which was popular not élitist in its soteriology. Conversion of pagans in large numbers could not be reconciled with the pristine theology of Jansenism; and the attempt to make that theology an acceptable part of orthodox teaching was, in the end, and with much difficulty, defeated.

The jurisdictional aspects of any conflict over the interpretation of orthodoxy remained after Trent, just as much as at the time of Luther; so did political complications, of secular and ecclesiastical authority. But the defeat of original, theological Jansenism was as undoubted, in the end, as the success of pastoral Jansenism: the interruption of missionary work overseas by the demand for a careful approach to the sacraments. That demand could not, in the end, be resisted, because the reassertion of the necessity of the sacraments in a hierarchical Church, at the Council of Trent, was the answer to Protestant doctrinal innovation; and Catholic rigorists and reformers naturally inculcated regard for the sacraments, as with devotion to the Reserved Sacrament, as well as veneration of saints and the Madonna. The effect of European religious conflict was thus, indirectly, felt in the missionfields, and the decision to insist on the strictest application of rules for admission to the sacraments, and so to Catholicism, interrupted the experiments of Jesuit missionaries in the alternative missionary method of assimilating non-European, and possibly anti-Christian practices, to Catholicism. The distinction between social values and religious was thus implicit in Jesuit methods, denied in practice if not in theory by the eventual papal condemnation of such missionary methods. Outside Europe, as within it, political considerations were also crucial: the internal political developments of Japan, as well as Anglo-Dutch and French rivalry with Iberian power overseas. But Jansenist attitudes to

pastoral questions were triumphant overseas, at the beginning of
the eighteenth century, at the very time that Jansenist theology had
at last been defeated, despite continued resistance, in Europe. The
attack on Jesuit pastoral methods and their supposed laxism was
reinforced in Europe by the papal decision, in the end, against Jesuit
missionary methods abroad; and again political complications arose,
because of the alleged political attitudes of the Society of Jesus. The
Catholic erastianism of eighteenth-century Europe combined with
jurisdictional Jansenism, the assertion of episcopal independence
against both papacy and regulars, Jesuits above all, to force the
papacy to suppress Jesuit work in Europe and overseas, in subsequent developments. But the internal mission of both bishops and
regulars within Europe, to catechize and convert the masses, produced in turn a popular reaction against reforms imposed by secular
or independent episcopal authority.

The history of the Catholic missions overseas is thus essential for
any understanding of the Counter-Reformation in Europe. Both the
Protestant Reformation and the Counter-Reformation sprang from
a common unease, a consequent attention to Augustinian theology,
and an attempt to revitalize popular religious practice. But the different forms taken by Protestantism and by Catholic revival had an
impact on areas of differing size and importance. The export to
North America of the internal divisions of the Protestant world was
arguably of greater long-term importance than the export to the
Catholic overseas missions of the internal disputes of the European
Church: papal and royal authority and finance, bishops and regulars,
friars and Jesuits. But these latter divisions did play a part in determining the outcome of Catholicism, before 1800, as either a religion
confined to Europe and the European colonies of the Atlantic and
Pacific; or a truly Catholic, that is world-wide, religion. The failure
to allow continued experiment in assimilative missionary work in
China and India is more certain than the speculative results of the
alternative decision: in the event China and India, the Far East
generally, despite enclaves of Portuguese or French influence, were
not to become Catholic in the sense that parts of Europe, or even
much of Latin America were to be and to remain. The internal
divisions within the European Counter-Reformation were to affect
the history of the world religions and their relations on a much wider
scale. In return, the challenge of problems hardly faced within the
divisions of Western Christendom, except perhaps in the racial an-
tagonisms of the Iberian peninsula, affected the internal development
of the Counter-Reformation, producing one result from the Council

of Trent and its reforms, rather than another, despite the lack of attention at Trent to missionary questions extraneous to European concerns. One view of the Counter-Reformation might take the early eighteenth-century papal condemnations of the Chinese Rites as a logical point of conclusion; or alternatively the papal subjection to demands of Catholic rulers for the suppression of the Society of Jesus.

By the middle of the eighteenth century the transformation of the Jansenist problem from one primarily of theology to one primarily of jurisdiction was complete. The impatience of secular governments with internal doctrinal dispute in Catholic Europe only sharpened their attacks on clerical privilege, monastic ease, the educational influence of religious orders, and the investment of economic resources in ecclesiastical institutions. The confrontation of Catholicism with rationalism and unbelief replaced to a large degree the older controversy with Protestantism; while such rationalism and scepticism also represented, in part at least, a reaction against theological dispute, as much as against denominational conflict and war. The arguments drawn by such critics of Catholic and Christian Europe from the supposed nature of non-European, non-Christian society, again owed much to the reports of missionaries, at this date still largely Catholic, and not least Jesuit. The nature of the Counter-Reformation was in the end determined by three main factors: the working out of the relation between Church and state in Catholic Europe, following the lead of Protestant areas; the internal relations of authorities within the Church itself, papacy, Curia, bishops and regulars; and the geographical expansion and then limitation of the Catholic presence within Europe and beyond. As the relative achievements and failures of the Counter-Reformation were characterized by these developments, so the chronological limits of the Counter-Reformation are logically defined by them.

The internal missions of bishops and regulars in Catholic Europe in the seventeenth and eighteenth centuries represented both moral rigorism and theological concern for the salvation of all: a combination distinct from the alleged laxism of Jesuit spiritual direction and missionary conversion. The work of internal missions in eighteenth-century Italy, Spain and France prepared the way for the survival of European Catholicism during the Revolutionary and Napoleonic period. The influence of Liguori and the Redemptorists, in particular, was to prepare acceptance in the Catholic reaction of the nineteenth century of the questions, not settled at Trent, of the Immaculate Conception and of papal infallibility, determined by

revived papal authority and the combination of that and Conciliar
authority for the first time since the Tridentine Council. The Catholic restoration of the nineteenth century, in Europe and overseas,
saw the revival of contemplative orders, the foundation of more new
orders devoted to practical ends, educational, charitable and missionary, and the resurrection of the Society of Jesus. This revival
was stimulated by reaction to the Revolutionary changes in Europe
and their aftermath, even if building on foundations laid in the post-
Tridentine Church. The institutional position of the Church was
radically altered by the Revolution in France and its effects in other
European states, however, and the Napoleonic regime arguably made
such changes irreversible. The nineteenth-century papacy and hierarchy were unable to prevent, even when they tried, the development
of Catholic liberalism and Catholic nationalism.

This result suggested a new competition, between the Catholic or
non-Catholic state on the one hand, and laity, Catholic or not, on
the other, in place of the previous conflict between the institutional
Church and Catholic rulers; just as the renewed Catholic missionary
effort of the nineteenth century, beyond Europe, as well as new
developments in areas of Europe, England for example, represented
a rivalry with new Protestant missionary activity, at home and
abroad. The laity's position in the Church could not in fact be
reduced to that of the pre-Revolutionary state, whatever the theoretical implications, for laity as well as clerics, of the assertion of
papal infallibility, later in the century. Despite the economic importance of lay brothers and lay sisters, in the upkeep of monastic
institutions, until near the end of the Ancien Régime in Europe, the
laity proper, outside the cloister, had little more than a passive role
under the old order, unless they were rulers or politicians. The failure
of the hierarchical Church, as an essentially male institution, to
subject female convents in post-Tridentine Europe to perfect enclosure and absolute clerical control, demonstrated an earlier assertion of lay independence; not so much by the nuns, as by their
families. So too with the lay resources represented by charitable
institutions and confraternities, lay resistance to clerical control was
shown from the end of the Council of Trent to the later eighteenth
century. But after the disruption of the Revolution and Napoleonic
empire, educational and charitable provision were still more a secular
concern, with state regulation and intervention on a new scale, even
in Catholic Europe, alongside continued provision of these social
requirements by religious orders or other ecclesiastical agencies.
Only in the exceptional conditions of Catholic survival under

proscription had lay voluntary effort been possibly more important than clerical direction, in England for example; and even there much turned on extraneous forces of political and social development, not only at the time of the popish plot, but as late as the Gordon Riots, the reception of French émigrés, and the eventual Catholic Emancipation. The Catholic household remained the essential locus of Catholic life, necessarily, in England and Ireland, into the nineteenth century. A similar aspect of Catholic survival had been demonstrated by clandestine Catholicism in the Dutch Netherlands of the seventeenth century, where Catholic chapels occupied a floor in houses which necessarily presented an exterior aspect of normal domesticity. Such lay initiative could not easily be reversed, as the restored hierarchy in nineteenth-century England discovered.

But the evolution of a state clearly secular, though still Catholic, in nineteenth-century Italy, for example, had been prepared in the eighteenth century. From that period, and even from the preceding century, the Piedmontese state had taken a lead in controlling religious life, without, in fact, the demonstrative attitudes of Jansenist-inspired or Josephinist rulers. The social and intellectual controls exercised from Turin, where Rousseau became a Catholic, were those of the ducal and royal government, rather than of the Church. The intellectual tradition of Sarpi might be lacking, apparently, at Turin as opposed to Venice; the explicit claims of Gallicanism and the practical claims of regalism, in France, Naples, Sicily and Spain were not perhaps so openly advanced by the House of Savoy. But the regulation of educational life, for example, in eighteenth-century Piedmont and Sardinia was undoubtedly the concern of the state. The government of Piedmont exercised a moral control in the state, independent of either France or Spain, having often had cause to resist political pressure exercised by Bourbons or Habsburgs. This proved a paradigm for states in Catholic Europe, outside the Italian peninsula too, in the nineteenth century, both as a result of the uniform regulations of civil life imposed by Napoleonic reforms, and as a result of reaction to the Napoleonic regime. The development, in different ways and with differing degrees of success, in that century, of German national unification under the leadership of Protestant Prussia, and of Italian national unification, under that of Catholic Piedmont, suggests that the previous evolution of Catholic Europe, as opposed to Protestant, had in some respects represented variation rather than absolute distinction. The artistic and cultural, as well as the social and economic development of Catholic and Protestant Europe, by 1800, with the new universality of neo-classical and Romantic forms, also suggest the absence of any absolute distinction between the two areas in the preceding three centuries. The Reformation and Counter-Reformation no more represented an absolute clash between North and South in Europe, than between the Atlantic and the Mediterranean, or between progress and decline.

The necessity of judging the Counter-Reformation as a long-term process is evident from the immediate development of conflict between Church and state in Catholic Europe after the Council of Trent. The opposition between ecclesiastical plans for reform and the secular defence of existing privileges and traditions was not the result of the eighteenth century alone, nor even of late seventeenth-century Neapolitan thought. The conflicts which began, with the Spanish, Venetian and other Catholic governments, in the years immediately after the closure of the Council of Trent did not cease, on the other hand, with the death of Charles Borromeo in 1584, or in 1600. The long-term assessment of Catholic development in the Counter-Reformation must also take account of the convergence, to a degree, of the attitudes of states, Catholic as well as Protestant, towards questions of loyalty and obedience, dissent and toleration. The common assumption of states in both parts of Europe, at the beginning of the seventeenth century, was still that religious uniformity was necessary for stable government: experience seemed at the time to confirm this. Only changed experience suggested an alternative view, from the later seventeenth century, in some Protestant states, to the later eighteenth century, in some Catholic states. Despite a secular reaction, after the French Revolution, of European governments against certain forms of rationalism, the debate between belief and scepticism was to remain characteristic of the pluralist society of the nineteenth century. The Augustinian moment in Christian Europe, from the end of the fifteenth century to the beginning of the eighteenth, had given way to the age of secularism.

# NOTES

THE PURPOSE of these notes is to supply at least summary references to unpublished material, as opposed to published works, to which the Select Bibliography is intended to act as guide. More detailed and extensive presentation of such archival evidence it is hoped to provide in a monographic study of much less ambitious chronological, geographic and thematic range, to be published as soon as possible. The abbreviations used in these notes are:

| | |
|---|---|
| A.A.M. | Archivio Arcivescovile, Milan |
| A.G.S. | Archivo General de Simancas, Spain |
| A.S.C. | Archivio Storico Civico, Milan |
| A.S.M. | Archivio di Stato, Milan |
| A.S.V. | Archivio Segreto Vaticano |
| A.S.V. Spagna | Segreteria di Stato: Spagna |
| A.S.V. Venezia | : Venezia |
| A.S.Ven. | Archivio di Stato, Venice |
| B.A. | Biblioteca Ambrosiana, Milan |
| B.A.V. | Biblioteca Apostolica Vaticana |
| B.N.M. | Biblioteca Nazionale Marciana, Venice |

## 1 Introduction: the Counter-Reformation and Augustinian Europe

1 The arguments on both sides of the Jacobean debate, including those of Bellarmine, were also subject to the censorship of the Spanish Inquisition: R. García Cárcel, *Herejía y sociedad en el siglo XVI. La Inquisición en Valencia 1530-1609* (Barcelona 1980), p. 307.

2 Dalmatia and Loreto: A.S.Ven., Collegio, Relazioni, b. 66, 1639; b. 72, 1621. The Jesuit college founded at Vilna in Poland in 1570 became a university in 1579, by royal intervention, too: J.W. Woś, 'Il regno di Polonia e il Concilio di Trento', in *Il Concilio di Trento come crocevia*

*della politica europea*, ed. H. Jedin and P. Prodi (Bologna 1979), pp. 137–59: p. 158.

3 Though secular clergy, particularly canons, predominated as Inquisitors in Spain by the end of the sixteenth century, the influence of friars, Dominicans above all, acting as censors of the Holy Office there, was still pervasive. This was seen in Valencia, in the opposition to Jesuit entry into university theological teaching there and to Jesuit writings, including those of Saint Francis Borgia, who had attempted to promote Jesuit teaching at Gandía: R. García Cárcel, op. cit., pp. 47, 64f., 127, 134f., 324. Composition of the Supreme Council of the Inquisition in Spain, the Inquisitor General and the campaign launched against the Jesuits: A.S.V. Spagna, XXXIII, XXXIV, 1587–8.

4 China: A.S.V. Spagna, XXXIII, XXXIV, 1587–8; where also evidence of poor quality among Portuguese bishops overseas, despite the good work of the Council of Portugal.

5 Milan and English Catholicism: B.A., MS G.260 inf., fos 284 r–v, 319 v, 1595. Comparison of English Recusant martyrs with Catholics executed in Scandinavia was also made in Sweden, in the light of the failure of Catholic hopes there at the very time of the consolidation of Catholicism in the related kingdom of Poland: O. Garstein, *Rome and the Counter-Reformation in Scandinavia*, vol. II (1583–1622) (Oslo 1980), p. 365.

## 2 Religion and magic in Augustinian Europe

1 Difficulty of fulfilling the Tridentine rule for the appointment of canon theologians, e.g. in Venetian territory: A.S.V. Venezia, VII, 1569.

2 Catholic criticism of cabbalism, e.g. Federico Borromeo, *De Cabbalisticis Inventis* (Milan 1627). His demonological views in *Parallela Cosmographica de Sede et Apparitionibus Daemonum* (Milan 1624), *De Cognitionibus, quas habent daemones* (Milan 1624), *De Providentia Dei, et illius permissione cum malignis spiritibus* (Milan 1624).

3 His position during the epidemic: B.A., MS G.256 inf., fos 120 r ff.; and his works *De Pestilentia*, ed. A. Saba (Sora 1932), *Instruttioni, Ordini, et Avvisi … con l'occasione della pestilenza dell' anno 1630* (Milan) [1631]. His cosmological views: *De Christianae mentis iucunditate* (Milan 1632).

4 Valier's works, *Cardinalis*, *Episcopus* and *Vita B. Caroli Borromei* were published together in an edition of 1602 (Verona).

5 Frankness at Venice and Naples, among state officials, about the nature and purpose of female convents: B.N.M., MSS italiani, classe VII, no. 1556 (8890), fos 82 v f.; A.G.S., Estado, Negociación de Roma, Legajo 968, 1596.

6 Attempt at Milan to test the vocation of girls entered for conventual life:

A.S.C., Collezione Gride, 5/101, no. 17, 1626. Federico Borromeo's correspondence with nuns: C. Marcora, 'Lettere del Card. Federico Borromeo alle claustrali', *Memorie storiche della diocesi di Milano*, XI (1964), 177ff.

7 His views on possession: *De Ecstaticis Mulieribus, et Illusis* (Milan 1616), *De Naturali Ecstasi* [Milan 1617].

8 The Venetian Republic and the confraternity supporting the Inquisition: A.S.Ven., Senato, Dispacci di Rettori, Brescia, 1614. Armed familiars of the Roman Inquisition in Spanish Lombardy: A.G.S., Estado, Milan, Leg. 1272, fos 138ff., 1593. Hooded confraternity processions at Milan: B.A.V., MS Barb. Lat. 5484, fo. 141 v, [1596-7].

9 Episcopal mediation in feuds in Venetian territory, e.g. A.S.Ven., Capi del Consiglio dei Dieci, Lettere di Rettori, b. 87, no. 203 bis, Padua 1617.

10 Choice of the Capuchin, Lorenzo da Brindisi, to represent Neapolitan grievances at the Spanish court and complain of the viceroy, Ossuna: A.G.S., Estado, Napoles, Leg. 1881, fo. 192, 1618-19.

11 Absolution reserved to the archbishop of Milan, or his vicar general: A.A.M., Carteggio Ufficiale, vols 28, 41.

12 Interest rates at Vicenza and trouble over the Inquisition there: A.S.Ven., Collegio, Relazioni di Rettori, 51, 1598, 1603.

13 Neapolitan compromise over inspection of pious institutions: A.S.V. Spagna, XXXIV, 1587-8; cf. A.G.S., Secretaría Provincial, Napoles, Visitas y Diversos, Libro 100, 1617.

14 Ursulines of Varese and Novara: A.S.M., Culto p.a., P.G., Consulta del Senato, Tom. 6. The condition of the Ursulines at Bologna remained less restricted, following the greater relative liberality of Catholic reform there, from Paleotti to Lambertini: L. Ciammitti, 'Una santa di meno. Storia di Angela Mellini', in *Quaderni Storici*, anno XIV, Religioni delle classi popolari, ed. C. Ginzburg (Bologna 1979), pp. 603ff.

15 Venetian city tribunal for blasphemy and other affairs: A.S.Ven., Esecutori contra Bestemmia.

16 More evidently heretical blasphemy also treated by Republican authority: e.g. A.S.Ven., Capi del Consiglio dei Dieci, Lettere di Rettori, Padova, b. 87, no. 261, b. 88, no. 282, 1619, 1626.

17 Blasphemy and usury contested at Naples: A.G.S., Secretaría Provincial, Napoles, Visitas y Diversos, Libro 107.

18 Spanish Inquisition and other conditions in Sicily: A.G.S., Estado, Sicilia, Legs. 1136-71, 1885-95, 3478, 3512; Secretaría Provincial, Sicilia, Varios, Legs. 1319-1510, Libros 776, 779. Further evidence in Estado, Negociacion de Roma, and A.S.V. Spagna.

19 Contested summons of laity to Church courts and clerics to secular courts at Naples: A.G.S., Secretaría Provincial, Napoles, Visitas y Diversos, Libros 95, 107; Estado, Napoles, Leg. 1097, fo. 34. Venetian contests: A.S.V. Venezia, XXXVIII, XL, XLII (B), XLII (H), 1607-22.

20 Venetian procedures with respect to criminal clerics and ecclesiastical property: A.S.Ven., Capi X, Lettere di Rettori, Bergamo, b. 3, Brescia, b. 26-8; A.S.V. Venezia, XXXI, XLII (B), XLII (F); 1595-1621.

21 Sicilian parallels: A.G.S., Estado, Sicilia, Legs. 1148, 1167, 1170; Secretaría Provincial, Sicilia, Varios, Leg. 1510.

22 Lombard bishops' complaint: A.S.V., Archivium Arcis (Armaria Inferiora), no. 6546, 1586.

23 Armed police force at Milan but not in other Lombard dioceses: A.S.V. Spagna, LXII, 1623. Particular problem at Tortona: A.S.V., Instrumenta Miscellanea, no. 4495.

24 Rivalries within Spanish officialdom: e.g. A.G.S., Estado, Sicilia, Legs. 1147, 1149, 1154, 1155, 1160, 1161-2, 1885.

25 Fear of Neapolitan episcopal authority by Spain: e.g. A.G.S., Secretaría Provincial, Napoles, Visitas y Diversos, Libro 54, fos 49 v f.

26 Sicilian pensions on bishoprics, commendatory abbacies, papal nephews and Scipio Borghese: A.G.S., Estado, Sicilia, Legs. 1161, 1164. P. Partner, 'Papal financial policy in the Renaissance and Counter-Reformation', Past and Present (1980).

27 Ludovisi, Federico Borromeo and conclaves: B.A.V., MS Vat. Lat. 10714, 1621. Spanish outrage at papal parallels with heretics: A.S.V. Spagna, XLV, 1594.

28 Lombard sequestration procedure: B.A.V., MS Ottoboni Lat. 2361. Venetian post-Interdict policy: A.S.V. Venezia, XXXVIII, 1607; A.S.Ven., Senato, Dispacci di Rettori; Collegio, Relazioni di Rettori: 1613-28.

29 Choice of vicar general at Milan: B.A., MS G.258 inf., fo. 258 v, 1614.

30 Spanish view of Venetian bishops and Interdict: A.G.S., Secretaría Provincial, Sicilia, Varios, Leg. 1510.

31 Spanish assessment of Milanese ecclesiastical lands: A.G.S., Secretaría Provincial, Milan, Consultas, Leg. 1796, 1594; Varios, Leg. 2009.

32 Bergamo, Brescia and Padua: A.S.Ven., Capi X, Lettere di Rettori, Bergamo, b. 2ff.; Brescia, b. 23ff.; Padua, b. 83ff.

33 Bergamasco and ecclesiastical property: A.S.Ven., Collegio, Relazioni di Rettori, Bergamo, b. 35.

34 Lecco: La Pieve di Lecco ai tempi di Federico Borromeo. Dagli Atti della Visita Pastorale del 1608, ed. C. Marcora (Lecco 1979).

35 Rice, grain, quartering and taxation and Milanese ecclesiastical policy: A.G.S., Secretaría Provincial, Milan, Varios, Legs. 2009, 2017; Consultas, Leg. 1803.

36 Sicily and grain: A.G.S., Estado, Sicilia, Leg. 1162, fo. 145, 1607.

37 Papal taxation of Neapolitan clergy: A.G.S., Estado, Napoles, Leg. 1098, fo. 25, 1602.

38 Defence costs and clerical contributions in Lombardy and the Venetian

Republic: A.S.V. Spagna, LXIV, 1624; Venezia, XXXII, 1604; XLII (I), 1623.

39 Bergamo and the Bergamasco: A.S.Ven., Collegio, Relazioni di Rettori, Bergamo, b. 35, b. 36. Paduan canonries: A.S.Ven., Capi X, Lettere di Rettori, Padova, b. 83, 1575.

40 The 'fabbrica' fund in Spain (as also at Naples in fact): A.S.V. Spagna, XXXII, 1586.

41 Confraternities and indulgences: Archivio della S. Congregazione del S. Concilio (at A.S.V.), Visite ad limina, Milano, Relatio 1597, 1600, 1609, 1614.

42 'Crusade' indulgence in Spain (and Portugal too): A.S.V. Spagna, XXX–XXXV, 1584-9.

43 In Sicily: A.G.S., Secr. Prov., Sicilia, Varios, Leg. 1380, 1588.

44 Clerical estate's subsidies there: A.G.S., Estado, Sicilia, Leg. 1160, 1603.

45 Monreale: A.G.S., Estado, Sicilia, Leg. 1164, 1609.

46 For clarification of the reality of the 'Inquisition' in the Netherlands: A. Duke, 'Salvation by Coercion: The Controversy surrounding the "Inquisition" in the Low Countries on the Eve of the Revolt', *Reformation Principle and Practice. Essays in honour of A.G. Dickens*, ed. P.N. Brooks (London 1980), pp. 135-56.

47 Use of rural deans, as opposed to archdeacons, in Poland too: Woś, 'Il regno di Polonia', pp. 157f.

48 Venice and Romagna grain: A.S.Ven., Secreta Archivi Propri Roma, 17, 1565-6.

49 Portugal: A.S.V. Spagna, XXXVII, 1591.

50 Papal Collector expelled from Spain (as also the Nuncio Taverna in 1582, in fact): A.S.V. Spagna XXXII, XXXIII, 1586-7.

51 Spain and the provinces of religious orders (especially after the acquisition of Portugal): A.S.V. Spagna XXXIII-IV, 1588.

52 Appropriations in the Iberian peninsula: A.S.V. Spagna, XXXVII, 1591.

53 Padua, Venice, tithes and parochial redistribution: A.S.V. Venezia, XXXII, XXXIII, XXXV, XXXVIII, 1600-8.

54 Santiago: A.S.V. Spagna, XXXV, 1589.

55 Naples, Lombardy and Sicily: A.G.S., Secr. Prov., Napoles, Visitas y Diversos, Libros 99, 102.

56 Appeals and examination in Spain: A.S.V. Spagna, XXX, XXXI, XXXII, 1584-6.

57 Venice, Padua, books and students: A.S.Ven., Capi X, Lettere di Rettori, Padova, b. 83, b. 84, 1571-82; A.S.V. Venezia, XLII (D), (G), 1616-18.

58 Cardinal Acquaviva, archbishop of Naples, the riot of 1606, the Dominican convent and Ossuna: A.G.S., Estado, Napoles, Legs. 1103, 1104, 1881.

59 Observance of holy days and behaviour in church: Visite ad limina, Milano, Relatio 1600. Portugal: A.S.V. Spagna, XLIII, 1594.

60 Como and Milan: A.S.V. Spagna, XXXII, 1586.

61 Messina: A.G.S., Estado, Sicilia, Leg. 1144, 1575.

62 The Netherlands: A.S.Ven., Secreta Archivi Propri Roma, 17, 18, 1565-7.

63 Milanese seminarians subsequently received a more liberal education in their own institutions, as opposed to the Brera College of the Jesuits: *Acta Ecclesiae Mediolanensis*, ed. A. Ratti, IV (Milan 1897), col. 295; cf. F. Rivola, *Vita di Federico Borromeo* (Milan 1656), p. 721.

64 Education and ordination of Venetian clergy: A.S.V. Venezia, XXXVIII, 1607-8. Female convents at Venice: ibid.; A.S.Ven., Provveditori sopra Monasteri, b. 260.

65 Venice, Spain and Roman examination of nominated bishops: A.S.V. Venezia, XXXV, 1600; A.G.S., Estado, Negoc. de Roma, Leg. 972, 1600.

66 Spanish competition and examination for benefices: A.S.V. Spagna, XXXIV, 1587-8.

67 Milanese examination for benefices: A.S.M., Autografi (Ecclesiastici), cart. 19; cf. A.G.S., Secr. Prov., Milan, Varios, Leg. 2020.

68 Synodal decrees in Venetian territory: A.S.Ven., Senato, Dispacci di Rettori, Brescia, 1613. Spanish royal representatives and discouragement of synods: J.I. Tellechea Idigoras, 'Filippo II e il Concilio di Trento', in *Il Concilio di Trento come crocevia*, pp. 127ff. The early importance of synods, but danger of national separatism in Poland: Woś, 'Il regno di Polonia', pp. 142ff.

69 Venice, Spain and *ad limina* visits: A.G.S., Secr. Prov., Sicilia, Varios, Leg. 1510; A.S.V. Spagna, XXX ff., 1584 onwards.

## 3 Scholasticism and Science

1 Campanella: A.G.S., Estado, Napoles, Legs. 1095, 1096, 1097.

2 Padua: A.S.Ven., Relazioni di Rettori, Padova, b. 43, 1611; Capi X, Lettere di Rettori, Padova, b. 89, 1630.

3 Venetian educational and library provisions: A.S.Ven., Riformatori dello Studio di Padova, filza 64.

4 The remains of the Pinelli collection purchased for the Ambrosiana: B.N.M., MSS Italiani, Classe X, no. 69 (6710), 1609.

5 Spaniards for the Vatican Library: A.S.V. Spagna, XXXV, 1589. Spanish policy towards Venice: A.G.S., Estado, Negoc. de Roma, Leg. 986, 1607.

6 Venice and the threat of schism: A.S.Ven., Inquisitori di Stato, Lettere agli Ambasciatori a Roma, b. 165, 1594-5.

7 Venice and the export of fount: A.S.Ven., Riformatori dello Studio di Padova, filza 64, 1604.

8 Spanish tradition and Nuncio's protest: A.S.V. Spagna, XXXIV, 1588.
9 A classic study of popular heresy in Friuli is now available in English translation: C. Ginzburg, *The Cheese and the Worms: The Cosmos of a Sixteenth-Century Miller* (London 1980).
10 The Gregorian calendar in the Venetian Mediterranean empire: A.S.Ven., Collegio, Relazioni, b. 63, 1584.
11 Sicilian monasteries: A.G.S., Secr. Prov., Sicilia, Varios, Libro 776, 1586.
12 Sicily and Jewish merchants: A.G.S., Estado, Sicilia, Leg. 1171, 1609.
13 Expulsion of Lombard Jews: A.G.S., Secr. Prov., Milan, Varios, Leg. 2042; Consultas, Legs. 1795, 1796: 1587–1688.
14 Ministers of the Sick at Milan: A.A.M., Cart. Uff., vols 88, 101: 1629–30. In Sicily: A.G.S., Estado, Sicilia, Leg. 1161: 1604.
15 'German' bishops remaining at Trent, rather than 'imperial', since those remaining to represent the emperor's position were not from the empire itself, but from the other territories of Charles V.

## 4 New problems of Catholic expansion

1 Further information on the overseas Catholic missions is now available in English translation in *History of the Church*, ed. H. Jedin, vol. 5 (London 1980).
2 Nuncio's reports on the Armada: A.S.V. Spagna, XXXIV, 26 Sept., 10 Oct. 1588. Financial contribution of the Spanish Church: ibid., 31 Oct.
3 Venetian secular concern about Greek abuses: e.g. A.S.Ven., Collegio, Relazioni, b. 78.
4 Corfu and Zante: ibid., b. 62, 63, 66, 83, 84, 85, 87. Crete: ibid., b. 78, 79, 81, 83, 86; and Duca di Candia, Ducali e lettere ricevute, b. 5, 6.
5 Persia and the circumvention of the Turks: A.S.Ven., Capi x, Lettere di Ambasciatori, Roma, b. 26.
6 Attempted reform of Portuguese Benedictines: A.S.V. Spagna, XXXIII, 1587.
7 Greek veneration of St Francis in Crete: A.S. Ven., Collegio, Relazioni, b. 79, 1602.
8 Jesuit involvement in the education of St Thomas Christians: A.S.V. Spagna, XXX, XXXI, 1585.

## 5 Religious divisions and political similarities

1 Royal rights reserved in Spanish acceptance of the Tridentine decrees: this is clear from a secret letter of Philip II to the viceroy in Naples, of 1564, onwards, despite recent insistence on the unreserved quality of the public reception of the decrees in Spain. A.G.S., Secr. Prov.,

Napoles, Visitas y Diversos, Libros 54, 102; A.S.V. Spagna, XLV, 1594. Cf. Tellechea Idígoras, 'Filippo II e il Concilio di Trento'. Spanish episcopal dress: A.S.V. Spagna, XXXIV, XXXV, 1588. Visitation of Spanish monasteries and convents: ibid., XXXIII–IV, 1586–8. In Sicily: A.G.S., Estado, Sicilia, Legs. 1148, 1162; Secr. Prov., Sicilia, Varios, Leg. 1403. Non-residence in Spain and obstruction of *ad limina* visits to Rome: A.S.V. Spagna, XXXIII, XXXIV, XXXV, XLIII. Episcopal subjection in Spanish theory: A.G.S., Secr. Prov., Napoles, Visitas y Diversos, Libro 94. Legatine authority in Portugal granted to cardinal archduke, as viceroy: A.S.V. Spagna, XXXI, XLIII, XLV, 1584–94.

2 Archbishop Braganza of Evora: A.S.V. Spagna, XXXII, XXXIV. Portuguese and Castilian religious: ibid., XXXIII, XXXIV.

3 Calvin: see H.A. Lloyd, 'Calvin and the duty of the Guardians to resist', *Journal of Ecclesiastical History*, XXXII, 1 (1981), 65ff. The English Protestant disputes over discipline and doctrine were very similar in a way to those in the royal and episcopal Lutheran Church in the Scandinavian kingdoms: Garstein, *Rome and the Counter-Reformation*, II.

4 Botero, the supposed champion of the 'Counter-Reformation state'; reference to Borromean opposition to him: A.G.S., Secr. Prov., Milan, Consultas, Leg. 1798.

5 Grisons' right to trade at Milan: A.G.S., Estado, Milan, Leg. 1272. Vicentine noble: A.S.Ven., Capi X, Lettere di Ambasciatori, Roma, b. 25, 1569–70.

6 Plans to concentrate troops on the Neapolitan border of the papal states, under Philip III: A.G.S., Estado, Napoles, Leg. 1882, 1619.

7 Venetian claims to headship of the Greek Church in the Republic's territories: B.N.M., MSS Italiani, classe VII, nos. 1553, 1556.

8 Venetian diplomatic contacts with England or Henri of Navarre: ibid.; A.S.Ven., Inquisitori di Stato, Lettere agli Ambasciatori a Roma, b. 165, 1589.

9 Venetian diplomats during the Interdict; belated exclusion from Spanish royal chapel: A.G.S., Estado, Negoc. de Roma, Leg. 986.

10 Renewed activity of the Inquisitors of State, despite supposed secrecy about the very existence of the magistracy, from 1585, and relationship with the Heads of the Council of Ten, after the supposed reform of 1582: A.S.Ven., Inquisitori di Stato, loc. cit.

11 Second arrest of Pérez, followed by his flight to Aragon and use of the Crown Inquisition against him: A.S.V. Spagna, XXXI, 1585.

12 Venice and involvement of the Propaganda in the Republic's Mediterranean territories: *Relazioni degli Stati Europei lette al Senato dagli Ambasciatori Veneti nel secolo decimosettimo*, ed. N. Barozzi and G. Berchet, serie III, Italia, Roma, 1 (Venice 1877), 390.

13 Pius V: A.S.Ven., Capi X, Lettere di Ambasciatori, Roma, b. 25.

14 Sfondrato as real leader of the Milanese ecclesiastical province after the

succession of Archbishop Visconti: A.S.V., Arch. Arcis (Arm. Infer.), no. 6546.

15 Spanish protest over papal policy and the French succession: A.G.S., Estado, Negoc. de Roma, Leg. 965, 1595.

16 Morone and Genoa: Fondazione Cini, Venice, Microfilms, A.S.V., Segreteria di Stato, Nunziatura in Venezia, filza 266; 78, 1575.

17 Imperial reaction to papal grant of grand-ducal title to the Medici: A.S.Ven., Capi x, Lettere di Ambasciatori, Roma, b. 25, 1570-1.

18 The Emperor Leopold I also composed sacred music drama for Lenten performance.

19 Continued Roman protest at the arrest of Khlesl: B.A.V., MS Barb. Lat. 5538, 1622.


## 6 Catholic reform and Augustinianism

1 Emulation of Charles Borromeo in Spain: A.A.M., Cart. Uff., vol. 12. In Poland: B.A., MS G.256 inf., fo. 105 r-v. Ormaneto and nuns: A.S.Ven., Capi x, Lettere di Ambasc., Roma, b. 25.

2 E.g. of a cardinal's powers in diocesan appointments: Federico Borromeo, archbishop of Milan; Archivio di Stato di Roma, Miscellanea Famiglia, b. 30, fasc. 4, 1595. A.A.M., Cart. Uff., vols 68, 85. Cf. Archbishop Visconti's position: ibid., cart. 78, 1585.

3 Granvelle and Zapata as viceroys of Naples: A.G.S., Estado, Napoles, Legs. 1063, 1884: 1573, 1622. Doria as interim viceroy banning the work of Baronius: ibid., Sicilia, Leg. 1164, 1611.

4 Baronius and St James: A.G.S., Estado, Sicilia, Leg. 1161, 1604.

5 Philip III and patronage of S. Pietro in Montorio, Rome, in the face of French competition: ibid.; and Leg. 1163, 1608; cf. Negoc. de Roma, Leg. 1857, 1604.

6 Education of clergy of Milanese collegiate churches: e.g. A.A.M., Sezione x, Visita Pastorale: Città, S. Stefano in Brolio, vol. 1, Q.19, 20; 1619.

7 Menocchio's posthumous work: A.G.S., Secr. Prov., Milan, Consultas, Leg. 1799.

8 North Italian provinces of religious orders: A.S.V. Spagna, LX (B), 1614; Venezia, XL, 1610.

9 Borromean restriction of those seeking alms: A.A.M., Cart. Uff., vol. 68, 1596, 1608, 1620.

10 Examination of patriarch-elect: A.S.V. Venezia, xxxv, xxxviii, 1600-1, 1607-8.

11 Roman defence of Sicilian Basilians: A.G.S., Secr. Prov., Sicilia, Varios, Libros 776, 779.

12 Las Huelgas: A.S.V. Spagna, xxxiv, 1588.

13 Canons of S. Giorgio in Alga: A.S.V. Venezia, xxxviii.

14 Reform of Trinitarians: B.A., MS G.260 inf.
15 Roman co-operation of Theatines and Oratorians: B.A., MS G.173 bis inf., 1596.
16 Visconti, the Jesuits and the Oblates at Milan: A.A.M., Cart. Uff., vol. I, no. I, Q.I, 1586. B.A., MS G.145 inf., 1589.
17 Tarugi at Avignon: B.A., MS G.260 inf., 1593.
18 Problem about triennial election in Spain: A.S.V. Spagna, XXXIV, 1588.
19 Enclosure of female tertiaries problematic there too: ibid., XXXII, XXXIII, XLIII, 1586-93.
20 Criminal band of male Franciscan conventual tertiaries: A.S.Ven., Capi x, Lettere di Rettori, Padova, b. 85, 1597.
21 Regulars and charitable institutions in Spain: A.S.V. Spagna, XXXV, XLIII, XLV, 1589-93.
22 E.g. of regulars' appeal against synodal decrees, at Milan, Bergamo and Brescia: A.S.Ven., Senato, Dispacci di Rettori, Brescia, 1613.
23 Spanish bull-fights: A.S.Ven., Secreta Archivi Propri Roma, 18, 1567.
24 Nuncio and Spanish drama, even religious: A.S.V. Spagna, XXXIV, 1588.
25 Malta: A.S.V. Spagna, XXXII; A.G.S., Estado, Sicilia, Legs. 1148, 1151; Negoc. de Roma, Leg. 981: 1578-1605.
26 Residence of bishops in Venetian sees: A.S.V. Venezia, XXXII, XXXIII, XXXVIII, 1602-8.
27 Neapolitan sees: A.G.S., Estado, Negoc. de Roma, Leg. 981.
28 Valier's visitation: A.S.Ven., Collegio, Relazioni, b. 62, 1581.
29 Valier and Charles Borromeo in the epidemic of the mid-1570s: A.S.Ven., Capi x, Lettere di Rettori, Padova, b. 84.
30 Seneca: A.G.S., Estado, Milan, Leg. 1282. Owen Lewis: A.S.V. Spagna, XXXIV, 1587-8.
31 Paleotti at Albano and Sabina: Biblioteca Vallicelliana, Rome, MS E.48.
32 Problems of Aquileia: A.S.Ven., Capi x, Lettere di Ambasciatori, Roma, b. 25.
33 Torcello and convents: A.S.Ven., Provveditori sopra Monasteri, b. 260.
34 Istria and Dalmatia: e.g., A.S.V. Venezia, XXXII, XXXIII, XXXV, 1600-4.
35 Crete: ibid.; A.S.Ven., Collegio, Relazioni, b. 79, 81.
36 Ceneda: A.S.V. Venezia, VII, 1569.
37 Sienese reform of female convents: Cremona and Bologna too: A.S.C., Coll. Gride, 5/101, nos 14, 18.
38 Conditions of the Roman Inquisition in Venetian territory; compared with Milanese and Neapolitan traditions: A.S.Ven., Capi x, Lettere di Ambasciatori, Roma, b. 25, 26.
39 Secular claim to confiscations in the Milanese tribunal of the Roman Inquisition: Archivio della S. Congregazione del S. Concilio, Visite ad limina, Milano, 1597.

40 Sardinia: A.G.S., Estado, Negoc. de Roma, Leg. 937.
41 Creation of see of Crema, independent of Cremona, and relationship to Piacenza: A.S.Ven., Secreta Archivi Propri Roma, 17. Alessandria: A.G.S., Secr. Prov., Milan, Varios, Leg. 2009.
42 Diocesan visitation at Milan: A.A.M., Sezione x, Visita Pastorale, Città; Diocesi.
43 More and Fisher: B.A., MS G.260 inf., fo. 319 v, 1595.
44 S.M. della Scala: A.A.M., Sezione x, Visita Pastorale, Città, S. Fedele, vol. 20; A.S.M., Fondo Religione p.a., S.M. della Scala, Visite Arcivescovili.
45 Canons of Milan cathedral: A.A.M., Cart. Uff., vol. 25, Q.6. Other collegiate churches: Archivio della S. Congregazione del S. Concilio, Visite ad limina, Milano, 1592.
46 S. Ambrogio: A.A.M., Sezione x, Visita Pastorale, Città, S. Ambrogio, vols 21–2; Cart. Uff., vol. 115.
47 Diocesan seminary education and disciplinary control of Milanese clergy: Archivio della S. Congregazione del S. Concilio, Visite ad limina, Milano, 1597.
48 Problems in the training of priests for Alpine areas: A.A.M., Cart. Uff., vol. 115.
49 Control of regulars at Milan by 1630: A.A.M., Cart. Uff., vol. 88.
50 Schools of Christian Doctrine: Arch. della S. Congr. del S. Concilio, loc. cit., 1614.
51 Vagabond friars at Venice: A.S.V. Venezia, XXXIII, XXXVIII, 1602–7.
52 Padua: A.S.Ven., Riformatori dello Studio di Padova, filza 64, 1599–1601.
53 Iberian canons and bishops: A.S.V. Spagna, XXXIV, XXXVII, XLI, XLIII, 1588–94.
54 Cult of St Charles Borromeo in the Netherlands, as in France: B.A., MS G.256 inf.

## 7 Puritanism of the Right and Baroque effect

1 S. Stefano Rotondo: as also in the original decorations of the chapel at the Ven. English College, Rome.
2 Valladolid: A.S.V. Spagna, XLIII, XLV, 1593–4.
3 Sanctuary of the Chiesa Nuova: B.A., MS G.173 bis inf., fo. 225 r, 1596; A.G.S., Estado, Sicilia, Leg. 1161, 1604.
4 The Ambrosiana: B.A., MS G.194 bis inf., 1605.
5 Recording the pristine decoration of Roman churches: B.A.V., MS Barb. Lat. 7819, fo. 59 r, 1624.
6 Borromean division within churches: Arch. della S. Congreg. del S. Concilio, Visite ad limina, Milano, 1597.

7  Governors' and viceroys' thrones: A.G.S., Estado, Sicilia, Leg. 1164, 1610.
8  Charles Borromeo and the Ambrosian office: A.S.V., Arch. Arcis (Arm. Infer.), no. 5506.
9  Ambrosian chant at Milan and instruments other than the organ: A.S.M., Fondo Religione p.a., S.M. d. Scala, Visite Arcivescovili, 1623 Visita e Decreti Arcivescovili.
10 Castrati and Spain at an early date: A.S.V. Spagna, XXXII, 1586.
11 Flight of the arts from Italy: B.A., MS G.258 inf., fo. 30 r-v.
12 Borromean control at Varese: B.A.V., MS Barb. Lat. 7819, fo. 44 r, 1619.
13 Federico Borromeo's concern about a supposedly 'miraculous' statue contrasts with Charles's attitudes to a certain extent: B.A., MS G.258 inf., fo. 356 r-v.
14 Charles Borromeo's visit to the Roman churches in the Jubilee on foot: A.S.Ven., Capi x, Lettere di Ambasciatori, Roma, b. 26.
15 Baronius and Federico Borromeo's Roman house: B.A., G.195 inf., fo. 132 r, 1606.
16 Female convents in Venetian territory: A.S.Ven., Capi x, Lettere di Rettori, Padova, b. 88.
17 Venetian concern to distinguish official dress from clerical: A.S.V. Venezia, VII, 1569.
18 Continued Curial involvement in provisions and related financial exactions: ibid., Spagna, XXXII, XXXIII, XXXIV.
19 Jesuit interest in a native clergy overseas, in the face of superior compliance with royal refusal: A.S.V. Spagna, XXXI, 1584.
20 Lipsius, supposedly representative of Catholic neo-stoicism, certainly corresponded with Federico Borromeo: B.A., MSS G.256 inf., G.260 inf.
21 Portuguese, bishops and purity of blood: A.S.V. Spagna, XXXII-IV, 1586-7.
22 Spanish bishops and familiars of the Inquisition: ibid., XXXIV, 1588.
23 Military orders in Portugal: ibid., XXXVII, 1591.
24 Parochial reorganization in Italy: A.S.V. Venezia, XXXVIII, 1607-8.
25 Poland: Merton College, Oxford, MS Q.1.10.
26 Neapolitan charitable institutions: A.G.S., Estado, Napoles, Leg. 1097, 1600.
27 Episcopal oversight of these: ibid.

# SELECT BIBLIOGRAPHY

THIS select bibliography is intended to provide a critical guide to further reading. Wherever possible, works have been cited in the edition most likely to be available, and English translations of foreign works noted.

## 1 Introduction: the Counter-Reformation and Augustinian Europe

The best introductory work on the Counter-Reformation, apart from older and outmoded books by Kidd, Froude and others, remains A. G. Dickens, *The Counter Reformation* (London 1968). This excellent institutional and general account should be supplemented by the insights of H.O. Evennett, *The Spirit of the Counter-Reformation*, posthumously published, with a Postscript by J. Bossy (Cambridge 1968). For the integration of the political sequence of events with more strictly religious history, a valuable guide is M.R. O'Connell, *The Counter Reformation, 1559–1610* (New York 1974). The Council of Trent naturally assumes an important place in any account of the Counter-Reformation, and the modern, standard history of the council, by H. Jedin, contains useful discussion of many aspects of the period beyond the confines of the council itself; especially of the background to the summoning of the Fifth Lateran Council and then of Trent, at the beginning of volume 1 of the English translation, *A History of the Council of Trent* (London 1957–61). The second volume is also available in translation, but from the third volume, which discusses the translation of the council to Bologna, to the end of the fourth volume, and the end of the council, the German original must be consulted: *Geschichte des Konzils von Trient* (Freiburg 1949 onwards). However a summary account, by the same author, of the last stages of the council and its closure has been translated as *Crisis and Closure of the Council of Trent* (London 1967). Another invaluable guide to the late medieval and Renaissance Church, the Reformation, the period of the Council of Trent and the Counter-Reformation Church to the end of the eighteenth century is the French ecclesiastical history, *Histoire de l'Eglise*, generally known by its original editors' names, A. Fliche

and V. Martin (Paris 1934 onwards). The failure of fifteenth-century Conciliar reform is traced in volumes 14 i–ii. Volumes 15 and 16 deal with the
Renaissance and Reformation, vols 17 and 18 with the period of the Council
of Trent and early Catholic reform, vols 19 i and ii with the Catholic Church
in Europe and overseas to the end of the eighteenth century. This scholarly
but traditional account should be contrasted with the important, recent
works of the French historian Jean Delumeau, who has put forward a
radical argument about the transformation of medieval Western Europe by
the leaders of the Protestant Reformation and Counter-Reformation alike,
in two works, to be read together ideally: *Naissance et Affirmation de la
Réforme* (2nd ed. Paris 1968) and *Le Catholicisme entre Luther et Voltaire*
(Paris 1971). This latter now exists in English translation, as *Catholicism
from Luther to Voltaire* (London 1977) and the introduction by John Bossy
should be consulted, for a critical review of Delumeau's approach by the
historian who, within the English-speaking historical world, has perhaps
most nearly adopted Delumeau's method of analysis. See Bossy's article
'The Counter-Reformation and the People of Catholic Europe' in the journal *Past and Present* (May 1970). For an introduction to the early historiography of the Counter-Reformation, in Germany and elsewhere, and a
discussion of the titles 'Counter-Reformation' or 'Catholic Reformation',
see H. Jedin, *Katholische Reformation oder Gegenreformation?* (Lucerne
1946). The limitations which can arise from the use of the term 'Catholic
Reformation', stressing the undoubted positive aspects of internal reform
rather than the equally present elements of reaction against Protestantism,
are evident in the otherwise splendid book by P. Janelle, *The Catholic
Reformation* (Milwaukee 1949). An early example of sympathetic understanding of Catholic reform and the Counter-Reformation by a non-
Catholic writer in England can be found in L. Pullan, *Religion Since the
Reformation* (Oxford 1923). The decrees of the Council of Trent, as of the
Fifth Lateran Council, can be traced in the large, and not always easy to use,
volumes of the *Histoire des Conciles*, generally known by the name of the
editor, C.J. von Hefele. The volumes which discuss the formulation of the
decrees and present their final form, with a French translation, are 9 i, 9 ii,
10 for Trent; discussion of Lateran v in vol. 8 i (Paris 1917–38). See also
*The Canons and Decrees of the Sacred and Oecumenical Council of Trent* ed.
J. Waterworth (London 1888). A succinct discussion of the Fifth Lateran
Council and the first period of the Council of Trent is also to be found in
the *Histoire des Conciles Œcuméniques*, x, Latran v et Trente (Paris 1975),
by O. de la Brosse, J. Lecler *et al.* For the beginnings of Christian and
monastic renewal, as represented by the Brethren of the Common Life, it
is hard to better the brilliant and sympathetic conclusion to the volume in
the Pelican History of the Church by Sir Richard Southern, ii: *Western
Society and the Church in the Middle Ages* (London 1970). His earlier book,
*The Making of the Middle Ages* (London 1953), also includes a penetrating

study of the Anselmian doctrine of Atonement. For Saint Augustine nothing can replace a study of his works, especially the *City of God* and *Confessions*: of which English translations are available by various hands. But a brilliant, concise introduction to Augustine and the history of Augustinianism is H.J. Marrou, *Saint Augustine and his Influence through the Ages* (New York 1957).

The literature, in the English language alone, on the Protestant Reformation is vast. Luther in particular has attracted biographical attention on a vast scale, in a way that Calvin and Zwingli, in the English-speaking world, have not. There are biographies of these last two however by T.H.L. Parker, *John Calvin, a biography* (London 1975); and G.R. Potter, *Zwingli* (Cambridge 1976), who has also published a shorter work, *Ulrich Zwingli* (Historical Association, London 1977). For the radical Reformation a standard account remains G.H. Williams, *The Radical Reformation* (Philadelphia 1962); and there is the study of *The Pursuit of the Millennium* by Norman Cohn (revised ed. London 1970). For the Protestant Reformation and for Luther, apart from the French volumes already mentioned, the works of A.G. Dickens probably provide the best introduction in English. There are *Reformation and Society in Sixteenth-century Europe* (London 1966); *Martin Luther and the Reformation* (London 1967); *The German Nation and Martin Luther* (London 1974), arguably the best of these, as representing the fruits of a lifetime's study of the subject. Among biographies of Luther, which are too numerous to list, mention may be made of one English account which is unusual for its insight, from the viewpoint of a sympathetic Catholic observer, and for the clarity of exposition with which the questions of indulgences, theology, reform and authority in the late medieval Church and in Nominalist thought are treated: John Todd, *Martin Luther, a biographical study* (London 1964). Erasmus has also attracted a vast amount of attention, ever since his own lifetime. A famous biography, among many, is available in English by the great Netherlandish historian, J. Huizinga, *Erasmus of Rotterdam* (London 1952). The only satisfactory modern account of Pole's religious beliefs, finally revealing what was carefully obscured for contemporaries and subsequent historians, is the brilliant and sympathetic work of Dermot Fenlon, *Heresy and Obedience in Tridentine Italy: Cardinal Pole and the Counter Reformation* (Cambridge 1972). A more recent work, which is less satisfactory for Pole, but interesting on the contrasting figure of Vergerio, is P. Simoncelli, *Il caso Reginald Pole. Eresia e santità nelle polemiche religiose del Cinquecento* (Rome 1977). Most accounts of the crucial question of Protestant response to the Tridentine decree on Justification, and of Catholic reaction to Protestant doctrine, a matter involved in the ultimate loyalty of Pole to Rome but departure of some Italians for Protestantism in exile, are now out of date. They are thus misleading not only about Pole, but also about Contarini and the previously supposed success of the latter's moderation in negotiation

with German Protestants about Justification. As revolutionary as Fenlon's
revelation of Pole's views is P. Matheson, *Cardinal Contarini at Regensburg*
(Oxford 1972). But the conclusions of Matheson are at odds with virtually
every earlier account of the final division between Catholicism and Protestant theology in the mid-sixteenth century. Another brilliant exposition
of the nature of personal and doctrinal divisions in the age of Pole, Caraffa,
Morone and Contarini is contained in the works of J.I. Tellechea Idígoras,
especially his *Fray Bartolomé Carranza y el Cardenal Pole: Un navarro en
la restauración católica de Inglaterra (1554-8)* (Pamplona 1977). By contrast,
a work available in English on the division of the Italian reformers, between
those who remained within the Italian and Catholic world and those who
eventually fled to Protestant lands, P. McNair, *Peter Martyr in Italy* (Oxford 1967), is sadly limited in its usefulness, by the apparent assumption
that the latter course was somehow the only natural outcome; while the
more interesting problem of what sustained Pole, Carranza or Vittoria
Colonna remains unresolved. The eradication, to a large degree, of the
earlier Erasmian influences in the Iberian peninsula, and the transformation
of early Spanish reform of religious orders and clerical education to the
Counter-Reformation policy of Philip II's reign, are exhaustively studied
in the justly famous book by M. Bataillon, *Erasme et l'Espagne* (Paris 1937).
Compare H.D. Smith, *Preaching in the Spanish Golden Age* (Oxford 1978).
For the early reform within the existing Church in France, there is an
equally massive book by A. Renaudet, *Préréforme et humanisme à Paris* (2nd
ed. Paris 1953). Compare the volumes on Italian conditions of P. Tacchi
Venturi, *Storia della Compagnia di Gesù in Italia* (3rd ed. Rome 1950). The
transmission of Augustine's works in manuscript is catalogued by M. Ober-
leitner, *Die handschriftliche Überlieferung der Werke des heiligen Augustinus* (Vienna 1969). For Saint Thomas Aquinas and medieval thought, an
introductory account in English is by D. Knowles, *The Evolution of Medieval Thought* (London 1962). In English, the most profound, yet exciting
study of Augustine himself, and the development of his views at different
stages of his life, is the brilliant biography by P. Brown, *Augustine of Hippo*
(London 1967). A very different characterization of Renaissance Europe
and the subsequent history of Europe and the transatlantic world is to be
found in J. Pocock, *The Machiavellian Moment* (Princeton 1975).

The work of the scholarly reformed Benedictines of France, the Maurists,
as also of the Jesuit scholars of the Netherlands, the Bollandists, are dis-
cussed by Knowles in *Great Historical Enterprises* (London 1963). The
importance of Philippe de Champaigne as a painter associated with Port-
Royal and the French Jansenists is indicated by L. Marin, 'Philippe de
Champaigne et Port-Royal', in *Annales E.S.C.*, 25 (1970). The figure of
Sarpi has attracted a large and possibly disproportionate attention in the
English world, since his own lifetime and contacts with the ambassadors of
James I of England. The most balanced account of Sarpi is perhaps that

of a sympathetic historian of his native Venice, G. Cozzi, who has edited Sarpi's works, including his famous *History of the Council of Trent*. The introduction by G. Cozzi to the modern Italian edition, *Opere*, ed. G. and L. Cozzi (Milan 1969) is most rewarding. Treatment of Sarpi by English historians is less reliable, from the attraction shown by the liberal Catholic historian, Lord Acton onwards: see Acton's *Essays on Church and State* (London 1952). A more recent and more balanced treatment of one aspect of Sarpi is the article of Frances Yates, 'Paolo Sarpi's "History of the Council of Trent"', in the *Journal of the Warburg and Courtauld Institutes* (1944). For Wyclif and Lollardy see the excellent account in volume 14 ii of the *Histoire de l'Eglise* ed. Fliche and Martin. The relationship with Huss and Hussitism in Bohemia is discussed there too, and also in G. Leff, *Heresy in the Later Middle Ages* (2 vols Manchester 1967). The volume of K.B. McFarlane, *John Wycliffe and the beginnings of English non-conformity* (London 1952) may be compared with his later *Lancastrian Kings and Lollard Knights* (Oxford 1972). For Savonarola there is a biography, available in English translation, by R. Ridolfi, *The life of Girolamo Savonarola* (London 1959), which discusses the background of Florentine politics, the fall of the Medici, the French invasion of Italy, and papal policy leading up to the Fifth Lateran Council. A corrective view of the precise relations between Savonarola and the pope is to be found in the articles by R. de Maio, 'Savonarola, Alessandro VI e il mito dell'Anticristo', and 'Eresia e mito della potestà pontificia nel processo romano a Savonarola', published in his book *Riforme e miti nella Chiesa del Cinquecento* (Naples 1973). Compare D. Hay, *The Church in Italy in the Fifteenth Century* (Cambridge 1977). The *Institutes of the Christian Religion*, of Calvin, can be consulted in English translation. For the international importance of Arminianism and the Synod of Dort, see the essay by H.R. Trevor-Roper on 'Religion, the Reformation and Social Change', in his book of the same title (London 1967), and also the essay there on 'The Religious Origins of the Enlightenment'. The background of Dutch revolt against Spanish rule can be traced in the work of P. Geyl, *The Revolt of the Netherlands, 1555–1609* (2nd ed. London 1958). Compare the recent publications of an English historian, G. Parker, *The Dutch Revolt* (London 1977) and *The Army of Flanders and the Spanish Road, 1567–1659* (Cambridge 1972). Although there are more recent biographical studies of James VI and I of Scotland and England, the king's involvement in international religious debate is well brought out by D.H. Willson, *King James VI and I* (London 1963). But the earlier English debates on predestination, in later Elizabethan Oxford and Cambridge, are discussed in an often neglected account by M.H. Curtis, *Oxford and Cambridge in Transition, 1558–1642* (Oxford 1959). The career of Archbishop Laud is traced in the biography by H.R. Trevor-Roper (London 1940); but a more recent view of Laudianism is the challenging article by N. Tyacke, 'Puritanism, Arminianism and Counter-Revolution', in the book *The*

*Origins of the English Civil War* (London 1973) ed. by C. Russell. The history of Jansenism, above all French Jansenism, has produced an enormous literature. As well as the extended accounts, in French and English, of Jansenism and Port-Royal by Sainte-Beuve (Paris, 1840 onwards), and Saint Cyres (Chapter on 'The Gallican Church' in the *Cambridge Modern History*, vol. 5, Cambridge, 1908), there is an engagingly malicious account of both Jansenism and Quietism by R. Knox, in his sparkling book, *Enthusiasm* (Oxford 1950). A more sober and succinct account of the development of the French Church and its troubles, in the seventeenth century and into the eighteenth, can be traced in the volumes of the *Histoire de l'Eglise* edited by Fliche and Martin. The background of Gallicanism and royal policy receives sympathetic treatment in this account by Catholic but French authors. The balance of the volumes of this series is more seriously disturbed by a concentration on events in France, as opposed to those in Italy and elsewhere; particularly because of certain limitations and deficiencies in vol. 17 on the Tridentine and immediately post-Tridentine Church by L. Cristiani. A distinct Italian version of this volume, incorporating new material, has been produced by A. Galuzzi, *La Chiesa al tempo del Concilio di Trento* (Turin 1977). There is also an important new chapter in the Italian edition of vol. 19 i. See *Le lotte politiche e dottrinali nei secoli XVII e XVIII*, ed. L. Mezzadri (Turin 1974). But another incisive study of French Jansenism is that of L. Cognet, *Le jansénisme* (Paris 1961). See also N. Abercrombie, *The Origins of Jansenism* (Oxford 1936) and *Saint Augustine and French classical thought* (Oxford 1938). For the necessary history of political developments in Europe, from the French invasion of Italy to Louis XIV and beyond, reference may be made to the volumes of the *New Cambridge Modern History*, and, for accounts which are even more detailed, if now dated, to those of the old *Cambridge Modern History*.

The singular development of English Puritanism has produced a seemingly limitless literature, in the English language above all, but one study, by P. Collinson, *The Elizabethan Puritan Movement* (London 1967), may perhaps be recommended especially, despite its chronological limitations and the effect of these on its argument. By contrast, for the long-term development of largely continental Europe, in secular as well as ecclesiastical life, an admirable survey has been recently provided by W. Doyle, *The Old European Order 1660–1800* (Oxford 1978). For the intellectual and religious history of the preceding period another dazzling exposition is available in the translation, from the French, of the book by R. Mandrou, *From Humanism to Science, 1480 to 1700* (Harmondsworth 1978). The many works by Christopher Hill on religious, intellectual, political and literary aspects of English Puritanism are matched by his earlier work, arguably his best, on the *Economic Problems of the Church* (Oxford 1956). This should be contrasted with the essay of Tyacke, already mentioned, and compared to the essay on 'Sir Francis Knollys's Campaign Against the *Jure Divino*

Theory of Episcopacy', by W.D.J. Cargill Thompson in the book *The Dissenting Tradition*, ed. C.R. Cole and M.E. Moody (Athens, Ohio 1975). The most stately apologia for the English Church, Richard Hooker, *Of the Laws of Ecclesiastical Polity* (published 1593 onwards), can be found in modern editions: e.g. edited with introduction by C. Morris (2 vols London 1907). For Wesley, an interesting, and again sympathetic account is that by John Todd, *John Wesley and the Catholic Church* (London 1958); but of course Wesley too has stimulated an extensive range of biographies and studies, quite apart from his own *Journal*. For the divisions within the English Catholic community, by the end of Elizabeth's reign, and in that of James I, over questions of authority, secular and religious, and the overtones of relations with Catholic foreign powers, France and Spain, see the article by J. Bossy, 'Rome and the Elizabethan Catholics: A question of Geography', in *Historical Journal* (1964). Compare his important book on *The English Catholic Community 1570-1850* (London 1975). For the international debate on regicide and alleged Jesuit support of this in practice, see R. Mousnier, *The Assassination of Henry IV, the tyrannicide problem and the consolidation of the French absolute monarchy in the early seventeenth century* (London 1973). This English translation is also a revision of the French original. The Counter-Reformation at Bologna is comprehensively treated by P. Prodi, *Il cardinale Gabriele Paleotti* (2 vols Rome 1959-67). The educational policy of the Jesuits, in Italy and elsewhere, is discussed by G.P. Brizzi, *La formazione della classe dirigente nel Sei-Settecento* (Bologna 1976). For conditions in Bohemia after the Habsburg and Catholic victory at the White Mountain, see the article of R.J.W. Evans, 'The Significance of the White Mountain for the Culture of the Czech Lands', in the *Bulletin of the Institute of Historical Research* (1971); and compare his work on *Rudolf II and his World, a study in intellectual history, 1576-1612* (Oxford 1973), and *The Making of the Habsburg Monarchy, 1550-1700: an interpretation* (Oxford 1979). For the specialist seminaries in Rome, as for all aspects of papal policy, see the detailed and still valuable volumes of *The History of the Popes* by L. von Pastor, in the English edition (London 1891 onwards). An English work on Ignatius Loyola, the subject of so many books, which deals with the crucial early years, is J. Brodrick, *Saint Ignatius Loyola. The Pilgrim Years* (London 1956). The discussion of the real sources of Ignatian spirituality in Evennett's *Spirit of the Counter-Reformation* should not be missed, as antidote to much nonsense still written about the nature and purpose of the original Society of Jesus. The relative importance of the Jesuits, often exaggerated, is demonstrated in Evennett's excellent discussion of the 'New Orders' in the *New Cambridge Modern History*, vol. 2 (Cambridge 1958). For later Jesuit and other educational developments in Spain see the article by R. Kagan, 'Universities in Castile 1500-1700', in *Past and Present* (1970), and his book *Students and Society in early modern Spain* (Baltimore 1974). The *Spiritual Exercises* of Saint

Ignatius can also be studied in modern English translation: e.g. by T. Corbishley (Wheathampstead 1973). For Saint Teresa of Avila the best introduction is her autobiography: *The life of Saint Teresa of Avila, by herself*, ed. J.M. Cohen (Harmondsworth 1957). Apart from older and less well balanced accounts, there remains a single sound discussion in English of the Spanish Inquisition by H. Kamen (London 1965). The real effect of Jesuit interventions in the debates of the Council of Trent, and the careful moderation of different traditions of theology in the doctrinal decrees, are clarified by J.M. Rovira Belloso, despite other, irrelevant considerations, in his book, *Trento. Una interpretación teológica* (Barcelona 1979). For the background of Spanish political, religious and racial developments in Spain, see *Spain in the Fifteenth Century*, edited by J.R.L. Highfield (London 1972); and the article by the same author on 'Christians, Jews and Muslims in the same society: the fall of *Convivencia* in Medieval Spain', in *Studies in Church History*, ed. D. Baker, volume 15 (Oxford 1978). The importance of financial and other relations between Rome and Spain, particularly under Philip II, is discussed by J. Lynch, *Spain under the Habsburgs* (2 vols Oxford 1964–9). The importance of the Military Orders of Spain in this context is demonstrated by L.P. Wright, 'The Military Orders in Sixteenth and Seventeenth Century Spanish Society', *Past and Present* (1969). The use of papal authority by Henry VIII is discussed by W. Wilkie in *The Cardinal Protectors of England* (London 1974). The contrast between England and France at this time is shown by R.J. Knecht, 'The Early Reformation in England and France: A Comparison', in the journal *History* (1972).

The importance of Seripando, not least at the Council of Trent, as a Catholic Augustinian, in many senses, is shown in the English translation of Jedin's book, *Papal Legate at the Council of Trent: Cardinal Seripando* (St Louis 1947). For the Marian restoration in England see the works of P. Hughes, *The Reformation in England*, vol. 2 (London 1953), and *Rome and the Counter-Reformation in England* (London 1942): even if these represent an over-committed and now partly outmoded approach, they remain valuable, as a corrective to views of Tudor history which are too insular. Compare Bossy's article, 'The Character of Elizabethan Catholicism', in *Crisis in Europe*, ed. T. Aston (London 1965). For Fénelon and his relations with Bossuet, Louis XIV, Jesuits and Jansenists, as also his own Quietism, see H. Hillenaar, *Fénelon et les Jésuites* (The Hague 1967). Compare the *Memoirs* of Saint Simon, rich in anecdote, from the viewpoint of the *dévots* attached to the successionary interest under Louis XIV, and critical of the old king's policies. For Bérulle, the Jansenists and *dévots*, and the whole development of the French seventeenth-century Catholic revival, see the volumes of H. Bremond, *A Literary History of Religious Thought in France* (London 1928 onwards). Compare the account of Rancé, a non-Jansenist Catholic reformer and rigorist, by A. Krailsheimer (Oxford 1974). The evolution of France under Richelieu and Mazarin has now been studied, in

English, by R. Bonney: *Political Change in France under Richelieu and Mazarin* (Oxford 1978). See also R. Briggs, *Early Modern France 1560–1715* (Oxford 1977). There exists a large literature, in French and in English translation, as well as works written in English, on seventeenth-century France: this may be traced in Bonney's book. For the royal Gallicanism of Louis XIV see in particular the essays, in English, collected in *Louis XIV and the Craft of Kingship*, ed. J. Rule (Columbus, Ohio 1969). Italian Jansenism has been studied by many, not least A.C. Jemolo: *Il giansenismo in Italia, prima della rivoluzione* (Bari 1928). See also E. Codignola, *Illuministi, giansenisti e giacobini nell'Italia del settecento* (Florence 1947). The works of F. Venturi on eighteenth-century Italy, especially the second volume of his two-volume *Settecento Riformatore* (Turin 1969, 1976), are also most useful. But there is a danger, evident in Italian treatment of the subject, to read the history of Jansenism in Italy retrospectively, with reference to the subsequent story of the Risorgimento and Italian unification, rather than in the chronological perspective of earlier European theological and then jurisdictional debates. For an outline of developments in German-speaking Europe the section by E. Wangermann, on the later eighteenth century, in the *New Cambridge Modern History*, vol. 8 (Cambridge 1965) complements the account of Italian states by J.M. Roberts there. The Austrian developments and reaction can also be studied in the works by E. Wangermann, *The Austrian Achievement, 1700–1800* (London 1973); and *From Joseph II to the Jacobin Trials* (2nd ed. London 1969). The history of the overseas Catholic missions can be traced in the *Histoire de l'Eglise*, edited by Fliche and Martin; while in English the stirring account of R. Ricard, *The Spiritual Conquest of Mexico* (Berkeley 1966), has appeared in translation. The works written in English by J.H. Parry and C.R. Boxer respectively on *The Spanish Seaborne Empire* and *The Portuguese Seaborne Empire* (London 1966 and 1969) can be used together with the dramatic study by Boxer of *The Christian Century in Japan 1549–1650* (London 1951). In Europe, a contrast emerges in the view of popular disorder, including religious riot, adopted by N.Z. Davis, *Society and Culture in early modern France* (London 1975); and the careful demonstration of limited violence in the iconoclastic movement of the sixteenth-century Netherlands by P. Mack Crew, *Calvinist Preaching and Iconoclasm in the Netherlands 1544–69* (Cambridge 1978). Thomas More has been the subject of many works, some more hagiographic than scholarly. But a sound view remains that of R.W. Chambers, *Thomas More* (London 1935). Compare J.K. McConica, *Thomas More, a short biography* (London 1977). An account of Henry VIII and the precise nature of his matrimonial difficulties in relation to Church authority, sympathetic at once to royal interests and Catholic positions, which equally stands out from other treatments of the monarch and his reign, is that of J. Scarisbrick, *Henry VIII* (London 1968). For the question of the great witch-craze, Trevor-Roper's essay on the craze, in his book *Religion, the Reformation and Social Change*, is fundamental. The book by Norman Cohn, *Europe's Inner Demons* (London 1975) must also be considered, however; while a book which raises valuable cognate issues is J.M. Roberts, *The Mythology of the Secret Societies* (London 1972). For Alpine areas there is the treatment of witch-hunting by E. Monter, *Witchcraft in France and Switzerland, the borderlands during the Reformation* (Ithaca 1976); to be compared with H.C.E. Midelfort, *Witch hunting in Southwestern Germany, 1562-1684* (Stanford 1972). See also bibliography for Chapter 2, below.

On artistic development in Europe, a fundamental study is F. Haskell, *Patrons and Painters, a study in the relations between Italian art and society in the age of the Baroque* (London 1963). The Pelican *Outline of European Architecture* by N. Pevsner includes a brilliant introduction to the development of Mannerism, Baroque and Rococo from Renaissance building and decoration. See also an older but still classic analysis by H. Wölfflin, *Renaissance and Baroque*, in English translation (London 1964). Other works in the bibliography for Chapter 7, below.

## 2 Religion and magic in Augustinian Europe

For the state of religion in Alpine areas in the Tridentine period see M. Grosso and M.F. Mellano, *La Controriforma nella arcidiocesi di Torino, 1558-1610* (3 vols, Vatican City 1957). The study of one locality where medieval heresy took root has become famous: E. Le Roy Ladurie, *Montaillou: Cathars and Catholics in a French village, 1294-1324* (London 1978). Compare his book, *Peasants of Languedoc* (Urbana 1974). For the relations of lawyers to witch trials in France see R. Mandrou, *Magistrats et sorciers en France au XVIIᵉ siècle* (Paris 1968). An unusual study of French and other witch-belief, from its late Roman origins, is that of C.W.S. Williams, *Witchcraft* (London 1941). Compare the well-balanced remarks of C.S. Lewis in his 'New Ignorance and New Learning', the introduction to his *Oxford History of English Literature* volume on the sixteenth century (Oxford 1968). The exceptional conditions in England are studied by K. Thomas in a book of seminal importance, *Religion and the Decline of Magic. Studies in Popular Beliefs in Sixteenth- and Seventeenth-Century England* (London 1971). For the Counter-Reformation and the question of social relationships and private feuds, see two articles by J. Bossy: 'Blood and baptism: kinship, community and christianity in western Europe from the fourteenth to the seventeenth centuries', *Studies in Church History*, vol. 10 (1973); and 'The Social History of Confession in the Age of the Reformation', *Transactions of the Royal Historical Society* (1975). The social conditions, and economic differences between mountainous and lowland areas of the Mediterranean lands in the period, are brilliantly discussed in the great volume of F. Braudel, *La Méditerranée et le Monde méditerranéen à l'époque de Philippe II* (Paris 1949); now also available in English translation:

*The Mediterranean and the Mediterranean World in the Age of Philip II* (2 vols, 2nd ed. London 1972–3). For the Christian adoption of Neo-Platonism see D.P. Walker, *The Ancient Theology* (London 1972). The relations of Federico Borromeo and Galileo are studied by A. Favaro, *Federigo Borromeo e Galileo Galilei* (Milan 1910). Compare G. Cozzi, *Paolo Sarpi tra Venezia e l'Europa* (Turin 1979). Family economy and patterns of social behaviour at Venice are considered by J.C. Davis, *The Decline of the Venetian Nobility as a Ruling Class* (Baltimore 1962). Compare P. Burke, *Venice and Amsterdam* (London 1974); W.J. Bouwsma, *Venice and the Defense of Republican Liberty* (Berkeley 1968); F.C. Lane, *Venice, A Maritime Republic* (Baltimore 1973); B. Pullan, *Rich and Poor in Renaissance Venice* (Oxford 1971). Religious conditions in Tudor Lancashire are studied by C. Haigh, *Reformation and Resistance in Tudor Lancashire* (London 1975). Aspects of the reign of James VI and I, and the transformation of his views on witchcraft, are discussed in a book edited by A.G.R. Smith, *The Reign of James VI and I* (London 1973). The education of the English gentry is treated by H. Kearney, *Scholars and Gentlemen* (London 1970). The importance of Charles Borromeo in the tradition of episcopal reform after the Council of Trent is discussed by Jedin, in a book adapted by P. Broutin under the title, *L'évêque dans la tradition pastorale du xvie siècle* (Bruges 1953). Compare the distinct original published as *Il tipo ideale di vescovo secondo la riforma cattolica* (Brescia 1950). See also the stimulating essay by R. Briggs, 'The Catholic Puritans: Jansenists and Rigorists in France', in *Puritans and Revolutionaries* [collected essays in honour of Christopher Hill], ed. D. Pennington and K. Thomas (Oxford 1978); and also there the article by N. Tyacke on 'Science and Religion at Oxford before the Civil War'. On Augustinianism and legalism, see the two essays by Bouwsma, 'The Two Faces of Humanism. Stoicism and Augustinianism in Renaissance Thought', in *Itinerarium Italicum* [essays presented to P.O. Kristeller], ed. H.A. Oberman with T.A. Brady, Jr (Leiden 1975); and 'Lawyers in Early Modern Culture', *American Historical Review* (1953). The condition of female convents at Naples after the Council of Trent is discussed by C. Russo, *I monasteri femminili di clausura a Napoli nel secolo xvii* (Naples 1970). For Sicilian conditions under Spanish rule, including the position of the crown Inquisition in the island, see H. Koenigsberger, *The Government of Sicily under Philip II of Spain* (London 1951). Compare his article, 'Decadence or Shift? Changes in the Civilization of Italy and Europe in the Sixteenth and Seventeenth Centuries', *Transactions of the Royal Historical Society* (1960); and his article, 'Republics and Courts in Italian and European Culture in the Sixteenth and Seventeenth Centuries', *Past and Present* (1979). See also R. Quazza, *Preponderanza Spagnuola* (Milan 1950). For the state of Rome and the central papal states after the Council of Trent see J. Delumeau, *Vie économique et sociale de Rome dans la seconde moitié du xvie siècle* (2 vols, Paris 1957–9). See also his *Rome au xvie siècle* (Paris 1975).

The working of the English Church courts, for one area, after the Reformation is discussed by R. Marchant, *The Church under the Law. Justice, Administration and Discipline in the Diocese of York 1560-1640* (Cambridge 1969). See also R. Houlbrooke, *Church Courts and the People during the English Reformation, 1520-70* (Oxford 1979). C. Cairns has written a biographical study of Bollani as bishop: *Domenico Bollani* (Nieuwkoop 1976). The early Counter-Reformation activity at Bologna and Milan, as well as at Rome, after the Council of Trent, was described by an English Catholic exile, Gregory Martin, also involved in the Douai version of the English Bible. Under the title *Roma Sancta* he wrote his account in English and a modern edition has beeñ produced by G.B. Parks (Rome 1969). Compare, for female conventual conditions even at Milan, M. Mazzucchelli, *The Nun of Monza* (London 1963). For the often neglected importance of Neri and the Roman Oratory in the Counter-Reformation see L. Ponnelle and L. Bordet, *Saint Philip Neri and the Roman Society of his times (1515-95)* (London 1932). The best works on Baronius are in Italian and German; see below, under Chapter 6. There is also a study in English by C.R. Pullapilly, *Caesar Baronius, counter-reformation historian* (Notre Dame 1975). For popular culture in Europe in this period see P. Burke, *Popular culture in early modern Europe* (London 1978). Compare also the essays in *Religioni delle classi popolari* (Quaderni Storici 41) ed. C. Ginzburg (Bologna 1979) with the older essay by Evennett on the Counter-Reformation in *The Reformation Crisis* ed. J. Hurstfield (London 1965). In the book on *The Pursuit of Holiness in Late Medieval and Renaissance Religion* ed. C. Trinkaus and H. Oberman (Leiden 1974) is an important essay by T. Tentler on 'The Summa for Confessors as an Instrument of Social Control'. But this should be read in the light of the other essay there by L. Boyle, 'The Summa for Confessors as a Genre and its Religious Intent'; and other essays by Galpern, Becker, Weinstein, N.Z. Davis, Trinkaus, Kristeller and McConica. Tentler has also put forward his views in a book, *Sin and confession on the eve of the Reformation* (Princeton 1977). Other aspects of humanism in the era of the movement for Church reform and the Reformation are studied by R. Weiss, *Humanism in England during the fifteenth century* (Oxford 1941), and J. McConica, *English humanists and Reformation politics under Henry VIII and Edward VI* (Oxford 1965). For a useful corrective to the view of Catholic decline by the eighteenth century from the initial standards of reform, see J. McManners, 'Aristocratic vocations: the bishops of France in the eighteenth century', in *Studies in Church History*, vol. 15 (Oxford 1978), ed. D. Baker. An equally timely revision of accepted views of the supposed decline of Spain is provided by the article of H. Kamen, 'The Decline of Spain: a historical myth?' *Past and Present* (1978). Compare J.H. Elliott, 'Self-perception and decline in early seventeenth-century Spain', in the same journal (1977). For the important text of Italian reform tending to theological dissidence, the *Beneficio di Cristo*, see C.

Ginzburg and A. Prosperi, *Le due redazioni del 'Beneficio di Cristo': Eresia e riforma nell'Italia del '500* (Florence 1974), and *Giochi di pazienza. Un seminario sul 'Beneficio di Cristo'* (Turin 1975). See also the edition of S. Caponetto, *Benedetto da Mantova, Il Beneficio di Cristo con le versioni del secolo XVI. Documenti e testimonianze* (Florence 1972). Compare one aspect of the evolution of Italian exiles' radical propositions in the article of P. McNair, 'Ochino's Apology: Three Gods or Three Wives', *History* (1975). See also P. McNair and J. Tedeschi, 'New Light on Ochino', in *Bibliothèque d'Humanisme et Renaissance* (1973). The German peasants' revolt of the sixteenth century has recently received renewed attention, including the study edited by B. Scribner and G. Benecke, *The German peasant war of 1525: new viewpoints* (London 1979). The firm control of Catholic society by the state even more than by the Church, in the case of Piedmont in the seventeenth and eighteenth centuries, is revealed by G. Quazza, *La decadenza italiana nella storia europea. Saggi sul Sei-Settecento* (Turin 1971). The originally different intellectual world of Venice, in the development of printing, publishing and the edition of classical texts, is described by M. Lowry, *The World of Aldus Manutius* (Oxford 1979). Compare the views on the impact of printing of E. Eisenstein, *The printing press as an agent of change: communications and cultural transformation in early-modern Europe* (2 vols, Cambridge 1979). A comprehensive view of the evolution of European political thought is provided by Q. Skinner, *The foundations of modern political thought* (2 vols, Cambridge 1978). The transformation of both classical and religious ideals by the age of Winckelmann can be seen by reference to the essay of Walter Pater on Winckelmann in *The Renaissance* (London 1888). The more immediate effect of Tridentine restrictions on sepulchral display, leading to the use of side-altars as still effectively personal monuments, in Venetian territory, is illustrated in an article by K.B. Hiesinger, 'The Fregoso Monument: A Study in Sixteenth-century Tomb Monuments and Catholic Reform', *Burlington Magazine* (1976). The distinct subject of the erudite revival of paganism, at Rome not least, in the Renaissance may be studied in J. Seznec, *The Survival of the pagan gods* (Princeton 1972), or E. Wind, *Pagan Mysteries in the Renaissance* (London 1968). But an important article on popular superstition is that of P.C. Ioly Zorattini, 'Per lo studio della stregoneria in Italia nell'età moderna', *Rivista di storia della Chiesa in Italia* (1971). For the different impact of religious change in England on popular faith see J. Phillips, *The Reformation of Images* (Berkeley 1973). But for Italy again see C. Ginzburg, *I Benandanti* (Turin 1966). See also R. Weiss, *The Renaissance Discovery of Classical Antiquity* (Oxford 1969). An important collection of articles has been edited by C. Russo, *Società, chiesa e vita religiosa nell' 'Ancien Régime'* (Naples 1976). Compare A.N. Galpern, *The Religions of the People in sixteenth-century Champagne* (Cambridge, Mass. 1976), and V. Marchetti, *Gruppi ereticali senesi del cinquecento* (Florence 1975). Other relevant works are P. Lopez, *Il movimento valdesiano a Napoli. Mario Galeota e le sue vicende col Sant'Uffizio* (Naples 1976); M. Bendiscioli, *Dalla Riforma alla Controriforma* (Bologna 1974); and F. Molinari, *I tabù della storia della Chiesa moderna* (Turin 1973). See also H. Jedin, *Kirche des Glaubens, Kirche der Geschichte* (2 vols, Freiburg 1966) for Contarini in particular. For later developments, see also *Katholische Aufklärung und Josephinismus*, ed. E. Kovács (Munich 1979); and G. Klingenstein, *Staatsverwaltung und kirchliche Autorität im 18 Jahrhundert* (Vienna 1970). For an earlier period see *Il Concilio di Trento e la riforma tridentina. Atti del Convegno Storico*, Trento 1963 (2 vols, Rome 1965); and E. Stakemeier, *Der Kampf um Augustin auf dem Tridentinum* (Paderborn 1937). Other relevant studies are J. Semmler, *Das päpstliche Staatssekretariat in den Pontifikaten Pauls V. und Gregors XV. 1605–23* (Rome 1969); and K. Walf, *Das bischöfliche Amt in der Sicht josephinischer Kirchenrechtler* (Vienna 1975).

## 3   Scholasticism and science

Among the articles of C.M. Cipolla which discuss the economy of Italy and the role of Church property see 'Une crise ignorée: comment s'est perdue la propriété ecclésiastique dans l'Italie du Nord entre le XI$^e$ et le XVI$^e$ siècle', in *Annales E.S.C.* (1947), which has not won universal acceptance however. For French Church finance in the eighteenth century, see J. McManners, *French Ecclesiastical Society under the Ancien Régime* (Manchester 1960). The esoteric origins of experimental science are examined by Frances Yates in *The Rosicrucian Enlightenment* (London 1974). For the economic development of France and England, see J. Nef, *Industry and Government in France and England, 1540–1640* (Ithaca 1967). The relationship of scientific knowledge to Dutch economic development is assessed in C. Wilson, *The Dutch Republic* (London 1968). The arguments advanced by Max Weber and R.H. Tawney – see the latter's *Religion and the Rise of Capitalism* (Harmondsworth 1964) – about the relation of Protestantism and capitalism are ably refuted by K. Samuelsson, *Religion and Economic Action* (Stockholm 1961). The economy of Spain is examined by J.G. da Silva, under the delphic title, *En Espagne* (Paris 1965). Another useful survey of the interrelation between European, particularly Iberian, economies and the transatlantic colonies, in an age of inflation, is F. Mauro, *L'expansion européenne (1600–1870)* (Paris 1964). For the most recent and well-balanced treatment of the much disputed origins of English experimental science at Oxford and London, see the collected essays in honour of Christopher Hill, already mentioned, for the essay by N. Tyacke, 'Science and Religion at Oxford before the Civil War'. But see also C. Webster, *The Great Instauration* (London 1975) for the transformation of the Baconian tradition. For Descartes, compare the view of Frances Yates, in her book on the Rosicrucian Enlightenment mentioned above, with that of E. Gilson,

*Etudes sur le rôle de la pensée médiévale dans la formation du système cartésien* (Paris 1951). Bruno is the subject of a book by Frances Yates, *Giordano Bruno and the Hermetic Tradition* (London 1964). For Campanella and the background of Neapolitan unrest, see also R. Villari, *La rivolta antispagnola a Napoli: le origini (1585-1647)* (Bari 1967). Galileo has stimulated a vast literature. An interesting approach is that of A. Koestler, *The Sleepwalkers* (London 1968). A general account of the conditions of the Jewish communities in Italy is provided by C. Roth, *The History of the Jews in Italy* (Philadelphia 1946). For the work of Borromini, see P. Portoghesi, *Borromini* (London 1968) and A. Blunt, *Borromini* (London 1979). See also R. Wittkower, *Art and Architecture in Italy 1600-1750* (Harmondsworth 1958). European Universities are the subject of important volumes edited by L. Stone, *The University in Society* (2 vols, Princeton 1974). Medical practice and epidemic in seventeenth-century Italy are illustrated by C.M. Cipolla, *Cristofano and the Plague* (London 1973), and *Faith, Reason and the Plague* (Brighton 1979). Academic activity at Venice is discussed by P.L. Rose in an article, 'The Accademia Venetiana, science and culture in Renaissance Venice', in *Studi Veneziani*, 1969. On the Venetian book trade, see P. Grendler, *The Roman Inquisition and the Venetian Press 1540-1605* (Princeton 1977). For the Great Tew circles, see H.R. Trevor-Roper, *Edward Hyde, Earl of Clarendon* (Oxford 1975). On the question of the 'closing' of Spain to European influence under Philip II, see R. Menéndez Pidal, *Los españoles en la Historia* (2nd ed, Madrid 1971). For El Greco, see D. Davies, *El Greco* (Oxford 1976). J. Arthos has written on Milton and the Italian academies in his book, *Milton and the Italian cities* (London 1968). The economic and intellectual development of Italy, as well as religious, can be traced from the Middle Ages to the present in the monumental new history of Italy, published by Einaudi, under the general editorship of R. Romano and C. Vivanti: *Storia d'Italia* (Turin 1972 onwards, in 6 vols, some in more than one part, and including the 'Atlante' and documents, plus further 'Annali' volumes). See also the UTET *Storia d'Italia*, ed. G. Galasso (Turin 1979 onwards, to be completed in 23 vols, plus 'Atlante'). The financial consequences of papal policy under the Barberini are well illustrated in an article, published in *Rom in der Neuzeit*, ed. R. Elze *et al.* (Vienna–Rome 1976), by G. Lutz, 'Rom und Europa während des Pontifikats Urbans VIII'. Bernini's work in Rome, not least for the Barberini, is treated by R. Wittkower in his book on art and architecture in Italy, and also in his monograph on the artist: *Bernini* (2nd ed, London 1966). See also his treatment of the reception of Bernini in France: *Bernini's Bust of Louis XIV* (London 1951), and his book, edited with I.B. Jaffe, *Baroque art, the Jesuit contribution* (New York 1972). For the French Minims of the seventeenth century, see P.J.S. Whitmore, *The Order of Minims in seventeenth-century France* (The Hague 1967). For Christina of Sweden, see the English version of the biography by S. Stolpe (London

1966). On Salviati, there is a biography by P. Brown, *Lionardo Salviati* (Oxford 1974). Pascal has attracted a vast literature. The best initial approach is probably to read his own *Provincial Letters*, of which modern editions provide an English translation. The subject of James II and English religious polemic in the later seventeenth century is discussed in two works by J. Miller, *Popery and Politics in England 1660–88* (Cambridge 1973); and *James II; a study in kingship* (Hove 1978). See also an important article in *Studies in Church History*, vol. 10 (1978), by G. Bennett, 'The seven bishops: a reconsideration'. La Rochefoucauld can be studied in modern editions. An English translation of the *Maxims* was published in London, 1868. L. Goldmann's important treatment of Jansenism is translated under the title *The Hidden God* (London 1964). The plays of Racine, and the contrasting ones of Corneille can be studied in modern editions, and in English translations. Other, recent treatment of Jewish history in Counter-Reformation Italy can be found in two articles by B. Pullan: 'The Inquisition and the Jews of Venice: The Case of Gaspare Ribeiro, 1580–1', *Bulletin of the John Rylands University Library of Manchester* (1979); and '"A Ship with Two Rudders": "Righetto Marrano" and the Inquisition in Venice', *Historical Journal* (1977). For the English colleges and seminaries abroad, see A.C.F. Beales, *Education under Penalty* (London 1963). On the Cambridge Platonists, see B. Willey, *The English Moralists* (London 1964). For Newton there is an extensive literature; see especially F. Manuel, *The Religion of Isaac Newton* (Oxford 1974). Compare F.A. Yates, *The Occult Philosophy in the Elizabethan Age* (London 1979), for discussion of the Christian Cabala.

A work of wide scope is that of P. Hazard, *The European Mind 1680–1715* (London 1953). Universities are the study of S. d'Irsay, *Histoire des universités* (2 vols, Paris 1933–5). See also A.R. Hall, *The Scientific Revolution* (2nd ed, London 1967). L. Firpo has written on *Lo stato ideale della Controriforma* (Bari 1957). See also C. Vivanti, *Lotta politica e pace religiosa in Francia fra cinquecento e seicento* (Turin 1963). For Arminius, see the work of C. Bangs, *Arminius: a study in the Dutch reformation* (Nashville, N.Y. 1971). Another aspect of intellectual development is traced in J. Bignami Odier, *La bibliothèque Vaticane de Sixte IV à Pie XI: Recherches sur l'histoire des collections de manuscrits* (Vatican City 1973). Compare O. Chadwick, *Catholicism and history: the opening of the Vatican Archives* (Cambridge 1978). See also P.F. Grendler, *Critics of the Italian World 1530–60* (London 1969). Another work on the Bollandists is that of H. Delehaye, *L'œuvre des Bollandistes 1615–1915* (2nd ed, Brussels 1959). J.N. Figgis published a work on *Political Thought from Gerson to Grotius* which was edited in 1960 with an introduction by G. Mattingly (New York). See also F. Chabod, *La politica di Paolo Sarpi* (Venice-Rome 1962). An important work is that of A.C. Jemolo, *Stato e Chiesa negli scrittori italiani del Seicento e del Settecento* (2nd edition, ed. M. Broglio, Naples 1972). P.

Paschini, *Un Amico del Cardinal Polo: Alvise Priuli* (Rome 1921) has studied another important figure in Catholic reform. Compare P. Prodi, *Lo sviluppo dell'assolutismo nello stato pontificio (secoli XV-XVI)* (vol. I, Bologna 1968). The letters of Sarpi to Protestant correspondents have been edited by M.D. Busnelli and G. Gambarin: *Lettere ai Protestanti* (2 vols, Bari 1931). Compare the edition by B. Ulianich of his *Lettere ai Gallicani* (Wiesbaden 1961); and R. Briggs, *The Scientific Revolution of the seventeenth century* (London 1969). The international political overtones of Dutch Arminian debate are also noted by C. Wilson on the Dutch Republic, already mentioned. Other useful works include R. Menéndez Pidal, *Idea Imperial de Carlos V* (4th ed, Madrid 1955); L. Firpo, *Esecuzioni capitali in Roma (1567-1671)* (Florence 1974: Eresia e Riforma nell' Italia del Cinquecento, Miscellanea I); and P.O. Kristeller, *Medieval Aspects of Renaissance Learning* (Durham, N.C. 1974). Compare E. Garin, *Italian Humanism: philosophy and civic life in the Renaissance* (Oxford 1966); J.C. Nieto, *Juan de Valdés and the origins of the Spanish and Italian Reformation* (Geneva 1970); and A. Rotondò, *Studi e ricerche di storia ereticale italiana del '500: I* (Turin 1974). Works on aspects of French development include F.J. Baumgartner, *Radical Reactionaries, the political thought of the French Catholic League* (Geneva 1976); J.M. Hayden, 'The Social Origins of the French Episcopacy at the Beginning of the Seventeenth Century', in *French Historical Studies* (1977); and R. Taveneaux, *Jansénisme et prêt à intérêt* (Paris 1977). Compare P. Chaunu, 'Le XVIIᵉ siècle religieux', in *Annales E.S.C.* (1967), and J. Bodin, *Colloquium of the Seven about Secrets of the Sublime*, ed. M.L.D. Kuntz (Princeton 1975). For developments in German-speaking Europe see V. Pitzner, *Justinus Febronius. Das Ringen eines katholischen Irenikers um die Einheit der Kirche im Zeitalter der Aufklärung* (Göttingen 1976). Other questions are treated by J.A. Fernández-Santamaria, *The State, War and Peace: Spanish Political Thought in the Renaissance 1516-56* (Cambridge 1977); and in *The Damned Art, Essays in the Literature of Witchcraft*, ed. S. Anglo (London 1977). A further tradition can be pursued in the books edited by R. Bolgar, *Classical Influences on European Culture A.D. 1500-1700* (Cambridge 1976), and *Classical Influences on Western Thought A.D. 1650-1870* (Cambridge 1979); C.L. Stringer, *Humanism and the Church Fathers: Ambrogio Traversari (1386-1439) and Christian Antiquity in the Italian Renaissance* (Albany 1977); and A. Dupront, *L.A. Muratori, et la société européenne des pré-lumières* (Florence 1976). See also D. Koenigsberger, *Renaissance Man and Creative Thinking: a history of concepts of harmony 1400-1700* (Hassocks 1979); and R. Pfeiffer, *History of classical scholarship*, vol. 2, *1300-1850* (Oxford 1976). Other perspectives are provided by R. García-Villoslada, *Loyola y Erasmo* (Madrid 1965); and P. Hersche, *Der aufgeklärte Reformkatholizismus in Österreich* (Bern 1976).

## 4  New problems of Catholic expansion

The political history of Europe in the seventeenth century, and French
policy within that, during and after the Thirty Years War, is outlined with
clarity by D. Ogg, *Europe in the Seventeenth Century* (revised 8th ed.,
London 1961). For the Thirty Years War, see also the works on that subject
by S.H. Steinberg (London 1966) and C.V. Wedgwood (Harmondsworth
1961). Aldous Huxley has written on Père Joseph in his own personal
manner: *Grey Eminence* (London 1942). On the siege of Vienna there is a
monograph by J.W. Stoye, *The Siege of Vienna* (London 1964). For the
French Wars of Religion of the sixteenth century, see E. Armstrong, *The
French Wars of Religion* (2nd ed. facsimile, New York 1971). The questions
of the policy of Catherine de Medici and of the Massacre of Saint Bartholomew are discussed by N.M. Sutherland, *The Massacre of St. Bartholomew
and the European Conflict 1559-72* (London 1973); *Catherine de Medici and
the Ancien Régime* (London 1966, Historical Association); and 'The Cardinal of Lorraine and the Colloque of Poissy, 1561: a reassessment,' *Journal
of Ecclesiastical History* (1977). See also *The Massacre of Saint Bartholomew.
Reappraisals and Documents*, ed. A. Soman (The Hague 1974). Compare
the picture of Henri III given by Frances Yates in *The French Academies of
the Sixteenth Century* (London 1947). The militia service owed by English
prelates is described in an article by J.J.N. McGurk, 'The Clergy and the
Militia 1580-1610', in *History* (1975). Fénelon's *Télémaque* exists in modern
editions. Las Casas has inspired many writers. For an introduction, see the
article by M. Bataillon, 'The Idea of the Discovery of America among the
Spaniards of the Sixteenth Century', in the book, *Spain in the Fifteenth
Century*, edited by J.R.L. Highfield, already mentioned. Thomas More's
*Utopia* exists in modern editions. See also the article of D.B. Fenlon,
'Utopia and its aftermath', in *Transactions of the Royal Historical Society*
(1975).

K.S. Latourette has written a history of Christian expansion. See vol. 3,
*Three Centuries of Advance* (London 1940). See also the *Handbuch der
Kirchengeschichte*, edited by H. Jedin, vol. 4 (Freiburg 1967), for the section
on the missions. Francis Xavier is the subject of a study by J. Brodrick,
*Saint Francis Xavier* (London 1952). An extended and polyglot documen-
tary history of the overseas missions, in several volumes, is also being
published at Rome: ed. J. Metzler, *Sacrae Congregationis de Propaganda
Fide Memoria Rerum* (1971 onwards, to be completed in 3 vols). Consider-
ation of the Counter-Reformation in Ireland is to be found in *Historical
Studies*, ed. T.D. Williams, vol. 8 (Dublin 1971), by J. Bossy, 'The
Counter-Reformation and the People of Catholic Ireland, 1596-1641'. For
Catholicism in Scotland see D. Mathew, *Scotland under Charles I* (London
1955). Compare P. Anson, *Underground Catholicism in Scotland 1622-1878*
(Montrose 1970). On Chinese culture and that of Europe, see J. Needham,

abridged by C.A. Ronan, *The Shorter Science and Civilization in China*, vol. 1 (Cambridge 1978). Among the many works of C.R. Boxer on the Portuguese overseas empire, a recent book on female life overseas, *Mary and Misogyny* (London 1975), touches on questions of religious belief and practice. On the Inquisition in Mexico there is a monograph by R. Greenleaf, *The Mexican Inquisition of the Sixteenth Century* (Albuquerque 1969). For the operation of the secular courts in the Spanish overseas empire, in the case of New Galicia, see J.H. Parry, *The Audiencia of New Galicia in the Sixteenth Century* (Cambridge 1948). Other works on Spanish America and Brazil which are useful, as for the Far East too, include C.R. Boxer, *The Church Militant and Iberian Expansion 1440-1770* (Baltimore 1978); R.E. Greenleaf, ed., *The Roman Catholic Church in Colonial Latin America* (New York 1971); R. Hanke, ed., *History of Latin American Civilization*, 1 (London 1969); and B.W. Diffie and G.D. Winus, *Foundations of the Portuguese Empire 1415-1580* (Oxford 1977). On Japan, see also H.H. Gowen, *An Outline History of Japan* (New York 1927); G.B. Sansom, *The Western World and Japan* (London 1950), and *A History of Japan 1334-1615* (Stanford 1961), and *1615-1867* (1963).

For China see also K.S. Latourette, *A History of Christian Missions in China* (London 1929). The Christians of Saint Thomas, in India, are the subject of a monograph by L.W. Brown, *The Indian Christians of Saint Thomas* (Cambridge 1956). There is also a general work by S. Neill, *Colonialism and Christian Missions* (London 1966). For Poland, see *The Cambridge History of Poland*, ed. W.F. Reddaway *et al.* (2 vols, Cambridge 1950-1).

## 5  Religious divisions and political similarities

Some works relevant to the political history of Europe have been mentioned in the preceding sections of the bibliography. Other useful works include H.O. Evennett, *The Cardinal of Lorraine and the Council of Trent. A Study in the Counter-Reformation* (Cambridge 1930); J. Elliott, *Imperial Spain, 1469-1716* (London 1969), and *The Revolt of the Catalans* (Cambridge 1963). There is also the work of G. Albion, *Charles 1 and the Court of Rome* (London 1935). See also the books of J. Brodrick, *Saint Peter Canisius S.J. 1521-97* (London 1935), and *The Life and Work of Blessed Robert Francis Cardinal Bellarmine* (2 vols, London 1928). A most useful survey of Catholic reform in German lands is provided by G. Schreiber, 'Tridentinische Reformdekrete in deutschen Bistümern', reprinted in *Concilium Tridentinum*, ed. R. Bäumer (Darmstadt 1979). Compare the general study of O. Logan, *Culture and Society in Venice 1470-1790. The Renaissance and its Heritage* (London 1972). For an earlier period there is P. Partner, *Renaissance Rome* (London 1976), and M. Mallett, *The Borgias* (London 1969). Two accounts of precise topics are A. Pastore, *Nella Valtellina del tardo cinquecento: fede, cultura, società* (Milan 1975), and C. Wilson, *Queen Elizabeth and the Revolt of the Netherlands* (London 1970). Compare the collected essays by various authors in *Crisis in Europe, 1560–1660* (London 1965), ed. T. Aston, which discuss the revolts of the mid-seventeenth century and examine the possibility of a 'general crisis'. An important revision of earlier views of Joseph II's ecclesiastical policies is contained in the article by D. Beales, 'The False Joseph II', in *Historical Journal* (1975). For an early example of the evolution of Neapolitan legal theory, see V.I. Comparato on Valletta: *Giuseppe Valletta* (Naples 1970). An introduction to conditions in eighteenth-century France is provided in the first volume of the (Pelican) History of Modern France, by A. Cobban: *Old Régime and Revolution 1715–99* (3rd ed., Harmondsworth 1963). The *Leviathan* of Hobbes can be read in modern editions. For Locke, see *Two Treatises of Government*, ed. P. Laslett (2nd ed., Cambridge 1967). For the late sixteenth-century French development of political thought, under Calvinist inspiration, the *Vindiciae contra Tyrannos: A Defence of Liberty against Tyrants* [etc.] was published in English in 1689. See the modern English version in *Constitutionalism and Resistance in the sixteenth century*, ed. J.H. Franklin (New York 1969). D. Hay, in his book *Annalists and Historians* (London 1977), discusses Muratori. An elaborate edition of Muratori's correspondence, in many volumes, is being published by Olschki at Florence: *Edizione nazionale del carteggio di L.A. Muratori* (1975 onwards). For discussion of papal diplomacy and the transformation of the papal Nunciatures, see vol. 4 of the *Handbuch der Kirchengeschichte* already mentioned. The development of Sicily can be traced in a volume on the history of the island by D. Mack Smith, *Medieval Sicily 800–1713* (London 1968). For the Church in Tuscany after the Council of Trent, see A. d'Addario, *Aspetti della Controriforma a Firenze* (Rome 1972). The cult of Saint Teresa, and other saints in the Counter-Reformation, is discussed by C. Dejob, *De l'influence du Concile de Trente sur la littérature et les beaux-arts chez les peuples catholiques* (Paris 1884). See also *The Art of Ecstasy* by R.J. Petersson (London 1970). For the revival of Anglo-papal diplomatic relations, at the end of the eighteenth century, see the short work by Cardinal (F.A.) Gasquet, *Great Britain and the Holy See, 1792–1806* (Rome 1919). For the exiled Stuart court at Rome, and the world of art collectors and freemasons associated with it, see Lesley Lewis, *Connoisseurs and Secret Agents in eighteenth-century Rome* (London 1961). On the background to early Tudor reforms in government and planning of social legislation and economic direction, see W. Zeeveld, *Foundations of Tudor Policy* (Cambridge, Mass. 1948); and G.R. Elton, *Reform and Renewal. Thomas Cromwell and the Common Weal* (Cambridge 1973). The education of Pole has been studied by Cardinal Gasquet: *Cardinal Pole and his Early Friends* (London 1927). The *Prince* of Machiavelli is available in translation, in modern editions. See also *A Machiavellian Treatise*, ed. P.S. Donaldson (Cambridge

1975), who attributes it to Stephen Gardiner. The English evolution of the literal belief in Anti-Christ is shown by Christopher Hill, *Anti-Christ in Seventeenth-Century England* (London 1971). For the penal laws and the condition of English Catholics in Recusant times, there are many accounts, of varying degrees of scholarship. But a recent and simple guide, by a Catholic historian, is that of A. Morey, *The Catholic Subjects of Elizabeth I* (London 1978). The relations of different religious persuasions in the earlier seventeenth century in Europe are examined by H.R. Trevor-Roper, in an article in *Studies in Church History*, vol. 15, 'The Church of England and the Greek Church in the time of Charles I'. The Counter-Reformation in action, in the visitation by Charles Borromeo of Bergamo, in Venetian territory, can be studied in the Acts of the visitation, published in the volumes prepared by the future Pope John XXIII: A.G. Roncalli *et al.*, *Gli Atti della Visita Apostolica . . . a Bergamo* (Florence 1936 onwards). The travel accounts of Coryat, Fynes Moryson and Evelyn can be read in modern editions. For Evelyn see his *Diary* ed. E.S. de Beer (6 vols, Oxford 1955). O. Garstein has written on *Rome and the Counter-Reformation in Scandinavia*, vol. 1 (Copenhagen 1963).

Other material relevant to English developments includes H.A. Kelly, *The Matrimonial Trials of Henry VIII* (Stanford 1976). R.S. Bosher, *The Making of the Restoration Settlement* (London 1951) is still valuable, despite much criticism of the arguments put forward there. See also a more recent study, however, by I.M. Green, *The Re-establishment of the Church of England, 1660-3* (Oxford 1978). A useful corrective to oversimplified views of the relations of Puritans or parliamentary leaders with Catholics or courtiers is provided by R.M. Smuts, 'The Puritan followers of Henrietta Maria in the 1630s', in the *English Historical Review* (1978). For the *Political Testament* of Cardinal Richelieu, a translation of selected passages can be found in an edition by H.B. Hill (Madison 1965). The political and social evolution of Catholic Spain has been amply studied in the works of A. Domínguez Ortiz, *El Antiguo Régimen: los Reyes Catolicos y los Austrias* (5th ed., Madrid 1978); and *The Golden Age of Spain, 1516-1659* (London 1971). See also the article of A.W. Lovett, 'A cardinal's papers: the rise of Mateo Vázquez de Leca', *English Historical Review* (1973), and his book, *Philip II and Mateo Vázquez de Leca, The Government of Spain 1572-92* (Geneva 1977); and compare the book of I.A.A. Thompson, *War and Government in Habsburg Spain 1560-1620* (London 1976). For earlier foundations of royal control of ecclesiastical affairs in the Iberian peninsula, see E.A. Thompson, *The Goths in Spain* (Oxford 1969); and compare *Visigothic Spain: New Approaches* ed. E. James (Oxford 1980). For the Christian humanist education of Charles V and his consequent view of Church reform, at odds with papal plans for a Council, see the article of G. Müller, 'Zur Vorgeschichte des Tridentinums. Karl V. und das Konzil während des Pontifikates Clemens VII.', reprinted in *Concilium Tridentinum* ed. R.

Bäumer (Darmstadt 1979). The later evolutions of Catholic policy in Habsburg lands can be traced in the study of Jansenism in Austria by P. Hersche, *Der Spätjansenismus in Österreich* (Vienna 1977). See also E. Wangermann, *Aufklärung und staatsbürgerliche Erziehung, G. van Swieten als Reformator des österreichischen Unterrichtswesens 1781-91* (Vienna 1978). The evolution of Tuscany under the Medici, especially before the advent of Austrian reform there, is shown by E. Cochrane, *Florence in the Forgotten Centuries 1527-1800* (Chicago 1973). See also for Medicean control of learning, G.C. Pratilli, *L'università e il principe: Gli studi di Siena e di Pisa tra Rinascimento e Controriforma* (Florence 1975), and V.G. Stacchini and G. Bianchini, *Le Accademie dell' Aretino nel XVIIe XVIII secolo* (Florence 1978). The problem of Venetian development and social control by political means, as well as the question of relations with Rome, are touched on by M. Lowry in his article 'The reform of the Council of x, 1582-3: an unsettled problem?' in *Studi Veneziani*, vol. 13 (1971). But see the recent book of G. Cozzi, *Paolo Sarpi tra Venezia e l'Europa* (Turin 1979). The early Catholic reform, in Venetian territory, of Giberti, bishop of Verona, should be studied in A. Prosperi, *Tra Evangelismo e Controriforma: G.M. Giberti* (Rome 1969). Compare the article on Ormaneto as bishop of Padua by P. Preto, 'Un aspetto della Riforma cattolica nel Veneto: l'episcopato padovano di Niccolò Ormaneto', *Studi Veneziani*, vol. 11 (1969). For the brief and unhappy effects of Catholic reassertion under Venetian rule at Chios, see P. Argenti, *The Occupation of Chios by the Venetians (1694)* (London 1935). See also G. Benzoni, *Venezia nell' età della controriforma* (Milan 1973). A most important article on Venetian development is that of P. Prodi, 'The structure and organization of the church in Renaissance Venice: suggestions for research', in the book, *Renaissance Venice*, ed. J.R. Hale (London 1973). Other background information can be found in *Crisis and Change in the Venetian Economy*, ed. B. Pullan (London 1968). Compare the articles of S.J. Woolf, 'The Aristocracy in Transition: a continental comparison', in *Economic History Review* (1970); and C.M. Cipolla, 'The Decline of Italy', in the same journal (1952-3), and 'The so-called "Price Revolution". Reflections on "The Italian Situation"', in *Economy and Society in Early Modern Europe*, ed. P. Burke (London 1972). See also F. Chabod, *Per la storia religiosa dello stato di Milano durante il dominio di Carlo v* (2nd ed., Rome 1962), and *Lo stato e la vita religiosa a Milano nell' epoca di Carlo v* (Turin 1971). Compare D. Cantimori, *Prospettive di storia ereticale italiana del Cinquecento* (Bari 1960); R. de Maio, *Savonarola e la curia romana* (Rome 1969); or M. Bendiscioli, *Dalla riforma alla controriforma* (Bologna 1974). There is also a study by L. Càstano of *Gregorio XIV* (Turin 1957).

The political agitation experienced by the Jewish diaspora is discussed by G. Scholem, *Sabbatai Sevi: the mystical Messiah, 1626-76* (Princeton 1976). For the question of Catholicism in Spain at an earlier date, see R. Menéndez Pidal, *Los Reyes Catolicos y Otros Estudios* (Buenos Aires 1962).

There is also a book by A. Lynn Martin, *Henry III and the Jesuit politicians* (Geneva 1973). Botero's *Reason of State* is edited by P.J. and D.P. Waley (New Haven 1956). See also T.H. Clancy, *Papist Pamphleteers. The Allen-Persons Party and the Political Thought of the Counter-Reformation in England 1572–1615* (Chicago 1964). Compare F.A. Yates, *Astraea: the Imperial Theme in the Sixteenth Century* (London 1975). For the reality of lay reaction to the papal Interdict in the Venetian mainland dominions, see A. Sambo, 'Città, campagna e politica religiosa: l'interdetto del 1606–7 nella Repubblica di Venezia', *Atti dell' Istituto Veneto*, 1976. See also W.J. Bouwsma, *Venice and the Defense of Republican Liberty: Renaissance Values in the Age of the Counter-Reformation* (Berkeley 1968); R.T. Rapp, *Industry and economic decline in seventeenth-century Venice* (Cambridge, Mass. 1976); A. Tenenti, *Piracy and the Decline of Venice 1580–1615* (London 1967); and F.C. Lane, *Venice and History* (Baltimore 1966). Compare the perspectives of B. Croce, *Storia dell' età barocca in Italia* (2nd ed., Bari 1946); and J.W. Stoye's volume in the Fontana History of Europe, *Europe Unfolding 1648–88* (London 1969). H.G. Koenigsberger discusses 'The Italian Parliaments from their Origins to the End of the 18th Century', in the *Journal of Italian History* (1978). R. Mousnier has provided a concise study of *Louis XIV* (London 1974, Historical Association). J. Bossy's study of 'The English Catholic Community 1603–25', in *The Reign of James VI and I*, ed. A.G.R. Smith (London 1973), can be compared with his article, 'Henri IV, the Appellants and the Jesuits', in *Recusant History* (1965). Cardinal de Retz on the Frondes can be studied in the translation of his *Memoirs* (London c. 1904, Grolier Society), as well as in modern French editions. See also M. Rosa, *Politica e religione nel '700 europeo* (Florence 1974). For Saint Peter Canisius, see E.M. Buxbaum, *Petrus Canisius und die kirchliche Erneuerung des Herzogtums Bayern, 1549–56* (Rome 1973). Compare A.J. Loomie, *The Spanish Elizabethans: The English Exiles at the Court of Philip II* (New York 1963); and J.J. Scarisbrick, 'Robert Persons's plans for the "True" Reformation of England', in *Historical Perspectives: Studies in Honour of J.H. Plumb*, ed. N. McKendrick (London 1974). J.V. Polišensky has taken a general view of *War and Society in Europe, 1618–48* (Cambridge 1978); while, for eighteenth-century Spain, there is a monograph by L. Rodríguez Díaz, *Reforma e Ilustración en la España del siglo XVIII: Pedro Rodríguez de Campomanes* (Madrid 1975).

## 6 Catholic reform and Augustinianism

Reform within the Augustinian friars has been discussed by K. Walsh in an article, 'The Observance: Sources for a History of the Observant Reform Movement in the Order of Augustinian Friars in the fourteenth and fifteenth centuries', in *Rivista di storia della Chiesa in Italia* (1977). There is a study of Sadoleto by R.M. Douglas, *Jacopo Sadoleto, 1477–1547*

(Cambridge, Mass. 1959). A passage, in English translation, on the work
of Paleotti, by his biographer Prodi, is included in the book, edited by E.
Cochrane, *The Late Italian Renaissance* (London 1970). Prodi has also
written in French an article, 'Charles Borromée, archevêque de Milan et la
papauté', in *Revue d'histoire ecclésiastique* (1967). An English version of the
life of Charles Borromeo is that by M. Yeo, *A Prince of Pastors* (London
1938). But the French life by A. Deroo is better: *St. Charles Borromée* (Paris
1963). A short study in Italian is that of H. Jedin, *Carlo Borromeo* (Rome
1971). For the end of monasticism in England, see vol. 3 of D. Knowles,
*The Religious Orders in England* (Cambridge 1959). G. Cozzi has written a
biography of *Il Doge Nicolò Contarini. Ricerche sul patriziato veneziano agli
inizi del Seicento* (Venice 1958). For Catholic relief work in epidemics, the
careful historical research incorporated in the famous account of the North
Italian plague of 1630-1 at Milan, by Alessandro Manzoni, in his early
nineteenth-century romantic novel, *The Betrothed*, makes vivid reading.
His picture of Federico Borromeo is also very balanced. Compare the theory
of Jordan about the Protestant and Catholic motivations for charity in his
book: W.K. Jordan, *Philanthropy in England 1480-1660. A Study of the
changing pattern of English social aspirations* (London 1959). The criticism
of his arguments on the basis of the effects of inflation, reducing the real as
opposed to face value of charitable bequests, is to be found in an article by
W.G. Bittle and R.T. Lane, 'Inflation and Philanthropy in England', *Economic History Review* (1976). But see further 'A Re-assessment Reiterated',
in the same journal (1978) in answer to preceding critical comments by
other writers. See also, for contemporary views, John Stow's survey of
Elizabethan London, in a modern edition: *The Survey of London* (London
1923). French charity and eighteenth-century developments are treated by
J.P. Gutton, *La Société et les pauvres: l'exemple de la généralité de Lyon,
1534-1789* (Paris 1971); and O. Hufton, *The poor of eighteenth-century
France* (Oxford 1974). For Dominican reform, see the essays in *Spain in
the Fifteenth Century*, edited by J.R.L. Highfield, by V. Beltrán de Heredia,
on 'The Beginnings of Dominican Reform in Castile'; and J. Goñi Gaztam-
bide, on 'The Holy See and the Reconquest of the Kingdom of Granada
(1479-92)'. The poems of Saint John of the Cross can be read in translation,
e.g. by Roy Campbell (Harmondsworth 1960). The New Oxford History
of Music, vol. 5, ed. Sir Anthony Lewis, *Opera and Church Music 1630-
1750* (London 1975), provides a succinct guide to the subject. For the
connection between the 'New Music' of later sixteenth-century Florence,
and the development of the oratorio at Neri's Roman Oratory, and also for
discussion of the music of Lassus, see vol. 4, *The Age of Humanism 1540-
1630* (1968), ed. G. Abraham. The plays of Calderón can be read in translation: e.g. P. Calderón de la Barca, *Six Dramas* ed. H. Oelsner (London
1907). Compare those of other playwrights of the Golden Age, especially
Lope de Vega and Tirso de Molina. Compare also the *Romances* of Gongora.

For Mazarin and the Barberini, and political and artistic links, see the English version of G. Dethan, *The Young Mazarin* (London 1977). On the subject of French music drama at the royal court, in contrast to Jansenist and rigorist opposition to the theatre, compare the book by R.M. Isherwood, *Music in the Service of the King: France in the seventeenth century* (Ithaca 1973). For a general survey of diocesan reform in Italy, see the article by G. Alberigo, 'Studi e problemi relativi all' applicazione del Concilio di Trento in Italia', *Rivista storica italiana* (1958). See also his 'Carlo Borromeo come modello di vescovo nella Chiesa post-tridentina' in the same review (1967).

The French clergy and Gallicanism in seventeenth-century France have been studied by P. Blet: *Le clergé de France et la monarchie: étude sur les assemblées générales du clergé de 1615 à 1666* (2 vols, Rome 1959); and *Les assemblées du clergé et Louis XIV de 1670 à 1693* (Rome 1972). The jurisdictional nature of even French Jansenists in the eighteenth century is revealed by D. van Kley, *The Jansenists and the Expulsion of the Jesuits from France 1757-65* (New Haven 1975). Compare two recent studies of Jansenists and convulsionaries, A. Sedgwick, *Jansenism in Seventeenth Century France. Voices from the Wilderness* (Charlottesville 1978); and B.R. Kreiser, *Miracles, Convulsions and ecclesiastical politics in early eighteenth-century Paris* (Princeton 1978). The nature of eighteenth-century French Jansenism is also discussed by J. McManners, in an article in *Studies in Church History*, vol. 12 (Oxford 1975) ed. D. Baker: 'Jansenism and politics in the eighteenth century'. The role of Saint-Sulpice in eighteenth-century society is reflected in the famous proto-romantic novel, *Manon Lescaut* by the Abbé Prévost. For the early development of scepticism, see R. Pintard, *Le libertinage érudit dans la première moitié du XVII^e siècle* (Paris 1943). Contrast the picture of popular heresy in sixteenth-century Friuli presented by C. Ginzburg, *Il formaggio e i vermi* (Turin 1976). A review of aspects of European religion in practice is provided by P. Burke in the Companion Volume of the *New Cambridge Modern History* (vol. 13 ed. P. Burke, Cambridge 1979). Some figures in the circles of early Catholic reform in Italy are discussed by V. Cian, *Un illustre nunzio pontificio del Rinascimento, Baldassar Castiglione* (Vatican City 1951). There is an English translation by G. Bull of Castiglione's *Book of the Courtier* (Harmondsworth 1967). Works published by French historians which begin an assessment of popular religion in pre-Revolutionary France include: P. Ariès, *L'homme devant la mort* (Paris 1977); P. Chaunu, *La mort à Paris: 16^e, 17^e et 18^e siècles* (Paris 1978); F. Lebrun, *Les hommes et la mort en Anjou aux 17^e et 18^e siècles* (Paris 1971); M. Vovelle, *Piété baroque et déchristianisation en Provence au XVIII^e siècle* (Paris 1973), and *Mourir autrefois* (Paris 1974). Most important are the articles in *Church and society in Catholic Europe of the eighteenth century*, ed. W.J. Callahan and D. Higgs (Cambridge 1979). The trials of an earlier Catholic reforming prelate, whose work was necessarily short-lived, are further illuminated by J.I. Tellechea Idígoras, *Melanchton y Carranza. Préstamos y afinidades* (Salamanca 1979). A further article on the Council of Trent is that by A. Dupront, 'Du Concile de Trente: réflexions', in *Revue historique* (1951). See also another article of wide scope, on the question of the movement for Church reform and the Reformation, D.B. Fenlon, ' "Encore une question". Lucien Febvre, the Reformation and the School of "Annales" ', in *Historical Studies*, vol. 9 ed. J.G. Barry (Belfast 1974). Two important articles by O.M.T. Logan are 'Grace and Justification: Some Italian Views of the Sixteenth and Seventeenth Centuries', in the *Journal of Ecclesiastical History* (1969), and 'The Ideal of the Bishop and the Venetian Patriciate', in the same journal (1978). An older study of Pole, including his work in England, by W. Schenk (London 1950), may be compared with the rather disparaging views of D.M. Loades in his study of Mary Tudor: *The Reign of Mary Tudor: Politics, Government and Religion in England 1553-8* (London 1979). For Baronius see H. Jedin, *Kardinal Caesar Baronius* (Münster 1978). A further study of Charles Borromeo is that of R. Mols, *S. Carlo Borromeo iniziatore della pastorale moderna* (Milan 1961). See also the article of P. Prodi, 'San Carlo Borromeo e il Cardinale Gabriele Paleotti. Due vescovi della Riforma cattolica', *Critica storica* (1964). C. Robinson, *Nicolo Ormaneto, a papal envoy in the sixteenth century* (London 1920) is of limited value; but more stimulating is the short account of Baronius by the future Pope John XXIII: A.G. Roncalli, *Il Cardinale Cesare Baronio* (Rome, republished 1961). There is also an important article by P. Paschini, 'I Monasteri femminili in Italia nel '500', in *Italia Sacra*, vol. 2 (Padua 1960). On a particular aspect of papal Rome and its society, see L. Poliakov, 'La communauté juive à Rome aux XVI et XVII siècles', *Annales E.S.C.* (1957). Other works on the application of Catholic reform after the Council of Trent in local churches can be found in the ample bibliography of Delumeau's work, already mentioned, *Le Catholicisme*. See also, on the French clergy of the eighteenth century, T. Tackett, *Priest and parish in eighteenth-century France* (Princeton 1977). G. Alberigo has written on *I vescovi italiani al Concilio di Trento (1545-7)* (Florence 1959). See also his article, 'The Council of Trent: New Views on the Occasion of its Fourth Centenary', in *Concilium*, vol. 7 number 1 (1965). Compare M. Rosa, *Religione e società nel Mezzogiorno tra '500 e '600* (Bari 1976). Other relevant works include the article by E. Cattaneo, 'Influenze veronesi nella legislazione di San Carlo', in *Problemi di vita religiosa in Italia nel Cinquecento* (Padua 1960); A. Cistellini, *Figure della riforma pretridentina* (Brescia 1948); and Crisógono de Jesús, *The Life of St John of the Cross* (London 1958). Two other figures are studied by C.J. von Hefele, *The Life of Cardinal Ximenes* (London 1860); and H. Jedin, *Tommaso Campeggio (1483-1564): tridentinische Reform und kuriale Tradition* (Münster 1958). The same author has also written on *Ecumenical Councils of the Church* (Freiburg-im-B., 1960). Compare P. Paschini, *Tre ricerche sulla storia della*

*Chiesa del Cinquecento* (Rome 1945); and C. Ginzburg, *Il nicodemismo* (Turin 1970). See also the studies by E. Gleason, 'Sixteenth Century Italian Interpretations of Luther', *Archiv für Reformationsgeschichte* (1969); and P. Paschini, *Venezia e l'inquisizione romana da Giulio III a Pio IV* (Padua 1959). C. Gutiérrez has published an account of *Españoles en Trento* (Valladolid 1951), while S.J. Miller traces the later relations of *Portugal and Rome c. 1748-1830: an aspect of the Catholic Enlightenment* (Rome 1978). See also, for that uneasy relationship, A. Santos Hernandez, *Las misiones bajo el Patronato portugués* (Madrid 1977). B. Bennassar with others has written on *L'inquisition espagnole, XVe-XIXe siècles* (Paris 1979). Compare D. Pastine and others on the subject of *L'europa cristiana nel rapporto con le altre culture del secolo XVII* (Florence 1978); and the study by D. Pastine of *La nascita dell' idolatria. L'Oriente religioso di Athanasius Kircher* (Florence 1978). For the English College, Rome, in the mid-sixteenth century, see Anthony Munday, *The English Roman Life*, ed. P.J. Ayres (Oxford 1980); and for Roman conditions see also D. Beggiao, *La visita pastorale di Clemente VIII (1592-1600). Aspetti di riforma post-tridentina a Roma* (Rome 1978). The Roman synod of Benedict XIII is the subject of L. Fiorani, *Il Concilio romano del 1725* (Rome 1978); while a broader sweep of Italian history is treated by S.J. Woolf, *A History of Italy 1700-1860: The Social Constraints of Political Change* (London 1979). Roman conditions at different dates can also be studied in D. Chiomenti Vassalli, *Donna Olimpia, o del nepotismo nel seicento* (Milan 1979); and J.W. O'Malley, *Praise and blame in Renaissance Rome: Rhetoric, Doctrine and reform in the Sacred Orators of the papal court c. 1450-1521* (Durham N.C., 1979). See also M. Monaco, *Le finanze pontificie al tempo di Paolo V (1605-21). La fondazione del primo banco pubblico in Roma* (Rome 1974); W. Reinhard, *Papstfinanz und Nepotismus unter Paul V. (1605-21)* (Stuttgart 1974) [2 vols]; and M. Caravale, *La finanza pontificia nel '500: le provincie del Lazio* (Camerino 1974). There is also M. Petrocchi, *Roma nel seicento* (Bologna 1975).

The account by M.N. Hamilton of *Music in Eighteenth Century Spain* (Urbana 1937) was reprinted in New York in 1979; as was R.M. Stevenson, *Spanish Cathedral Music in the Golden Age* (Berkeley 1961). G. Parker published a study of *Philip II* (London 1978), while M. Fernandez Alvarez published *Charles V: elected emperor and hereditary ruler* (London 1976). See also J. García Oro, *Cisneros y la reforma del clero español en tiempo de los reyes católicos* (Madrid 1971). Other Italian themes are treated by G. Piaia, *Marsilio da Padova nella Riforma e nella Controriforma: fortuna ed interpretazione* (Padua 1977); J.C. Olin, *The Catholic Reformation: Savonarola to Ignatius Loyola: reform in the Church 1495-1540* (London 1969); and B. Nicolini, *Studi cinquecenteschi II: Aspetti della vita religiosa, politica e letteraria* (Bologna 1974). Three other related works are S. Bertelli, *Ribelli, libertini e ortodossi nella storiografia barocca* (Florence 1973); A. Lauro, *Il giurisdizionalismo pregiannoniano nel Regno di Napoli* (Rome 1974); and P.

Lopez, *Sul libro a stampa e le origini della censura ecclesiastica* (Naples 1972). Italian local developments are also considered by P. Preto, *Venezia e i Turchi* (Florence 1975); R. de Maio, *Alfonso Carafa, Cardinale di Napoli* (Vatican City 1961); and P. Lopez, *Il movimento valdesiano a Napoli. Mario Galeota e le sue vicende col Sant' Uffizio* (Naples 1976). A wider perspective, for a later period, is that of A. Dupront, *L.A. Muratori et la société européenne des pré-lumières* (Florence 1976). Other Spanish subjects are treated by D. Gutiérrez, O.S.A., *Los Agostinos desde el protestantismo hasta la restauración católica 1518-1648* (Rome 1971); A. Márquez, *Los alumbrados: orígenes y filosofía 1525-59* (Madrid 1972); and A.F.G. Bell, *Luís de León* (Oxford 1925). Compare B. Reckers on *Benito Arias Montano* (London 1972); and J.L. de Orella y Unzue, *Respuestas católicas a las centurias de Magdeburgo (1559-88)* (Madrid 1976). For Molinos, see his *Spiritual Guide*, of which a seventeenth-century English translation has been edited (6th ed., London 1950). The history of Catholic reform, from a German viewpoint, has received the attention of R. Bireley, *Maximilian von Bayern, Adam Contzen S.J. und die Gegenreformation in Deutschland 1624-35* (Göttingen 1975); and K.D. Schmidt, *Die katholische Reform und die Gegenreformation* (Göttingen 1975). For a later period there are the works of E. Kovács, *Ultramontanismus und Staatskirchentum im theresianisch-josephinischen Staat: der Kampf der Kardinäle Migazzi und Franckenberg gegen Ferdinand Stöger* (Vienna 1975); F. Engel-Janosi, *Formen der europäischen Aufklärung: Untersuchungen zur Situation von Christentum Bildung und Wissenschaft* (Munich 1976); and V. Pitzner, *Justinus Febronius. Das Ringen eines katholischen Irenickers um die Einheit der Kirche im Zeitalter der Aufklärung* (Göttingen 1976). For the troubled history of Catholicism in the Netherlands, see M.G. Spietz, *L'église catholique des Provinces-Unies et le Saint-Siège pendant la deuxième moitié du XVIIᵉ siècle* (Louvain 1975). The contrasting conditions of Catholicism in Savoy and Piedmont after the Council of Trent are thoroughly examined by A. Erba, *La Chiesa Sabauda tra cinque e seicento. Ortodossia tridentina, gallicanesimo savoiardo e assolutismo ducale (1580-1630)* (Rome 1979).

## 7   Puritanism of the right and Baroque effect

On aspects of Mannerism, see the short work by Lord Clark, *A Failure of Nerve: Italian painting, 1520-35* (Oxford 1967). There is also a book by L. Murray, *The High Renaissance and Mannerism. Italy, the North and Spain 1500-1600* (London 1978). A useful introductory article on Baroque painting and religious art is that by E. Waterhouse, 'Some painters and the Counter-Reformation before 1600', *Transactions of the Royal Historical Society* (1972). Fundamental is the work of E. Mâle, *L'art religieux après le Concile de Trente* (Paris 1932). V.L. Tapié has published a book translated as *The Age of Grandeur* (London 1960). *The Age of the Baroque* is a general treatment of artistic and other history by C.J. Friedrich (New York 1962). On Baroque music see M. Bukofzer, *Music in the Baroque Era* (London 1948). The Baroque concerto is discussed by A. Hutchings, *The Baroque Concerto* (London 1961). There is a biography of the composer *Gesualdo* by G. Watkins (London 1973); compare D. Arnold, *Giovanni Gabrieli* (London 1979). The writings on Church art and furnishings by Charles Borromeo and Gabriele Paleotti are published in P. Barocchi, *Trattati d'Arte del '500, fra Manierismo e Controriforma,* vols 2–3 (Bari 1961–2). See also the works on artistic theory by A. Blunt and D. Mahon respectively: *Artistic Theory in Italy 1450–1600* (London 1973); and *Studies in Seicento Art and Theory* (London 1947). A. Blunt has also produced the beautiful and monumental study of *Neapolitan Baroque and Rococo Architecture* (London 1975), as well as a shorter study of *Sicilian Baroque* (London 1968). For French funerary imagery, as well as the general relation of the visual and literary arts of the Baroque, see J. Rousset, *La littérature de l'âge baroque en France* (Paris 1965). Compare M. Praz, *Studies in Seventeenth-Century Imagery* (2nd ed., Rome 1964). Michelangelo has been the subject of numerous studies. One which sheds useful light on his learning, despite some criticism, is that of R. Schott, *Michelangelo* (London 1963). Bernini's life was written by a famous art critic in the circle of Christina of Sweden, and is published in translation: F. Baldinucci, *The Life of Bernini* (London 1966). Rubens has attracted much attention, particularly recently. For an interesting approach to one aspect of his work, see the article by A. Blunt, 'Rubens and architecture', *Burlington Magazine* (September 1977). A. Blunt has also published a major work on Poussin, *Nicholas Poussin* (2 vols, New York 1967), as well as a critical catalogue of his paintings. Illusionistic art is the subject of a work by M. Pirenne, *Optics, Painting and Photography* (Cambridge 1970). Vasari's own elevation of Michelangelo as the supreme master of painting and the arts is evident from the final version of his life of the great man. See the modern edition of Vasari's *Lives of the Artists*, in translation, selected by G. Bull (Harmondsworth 1965). For the dramatic life of Caravaggio, see the account of G.P. Bellori, *Le Vite de' Pittori, Scultori e Architetti Moderni*, edited by E. Borea (Turin 1976). H.R. Trevor-Roper has discussed Habsburg patronage in *Princes and artists: patronage and ideology at four Habsburg courts* (London 1976). For Haydn at Esterháza, see H.C. Robbins Landon, *Haydn at Esterháza, 1766–90* (London 1978). For Stuart royal masques, see S.K. Orgel and R. Strong, *Inigo Jones: the theatre of the Stuart court* (2 vols, London 1973). Compare the discussion of Inigo Jones by Sir John Summerson (Harmondsworth 1966). The arts in seventeenth-century France are discussed by A. Blunt and E. Lockspeiser, *French art and music since 1500* (London 1974). The discussion by C.S. Lewis of euphuism and other aspects of English literature in the sixteenth century includes some original considerations on the question of European witch-belief. See his introduction to the Oxford History of

English Literature, vol. 3, *English Literature in the Sixteenth Century* (Oxford 1968). Southwell's works can be consulted: see *The Poems of Robert Southwell, S.J.*, ed. J.H. McDonald and N.P. Brown (Oxford 1967). Voltaire's account of Louis xiv can be read in a modern translation: *The Age of Louis xiv* (London 1961). For Tiepolo, see the discussion of the father's work, as opposed to his son Domenico, in A. Morassi, *G.B. Tiepolo, His life and work* (London 1955). Palladio is the subject of a study by J. Ackerman, *Palladio* (Harmondsworth 1972). Among many works on Rembrandt, see the introduction by H. Focillon and notes of L. Goldscheider in *Rembrandt* (2nd ed., London 1964). Compare the importance of Rubens in relation to Italian art as studied by M. Jaffé, *Rubens and Italy* (Oxford 1977). Piranesi has lately received renewed attention; among other works, see that of J. Wilton-Ely, *The Mind and Art of G.B. Piranesi* (London 1978). Two important works by E. Waterhouse are *Baroque painting in Rome, the seventeenth century* (London 1937), and *Roman Baroque Painting* (London 1976). Two other useful treatments of musical themes are H.E. Smither, *A History of the Oratorio:* vol. 1: *The Oratorio in the Baroque Era: Italy* [etc.] (Chapel Hill 1977); and J. Glover, *Cavalli* (London 1978).

Studies of regional architectural developments include H. Aurenhammer, *J.B. Fischer von Erlach* (London 1973); W. Pinder, *Deutscher Barock. Die grossen Baumeister des 18. Jahrhunderts* (Königstein im Taunus 1929); and H.W. Hegemann, *Deutsches Rokoko* (Königstein i.T. 1958). Compare J.W. Franklin, *The Cathedrals of Italy* (London 1958); and J. Harvey, *The Cathedrals of Spain* (London 1957). R. Wittkower has studied 'Gothic' plans for the completion of earlier Italian basilicas in the Baroque age in *Gothic versus Classic: architectural projects in seventeenth century Italy* (London 1974). The interaction of Italian and Spanish culture in the age of the Renaissance and Baroque is the subject of the study by B. Croce, *La Spagna nella vita italiana durante la Rinascenza* (2nd ed., Bari 1922). Another work on Medicean Florence is that of J.R. Hale, *Florence and the Medici, the pattern of control* (London 1977). The letters of Mozart, including his initial experiences of Italy, have been translated and edited in selection by A.H. King and M. Carolan, *The Letters of Mozart and his family* (2 vols, London 1966).

For the French Catholic revival of the seventeenth century there is a vast literature. The figures of Vincent de Paul and Le Camus can be approached through the work of H. Lavedan, *Monsieur Vincent* (Paris 1928); the *Lettres de S. Vincent de Paul* (2 vols, Paris 1882); and the *Lettres du Cardinal Le Camus. Evêque et Prince de Grenoble (1632–1707)*, ed. P. Ingold (Paris 1892). The monumental work of H. Bremond, *Histoire littéraire du sentiment religieux en France depuis la fin des guerres de religion jusqu'à nos jours* (12 vols, Paris 1916–36), should be consulted, since only the first three volumes were translated as *A literary history of religious thought in France*, already mentioned. Other major figures, such as Olier and Bérulle, are discussed by G. Letourneau, *Le ministère pastorale de Jean-Jacques Olier, curé de Saint-Sulpice 1642–52* (Paris 1905); and J. Dagens, *Bérulle et les Origines de la Restauration Catholique (1575–1611)* (Paris 1952). Among the most prolific writers on aspects of the seventeenth-century French Church and its relations with government and society are P. Blet, whose important article 'Louis XIV et le Saint-Siège' can be found in the journal *XVIIᵉ siècle* for April–June 1979 (devoted to Louis XIV); and B. Neveu, whose work includes the articles 'Episcopus et Princeps Urbis: Innocent XI réformateur de Rome d'après des documents inédits (1676–89)', in *Römische Kurie. Kirchliche Finanzen. Vatikanisches Archiv. Studien zu Ehren von Hermann Hoberg* ed. E. Gatz (vol. 2, Rome 1979), and 'Politique ecclésiastique et controverses doctrinales à Rome de 1683 à 1705', in *Bulletin de la Société d'Histoire Moderne* (1975). See also the article by H.G. Judge on 'Louis XIV and the Church' in the book *Louis XIV and the Craft of Kingship*, ed. J.C. Rule (Ohio 1969). For St Francis de Sales see M. de la Bedoyère, *François de Sales* (London 1960). Most important are the two volumes of P. Broutin, *La réforme pastorale en France au XVIIᵉ siècle* (Paris 1956). Compare V. Martin, *Le gallicanisme politique et la réforme catholique* (Paris 1919), and his other works on Gallicanism. A more modern approach to the state of seventeenth-century French Catholicism is that of J. Ferté, *La vie religieuse dans les campagnes parisiennes 1622–95* (Paris 1962). See also B. Plongeron, *La vie quotidienne du clergé français au XVIIIᵉ siècle* (Paris 1974). Another relevant study is that of C.C. Fairchilds, *Poverty and charity in Aix-en-Provence 1640–1789* (Baltimore 1976). B. Pullan has written on 'Catholics and the Poor in Early Modern Europe', in *Transactions of the Royal Historical Society* (1976). Compare C. Cipolla, *I pidocchi e il Granduca: Crisi economica e problemi sanitari nella Firenze del '600* (Bologna 1979). Educational activity is discussed by W.J. Battersby, *De la Salle: a pioneer of modern education* (London 1949). Related questions are treated by J. Orcibal, *Le premier Port-Royal: Réforme ou Contre-Réforme?* (Paris 1956), and *Saint-Cyran et le Jansénisme* (Paris 1961). Compare L. Cognet, *Les origines de la spiritualité française au XVIIᵉ siècle* (Paris 1949); and P. Guilday, *The English Catholic refugees on the continent* (London 1914). Fundamental to the new approaches to French religious history were the books of G. Le Bras, *Introduction à l'histoire de la pratique religieuse en France* (2 vols, Paris 1942–5), and *L'église et le village* (Paris 1976). Compare the literary figure of *Rabelais* in the biography by M. Screech (Ithaca 1979).

For developments in the visual arts which included the picaresque, see B. Nicolson, *The International Caravaggesque Movement, 1590 to 1650* (Oxford 1979). Compare M.R. Maniates, *Mannerism in Italian music and culture, 1530–1630* (Manchester 1979). Other treatment of artistic imagery can be found in J. Brown, *Images and Ideas in seventeenth-century Spanish painting* (Princeton 1980); and J.R. Martin and G. Feigenbaum, *Van Dyck as religious artist* (Princeton 1980). Two influential texts on the imagery of the art of the period have been reprinted in facsimile editions: the two volumes of the formative *Iconology* of C. Ripa (New York, 1979, using an eighteenth-century English translation of the 1603 original text); and V. Cartari, *Vere e nove imagini* (New York 1979, from the 1615 edition at Padua). There is similarly an edition of P. Giovio, *Dialogo dell' imprese* [1574], from an English translation of 1585 (New York 1979). See also R. Pallucchini, *Tiziano e il manierismo europeo* (Florence 1978); and G. Spini, *Architettura e politica da Cosimo I a Ferdinando I* (Florence 1976). M.B. Hall has written on *Renovation and counter-reformation: Vasari and Duke Cosimo in Sta Maria Novella and Sta Croce 1565-77* (Oxford 1979); and A. Blunt on *Some uses and misuses of the terms baroque and rococo as applied to architecture* (London 1973). Studies of individual artists are provided by A.W.A. Boschloo, *Annibale Carracci in Bologna: visible reality in art after the Council of Trent* (2 vols, The Hague 1974); B. Nicolson and C. Wright, *Georges de la Tour* (London 1974); and C. Gould, *The paintings of Correggio* (London 1976). See also J.B. Knipping, *Iconography of the Counter-Reformation in the Netherlands: heaven on earth* (2 vols, Nieuwkoop 1974); and T.L. Glen, *Rubens and the Counter-Reformation: studies in his religious paintings 1609-20* (London 1977). Roman themes are discussed by R. de Maio, *Michelangelo e la Controriforma* (Bari 1978); and M.S. Weil, *History and Decoration of the Ponte S. Angelo* (London 1974). Compare D. Howard, *Jacopo Sansovino, architecture and patronage in Renaissance Venice* (London 1975); and C. Dempsey, *Annibale Carracci and the beginnings of Baroque style* (Glückstadt 1977). *Borromini* has also been studied by G.C. Argan (Milan 1978); while two other related books are H.J. Jensen, *The muses' concord: literature, music and the visual arts in the Baroque age* (London 1976); and M. Praz, *Il giardino dei sensi: studi sul manierismo e il barocco* (Milan 1975).

By contrast, popular culture is the subject of G. Bollème, *La bibliothèque bleue: littérature populaire en France du XVIIᵉ au XIXᵉ siècle* (Paris 1971). See also B. Plongeron, *La religion populaire dans l'occident chrétien: approches historiques* (Paris 1976). Religious and political questions are involved in the social strife studied by E. Le Roy Ladurie in *Carnival. A People's Uprising in Romans 1579-80* (London 1980). Compare the classic work of L. Febvre, *Au cœur religieux du XVIᵉ siècle* (2nd ed., Paris 1968); and N.M. Sutherland, *The Huguenot Struggle for Recognition* (New Haven 1980). Further studies of the impact of French Catholic reform on popular behaviour are L. Cristiani, *St Vincent de Paul 1581-1660* (Boston, Mass. 1977); and J. Godel, *Cardinal des montagnes: Etienne Le Camus, évêque de Grenoble 1671-1707* (Grenoble 1974). Related questions involving other areas are examined in P. Preto, *Peste e società a Venezia 1576* (Vicenza 1978); and V. Pinot, *La Chine et la formation de l'esprit philosophique en France (1640-1740)* (Paris 1932). Popular and élite religious life may again be contrasted in the works of R. Sauzet, *Les visites pastorales dans le diocèse de Chartres pendant la première moitié du XVIIᵉ siècle: essai de sociologie religieuse* (Rome 1975); and F.E. Weaver, *The evolution of the reform of Port-Royal, from the rule of Cîteaux to Jansenism* (Paris 1979). Compare R. Taveneaux, *La vie quotidienne des jansénistes aux XVIIᵉ et XVIIIᵉ siècles* (Paris 1973); and P. Jansen, *Le Cardinal Mazarin et le mouvement janséniste français (1653-9)* (Paris 1967). A similar contrast may be traced in Y.M. Bercé, *Fête et révolte: des mentalités populaires du XVIᵉ au XVIIIᵉ siècle* (Paris 1976); and A. Tenenti, *Credenze, ideologie, libertinismi tra Medioevo ed Età Moderna* (Bologna 1978). The notorious attack by M. Mersenne, of 1624, *L'impiété des déistes, athées et libertins de ce temps combatue et renversée* has been reproduced in facsimile (Stuttgart 1975). Another famous work of the century, J.-B. Bossuet, *Discourse on Universal History*, has been edited in translation by O. Ranum (Chicago 1976). Other aspects of French religious history are treated by J. Orcibal, *Louis XIV contre Innocent XI* (Paris 1949); and A.G. Martimort, *Le gallicanisme de Bossuet* (Paris 1953). Wider questions are examined by M. Lee Jr in *James I and Henri IV* (Urbana 1970); and in the book, *Religion and the People 800-1700*, ed. J. Obelkevich (Chapel Hill 1979). On Jansenism, as an ecclesiastical development linking France to other areas, see the *Colloque sur le Jansénisme, Rome 1973: Actes du colloque* (Louvain 1977); and *Miscellanea Jansenistica offerts à Lucien Ceyssens O.F.M.* (Louvain 1963). While the history of Jansenism has been much illuminated by the documentary volumes of Ceyssens himself, there are other studies of the complicated evolution of the *dévots*, such as P. Erlanger, *Mme de Longueville: De la révolte au mysticisme* (Paris 1977); and R. Allier, *La Cabale des Dévots 1627-66* (Paris 1902). There is again a contrast of theme, as well as of geographical area, to be seen in the article of A. Dupront, 'La religion populaire dans l'histoire de l'Europe occidentale', in *Revue d'histoire de l'église de France* (1978); and A. Erba, *La Chiesa sabauda tra '500 e '600: Ortodossia tridentina, gallicanesimo savoiardo e assolutismo ducale (1580-1630)* (Rome 1979). A later period is discussed by N. Ravitch, in *Sword and Mitre: Government and episcopate in France and England in the age of aristocracy* (The Hague 1966).

# INDEX

Abbot, George, archbishop, 14
abortion, 54
absolutism, 150, 159, 164, 173
academies, 88-9, 228, 245
a cappella singing, 232
Acarie, Mme, 247
Acquapendente, 86, 95
Acquaviva, archbishop of Naples, 210, 287
Acquaviva, Claudio, S.J. general, 252-3
actors, 75
adiaphorism, 165
ad limina visits, 81, 222, 288, 290
Africa, 9, 19, 120, 128, 132, 140, 200, 211
Albano, 192, 215, 292
Albani, see Clement XI
Albanians, 214
Alberoni, cardinal, 174, 178-9
Albert, cardinal, archduke, 142, 150, 290
Alcalá, 87-8
alchemy, 85, 93
Aldobrandini family, 165, 176; see also Clement VIII
Aleander, 209
Alessandria, 217, 293
Alexander VII, 129, 177, 256
Alfonso Liguori, saint, 206-7, 279
Allegri, 233
Allen, cardinal, 93, 154
Altieri, cardinal, 177; see also Clement X
Ambrose, saint, 189
Ambrosian chant, 189, 232, 294; rite, 189, 232, 294
Ambrosiana, the, 46, 77, 87, 229, 238, 288, 293

America, 13, 31-3, 35, 50, 66, 122, 125-31, 134, 136, 140-4, 170, 175, 198, 238, 250, 277-8
Amsterdam, 99
Anagni, 215
anatomy, 86
Ancients and Moderns, quarrel, 93
Ancona, 62
Anglican Church, 11-12, 37, 49, 55, 57-8, 64, 69, 94, 106, 113, 122, 147, 151, 154-5, 158-61, 165, 190, 211, 237
Angola, 132
Animal Spirits, 120
Annales, 82, 87, 227, 253
Anne of Austria, 27, 89
Anselm, saint, 7, 10
anti-Curialism, 29, 65, 83, 166
Antonino, saint, 54
Antwerp, 38, 224
apostolic delegates, bishops as, 14-15, 39, 191
Aquileia, 215, 292
Aquinas, Thomas, saint, 4, 23, 26, 38, 84
Aragon, 18, 99, 171, 290
archdeacons, 68, 143, 287
Ariosto, 241
Aristotelianism, 4, 23, 45-6, 84-6, 122
Arizona, 128
Armada, Spanish, 122, 161, 289
Armenia, 146
Arminians, 10, 36, 43, 162, 173
Arnauld, family, 25-6, 144
Arnobius the Younger, 5
Asam, the, 239
Ascham, 93
Assisi, 193